SHONEN JUMP ADVANCED MANGA

DEATH NOTE
デスノート

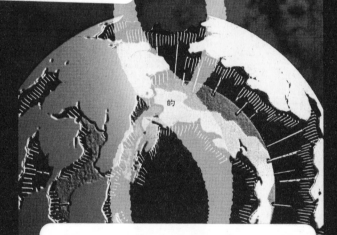

的

Vol. 8
Target

Story by Tsugumi Ohba
Art by Takeshi Obata

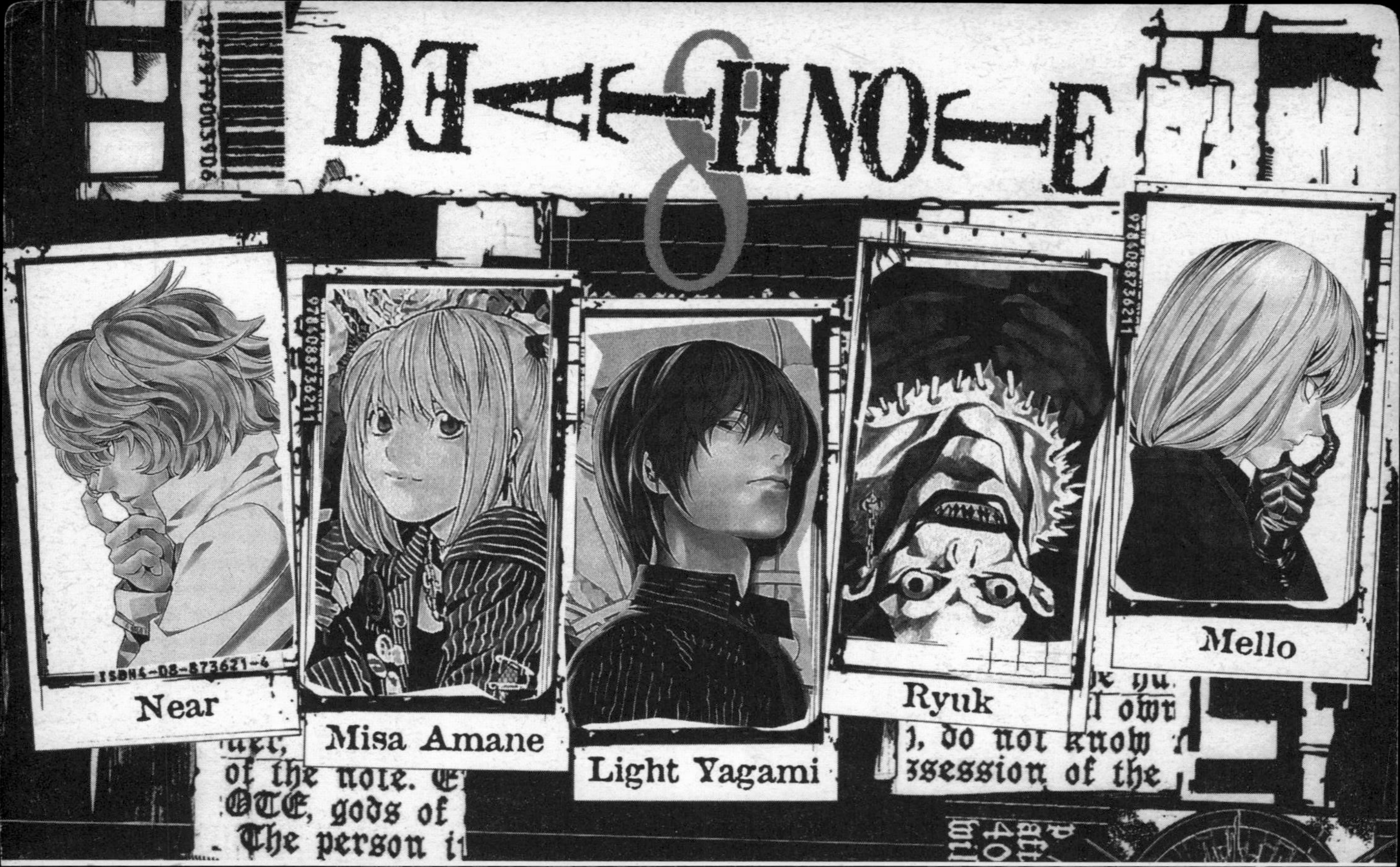
DEATH NOTE
8
ISBN4-08-873621-4
Near
Misa Amane
Light Yagami
Ryuk
Mello
of the note.
gods of
The person
1, do not know
ssession of the

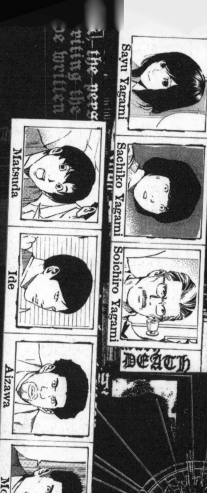

Sayu Yagami

Sachiko Yagami

Soichiro Yagami

Matsuda

Ide

Aizawa

Mogi

DEATH

AME IS WRITTEN IN THIS NOTE SHALL DIE"... LIGHT YAGAMI, A STRAIGHT-A HIGH SCHOOL HONORS STUDENT, PICKS UP THE
D BY THE SHINIGAMI RYUK INTO THE HUMAN WORLD. HALF DISBELIEVING, LIGHT USES THE NOTEBOOK, ONLY TO SEE THE
S HE HAS WRITTEN DROP DEAD! INITIALLY HORRIFIED BY THE NOTEBOOK'S POWERS, LIGHT EVENTUALLY DECIDES TO US
URGE THE WORLD OF VIOLENT CRIMINALS AND CREATE AN IDEAL SOCIETY. MEANWHILE, AS CRIMINALS WORLDWIDE STA
THE ENIGMATIC L, A SECRETIVE GENIUS WHO SPECIALIZES IN SOLVING UNSOLVED CASES, ENTERS THE PICTURE. HE US
NNOUNCE HE WILL CATCH WHOEVER IS RESPONSIBLE, SETTING OFF AN ALMIGHTY BATTLE OF THE WITS BETWEEN LIGH

APPEARANCE AS THE SECOND KIRA. L'S DOUBTS ABOUT LIGHT DEEPEN. IN ORDER TO FREE HIMSELF OF L'S SUSPICION, L
AND GIVES UP OWNERSHIP OF THE DEATH NOTE, LOSING ALL HIS MEMORIES OF THE DEATH NOTE AND HIS ACTIONS AS
RA APPEARS, LIGHT IS RELEASED IN ORDER TO WORK WITH L TO CATCH THIS NEWEST KIRA. THE TASKFORCE DISCOVERS
E OF THE HUGE YOTSUBA GROUP, IS KIRA DURING THE ARREST. THE TASKFORCE LEARNS ABOUT THE DEATH NOTE AND
HINIGAMI. AND LIGHT, ONCE HE TOUCHES THE NOTEBOOK, REGAINS ALL HIS MEMORIES AND KILLS HIGUCHI ON THE SPOT
ULD TELL. THE TASKFORCE ABOUT THE DEATH NOTE IS DEAD, AND THE SHINIGAMI WON'T GIVE THEM ANY USEFUL INFO
BUT IN MOTION BEFORE HE RELINQUISHED THE DEATH NOTE AND LOST HIS MEMORY, HAVE COME TO FRUITION, AND HE
EXT STAGE OF HIS MASTER PLAN-KILLING L. BY MANIPULATING MISA AND THE SHINIGAMI REM, LIGHT GETS RID OF L AND
FOUR YEARS LATER, LIGHT HAS JOINED THE POLICE FORCE AND CONTINUED TO SHAPE THE WORLD AS KIRA. BUT L'S TW
UN TO MAKE THEIR MOVE. NEAR TELLS THE PRESIDENT OF THE UNITED STATES ABOUT THE DEATH NOTE AND FORMS TH
FOR KIRA! MELLO SNATCHES THE DIRECTOR OF THE JAPANESE NPA, DEMANDING A RANSOM OF THE DEATH NOTE HELD
WHEN THE DIRECTOR DIES, MELLO SNATCHES LIGHT'S YOUNGER SISTER SAYU AND DEMANDS ANOTHER EXCHANGE

DEATH NOTE
Vol. 8

CONTENTS

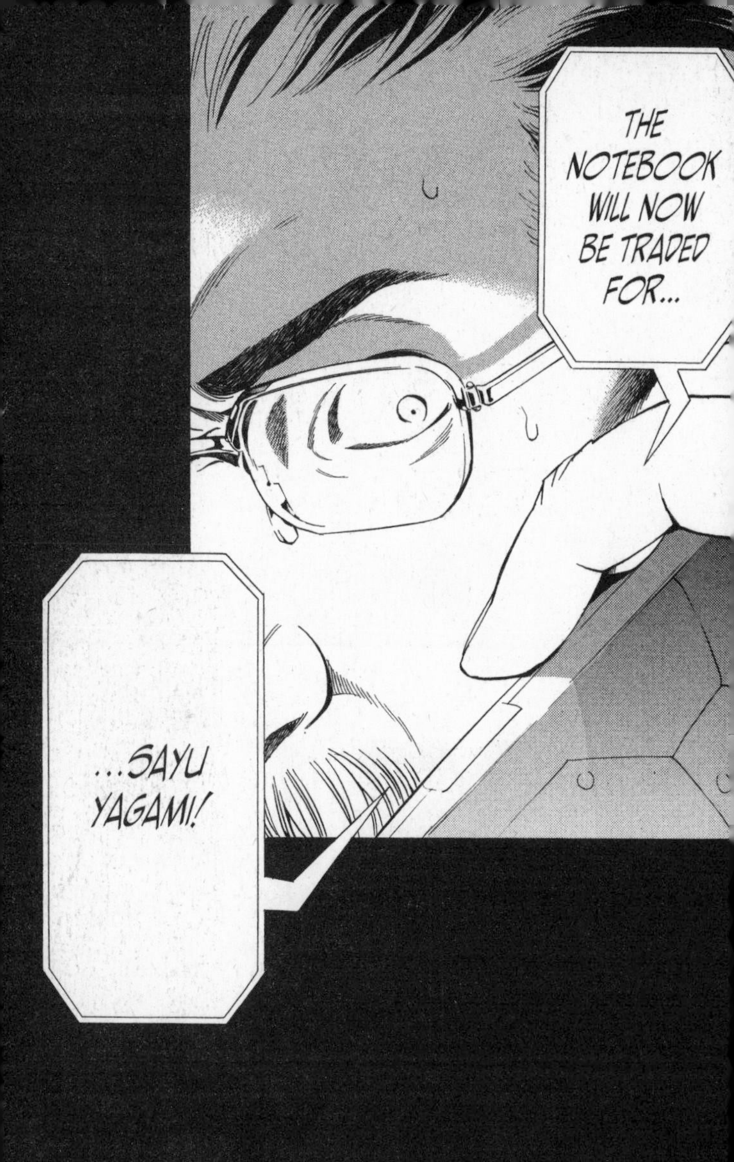

chapter 62 Decision

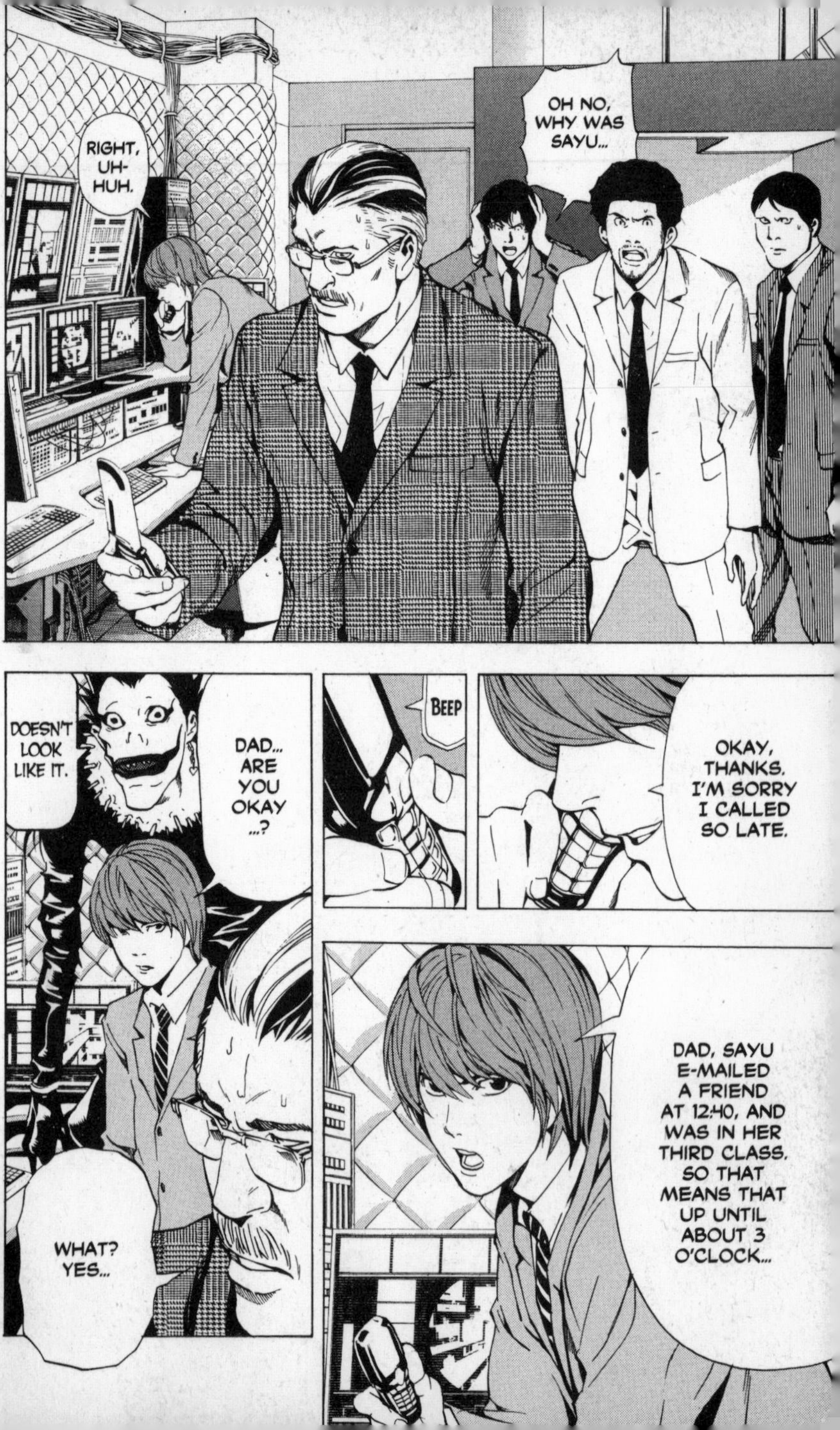
OH NO, WHY WAS SAYU...
RIGHT, UH-HUH.
OKAY, THANKS. I'M SORRY I CALLED SO LATE.
BEEP
DAD, SAYU E-MAILED A FRIEND AT 12:40, AND WAS IN HER THIRD CLASS. SO THAT MEANS THAT UP UNTIL ABOUT 3 O'CLOCK...
DAD... ARE YOU OKAY ...?
DOESN'T LOOK LIKE IT.
WHAT? YES...

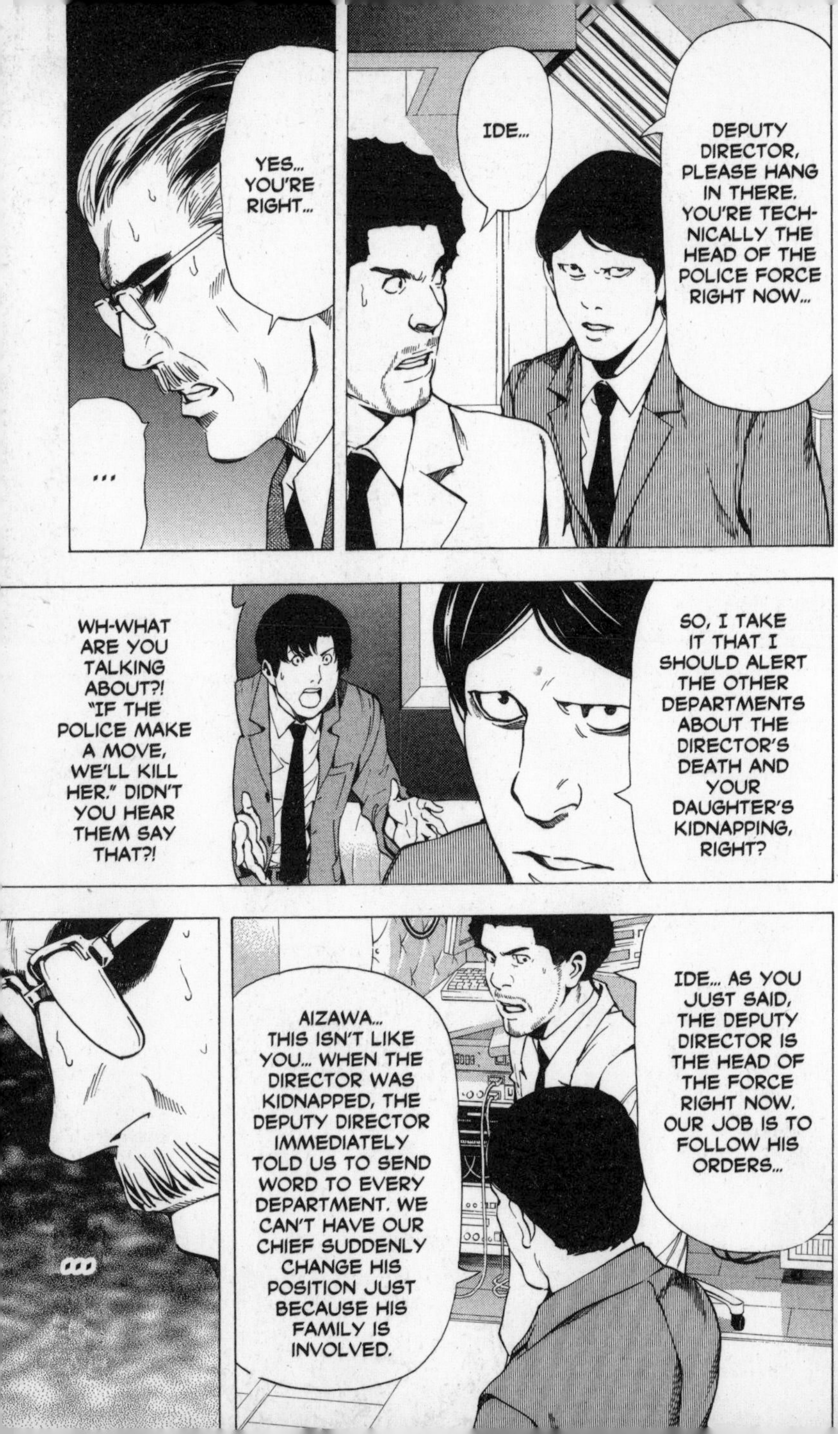
DEPUTY DIRECTOR, PLEASE HANG IN THERE. YOU'RE TECHNICALLY THE HEAD OF THE POLICE FORCE RIGHT NOW...
IDE...
YES... YOU'RE RIGHT...
...
SO, I TAKE IT THAT I SHOULD ALERT THE OTHER DEPARTMENTS ABOUT THE DIRECTOR'S DEATH AND YOUR DAUGHTER'S KIDNAPPING, RIGHT?
WH-WHAT ARE YOU TALKING ABOUT?! "IF THE POLICE MAKE A MOVE, WE'LL KILL HER." DIDN'T YOU HEAR THEM SAY THAT?!
IDE... AS YOU JUST SAID, THE DEPUTY DIRECTOR IS THE HEAD OF THE FORCE RIGHT NOW. OUR JOB IS TO FOLLOW HIS ORDERS...
AIZAWA... THIS ISN'T LIKE YOU... WHEN THE DIRECTOR WAS KIDNAPPED, THE DEPUTY DIRECTOR IMMEDIATELY TOLD US TO SEND WORD TO EVERY DEPARTMENT. WE CAN'T HAVE OUR CHIEF SUDDENLY CHANGE HIS POSITION JUST BECAUSE HIS FAMILY IS INVOLVED.
...

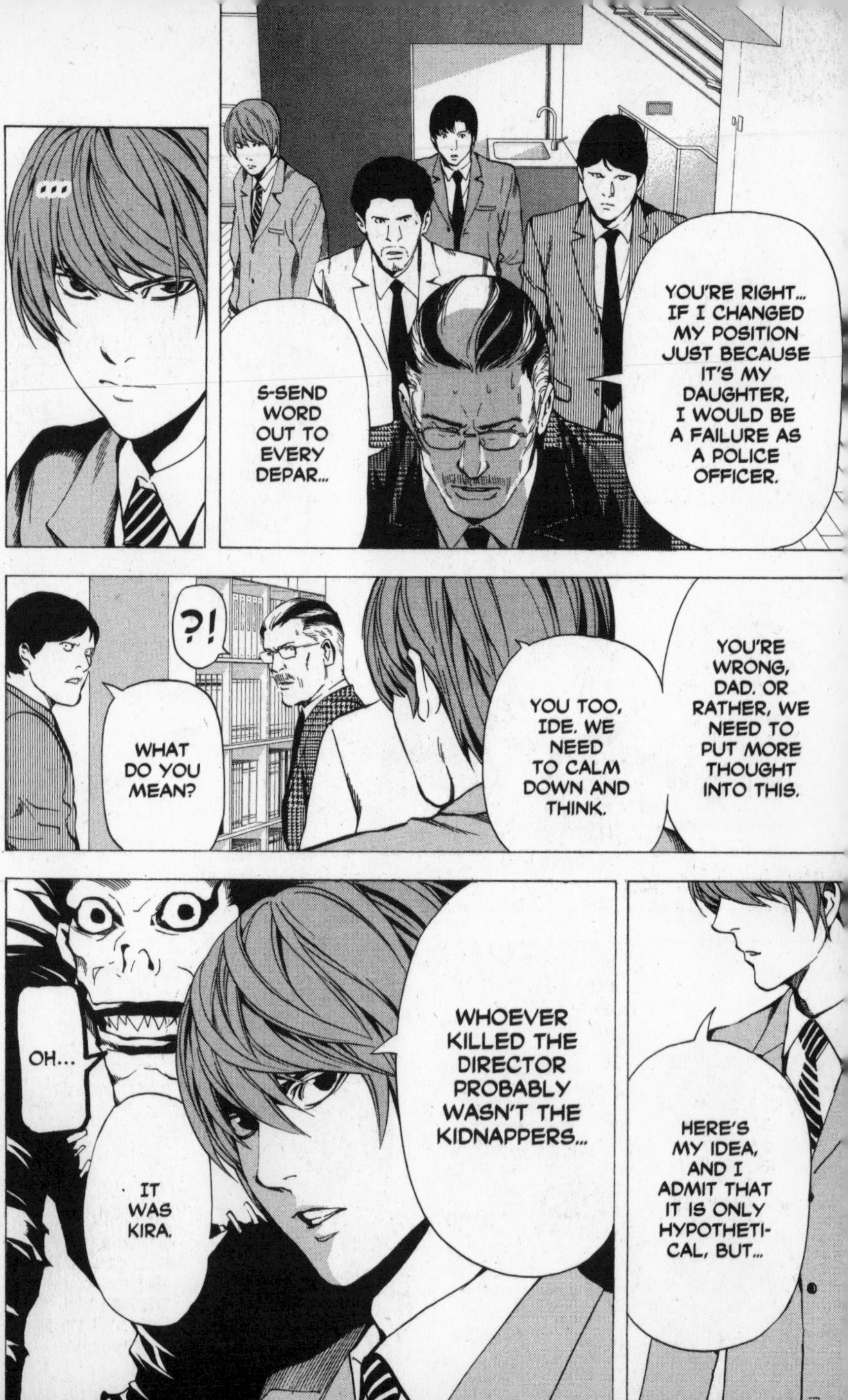

YOU'RE RIGHT... IF I CHANGED MY POSITION JUST BECAUSE IT'S MY DAUGHTER, I WOULD BE A FAILURE AS A POLICE OFFICER.
S-SEND WORD OUT TO EVERY DEPAR...
...
YOU'RE WRONG, DAD. OR RATHER, WE NEED TO PUT MORE THOUGHT INTO THIS.
YOU TOO, IDE. WE NEED TO CALM DOWN AND THINK.
?!
WHAT DO YOU MEAN?
HERE'S MY IDEA, AND I ADMIT THAT IT IS ONLY HYPOTHETICAL, BUT...
WHOEVER KILLED THE DIRECTOR PROBABLY WASN'T THE KIDNAPPERS...
IT WAS KIRA.
OH...

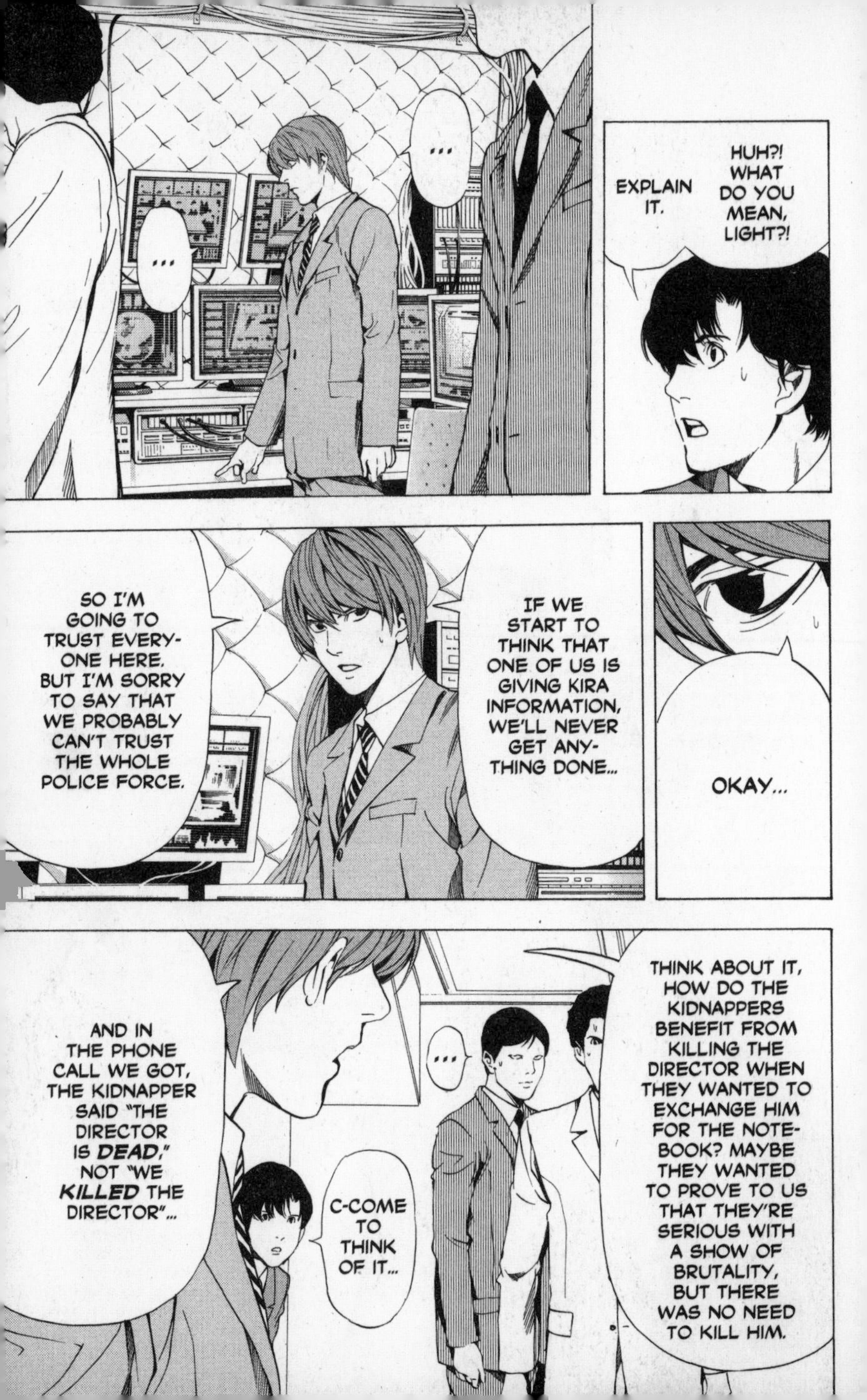
HUH?! WHAT DO YOU MEAN, LIGHT?!
EXPLAIN IT.
...
...
OKAY...
IF WE START TO THINK THAT ONE OF US IS GIVING KIRA INFORMATION, WE'LL NEVER GET ANY-THING DONE...
SO I'M GOING TO TRUST EVERY-ONE HERE. BUT I'M SORRY TO SAY THAT WE PROBABLY CAN'T TRUST THE WHOLE POLICE FORCE.
THINK ABOUT IT, HOW DO THE KIDNAPPERS BENEFIT FROM KILLING THE DIRECTOR WHEN THEY WANTED TO EXCHANGE HIM FOR THE NOTE-BOOK? MAYBE THEY WANTED TO PROVE TO US THAT THEY'RE SERIOUS WITH A SHOW OF BRUTALITY, BUT THERE WAS NO NEED TO KILL HIM.
...
AND IN THE PHONE CALL WE GOT, THE KIDNAPPER SAID "THE DIRECTOR IS DEAD," NOT "WE KILLED THE DIRECTOR"...
C-COME TO THINK OF IT...

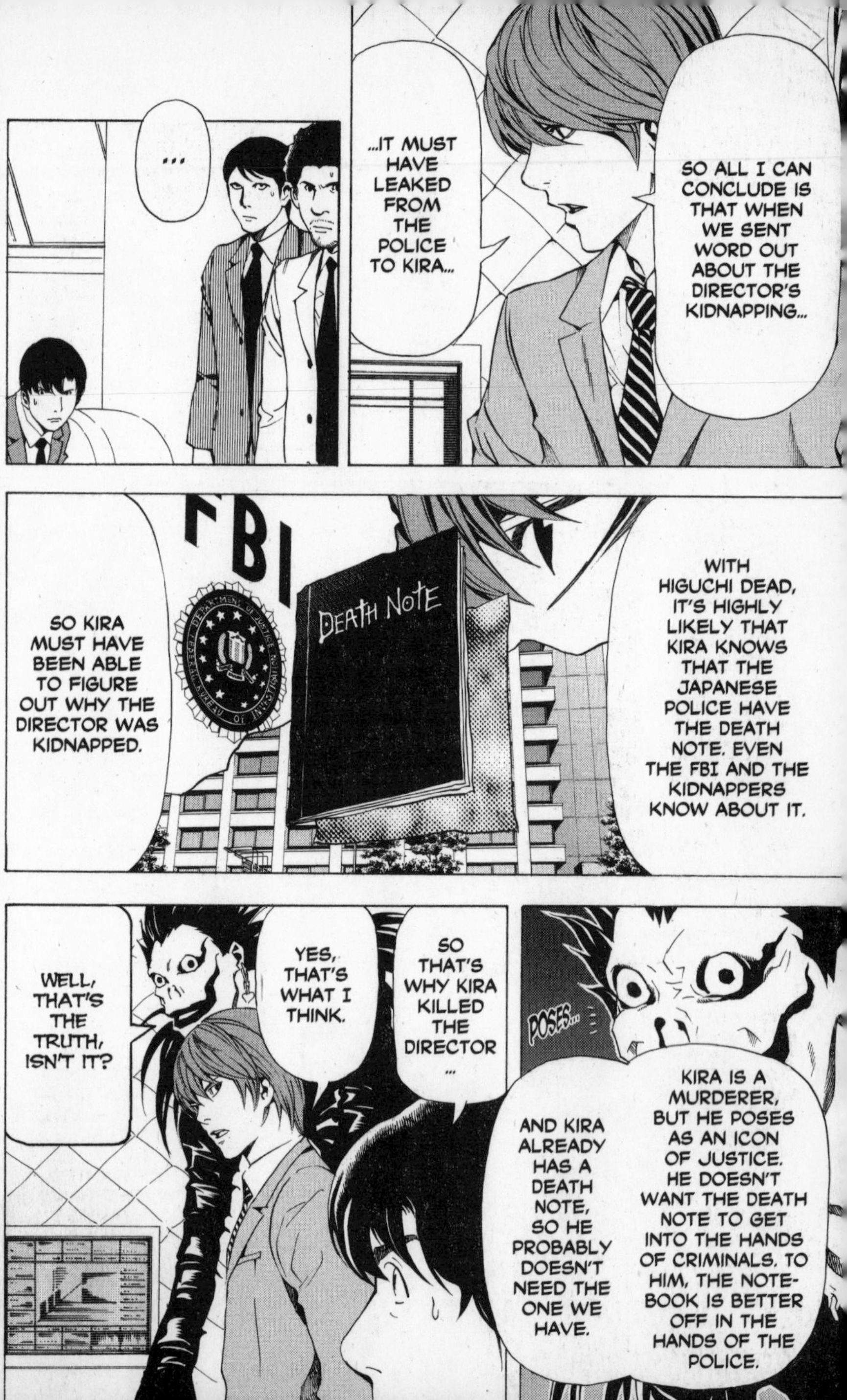
SO ALL I CAN CONCLUDE IS THAT WHEN WE SENT WORD OUT ABOUT THE DIRECTOR'S KIDNAPPING...
...IT MUST HAVE LEAKED FROM THE POLICE TO KIRA...
...
FBI
DEATH NOTE
WITH HIGUCHI DEAD, IT'S HIGHLY LIKELY THAT KIRA KNOWS THAT THE JAPANESE POLICE HAVE THE DEATH NOTE. EVEN THE FBI AND THE KIDNAPPERS KNOW ABOUT IT.
SO KIRA MUST HAVE BEEN ABLE TO FIGURE OUT WHY THE DIRECTOR WAS KIDNAPPED.
POSES...
KIRA IS A MURDERER, BUT HE POSES AS AN ICON OF JUSTICE. HE DOESN'T WANT THE DEATH NOTE TO GET INTO THE HANDS OF CRIMINALS. TO HIM, THE NOTE-BOOK IS BETTER OFF IN THE HANDS OF THE POLICE.
AND KIRA ALREADY HAS A DEATH NOTE, SO HE PROBABLY DOESN'T NEED THE ONE WE HAVE.
SO THAT'S WHY KIRA KILLED THE DIRECTOR...
YES, THAT'S WHAT I THINK.
WELL, THAT'S THE TRUTH, ISN'T IT?

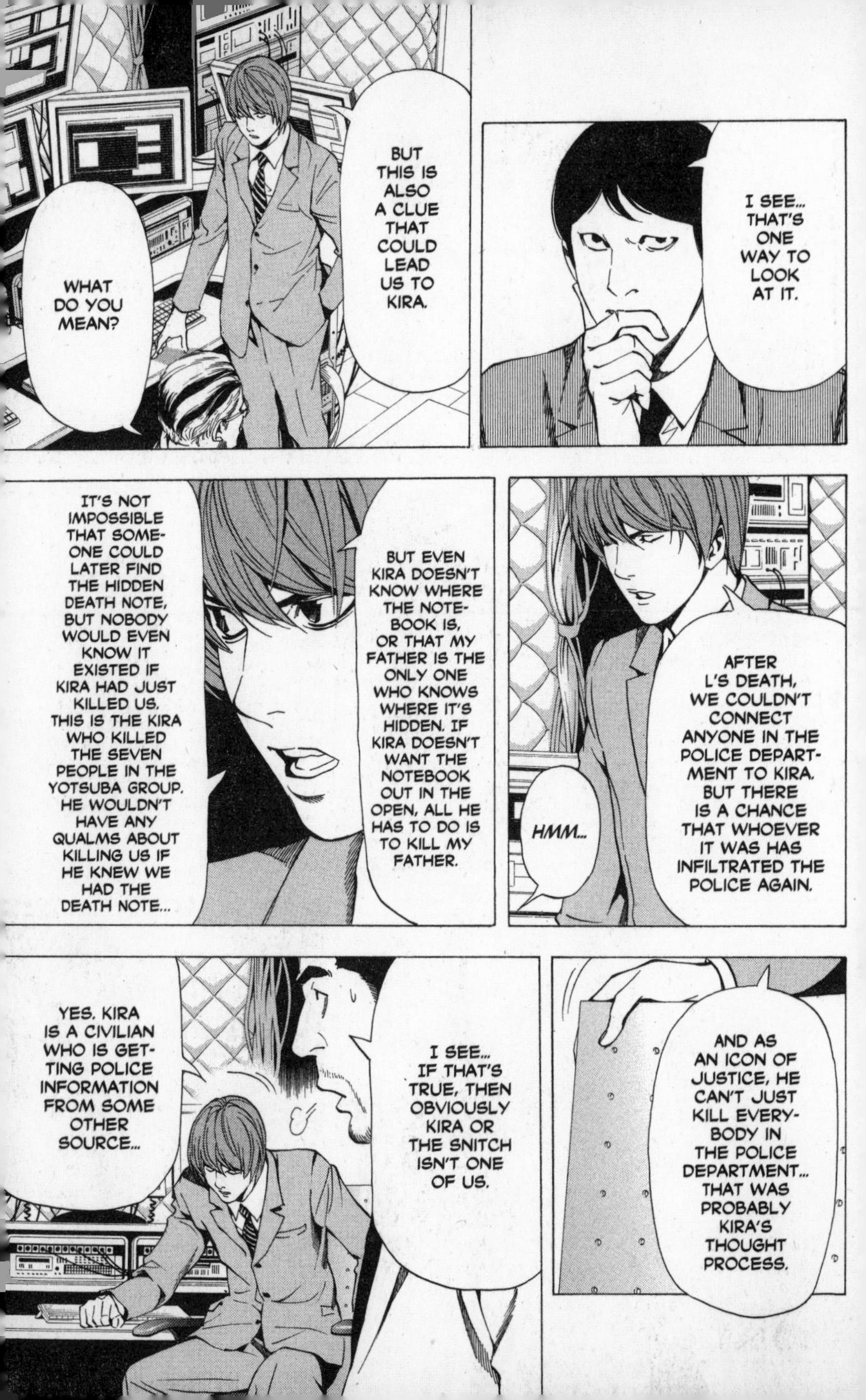
I SEE... THAT'S ONE WAY TO LOOK AT IT.
BUT THIS IS ALSO A CLUE THAT COULD LEAD US TO KIRA.
WHAT DO YOU MEAN?
AFTER L'S DEATH, WE COULDN'T CONNECT ANYONE IN THE POLICE DEPARTMENT TO KIRA. BUT THERE IS A CHANCE THAT WHOEVER IT WAS HAS INFILTRATED THE POLICE AGAIN.
HMM...
BUT EVEN KIRA DOESN'T KNOW WHERE THE NOTEBOOK IS, OR THAT MY FATHER IS THE ONLY ONE WHO KNOWS WHERE IT'S HIDDEN. IF KIRA DOESN'T WANT THE NOTEBOOK OUT IN THE OPEN, ALL HE HAS TO DO IS TO KILL MY FATHER.
IT'S NOT IMPOSSIBLE THAT SOMEONE COULD LATER FIND THE HIDDEN DEATH NOTE, BUT NOBODY WOULD EVEN KNOW IT EXISTED IF KIRA HAD JUST KILLED US. THIS IS THE KIRA WHO KILLED THE SEVEN PEOPLE IN THE YOTSUBA GROUP. HE WOULDN'T HAVE ANY QUALMS ABOUT KILLING US IF HE KNEW WE HAD THE DEATH NOTE...
AND AS AN ICON OF JUSTICE, HE CAN'T JUST KILL EVERYBODY IN THE POLICE DEPARTMENT... THAT WAS PROBABLY KIRA'S THOUGHT PROCESS.
I SEE... IF THAT'S TRUE, THEN OBVIOUSLY KIRA OR THE SNITCH ISN'T ONE OF US.
YES. KIRA IS A CIVILIAN WHO IS GETTING POLICE INFORMATION FROM SOME OTHER SOURCE...

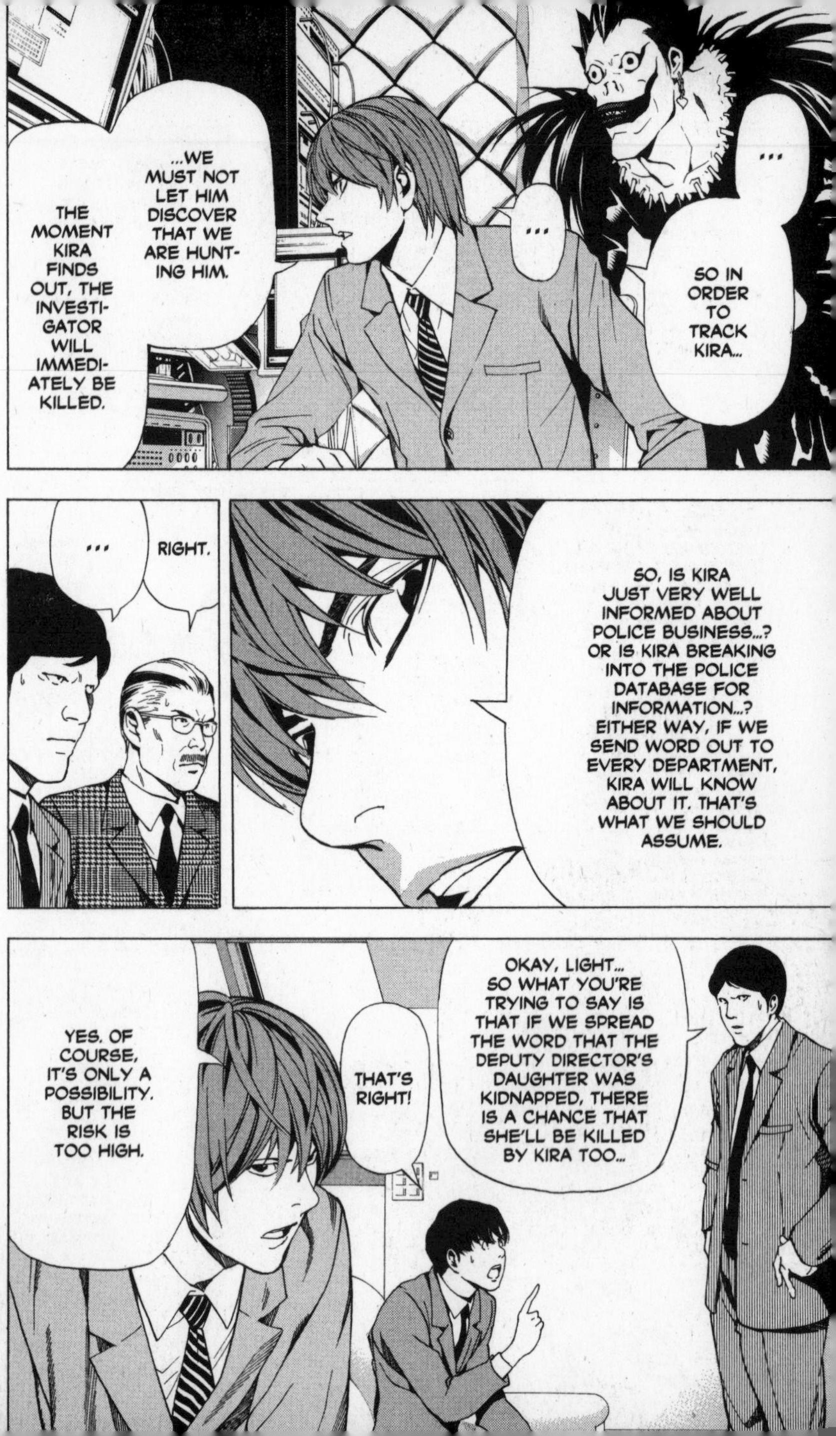
...
SO IN ORDER TO TRACK KIRA...
...
...WE MUST NOT LET HIM DISCOVER THAT WE ARE HUNTING HIM.
THE MOMENT KIRA FINDS OUT, THE INVESTIGATOR WILL IMMEDIATELY BE KILLED.
SO, IS KIRA JUST VERY WELL INFORMED ABOUT POLICE BUSINESS...? OR IS KIRA BREAKING INTO THE POLICE DATABASE FOR INFORMATION...? EITHER WAY, IF WE SEND WORD OUT TO EVERY DEPARTMENT, KIRA WILL KNOW ABOUT IT. THAT'S WHAT WE SHOULD ASSUME.
RIGHT.
...
OKAY, LIGHT... SO WHAT YOU'RE TRYING TO SAY IS THAT IF WE SPREAD THE WORD THAT THE DEPUTY DIRECTOR'S DAUGHTER WAS KIDNAPPED, THERE IS A CHANCE THAT SHE'LL BE KILLED BY KIRA TOO...
THAT'S RIGHT!
YES. OF COURSE, IT'S ONLY A POSSIBILITY. BUT THE RISK IS TOO HIGH.

READ THIS WAY

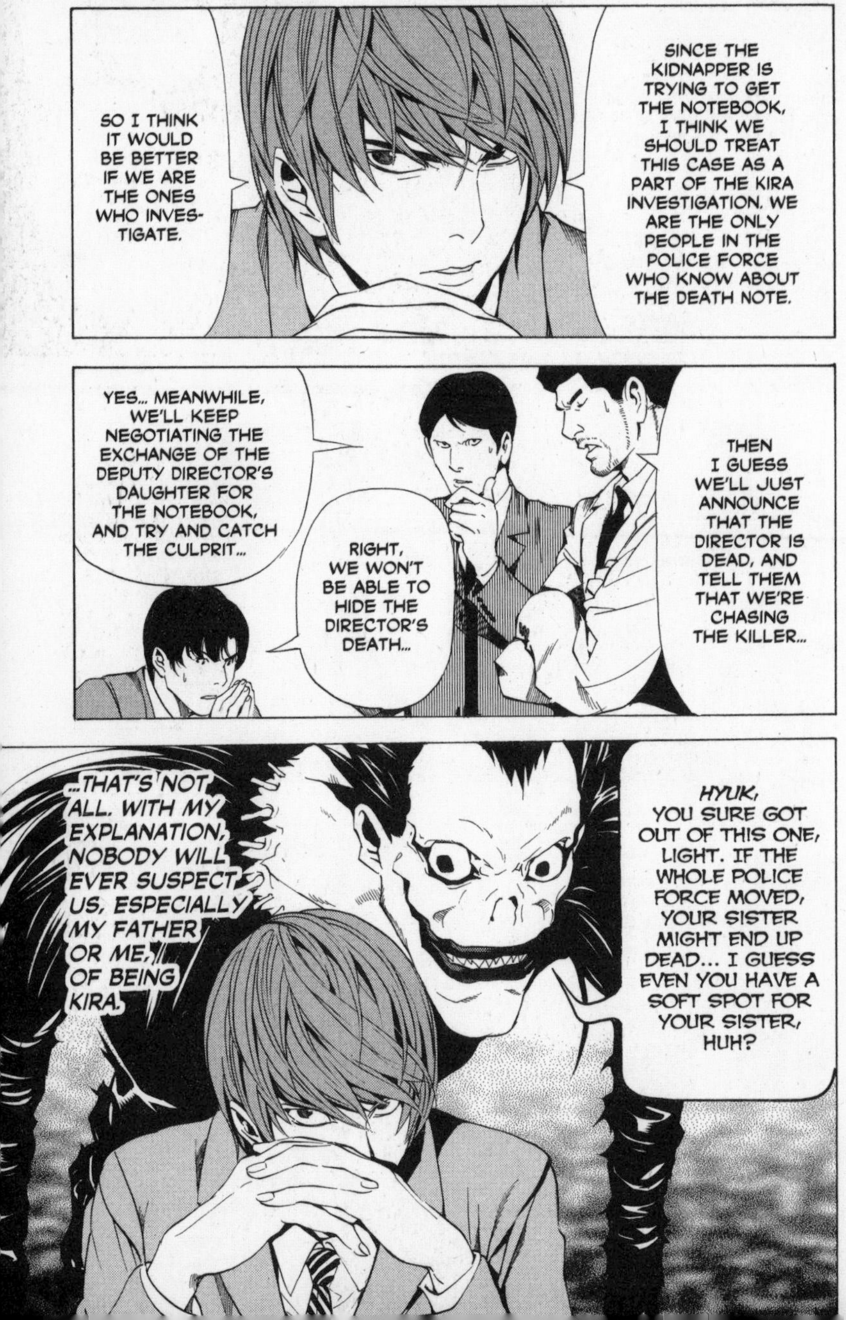

SINCE THE KIDNAPPER IS TRYING TO GET THE NOTEBOOK, I THINK WE SHOULD TREAT THIS CASE AS A PART OF THE KIRA INVESTIGATION. WE ARE THE ONLY PEOPLE IN THE POLICE FORCE WHO KNOW ABOUT THE DEATH NOTE.
SO I THINK IT WOULD BE BETTER IF WE ARE THE ONES WHO INVES-TIGATE.
THEN I GUESS WE'LL JUST ANNOUNCE THAT THE DIRECTOR IS DEAD, AND TELL THEM THAT WE'RE CHASING THE KILLER...
RIGHT, WE WON'T BE ABLE TO HIDE THE DIRECTOR'S DEATH...
YES... MEANWHILE, WE'LL KEEP NEGOTIATING THE EXCHANGE OF THE DEPUTY DIRECTOR'S DAUGHTER FOR THE NOTEBOOK, AND TRY AND CATCH THE CULPRIT...
HYUK, YOU SURE GOT OUT OF THIS ONE, LIGHT. IF THE WHOLE POLICE FORCE MOVED, YOUR SISTER MIGHT END UP DEAD... I GUESS EVEN YOU HAVE A SOFT SPOT FOR YOUR SISTER, HUH?
...THAT'S NOT ALL. WITH MY EXPLANATION, NOBODY WILL EVER SUSPECT US, ESPECIALLY MY FATHER OR ME, OF BEING KIRA.

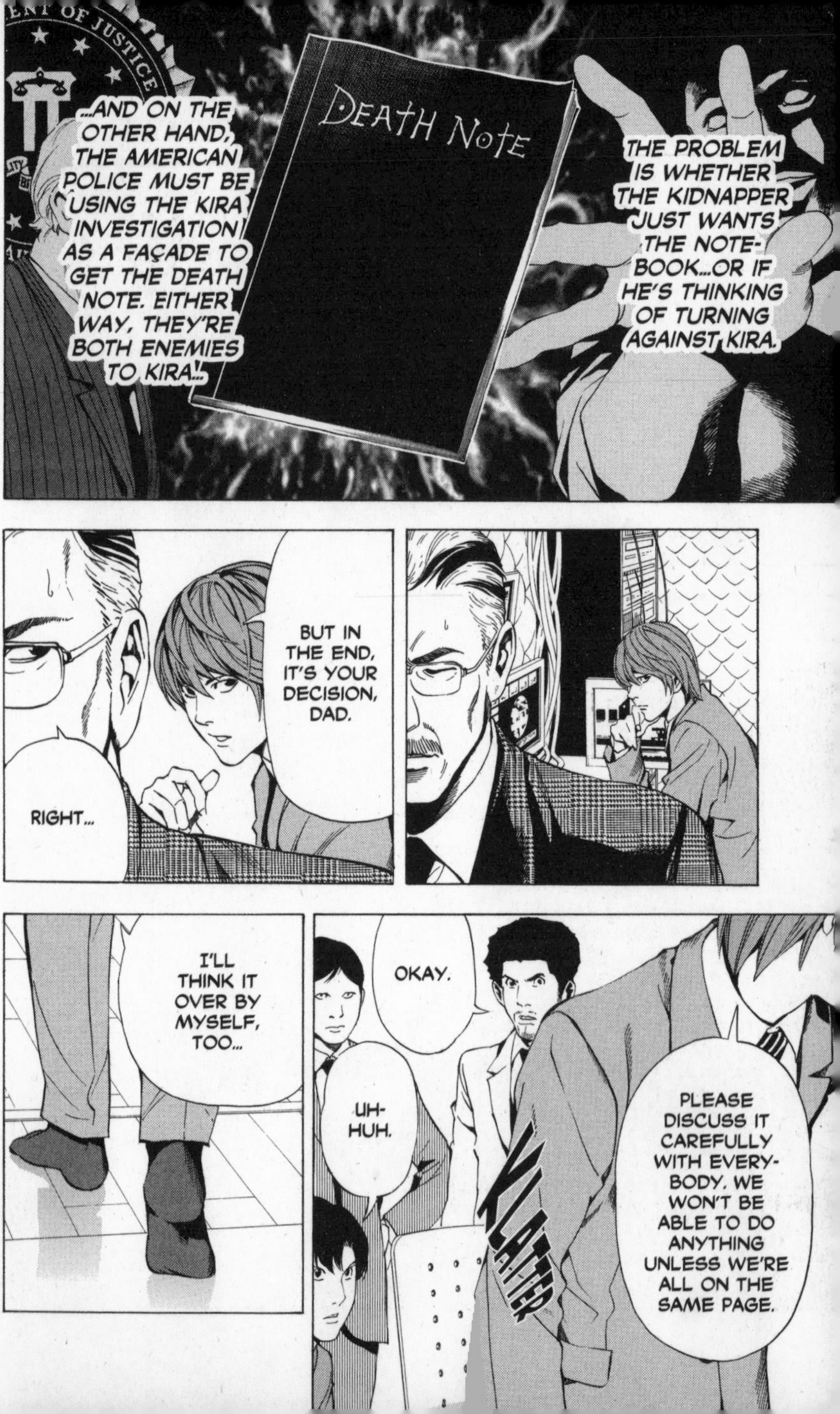
THE PROBLEM IS WHETHER THE KIDNAPPER JUST WANTS THE NOTE-BOOK...OR IF HE'S THINKING OF TURNING AGAINST KIRA.
DEATH NOTE
...AND ON THE OTHER HAND, THE AMERICAN POLICE MUST BE USING THE KIRA INVESTIGATION AS A FAÇADE TO GET THE DEATH NOTE. EITHER WAY, THEY'RE BOTH ENEMIES TO KIRA...
BUT IN THE END, IT'S YOUR DECISION, DAD.
RIGHT...
PLEASE DISCUSS IT CAREFULLY WITH EVERY-BODY. WE WON'T BE ABLE TO DO ANYTHING UNLESS WE'RE ALL ON THE SAME PAGE.
OKAY.
UH-HUH.
KLATTER
I'LL THINK IT OVER BY MYSELF, TOO...

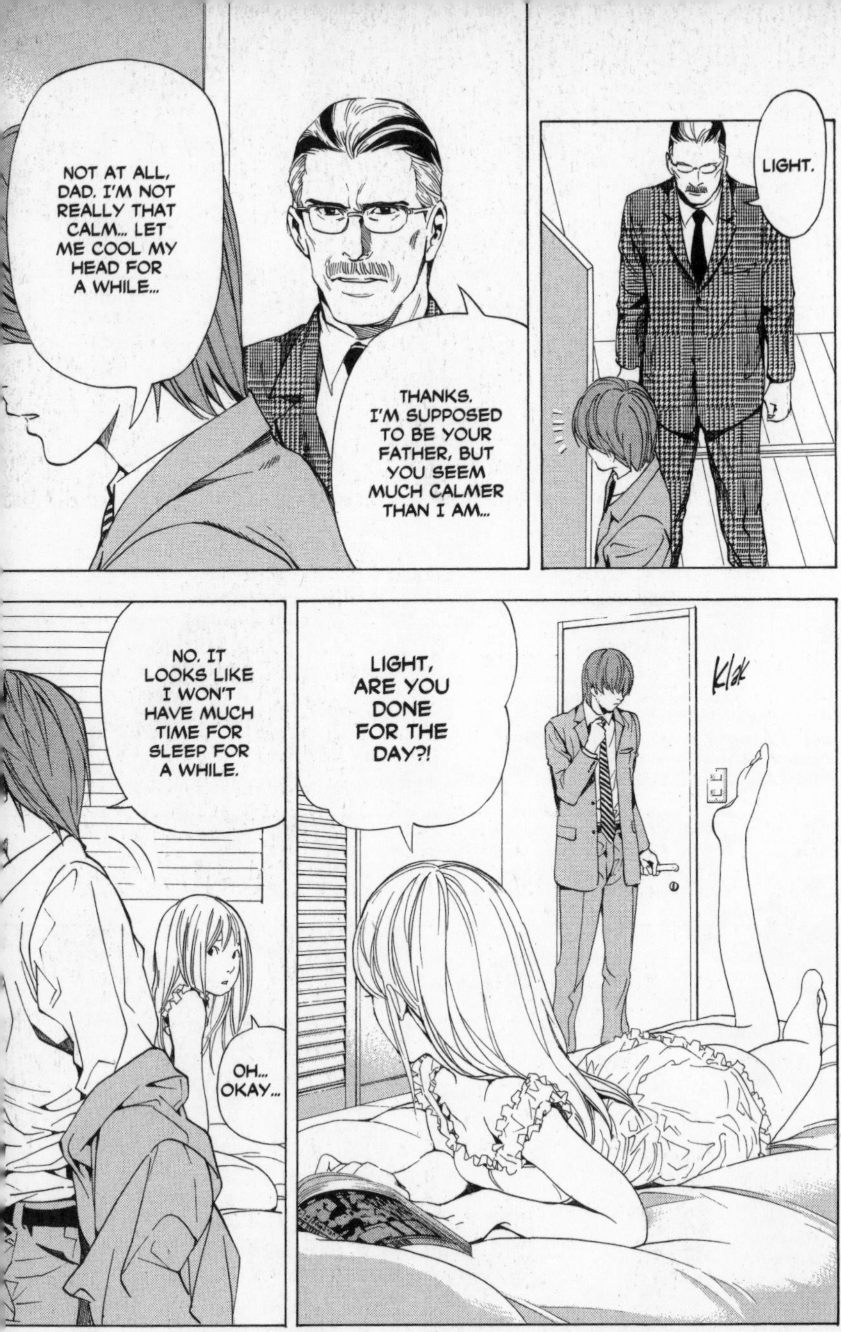
LIGHT.
THANKS. I'M SUPPOSED TO BE YOUR FATHER, BUT YOU SEEM MUCH CALMER THAN I AM...
NOT AT ALL, DAD. I'M NOT REALLY THAT CALM... LET ME COOL MY HEAD FOR A WHILE...
KLAK
LIGHT, ARE YOU DONE FOR THE DAY?!
NO. IT LOOKS LIKE I WON'T HAVE MUCH TIME FOR SLEEP FOR A WHILE.
OH... OKAY...

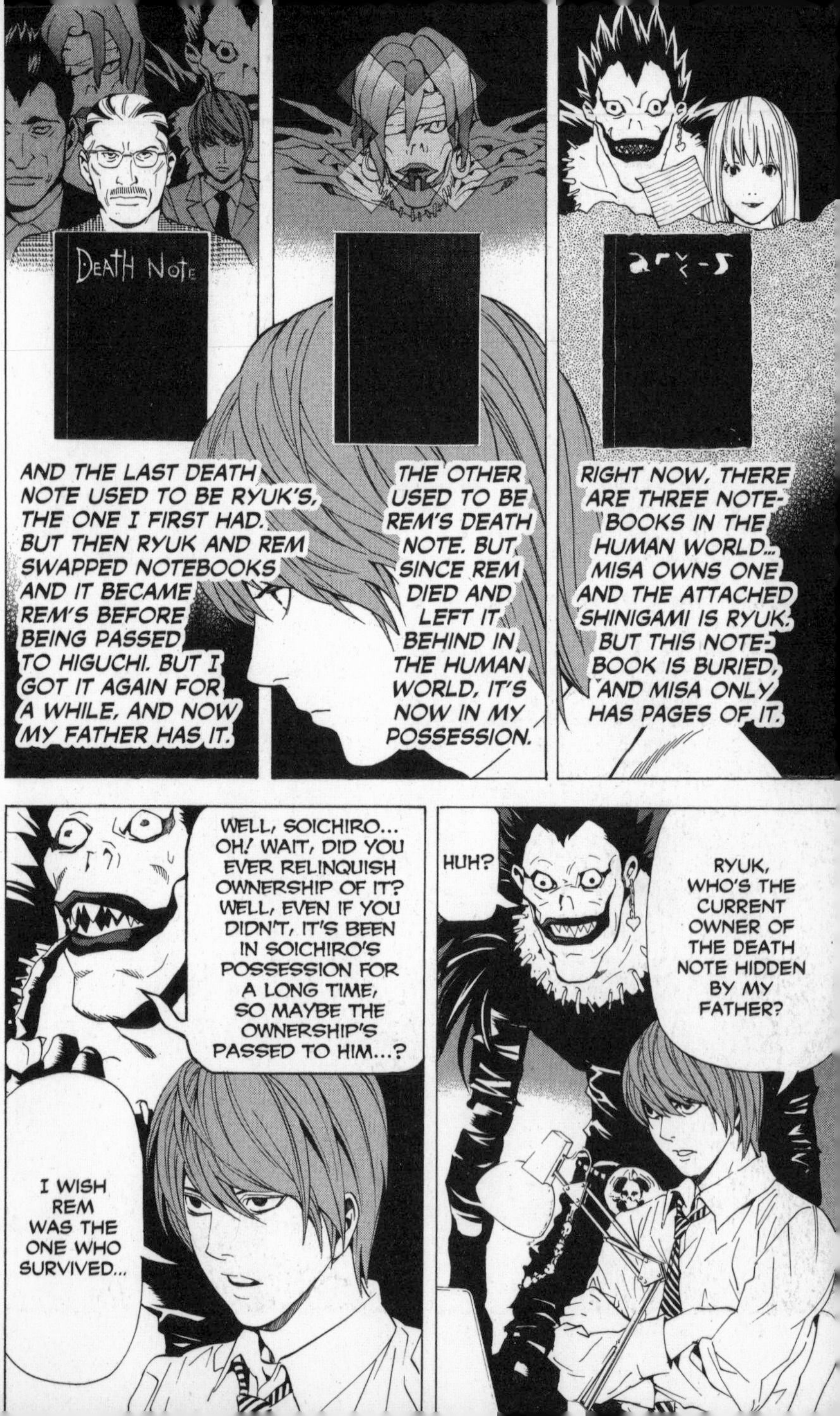
RIGHT NOW, THERE ARE THREE NOTE-BOOKS IN THE HUMAN WORLD... MISA OWNS ONE AND THE ATTACHED SHINIGAMI IS RYUK. BUT THIS NOTE-BOOK IS BURIED, AND MISA ONLY HAS PAGES OF IT.
THE OTHER USED TO BE REM'S DEATH NOTE. BUT, SINCE REM DIED AND LEFT IT BEHIND IN THE HUMAN WORLD, IT'S NOW IN MY POSSESSION.
DEATH NOTE
AND THE LAST DEATH NOTE USED TO BE RYUK'S, THE ONE I FIRST HAD. BUT THEN RYUK AND REM SWAPPED NOTEBOOKS AND IT BECAME REM'S BEFORE BEING PASSED TO HIGUCHI. BUT I GOT IT AGAIN FOR A WHILE, AND NOW MY FATHER HAS IT.
RYUK, WHO'S THE CURRENT OWNER OF THE DEATH NOTE HIDDEN BY MY FATHER?
HUH?
WELL, SOICHIRO... OH! WAIT, DID YOU EVER RELINQUISH OWNERSHIP OF IT? WELL, EVEN IF YOU DIDN'T, IT'S BEEN IN SOICHIRO'S POSSESSION FOR A LONG TIME, SO MAYBE THE OWNERSHIP'S PASSED TO HIM...?
I WISH REM WAS THE ONE WHO SURVIVED...

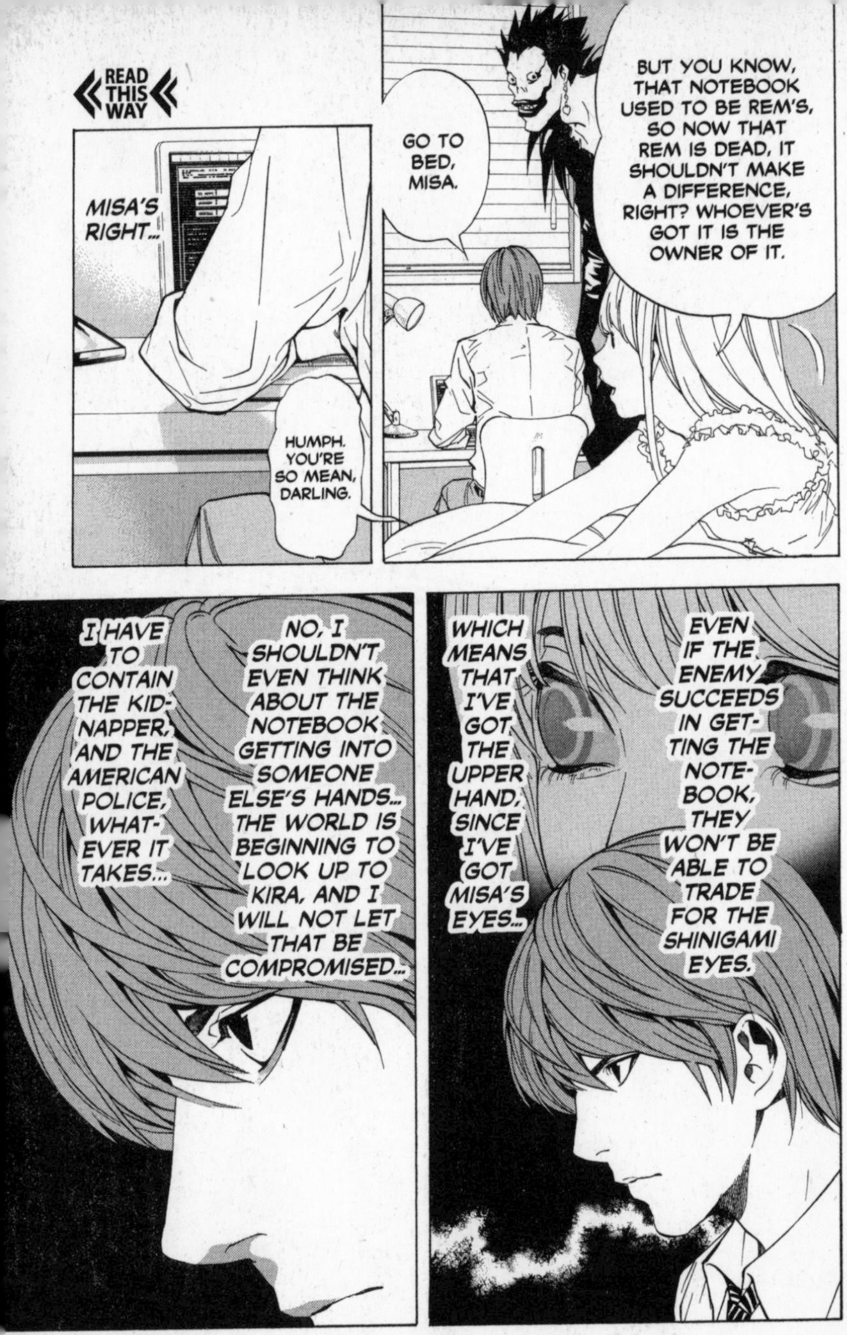
READ THIS WAY
BUT YOU KNOW, THAT NOTEBOOK USED TO BE REM'S, SO NOW THAT REM IS DEAD, IT SHOULDN'T MAKE A DIFFERENCE, RIGHT? WHOEVER'S GOT IT IS THE OWNER OF IT.
GO TO BED, MISA.
MISA'S RIGHT...
HUMPH. YOU'RE SO MEAN, DARLING.
EVEN IF THE ENEMY SUCCEEDS IN GETTING THE NOTEBOOK, THEY WON'T BE ABLE TO TRADE FOR THE SHINIGAMI EYES.
WHICH MEANS THAT I'VE GOT THE UPPER HAND, SINCE I'VE GOT MISA'S EYES...
NO, I SHOULDN'T EVEN THINK ABOUT THE NOTEBOOK GETTING INTO SOMEONE ELSE'S HANDS... THE WORLD IS BEGINNING TO LOOK UP TO KIRA, AND I WILL NOT LET THAT BE COMPROMISED...
I HAVE TO CONTAIN THE KIDNAPPER, AND THE AMERICAN POLICE, WHATEVER IT TAKES...

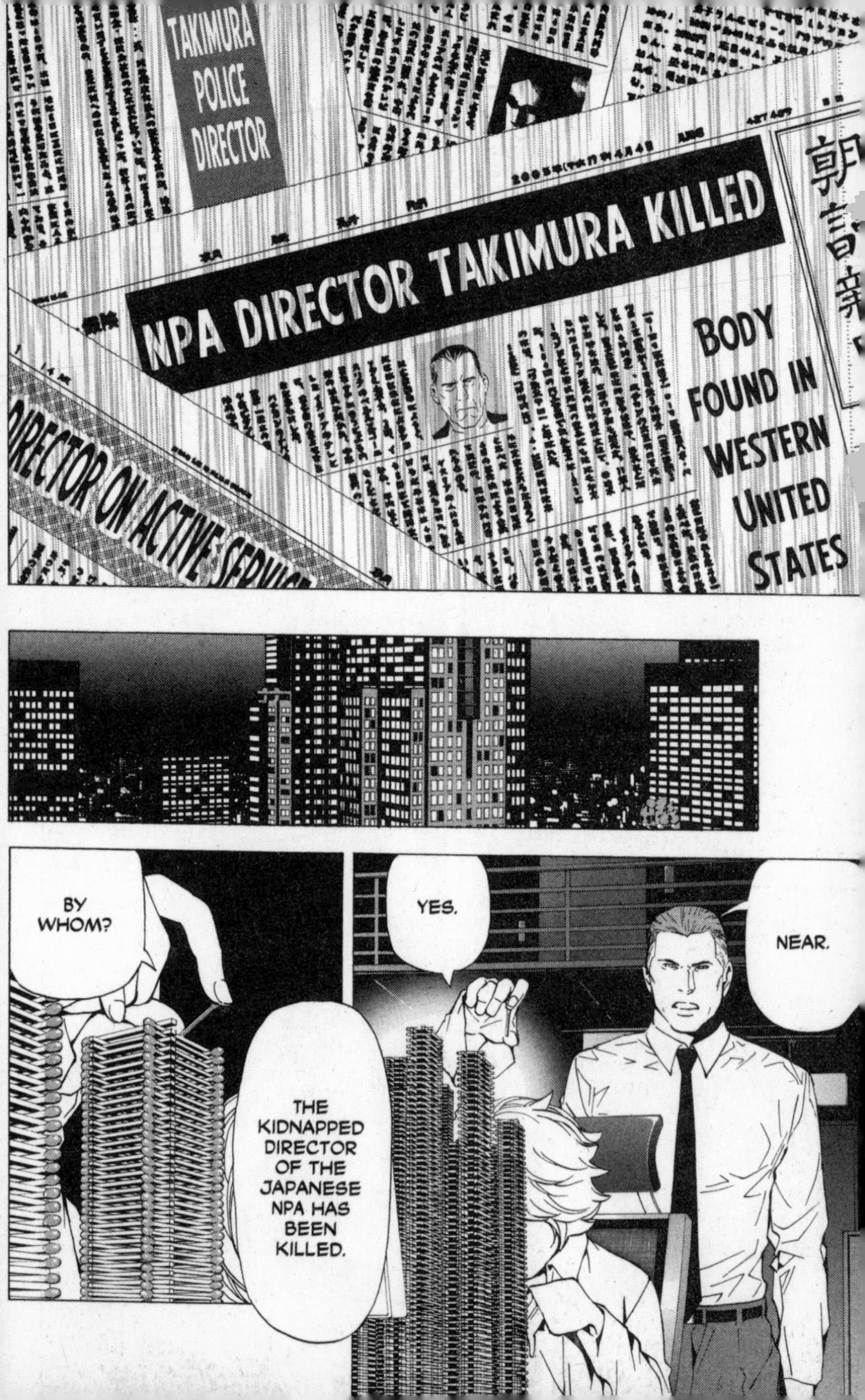

TAKIMURA POLICE DIRECTOR
NPA DIRECTOR TAKIMURA KILLED
BODY FOUND IN WESTERN UNITED STATES
DIRECTOR ON ACTIVE
NEAR.
YES.
THE KIDNAPPED DIRECTOR OF THE JAPANESE NPA HAS BEEN KILLED.
BY WHOM?

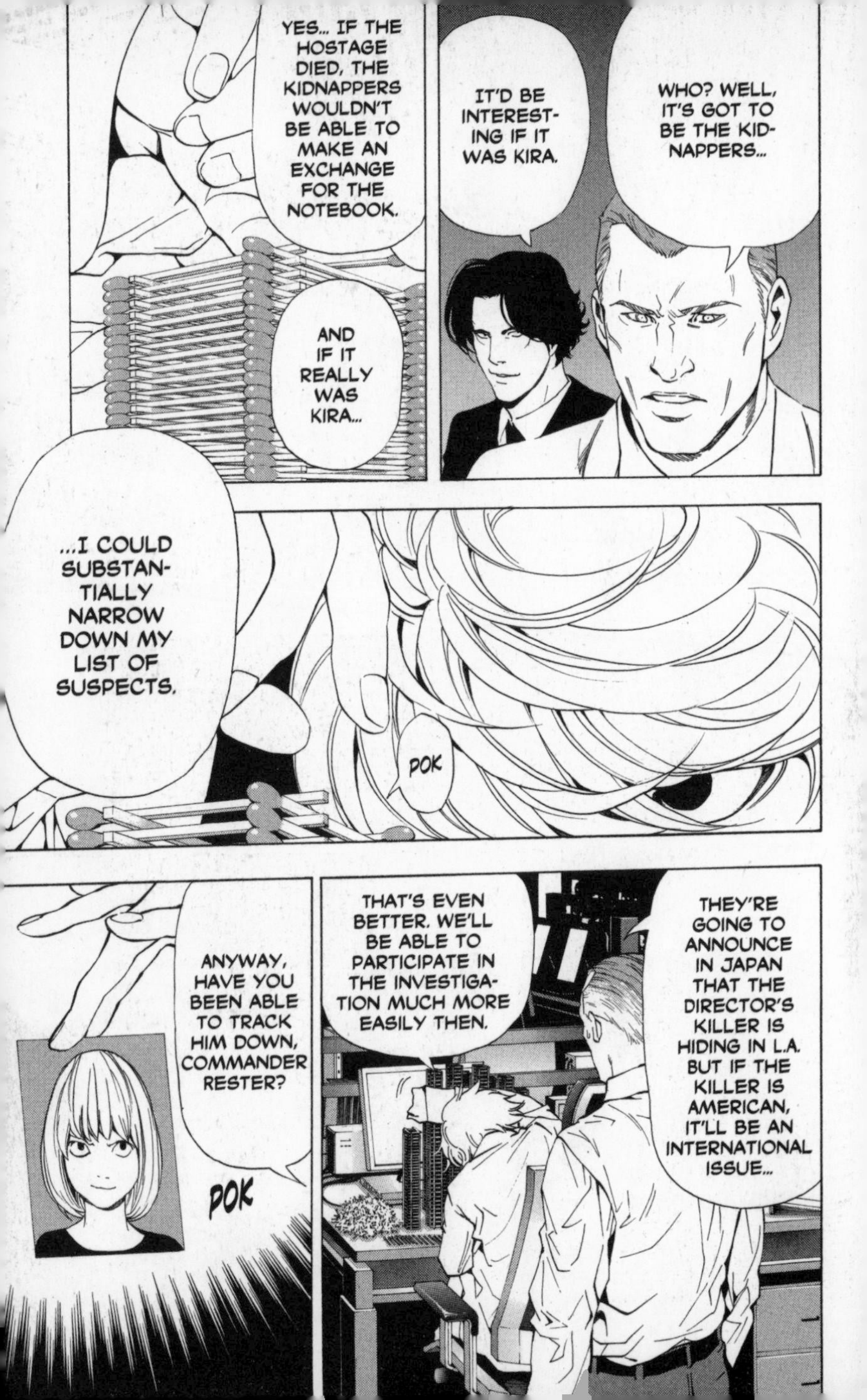
WHO? WELL, IT'S GOT TO BE THE KID-NAPPERS...
IT'D BE INTEREST-ING IF IT WAS KIRA.
YES... IF THE HOSTAGE DIED, THE KIDNAPPERS WOULDN'T BE ABLE TO MAKE AN EXCHANGE FOR THE NOTEBOOK.
AND IF IT REALLY WAS KIRA...
...I COULD SUBSTAN-TIALLY NARROW DOWN MY LIST OF SUSPECTS.
POK
THEY'RE GOING TO ANNOUNCE IN JAPAN THAT THE DIRECTOR'S KILLER IS HIDING IN L.A. BUT IF THE KILLER IS AMERICAN, IT'LL BE AN INTERNATIONAL ISSUE...
THAT'S EVEN BETTER. WE'LL BE ABLE TO PARTICIPATE IN THE INVESTIGA-TION MUCH MORE EASILY THEN.
ANYWAY, HAVE YOU BEEN ABLE TO TRACK HIM DOWN, COMMANDER RESTER?
POK

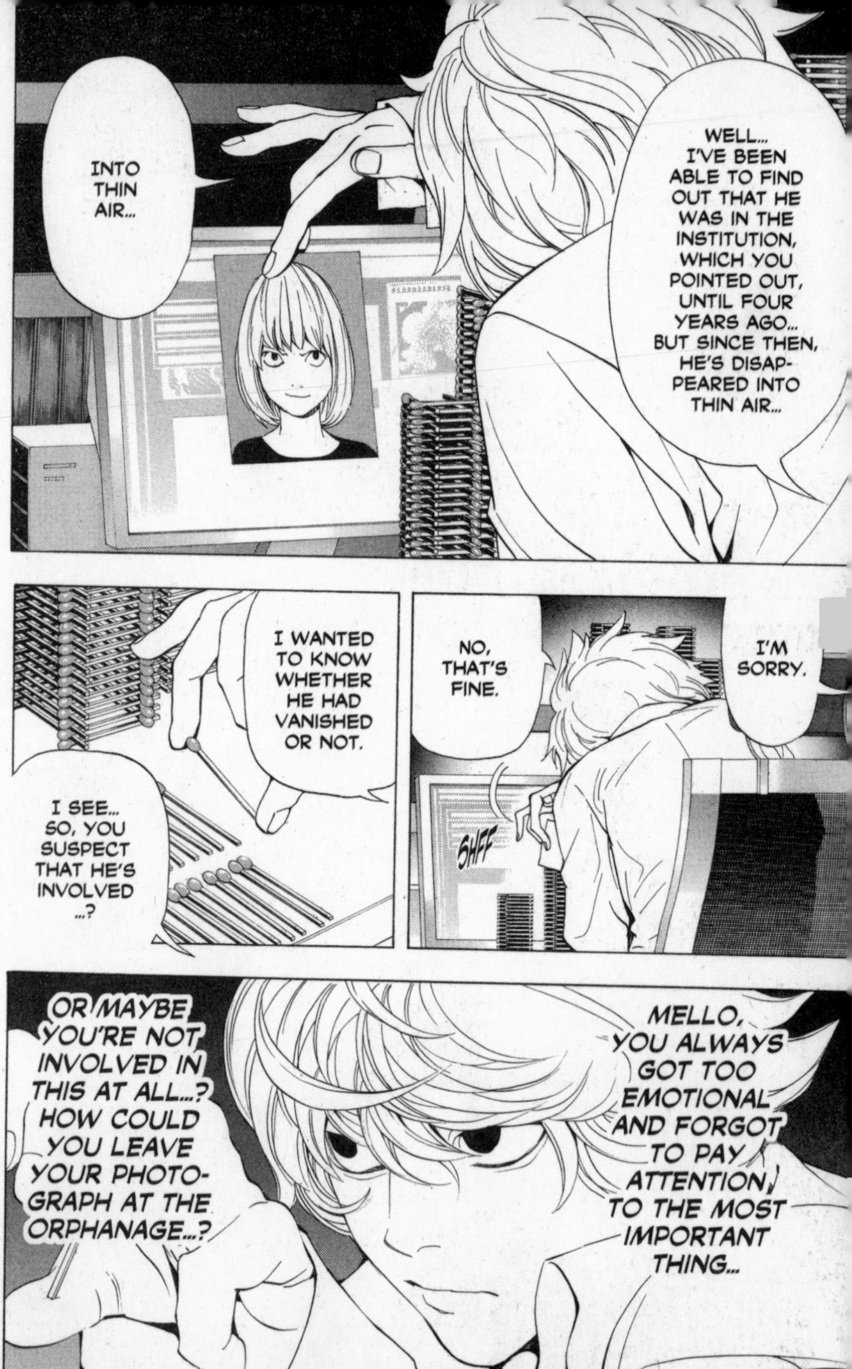
WELL... I'VE BEEN ABLE TO FIND OUT THAT HE WAS IN THE INSTITUTION, WHICH YOU POINTED OUT, UNTIL FOUR YEARS AGO... BUT SINCE THEN, HE'S DISAP-PEARED INTO THIN AIR...
INTO THIN AIR...
I'M SORRY.
NO, THAT'S FINE.
SHFF
I WANTED TO KNOW WHETHER HE HAD VANISHED OR NOT.
I SEE... SO, YOU SUSPECT THAT HE'S INVOLVED ...?
MELLO, YOU ALWAYS GOT TOO EMOTIONAL AND FORGOT TO PAY ATTENTION TO THE MOST IMPORTANT THING...
OR MAYBE YOU'RE NOT INVOLVED IN THIS AT ALL...? HOW COULD YOU LEAVE YOUR PHOTO-GRAPH AT THE ORPHANAGE...?

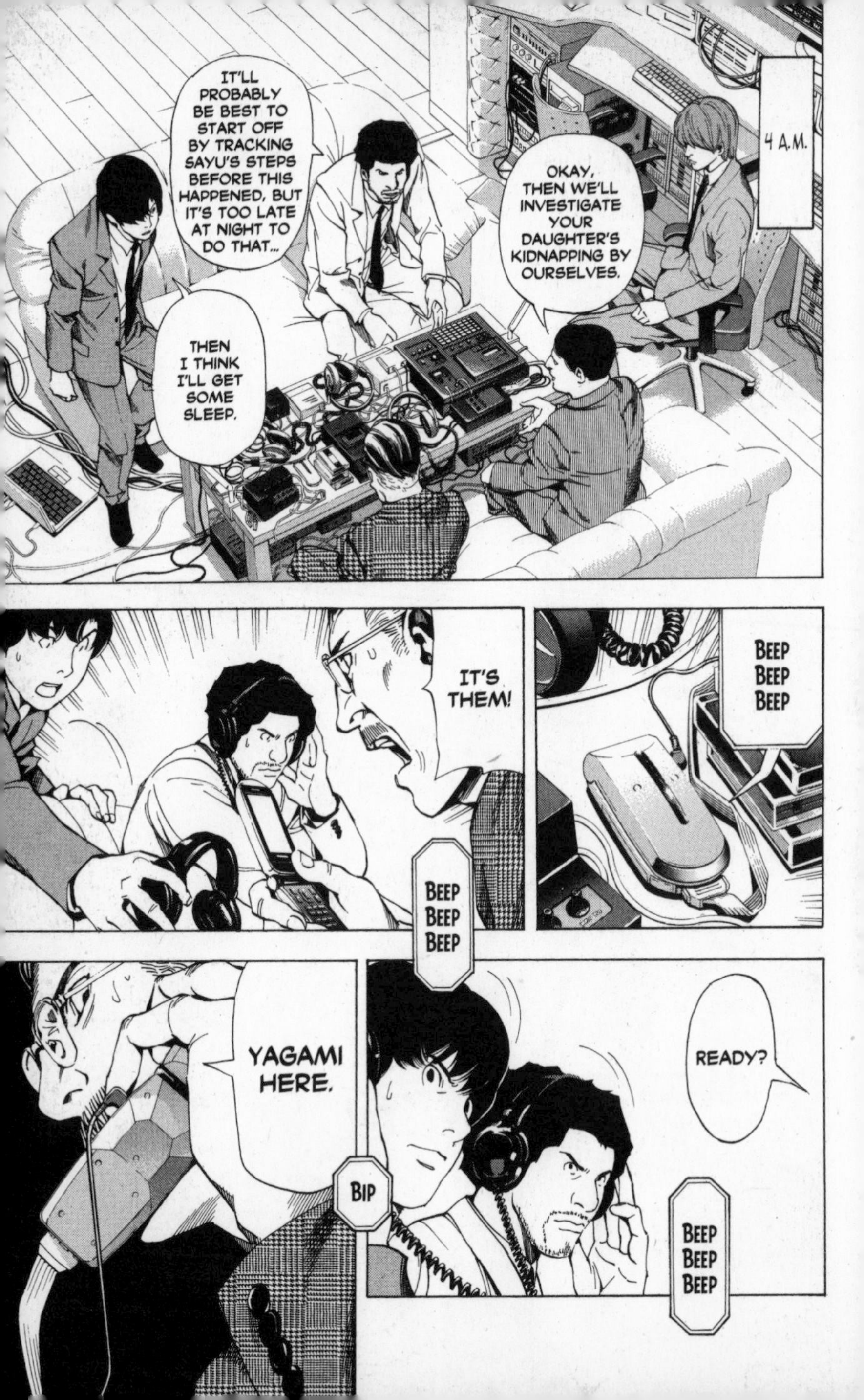
4 A.M.
OKAY, THEN WE'LL INVESTIGATE YOUR DAUGHTER'S KIDNAPPING BY OURSELVES.
IT'LL PROBABLY BE BEST TO START OFF BY TRACKING SAYU'S STEPS BEFORE THIS HAPPENED, BUT IT'S TOO LATE AT NIGHT TO DO THAT...
THEN I THINK I'LL GET SOME SLEEP.
BEEP BEEP BEEP
IT'S THEM!
BEEP BEEP BEEP
READY?
BEEP BEEP BEEP
YAGAMI HERE.
BIP

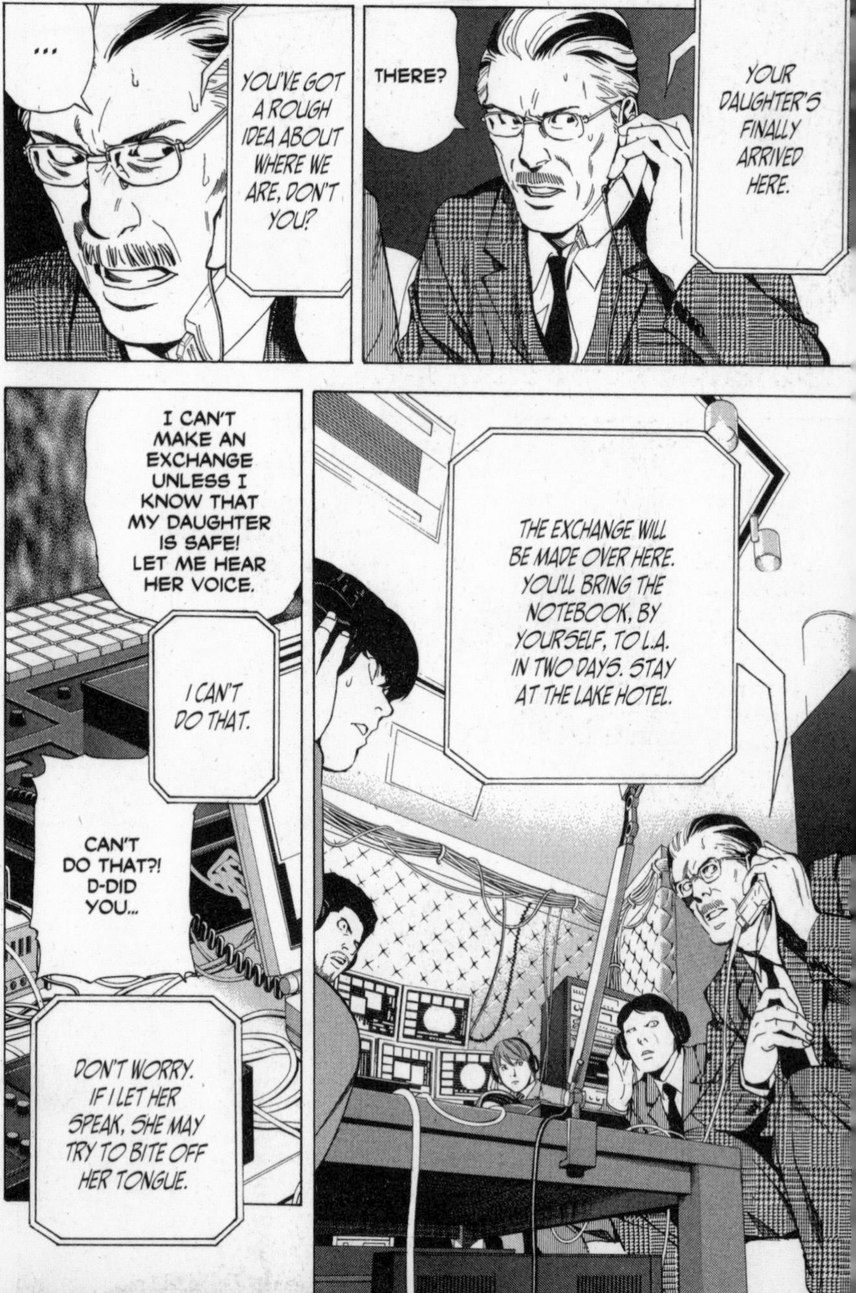
YOUR DAUGHTER'S FINALLY ARRIVED HERE.
THERE?
YOU'VE GOT A ROUGH IDEA ABOUT WHERE WE ARE, DON'T YOU?
...
THE EXCHANGE WILL BE MADE OVER HERE. YOU'LL BRING THE NOTEBOOK, BY YOURSELF, TO L.A. IN TWO DAYS. STAY AT THE LAKE HOTEL.
I CAN'T MAKE AN EXCHANGE UNLESS I KNOW THAT MY DAUGHTER IS SAFE! LET ME HEAR HER VOICE.
I CAN'T DO THAT.
CAN'T DO THAT?! D-DID YOU...
DON'T WORRY. IF I LET HER SPEAK, SHE MAY TRY TO BITE OFF HER TONGUE.

I CAN'T MAKE AN EXCHANGE IF THE HOSTAGE DIES AGAIN, RIGHT?

BUT, YOU KNOW...

...IF YOU OR I ANNOUNCE TO THE PUBLIC...

?!

...THAT THE KIDNAPPER IS ASKING FOR THE NOTEBOOK IN EXCHANGE FOR HER, I BET SHE'LL DIE...

BUT... I'M NOT THE POLICE, AND I'VE GOT NO INTENTION OF LEAKING THE INFORMATION. THAT GIVES YOU A GOOD REASON TO KEEP THIS BETWEEN US, YOU KNOW?

HYUK HYUK

WH-WHAT ARE YOU TALKING ABOUT?! I'M ASKING YOU FOR PROOF OF MY DAUGHTER'S SAFETY. THAT IS A PREREQUISITE FOR THIS EXCHANGE!

OKAY, OKAY. I'LL E-MAIL YOU A PICTURE.

CLICK

BEEEEP

BEEEEP

BEEP

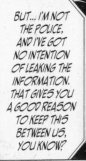

25

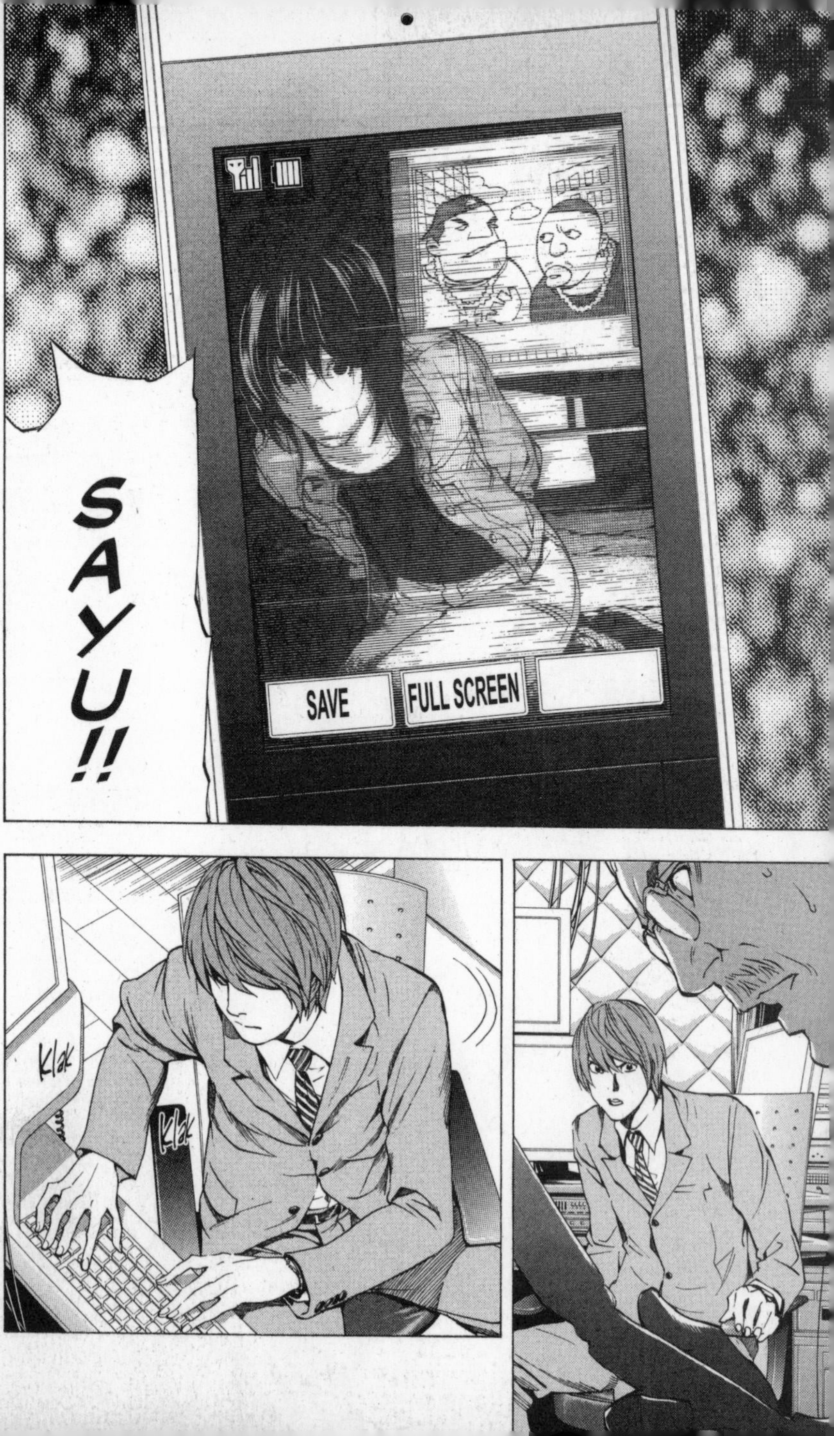
SAVE
FULL SCREEN
SAYU!!
Klak
Klak

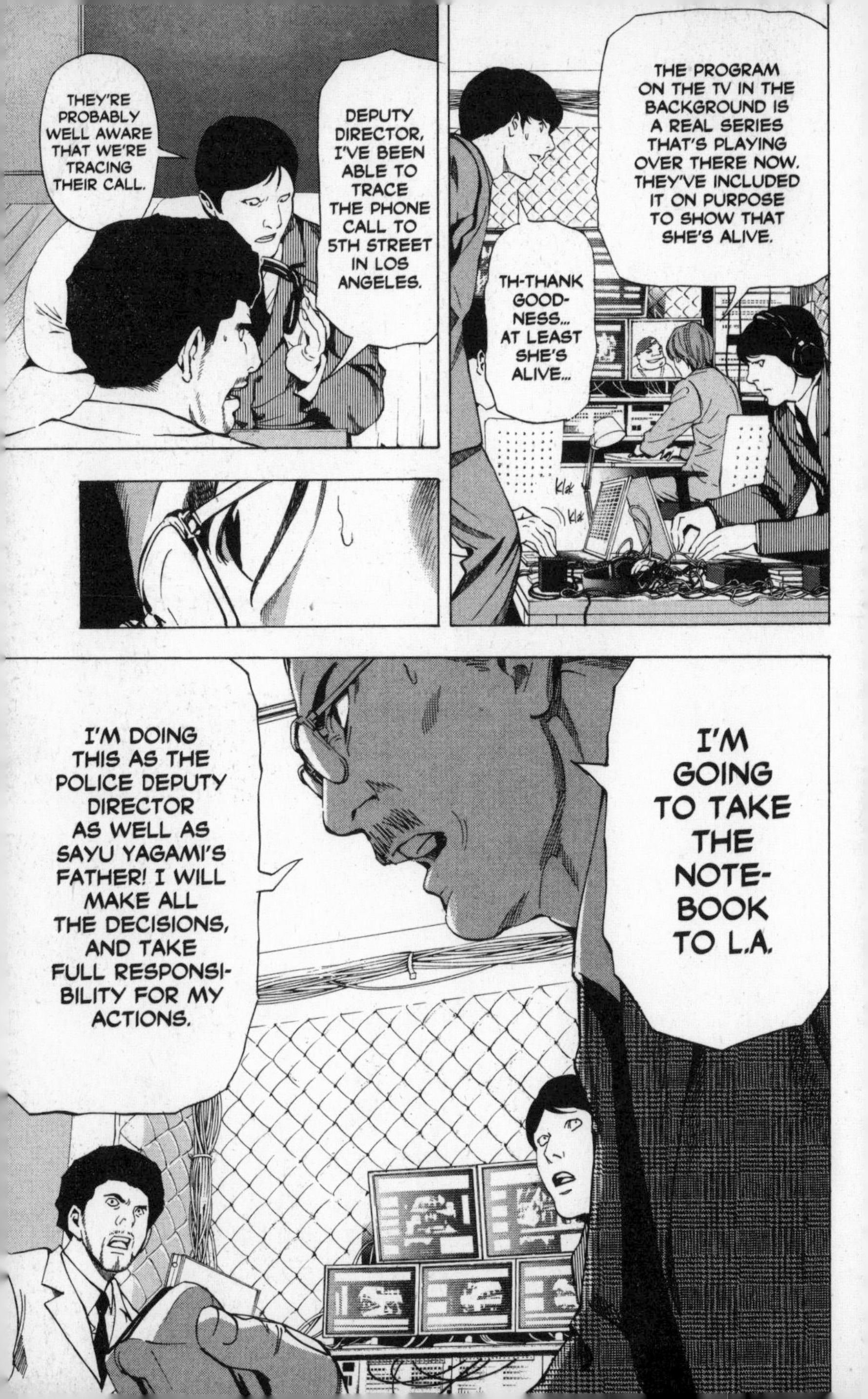
THE PROGRAM ON THE TV IN THE BACKGROUND IS A REAL SERIES THAT'S PLAYING OVER THERE NOW. THEY'VE INCLUDED IT ON PURPOSE TO SHOW THAT SHE'S ALIVE.
TH-THANK GOODNESS... AT LEAST SHE'S ALIVE...
Klak
Klak
DEPUTY DIRECTOR, I'VE BEEN ABLE TO TRACE THE PHONE CALL TO 5TH STREET IN LOS ANGELES.
THEY'RE PROBABLY WELL AWARE THAT WE'RE TRACING THEIR CALL.
I'M GOING TO TAKE THE NOTE-BOOK TO L.A.
I'M DOING THIS AS THE POLICE DEPUTY DIRECTOR AS WELL AS SAYU YAGAMI'S FATHER! I WILL MAKE ALL THE DECISIONS, AND TAKE FULL RESPONSI-BILITY FOR MY ACTIONS.

DEATH NOTE
How to use it
XLII

- The use of the DEATH NOTE in the human world sometimes affects other human's lives or shortens their original life-span, even though their names are not actually written in the DEATH NOTE itself. In these cases, no matter the cause, the god of death sees only the original life-span and not the shortened life-span.

人間界にデスノートがある事である人間の人生が変わり、
デスノートに書かれなくとも本来の寿命より前に死んでしまう事はある。
それがどんな死に方であろうと、その場合、やはり死神の目には
縮んだ寿命でなく本来の寿命が見える事になる。

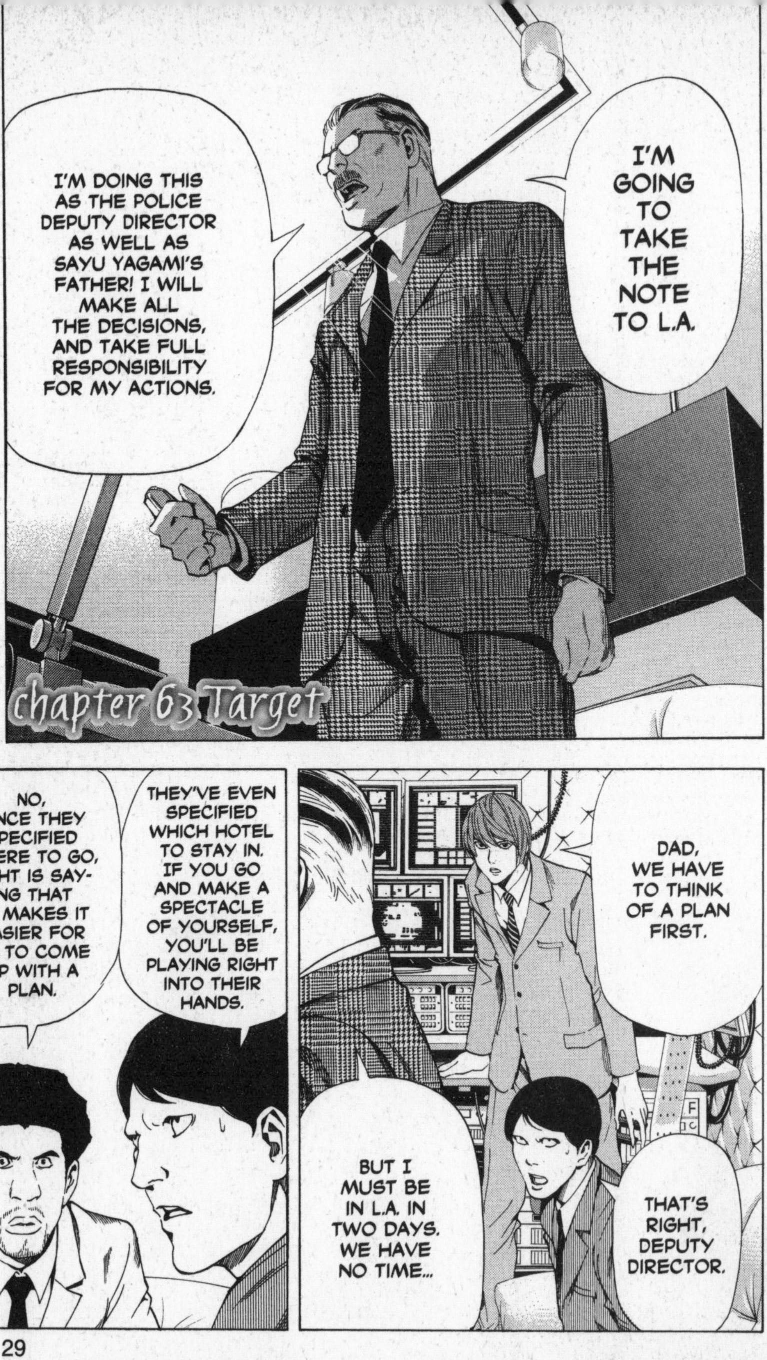
I'M GOING TO TAKE THE NOTE TO L.A.
I'M DOING THIS AS THE POLICE DEPUTY DIRECTOR AS WELL AS SAYU YAGAMI'S FATHER! I WILL MAKE ALL THE DECISIONS, AND TAKE FULL RESPONSIBILITY FOR MY ACTIONS.
chapter 63 Target
DAD, WE HAVE TO THINK OF A PLAN FIRST.
THAT'S RIGHT, DEPUTY DIRECTOR.
BUT I MUST BE IN L.A. IN TWO DAYS. WE HAVE NO TIME...
THEY'VE EVEN SPECIFIED WHICH HOTEL TO STAY IN. IF YOU GO AND MAKE A SPECTACLE OF YOURSELF, YOU'LL BE PLAYING RIGHT INTO THEIR HANDS.
NO, SINCE THEY SPECIFIED WHERE TO GO, LIGHT IS SAYING THAT IT MAKES IT EASIER FOR US TO COME UP WITH A PLAN.

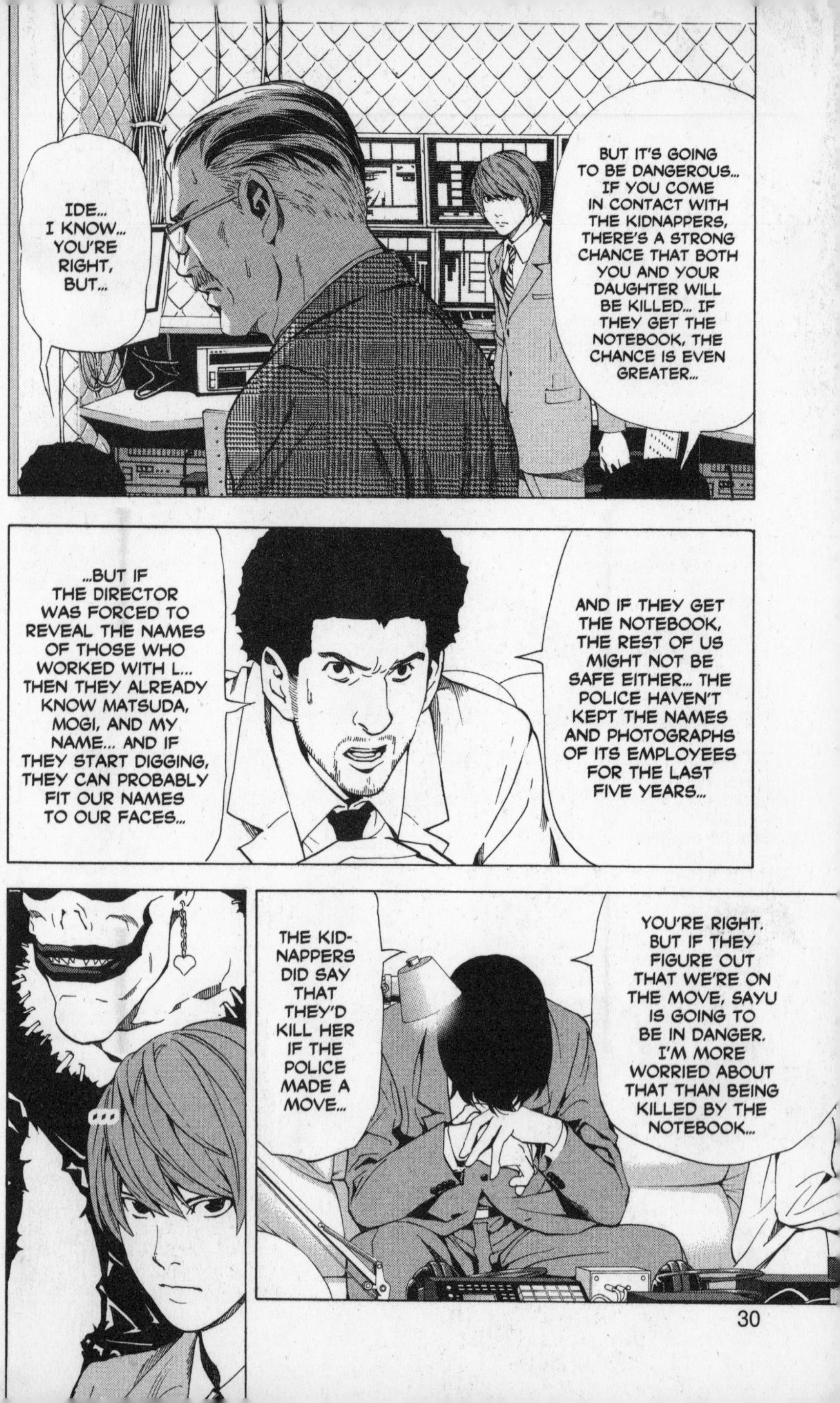
BUT IT'S GOING TO BE DANGEROUS... IF YOU COME IN CONTACT WITH THE KIDNAPPERS, THERE'S A STRONG CHANCE THAT BOTH YOU AND YOUR DAUGHTER WILL BE KILLED... IF THEY GET THE NOTEBOOK, THE CHANCE IS EVEN GREATER...
IDE... I KNOW... YOU'RE RIGHT, BUT...
AND IF THEY GET THE NOTEBOOK, THE REST OF US MIGHT NOT BE SAFE EITHER... THE POLICE HAVEN'T KEPT THE NAMES AND PHOTOGRAPHS OF ITS EMPLOYEES FOR THE LAST FIVE YEARS...
...BUT IF THE DIRECTOR WAS FORCED TO REVEAL THE NAMES OF THOSE WHO WORKED WITH L... THEN THEY ALREADY KNOW MATSUDA, MOGI, AND MY NAME... AND IF THEY START DIGGING, THEY CAN PROBABLY FIT OUR NAMES TO OUR FACES...
YOU'RE RIGHT. BUT IF THEY FIGURE OUT THAT WE'RE ON THE MOVE, SAYU IS GOING TO BE IN DANGER. I'M MORE WORRIED ABOUT THAT THAN BEING KILLED BY THE NOTEBOOK...
THE KID-NAPPERS DID SAY THAT THEY'D KILL HER IF THE POLICE MADE A MOVE...
...

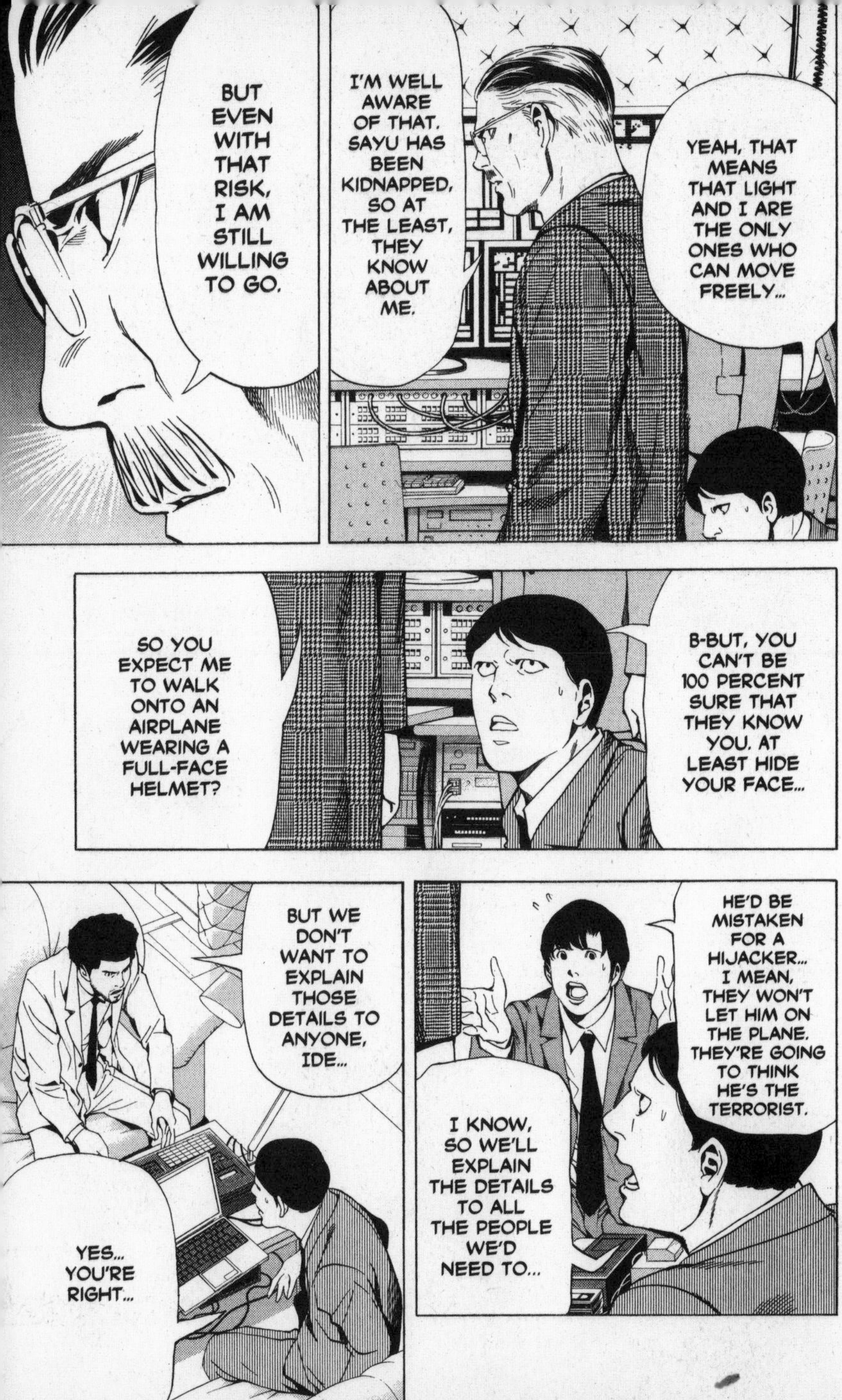
YEAH, THAT MEANS THAT LIGHT AND I ARE THE ONLY ONES WHO CAN MOVE FREELY...
I'M WELL AWARE OF THAT. SAYU HAS BEEN KIDNAPPED, SO AT THE LEAST, THEY KNOW ABOUT ME.
BUT EVEN WITH THAT RISK, I AM STILL WILLING TO GO.
B-BUT, YOU CAN'T BE 100 PERCENT SURE THAT THEY KNOW YOU. AT LEAST HIDE YOUR FACE...
SO YOU EXPECT ME TO WALK ONTO AN AIRPLANE WEARING A FULL-FACE HELMET?
HE'D BE MISTAKEN FOR A HIJACKER... I MEAN, THEY WON'T LET HIM ON THE PLANE. THEY'RE GOING TO THINK HE'S THE TERRORIST.
I KNOW, SO WE'LL EXPLAIN THE DETAILS TO ALL THE PEOPLE WE'D NEED TO...
BUT WE DON'T WANT TO EXPLAIN THOSE DETAILS TO ANYONE, IDE...
YES... YOU'RE RIGHT...

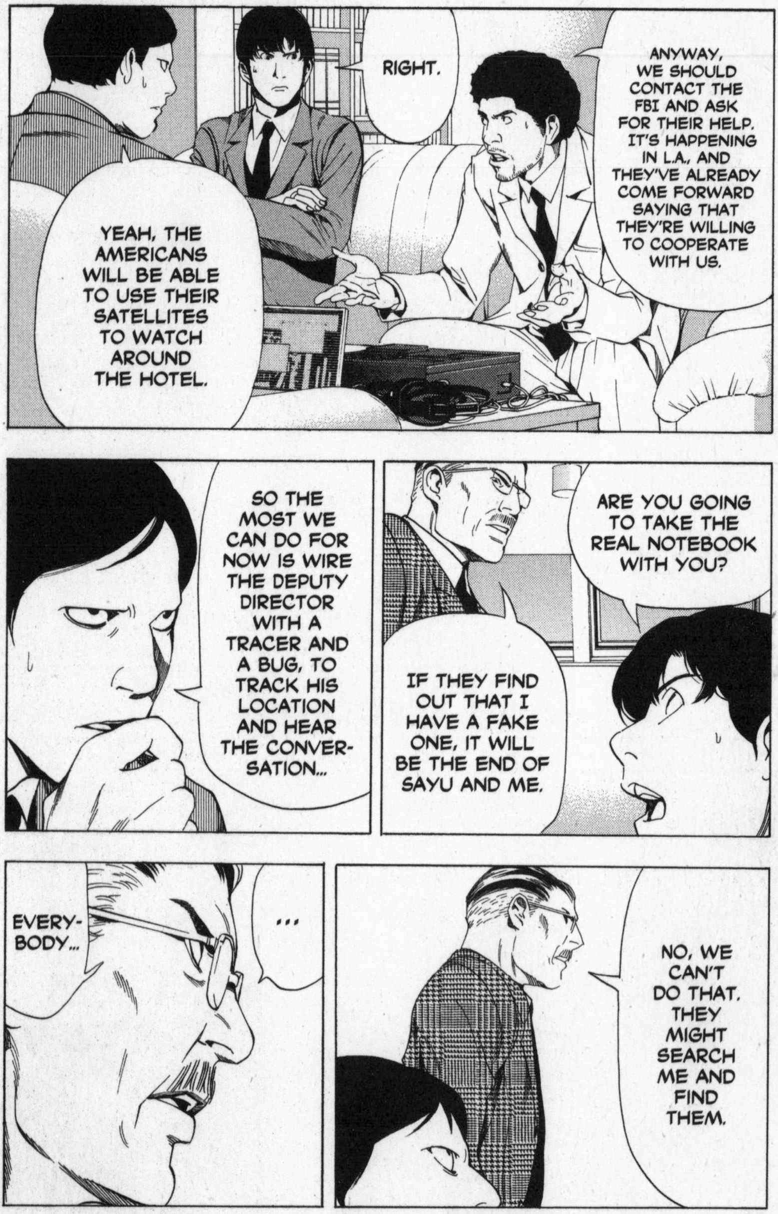

ANYWAY, WE SHOULD CONTACT THE FBI AND ASK FOR THEIR HELP. IT'S HAPPENING IN L.A., AND THEY'VE ALREADY COME FORWARD SAYING THAT THEY'RE WILLING TO COOPERATE WITH US.
RIGHT.
YEAH, THE AMERICANS WILL BE ABLE TO USE THEIR SATELLITES TO WATCH AROUND THE HOTEL.
ARE YOU GOING TO TAKE THE REAL NOTEBOOK WITH YOU?
IF THEY FIND OUT THAT I HAVE A FAKE ONE, IT WILL BE THE END OF SAYU AND ME.
SO THE MOST WE CAN DO FOR NOW IS WIRE THE DEPUTY DIRECTOR WITH A TRACER AND A BUG, TO TRACK HIS LOCATION AND HEAR THE CONVERSATION...
NO, WE CAN'T DO THAT. THEY MIGHT SEARCH ME AND FIND THEM.
...
EVERY-BODY...

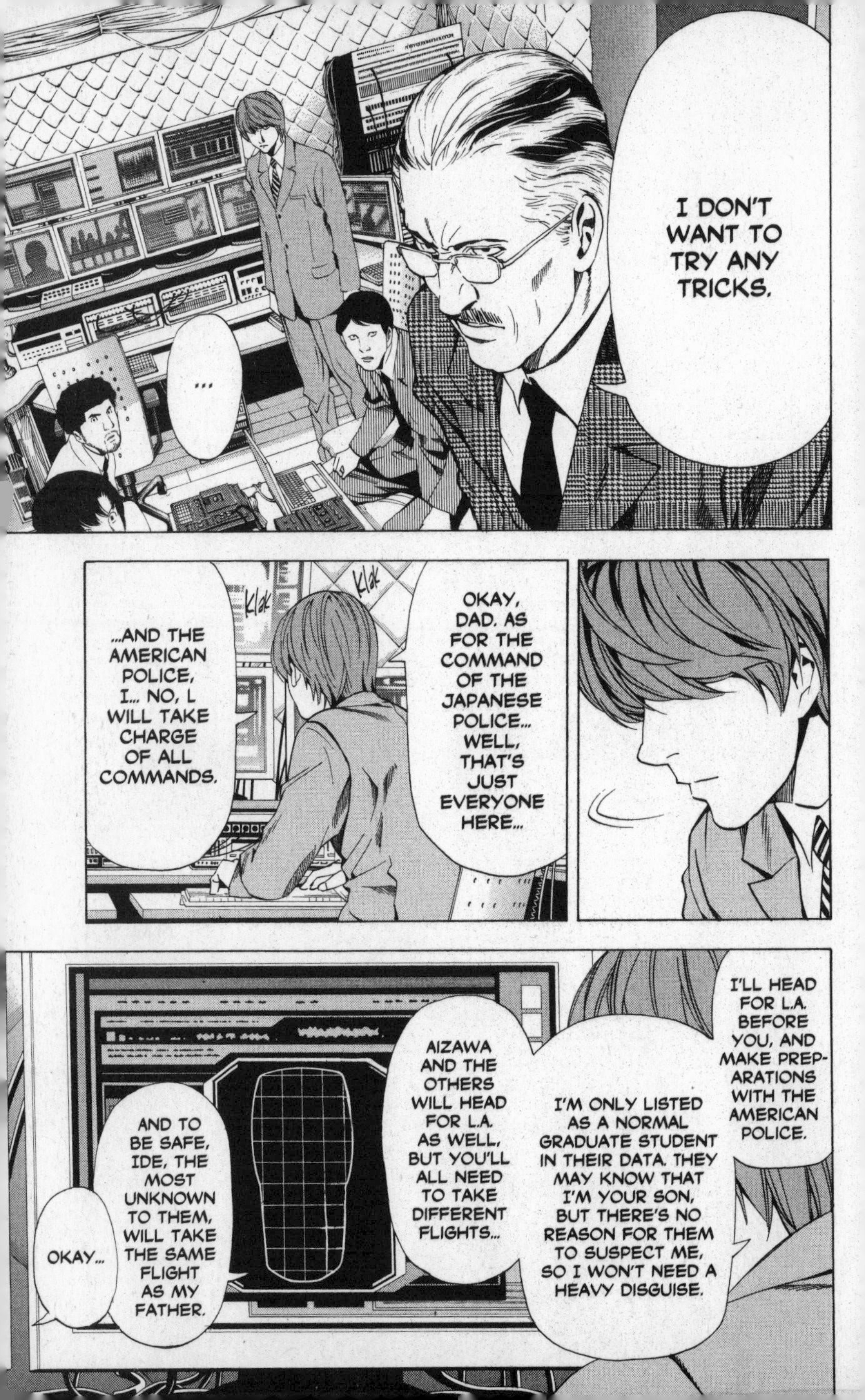
I DON'T WANT TO TRY ANY TRICKS.
...
Klak
Klak
OKAY, DAD. AS FOR THE COMMAND OF THE JAPANESE POLICE... WELL, THAT'S JUST EVERYONE HERE...
...AND THE AMERICAN POLICE, I... NO, L WILL TAKE CHARGE OF ALL COMMANDS.
I'LL HEAD FOR L.A. BEFORE YOU, AND MAKE PREPARATIONS WITH THE AMERICAN POLICE.
I'M ONLY LISTED AS A NORMAL GRADUATE STUDENT IN THEIR DATA. THEY MAY KNOW THAT I'M YOUR SON, BUT THERE'S NO REASON FOR THEM TO SUSPECT ME, SO I WON'T NEED A HEAVY DISGUISE.
AIZAWA AND THE OTHERS WILL HEAD FOR L.A. AS WELL, BUT YOU'LL ALL NEED TO TAKE DIFFERENT FLIGHTS...
AND TO BE SAFE, IDE, THE MOST UNKNOWN TO THEM, WILL TAKE THE SAME FLIGHT AS MY FATHER.
OKAY...

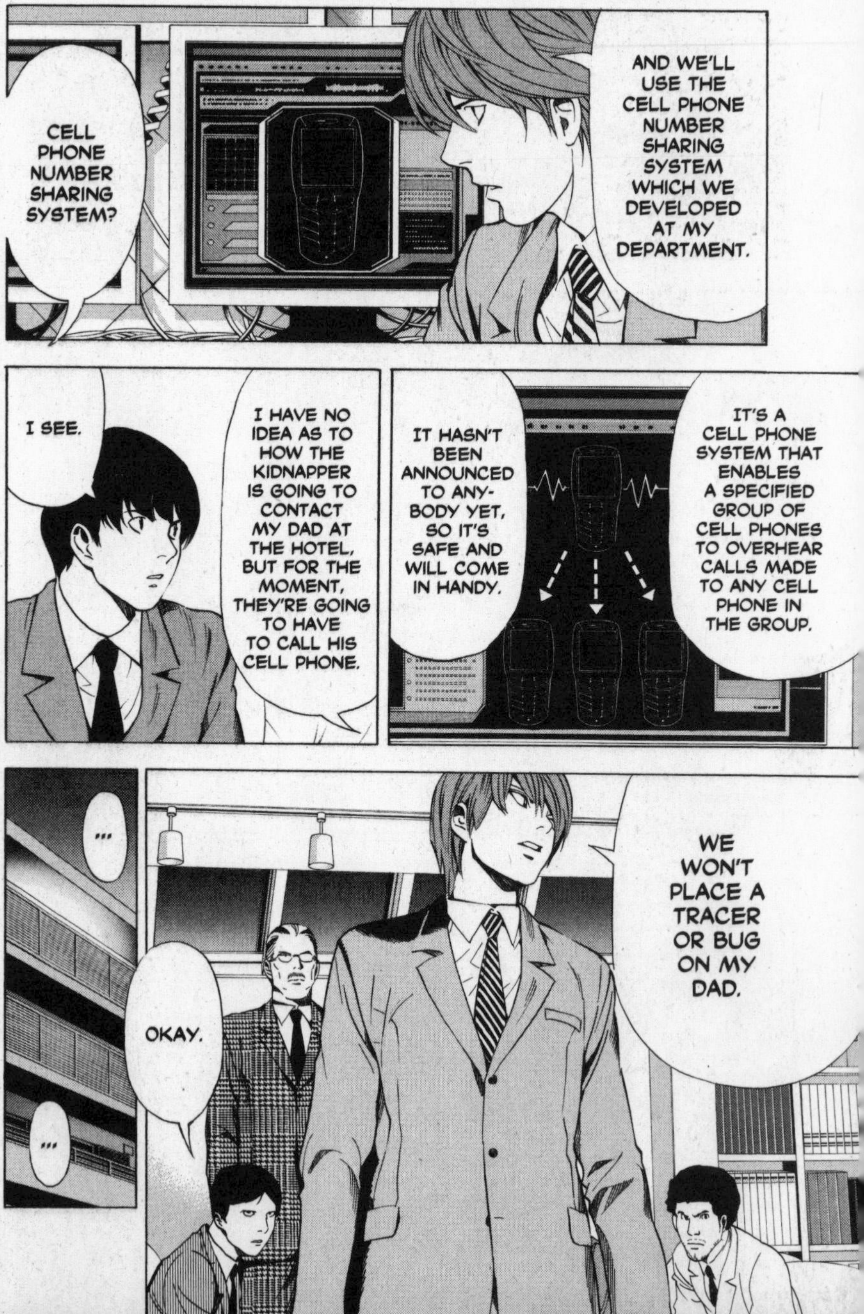
AND WE'LL USE THE CELL PHONE NUMBER SHARING SYSTEM WHICH WE DEVELOPED AT MY DEPARTMENT.
CELL PHONE NUMBER SHARING SYSTEM?
IT'S A CELL PHONE SYSTEM THAT ENABLES A SPECIFIED GROUP OF CELL PHONES TO OVERHEAR CALLS MADE TO ANY CELL PHONE IN THE GROUP.
IT HASN'T BEEN ANNOUNCED TO ANY-BODY YET, SO IT'S SAFE AND WILL COME IN HANDY.
I HAVE NO IDEA AS TO HOW THE KIDNAPPER IS GOING TO CONTACT MY DAD AT THE HOTEL, BUT FOR THE MOMENT, THEY'RE GOING TO HAVE TO CALL HIS CELL PHONE.
I SEE.
WE WON'T PLACE A TRACER OR BUG ON MY DAD.
OKAY.
...
...

READ THIS WAY

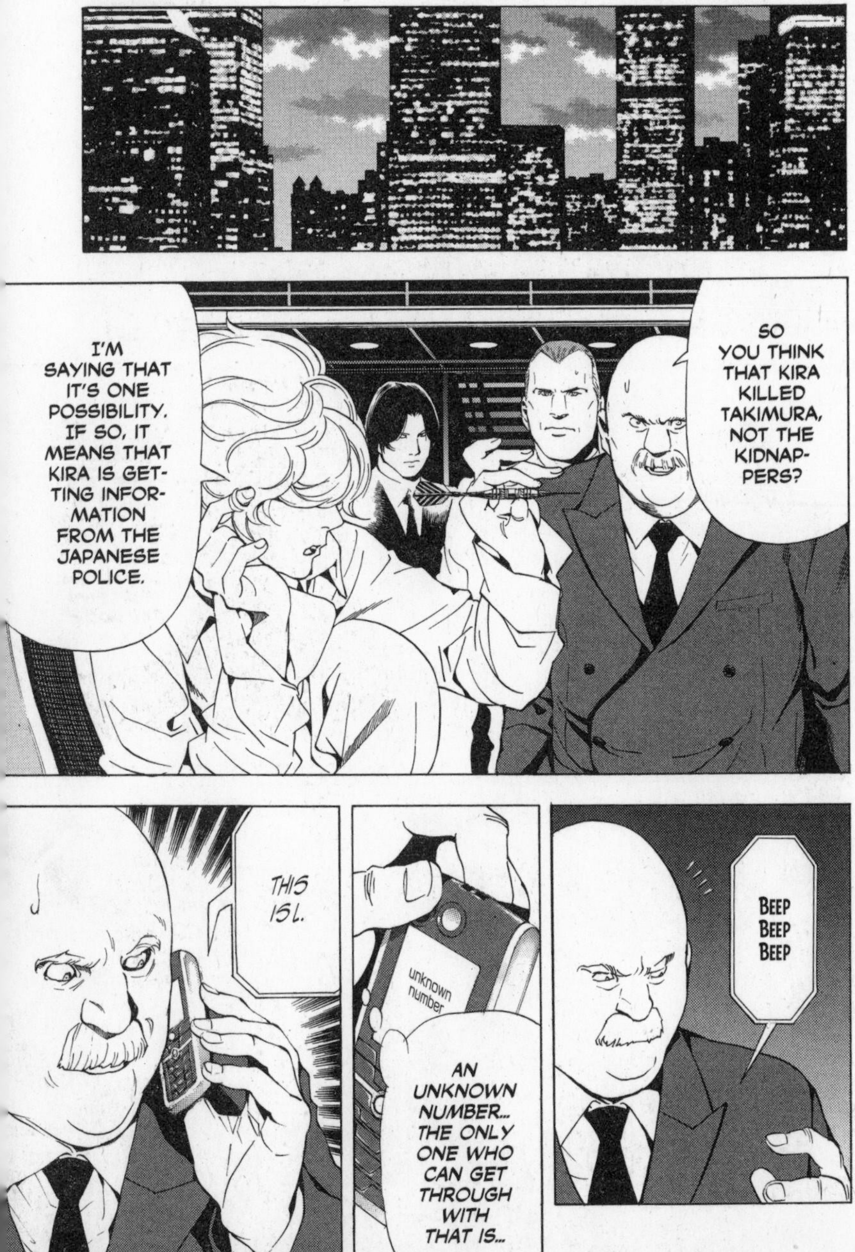

SO YOU THINK THAT KIRA KILLED TAKIMURA, NOT THE KIDNAPPERS?
I'M SAYING THAT IT'S ONE POSSIBILITY. IF SO, IT MEANS THAT KIRA IS GETTING INFORMATION FROM THE JAPANESE POLICE.
BEEP BEEP BEEP
unknown number
AN UNKNOWN NUMBER... THE ONLY ONE WHO CAN GET THROUGH WITH THAT IS...
THIS IS L.

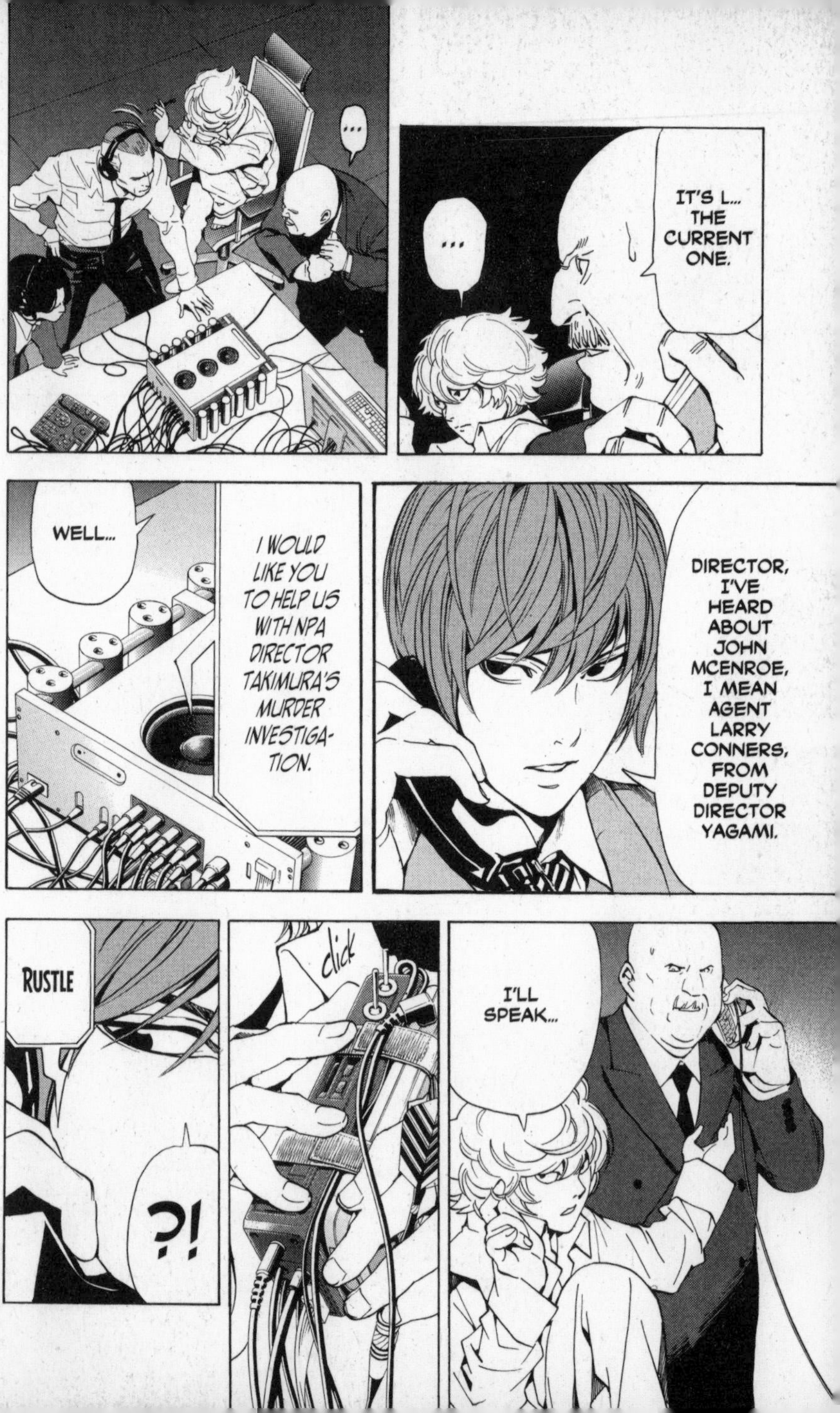
IT'S L... THE CURRENT ONE.
...
...
DIRECTOR, I'VE HEARD ABOUT JOHN MCENROE, I MEAN AGENT LARRY CONNERS, FROM DEPUTY DIRECTOR YAGAMI.
WELL...
I WOULD LIKE YOU TO HELP US WITH NPA DIRECTOR TAKIMURA'S MURDER INVESTIGATION.
I'LL SPEAK...
click
RUSTLE
?!

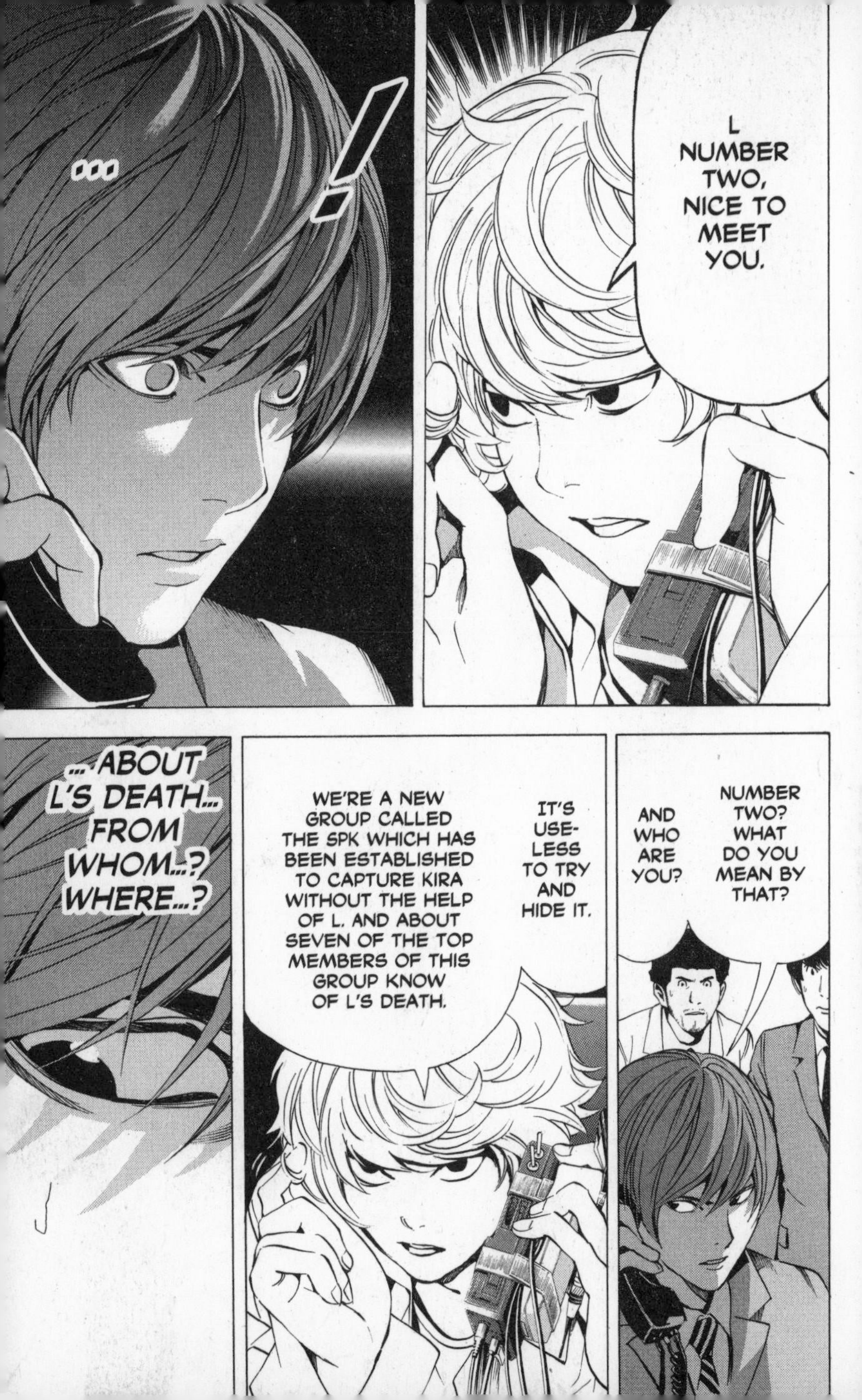
L NUMBER TWO, NICE TO MEET YOU.
...
!
NUMBER TWO? WHAT DO YOU MEAN BY THAT?
AND WHO ARE YOU?
IT'S USE- LESS TO TRY AND HIDE IT.
WE'RE A NEW GROUP CALLED THE SPK WHICH HAS BEEN ESTABLISHED TO CAPTURE KIRA WITHOUT THE HELP OF L. AND ABOUT SEVEN OF THE TOP MEMBERS OF THIS GROUP KNOW OF L'S DEATH.
...ABOUT L'S DEATH... FROM WHOM...? WHERE...?

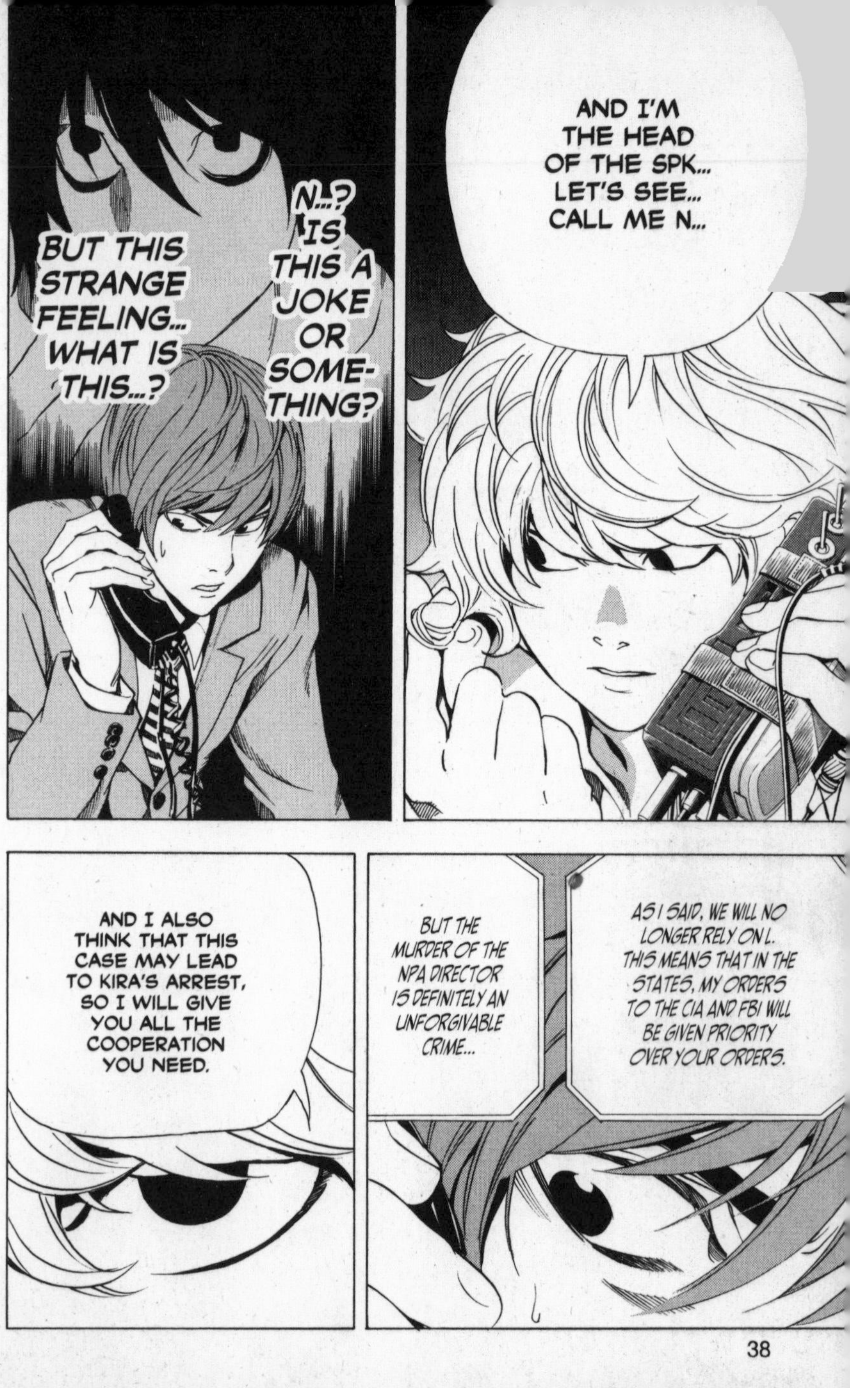
AND I'M THE HEAD OF THE SPK... LET'S SEE... CALL ME N...
N...? IS THIS A JOKE OR SOME-THING?
BUT THIS STRANGE FEELING... WHAT IS THIS...?
AS I SAID, WE WILL NO LONGER RELY ON L. THIS MEANS THAT IN THE STATES, MY ORDERS TO THE CIA AND FBI WILL BE GIVEN PRIORITY OVER YOUR ORDERS.
BUT THE MURDER OF THE NPA DIRECTOR IS DEFINITELY AN UNFORGIVABLE CRIME...
AND I ALSO THINK THAT THIS CASE MAY LEAD TO KIRA'S ARREST, SO I WILL GIVE YOU ALL THE COOPERATION YOU NEED.

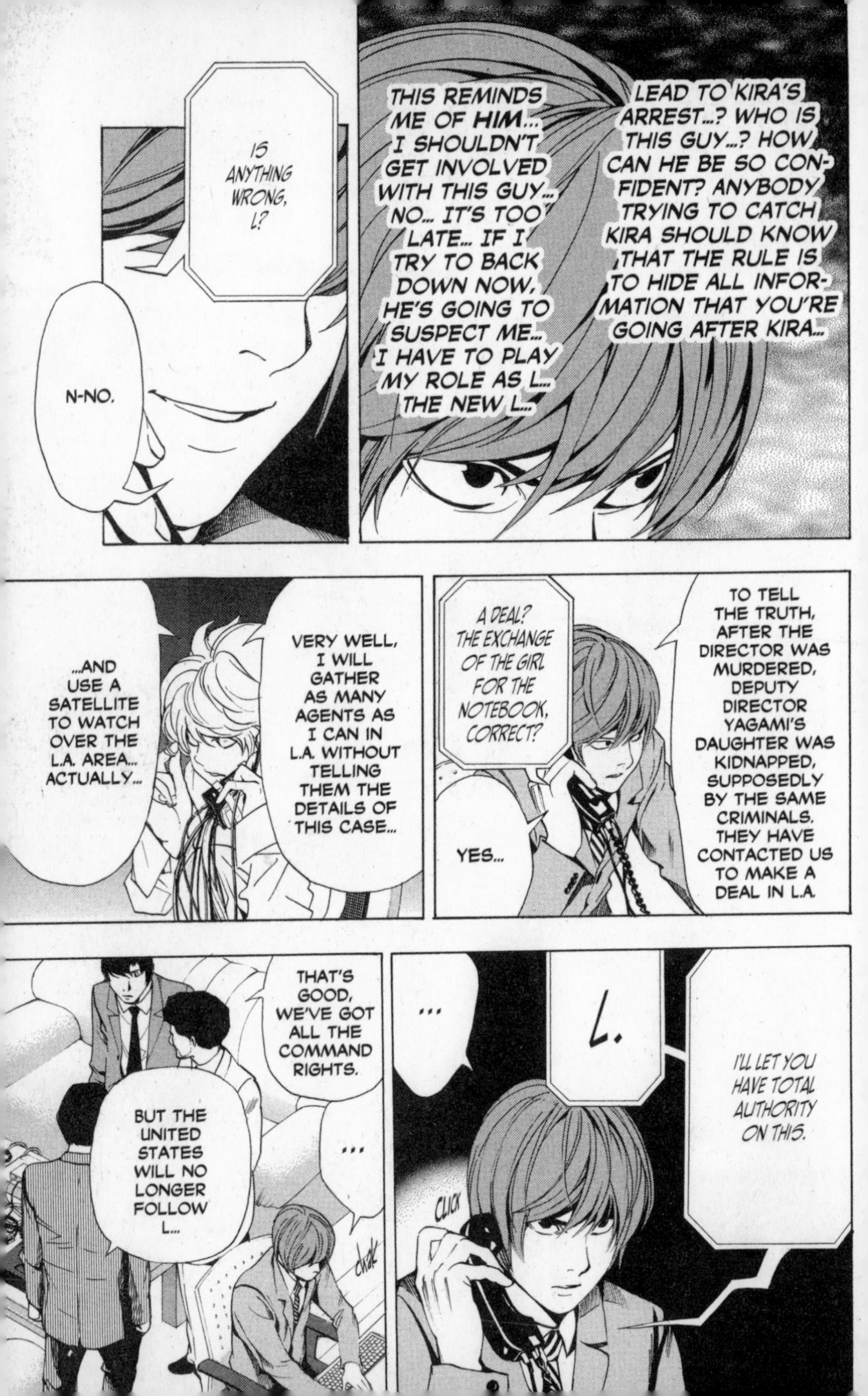
LEAD TO KIRA'S ARREST...? WHO IS THIS GUY...? HOW CAN HE BE SO CONFIDENT? ANYBODY TRYING TO CATCH KIRA SHOULD KNOW THAT THE RULE IS TO HIDE ALL INFORMATION THAT YOU'RE GOING AFTER KIRA...
THIS REMINDS ME OF HIM... I SHOULDN'T GET INVOLVED WITH THIS GUY... NO... IT'S TOO LATE... IF I TRY TO BACK DOWN NOW, HE'S GOING TO SUSPECT ME... I HAVE TO PLAY MY ROLE AS L... THE NEW L...
IS ANYTHING WRONG, L?
N-NO.
TO TELL THE TRUTH, AFTER THE DIRECTOR WAS MURDERED, DEPUTY DIRECTOR YAGAMI'S DAUGHTER WAS KIDNAPPED, SUPPOSEDLY BY THE SAME CRIMINALS. THEY HAVE CONTACTED US TO MAKE A DEAL IN L.A.
A DEAL? THE EXCHANGE OF THE GIRL FOR THE NOTEBOOK, CORRECT?
YES...
VERY WELL, I WILL GATHER AS MANY AGENTS AS I CAN IN L.A. WITHOUT TELLING THEM THE DETAILS OF THIS CASE...
...AND USE A SATELLITE TO WATCH OVER THE L.A. AREA... ACTUALLY...
I'LL LET YOU HAVE TOTAL AUTHORITY ON THIS.
L.
...
CLICK
THAT'S GOOD, WE'VE GOT ALL THE COMMAND RIGHTS.
...
BUT THE UNITED STATES WILL NO LONGER FOLLOW L...

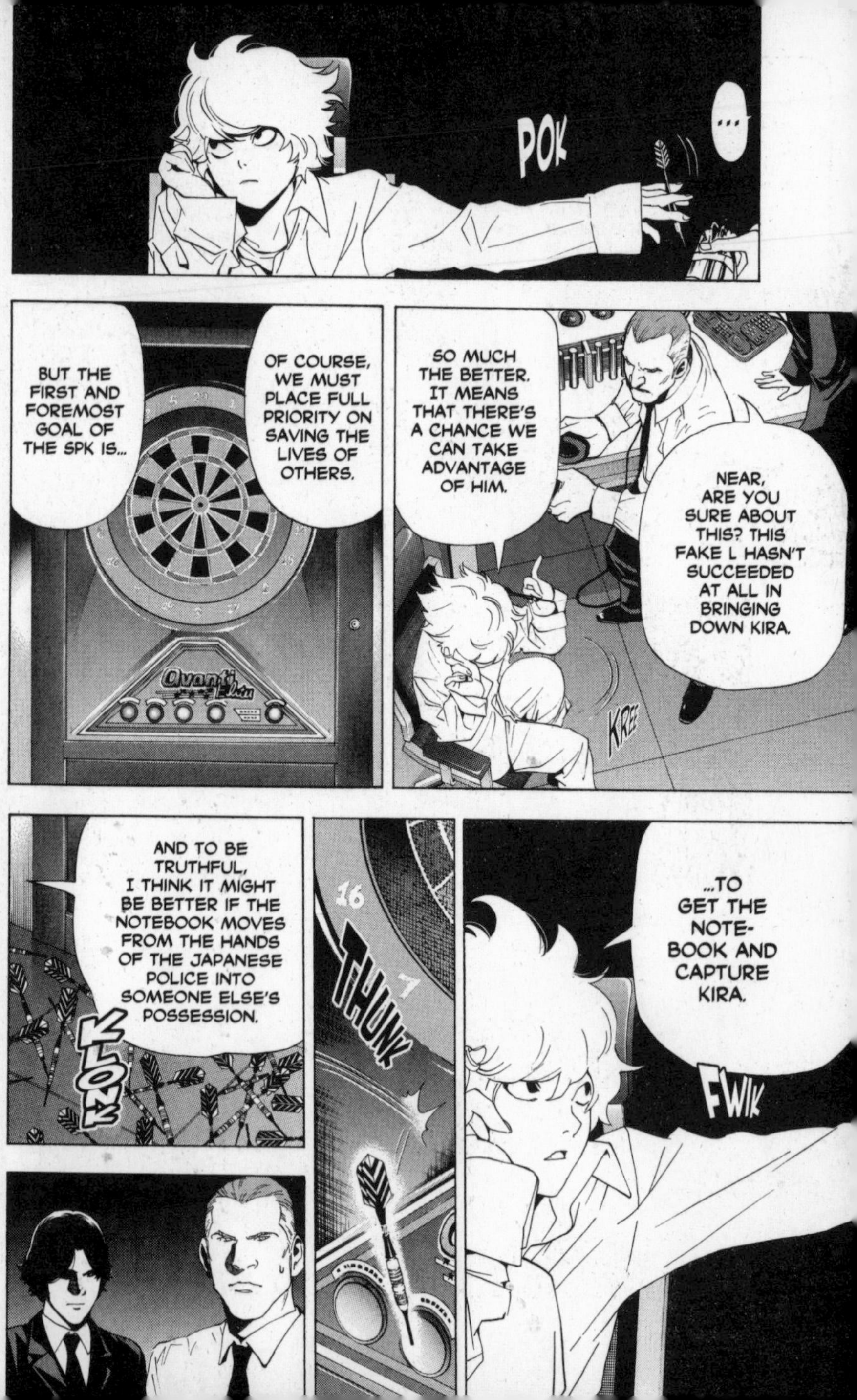
...
POK
NEAR, ARE YOU SURE ABOUT THIS? THIS FAKE L HASN'T SUCCEEDED AT ALL IN BRINGING DOWN KIRA.
SO MUCH THE BETTER. IT MEANS THAT THERE'S A CHANCE WE CAN TAKE ADVANTAGE OF HIM.
KREE
OF COURSE, WE MUST PLACE FULL PRIORITY ON SAVING THE LIVES OF OTHERS.
BUT THE FIRST AND FOREMOST GOAL OF THE SPK IS...
...TO GET THE NOTE-BOOK AND CAPTURE KIRA.
FWIK
THUNK
AND TO BE TRUTHFUL, I THINK IT MIGHT BE BETTER IF THE NOTEBOOK MOVES FROM THE HANDS OF THE JAPANESE POLICE INTO SOMEONE ELSE'S POSSESSION.
KLONK

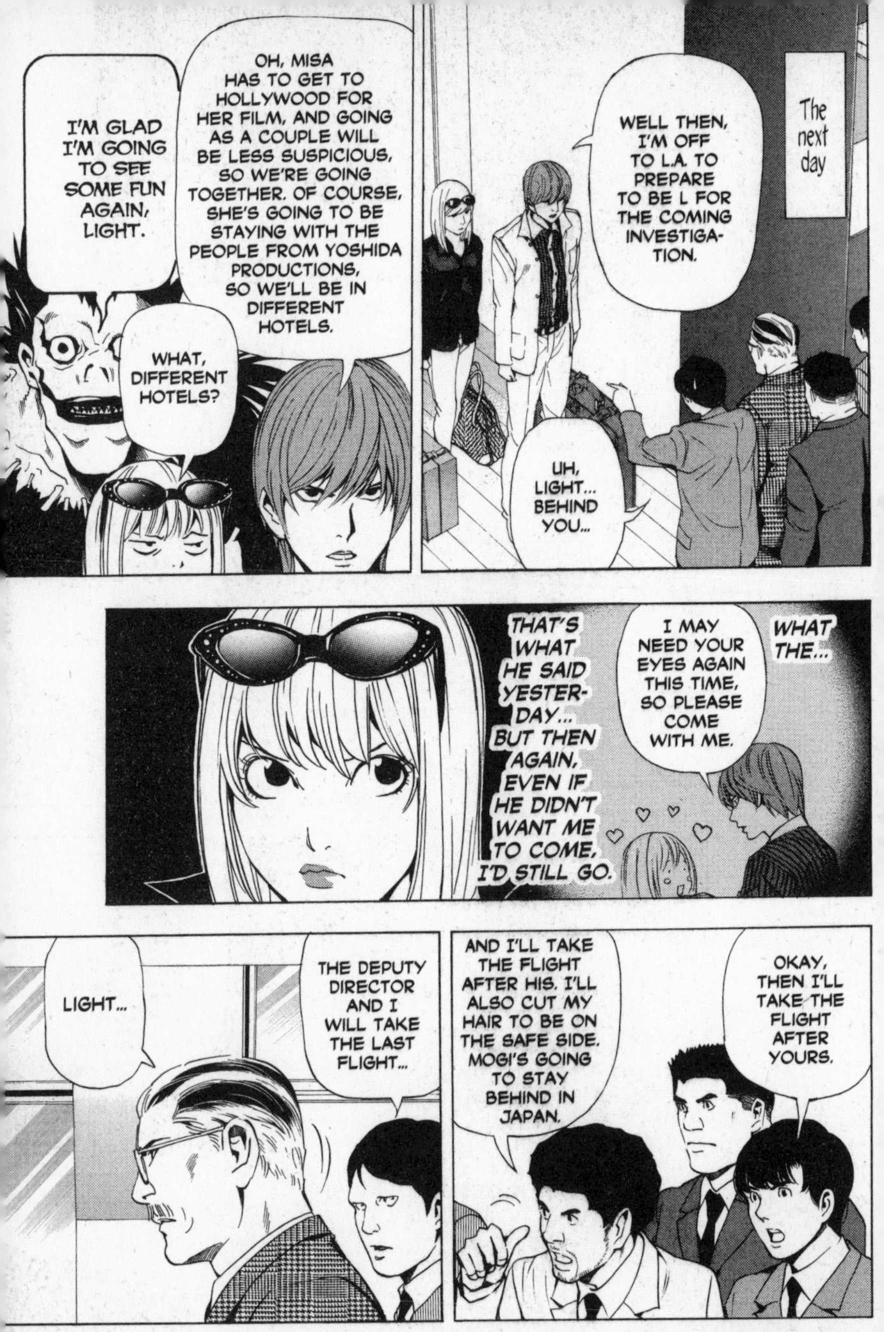
The next day
WELL THEN, I'M OFF TO L.A. TO PREPARE TO BE L FOR THE COMING INVESTIGATION.
UH, LIGHT... BEHIND YOU...
OH, MISA HAS TO GET TO HOLLYWOOD FOR HER FILM, AND GOING AS A COUPLE WILL BE LESS SUSPICIOUS, SO WE'RE GOING TOGETHER. OF COURSE, SHE'S GOING TO BE STAYING WITH THE PEOPLE FROM YOSHIDA PRODUCTIONS, SO WE'LL BE IN DIFFERENT HOTELS.
I'M GLAD I'M GOING TO SEE SOME FUN AGAIN, LIGHT.
WHAT, DIFFERENT HOTELS?
WHAT THE...
I MAY NEED YOUR EYES AGAIN THIS TIME, SO PLEASE COME WITH ME.
THAT'S WHAT HE SAID YESTERDAY... BUT THEN AGAIN, EVEN IF HE DIDN'T WANT ME TO COME, I'D STILL GO.
OKAY, THEN I'LL TAKE THE FLIGHT AFTER YOURS.
AND I'LL TAKE THE FLIGHT AFTER HIS. I'LL ALSO CUT MY HAIR TO BE ON THE SAFE SIDE. MOGI'S GOING TO STAY BEHIND IN JAPAN.
THE DEPUTY DIRECTOR AND I WILL TAKE THE LAST FLIGHT...
LIGHT...

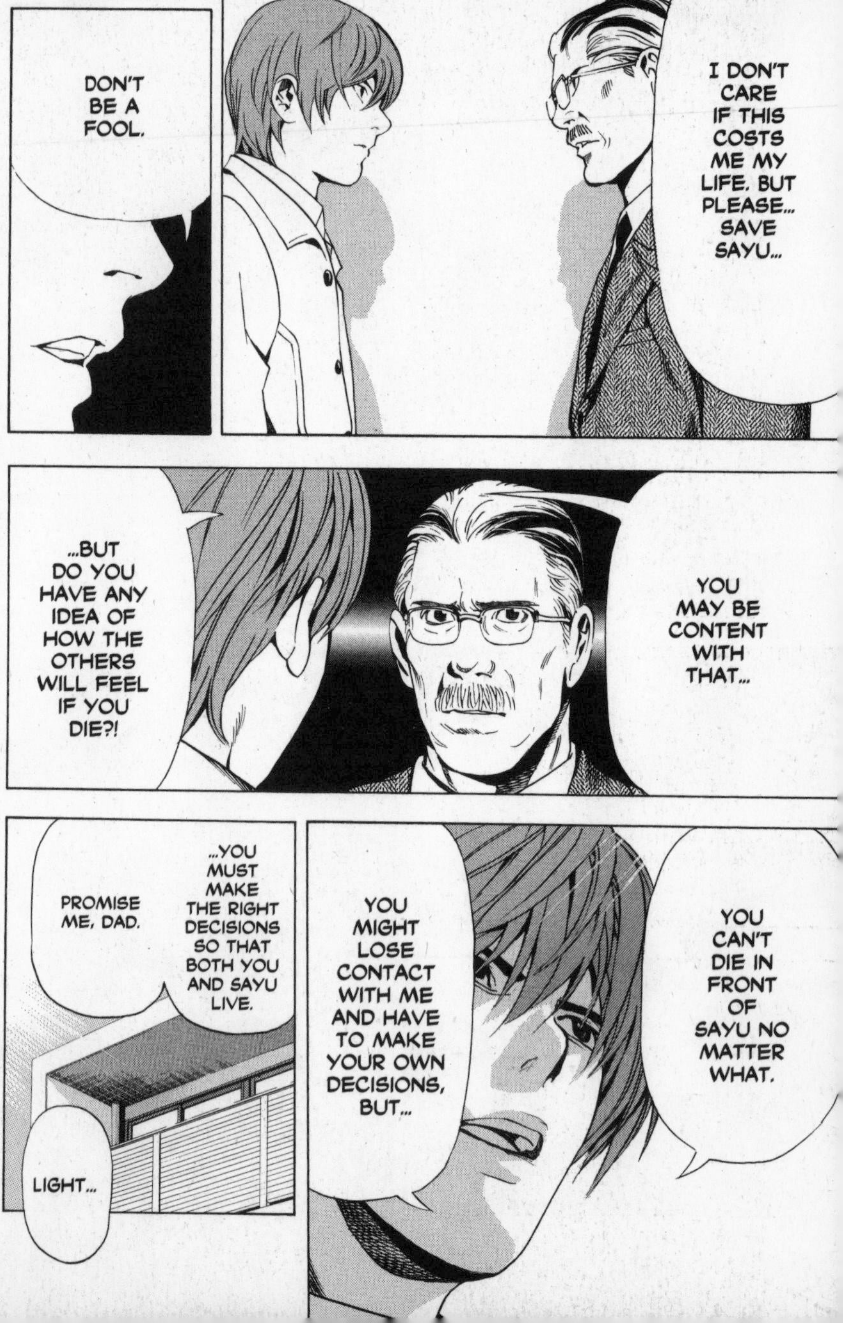
I DON'T CARE IF THIS COSTS ME MY LIFE. BUT PLEASE... SAVE SAYU...
DON'T BE A FOOL.
YOU MAY BE CONTENT WITH THAT...
...BUT DO YOU HAVE ANY IDEA OF HOW THE OTHERS WILL FEEL IF YOU DIE?!
YOU CAN'T DIE IN FRONT OF SAYU NO MATTER WHAT.
YOU MIGHT LOSE CONTACT WITH ME AND HAVE TO MAKE YOUR OWN DECISIONS, BUT...
...YOU MUST MAKE THE RIGHT DECISIONS SO THAT BOTH YOU AND SAYU LIVE.
PROMISE ME, DAD.
LIGHT...

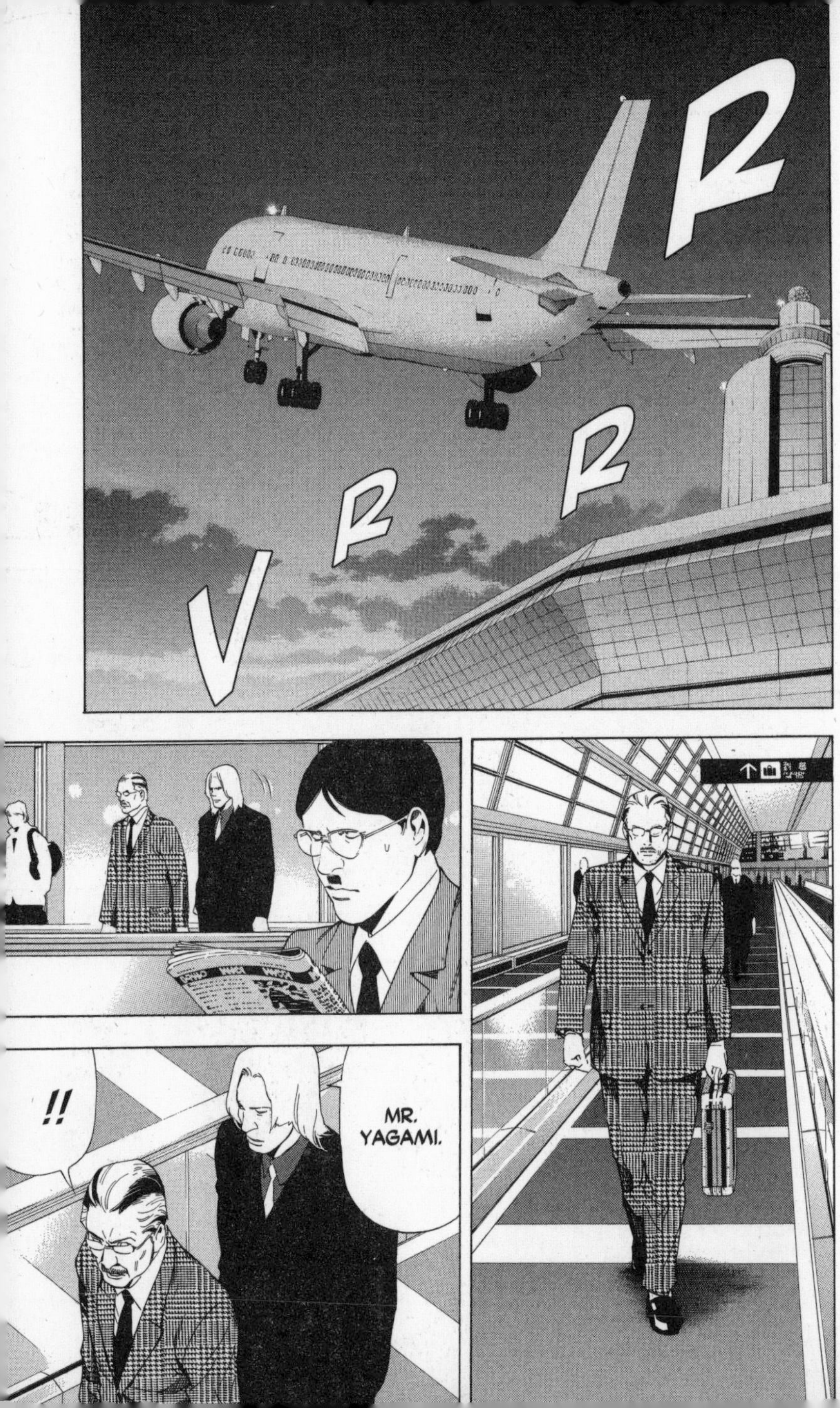
VRRR
MR. YAGAMI.
!!

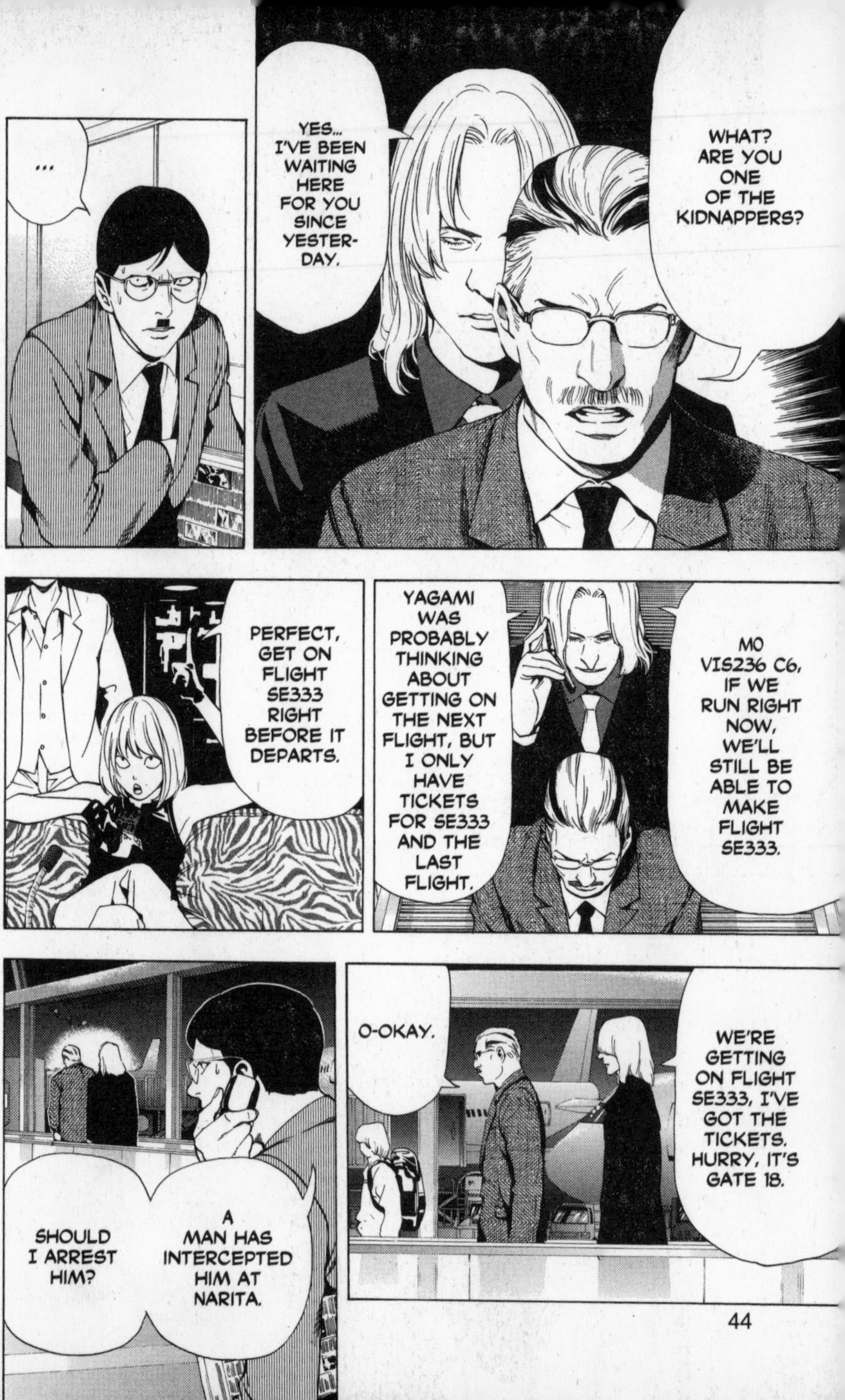
WHAT? ARE YOU ONE OF THE KIDNAPPERS?
YES... I'VE BEEN WAITING HERE FOR YOU SINCE YESTERDAY.
...
MO VIS236 C6, IF WE RUN RIGHT NOW, WE'LL STILL BE ABLE TO MAKE FLIGHT SE333.
YAGAMI WAS PROBABLY THINKING ABOUT GETTING ON THE NEXT FLIGHT, BUT I ONLY HAVE TICKETS FOR SE333 AND THE LAST FLIGHT.
PERFECT, GET ON FLIGHT SE333 RIGHT BEFORE IT DEPARTS.
WE'RE GETTING ON FLIGHT SE333, I'VE GOT THE TICKETS. HURRY, IT'S GATE 18.
O-OKAY.
A MAN HAS INTERCEPTED HIM AT NARITA.
SHOULD I ARREST HIM?

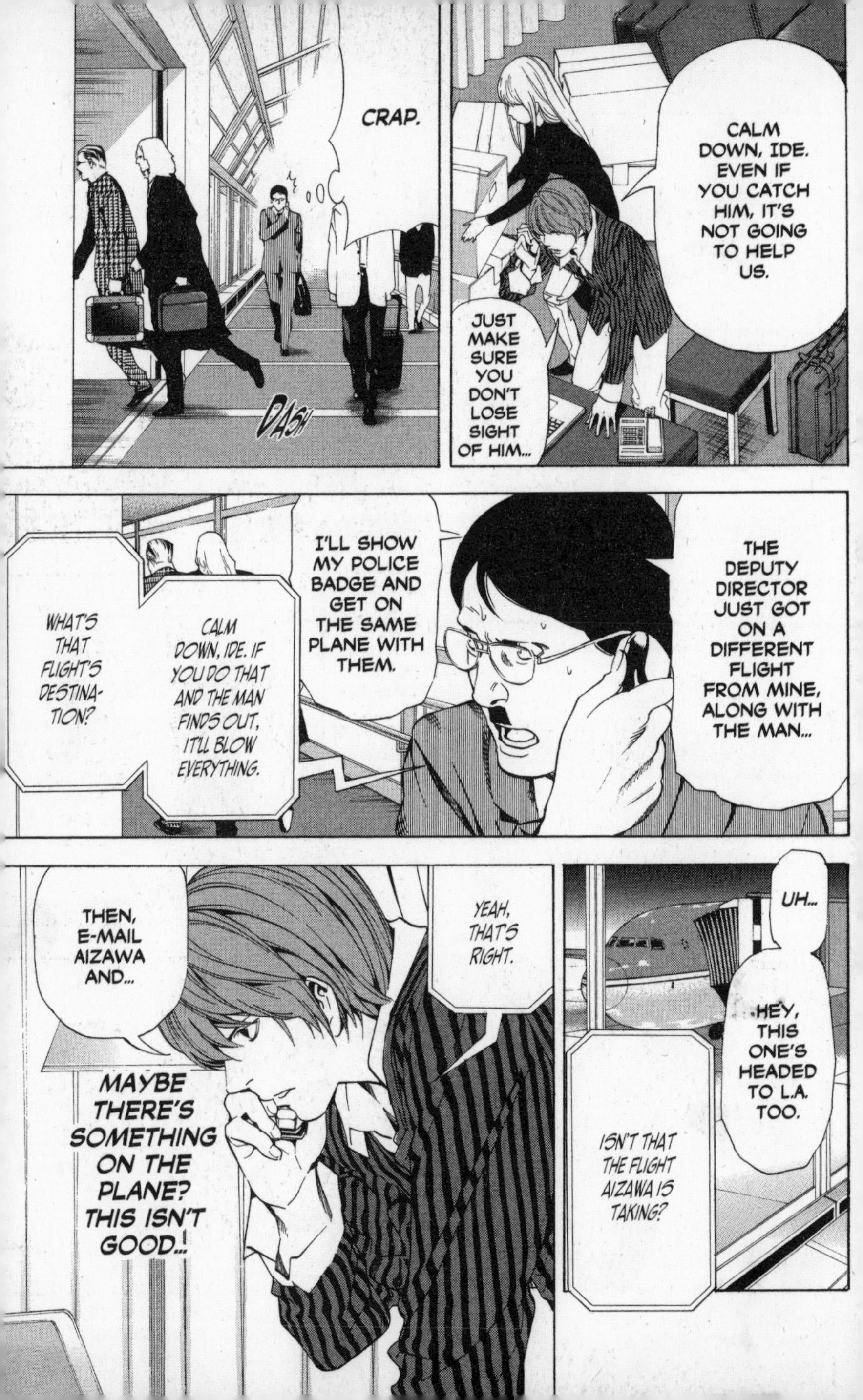
CALM DOWN, IDE. EVEN IF YOU CATCH HIM, IT'S NOT GOING TO HELP US.
JUST MAKE SURE YOU DON'T LOSE SIGHT OF HIM...
CRAP.
DASH
THE DEPUTY DIRECTOR JUST GOT ON A DIFFERENT FLIGHT FROM MINE, ALONG WITH THE MAN...
I'LL SHOW MY POLICE BADGE AND GET ON THE SAME PLANE WITH THEM.
CALM DOWN, IDE. IF YOU DO THAT AND THE MAN FINDS OUT, IT'LL BLOW EVERYTHING.
WHAT'S THAT FLIGHT'S DESTINATION?
UH...
HEY, THIS ONE'S HEADED TO L.A. TOO.
ISN'T THAT THE FLIGHT AIZAWA IS TAKING?
YEAH, THAT'S RIGHT.
THEN, E-MAIL AIZAWA AND...
MAYBE THERE'S SOMETHING ON THE PLANE? THIS ISN'T GOOD...!

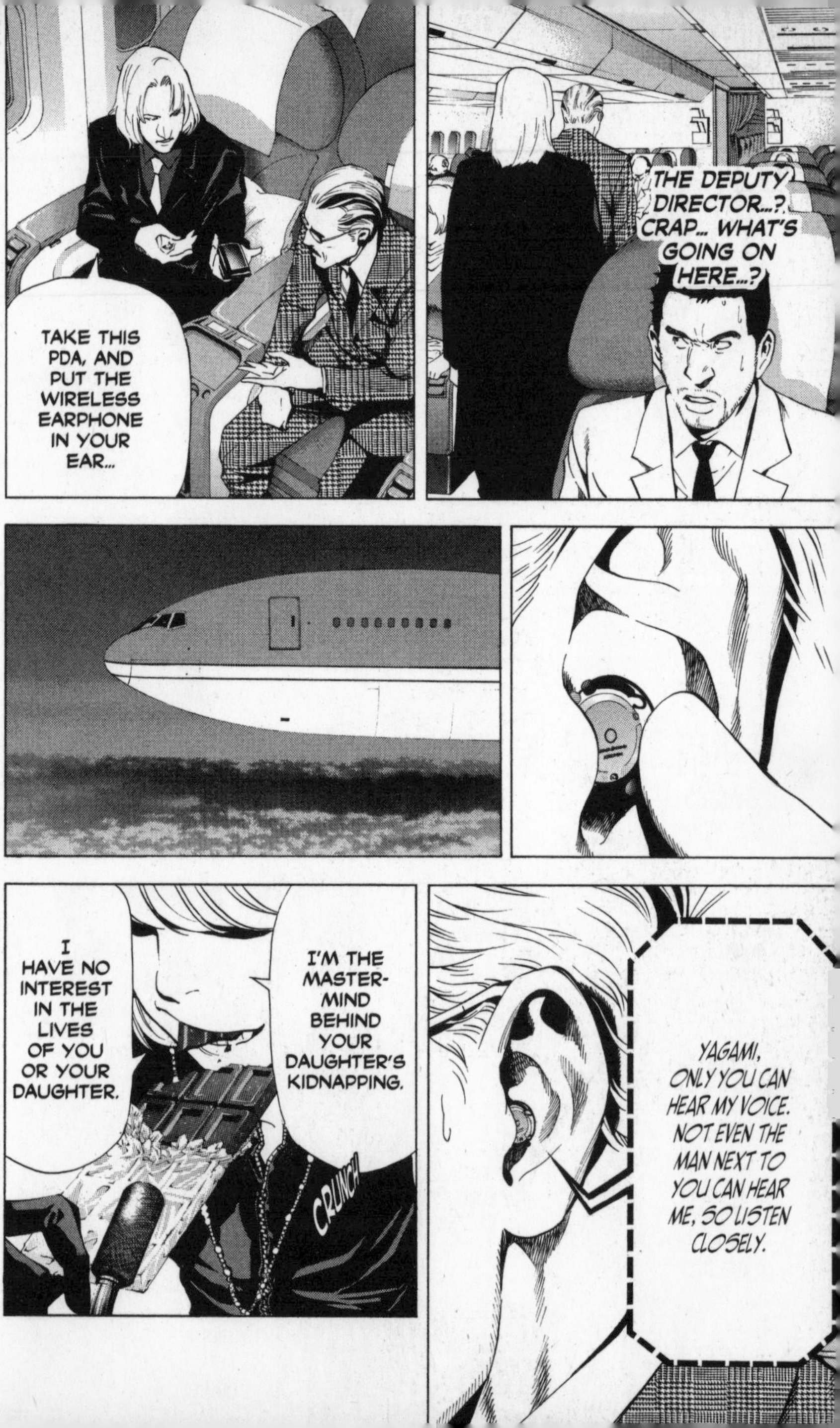
THE DEPUTY DIRECTOR...? CRAP... WHAT'S GOING ON HERE...?
TAKE THIS PDA, AND PUT THE WIRELESS EARPHONE IN YOUR EAR...
YAGAMI, ONLY YOU CAN HEAR MY VOICE. NOT EVEN THE MAN NEXT TO YOU CAN HEAR ME, SO LISTEN CLOSELY.
I'M THE MASTER-MIND BEHIND YOUR DAUGHTER'S KIDNAPPING.
I HAVE NO INTEREST IN THE LIVES OF YOU OR YOUR DAUGHTER.
CRUNCH

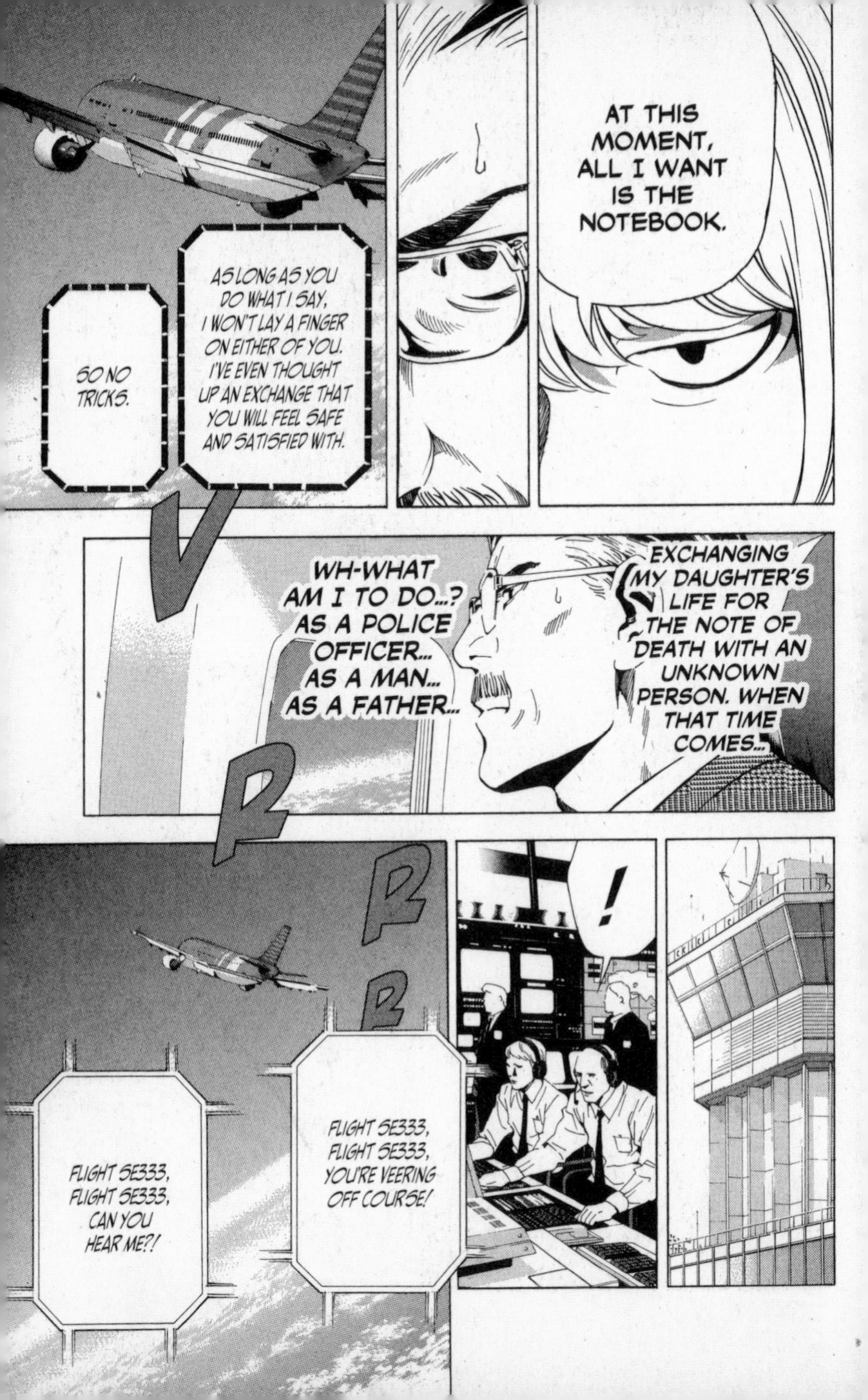
AT THIS MOMENT, ALL I WANT IS THE NOTEBOOK.
AS LONG AS YOU DO WHAT I SAY, I WON'T LAY A FINGER ON EITHER OF YOU. I'VE EVEN THOUGHT UP AN EXCHANGE THAT YOU WILL FEEL SAFE AND SATISFIED WITH.
SO NO TRICKS.
EXCHANGING MY DAUGHTER'S LIFE FOR THE NOTE OF DEATH WITH AN UNKNOWN PERSON. WHEN THAT TIME COMES...
WH-WHAT AM I TO DO...? AS A POLICE OFFICER... AS A MAN... AS A FATHER...
VRRR
!
FLIGHT SE333, FLIGHT SE333, YOU'RE VEERING OFF COURSE!
FLIGHT SE333, FLIGHT SE333, CAN YOU HEAR ME?!

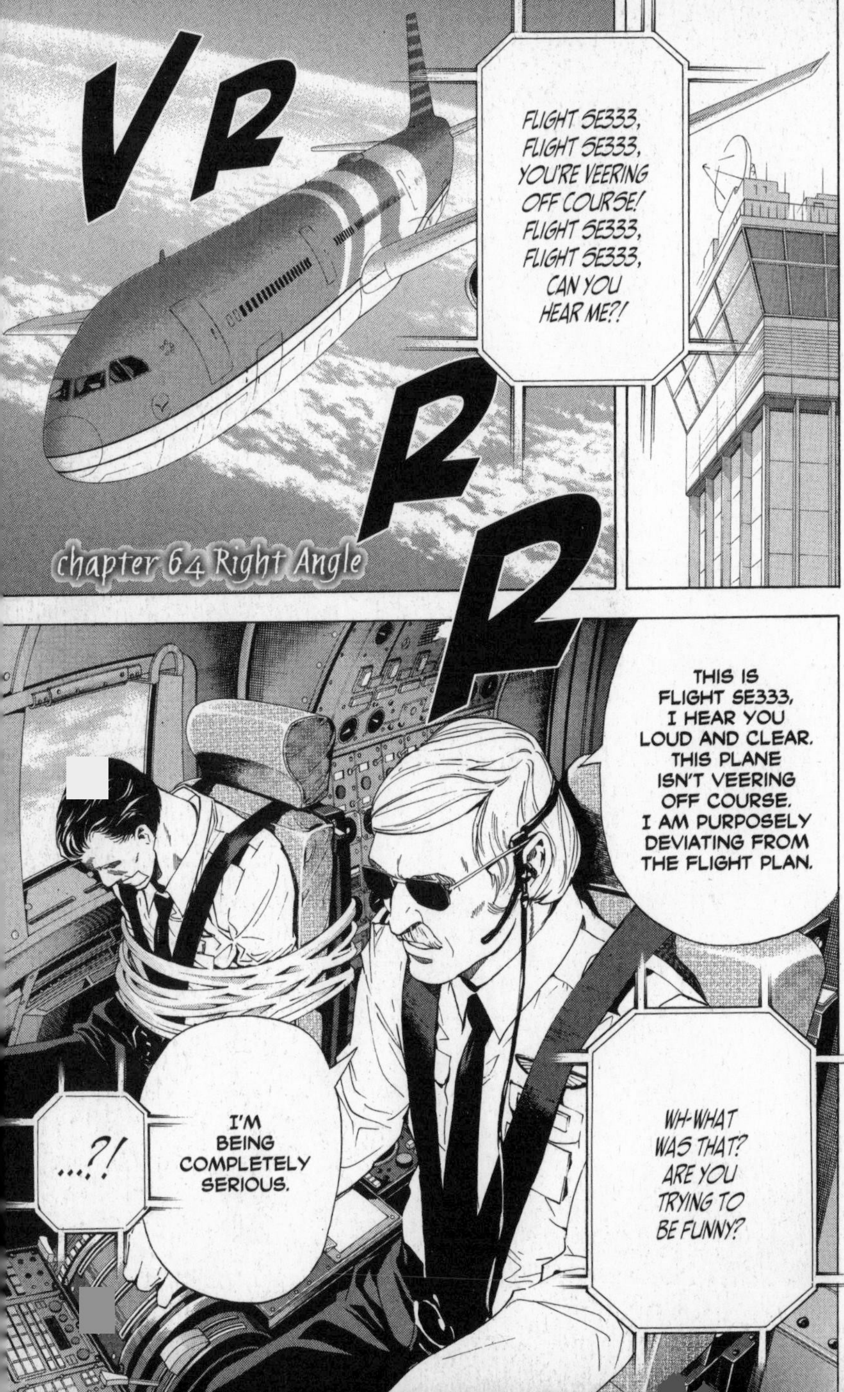
FLIGHT SE333, FLIGHT SE333, YOU'RE VEERING OFF COURSE! FLIGHT SE333, FLIGHT SE333, CAN YOU HEAR ME?!
VRRR
chapter 64 Right Angle
THIS IS FLIGHT SE333, I HEAR YOU LOUD AND CLEAR. THIS PLANE ISN'T VEERING OFF COURSE. I AM PURPOSELY DEVIATING FROM THE FLIGHT PLAN.
WH-WHAT WAS THAT? ARE YOU TRYING TO BE FUNNY?
I'M BEING COMPLETELY SERIOUS.
...?!

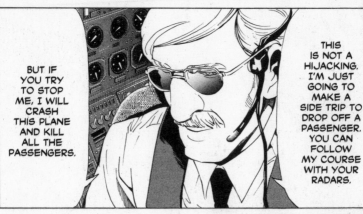

THIS IS NOT A HIJACKING. I'M JUST GOING TO MAKE A SIDE TRIP TO DROP OFF A PASSENGER. YOU CAN FOLLOW MY COURSE WITH YOUR RADARS.
BUT IF YOU TRY TO STOP ME, I WILL CRASH THIS PLANE AND KILL ALL THE PASSENGERS.
CLICK
CLICK
VRRRR
...
WH- WHAT? WHAT IS GOING ON...?

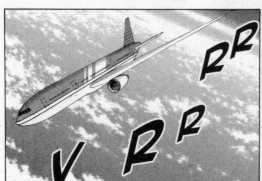

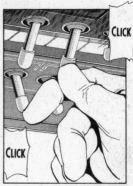

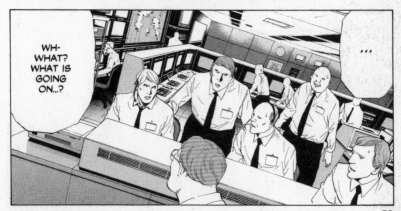

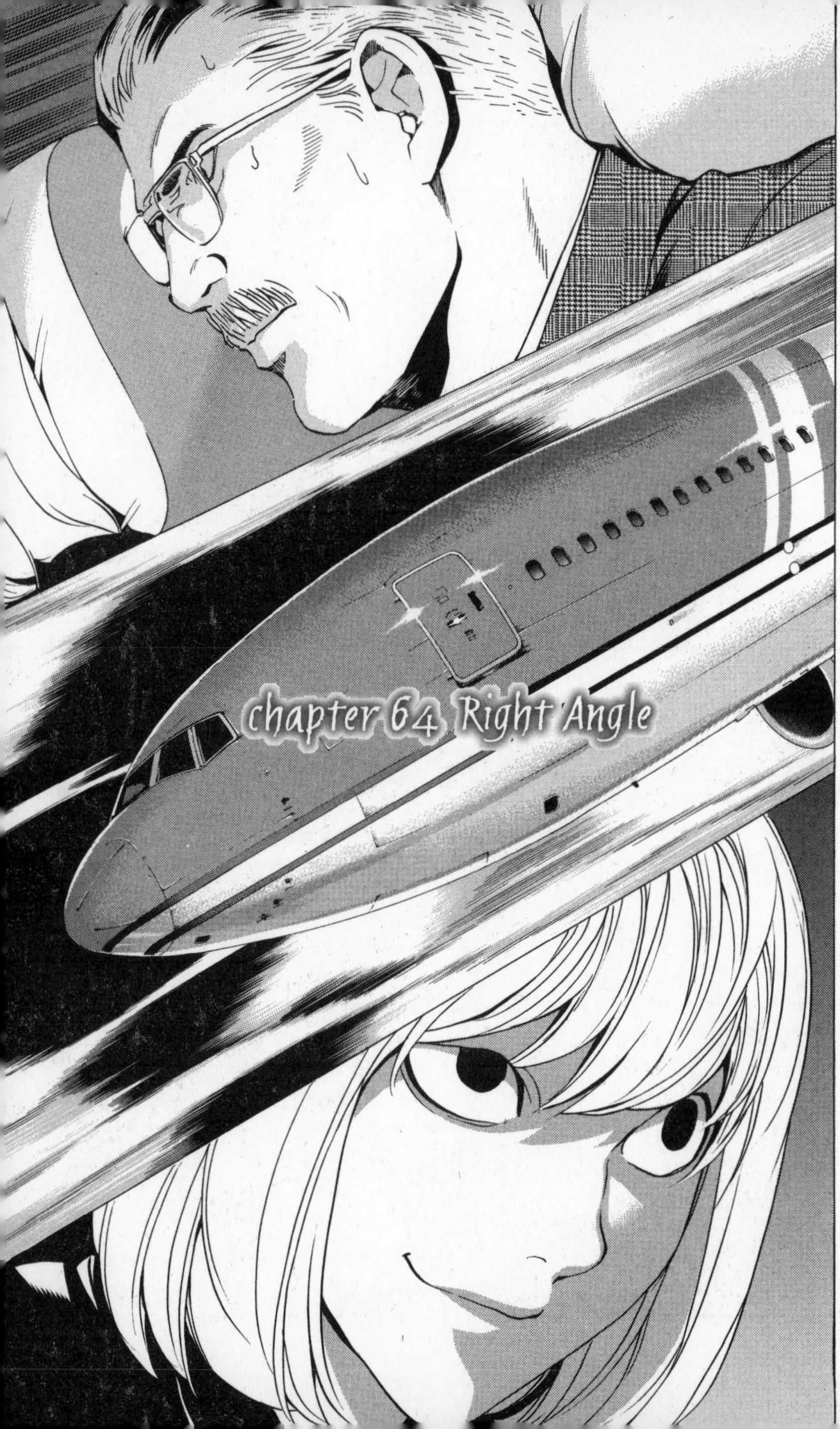
chapter 64 Right Angle

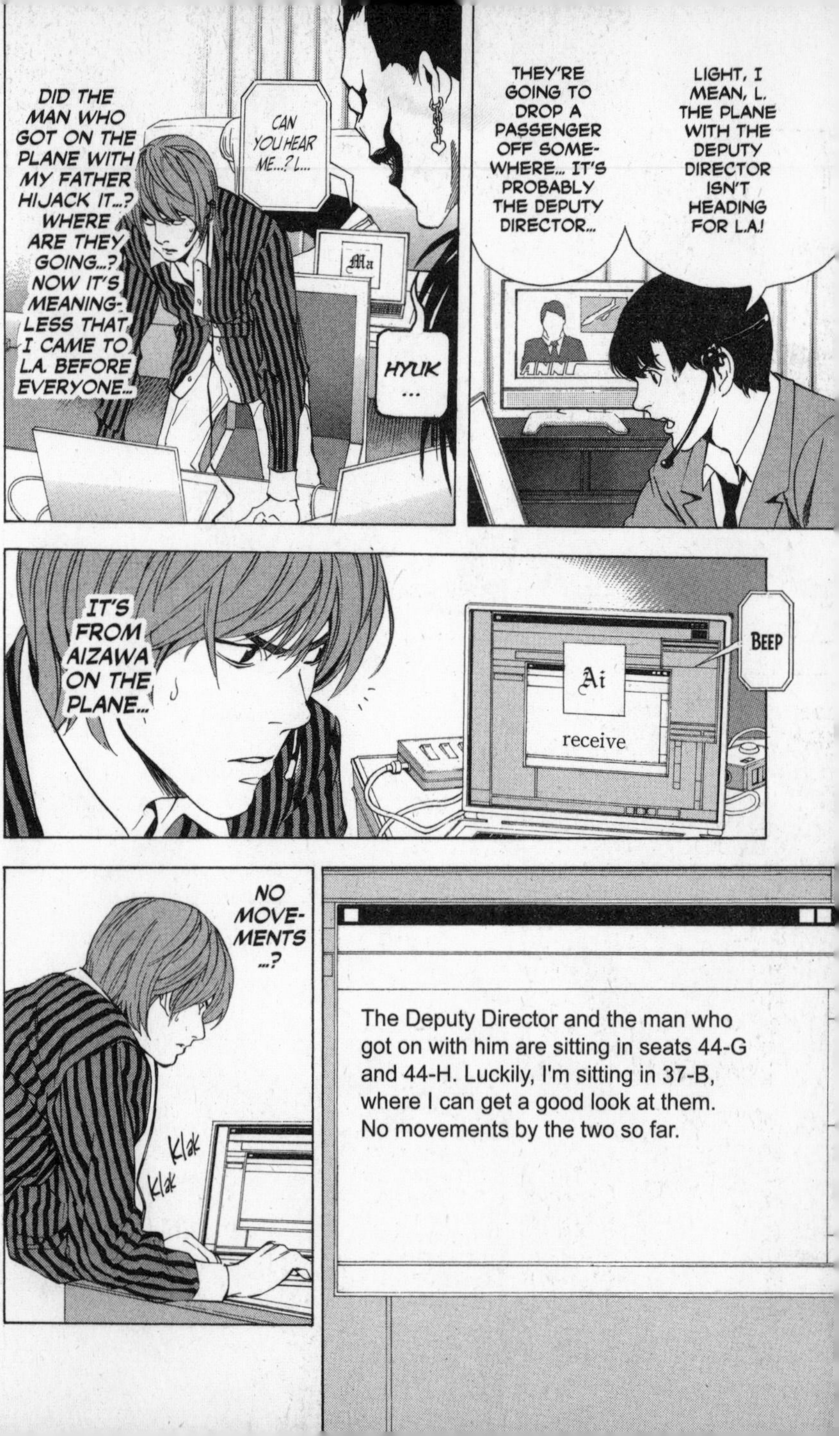
LIGHT, I MEAN, L. THE PLANE WITH THE DEPUTY DIRECTOR ISN'T HEADING FOR L.A.!
THEY'RE GOING TO DROP A PASSENGER OFF SOME-WHERE... IT'S PROBABLY THE DEPUTY DIRECTOR...
CAN YOU HEAR ME...? L...
HYUK ...
DID THE MAN WHO GOT ON THE PLANE WITH MY FATHER HIJACK IT...? WHERE ARE THEY GOING...? NOW IT'S MEANING-LESS THAT I CAME TO L.A. BEFORE EVERYONE...
Ma
BEEP
Ai
receive
IT'S FROM AIZAWA ON THE PLANE...
The Deputy Director and the man who got on with him are sitting in seats 44-G and 44-H. Luckily, I'm sitting in 37-B, where I can get a good look at them. No movements by the two so far.
NO MOVE-MENTS ...?
Klak
Klak

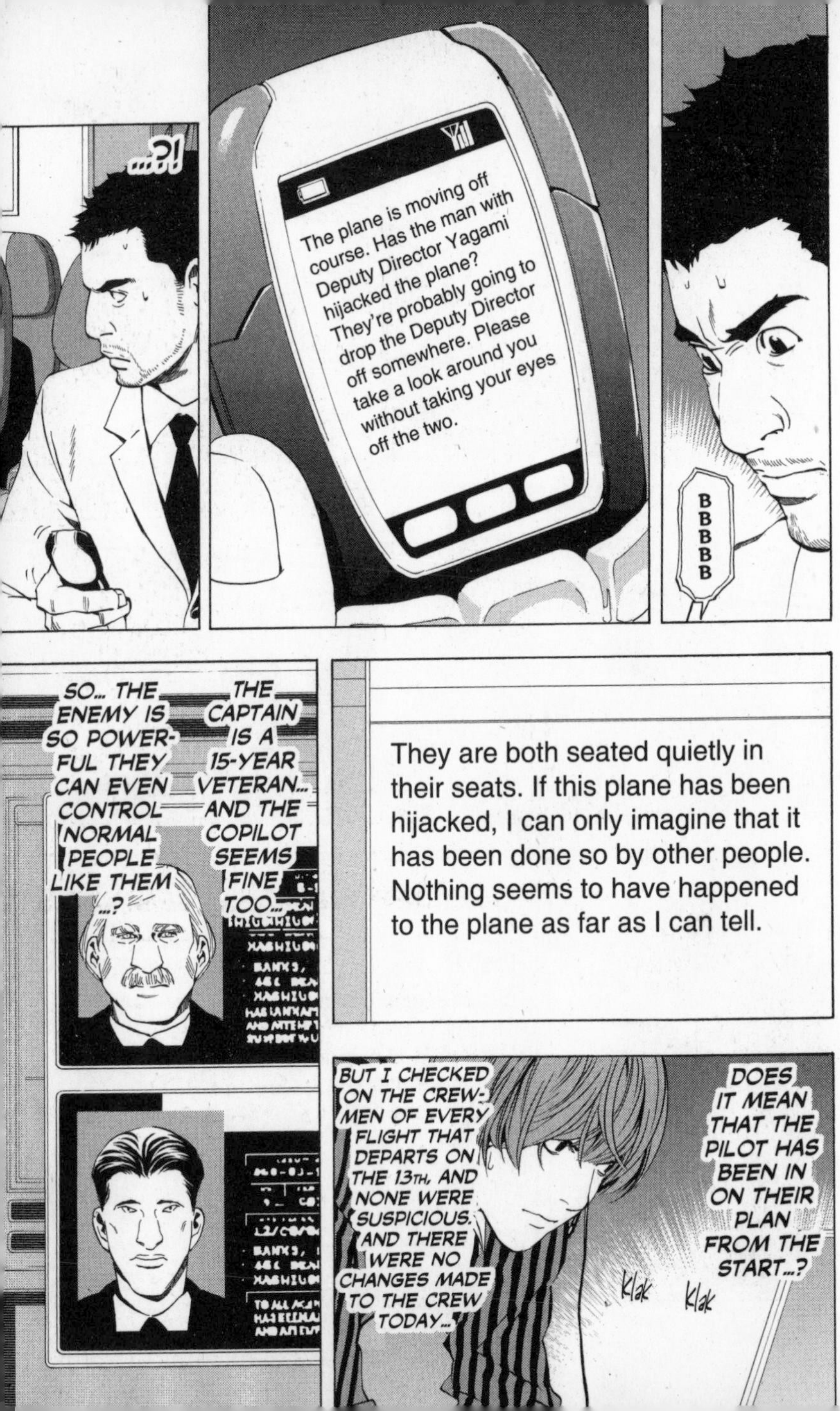
BBBBB
The plane is moving off course. Has the man with Deputy Director Yagami hijacked the plane? They're probably going to drop the Deputy Director off somewhere. Please take a look around you without taking your eyes off the two.
...?!
They are both seated quietly in their seats. If this plane has been hijacked, I can only imagine that it has been done so by other people. Nothing seems to have happened to the plane as far as I can tell.
DOES IT MEAN THAT THE PILOT HAS BEEN IN ON THEIR PLAN FROM THE START...?
BUT I CHECKED ON THE CREW-MEN OF EVERY FLIGHT THAT DEPARTS ON THE 13TH, AND NONE WERE SUSPICIOUS. AND THERE WERE NO CHANGES MADE TO THE CREW TODAY...
Klak Klak
THE CAPTAIN IS A 15-YEAR VETERAN... AND THE COPILOT SEEMS FINE TOO...
SO... THE ENEMY IS SO POWER-FUL THEY CAN EVEN CONTROL NORMAL PEOPLE LIKE THEM ...?

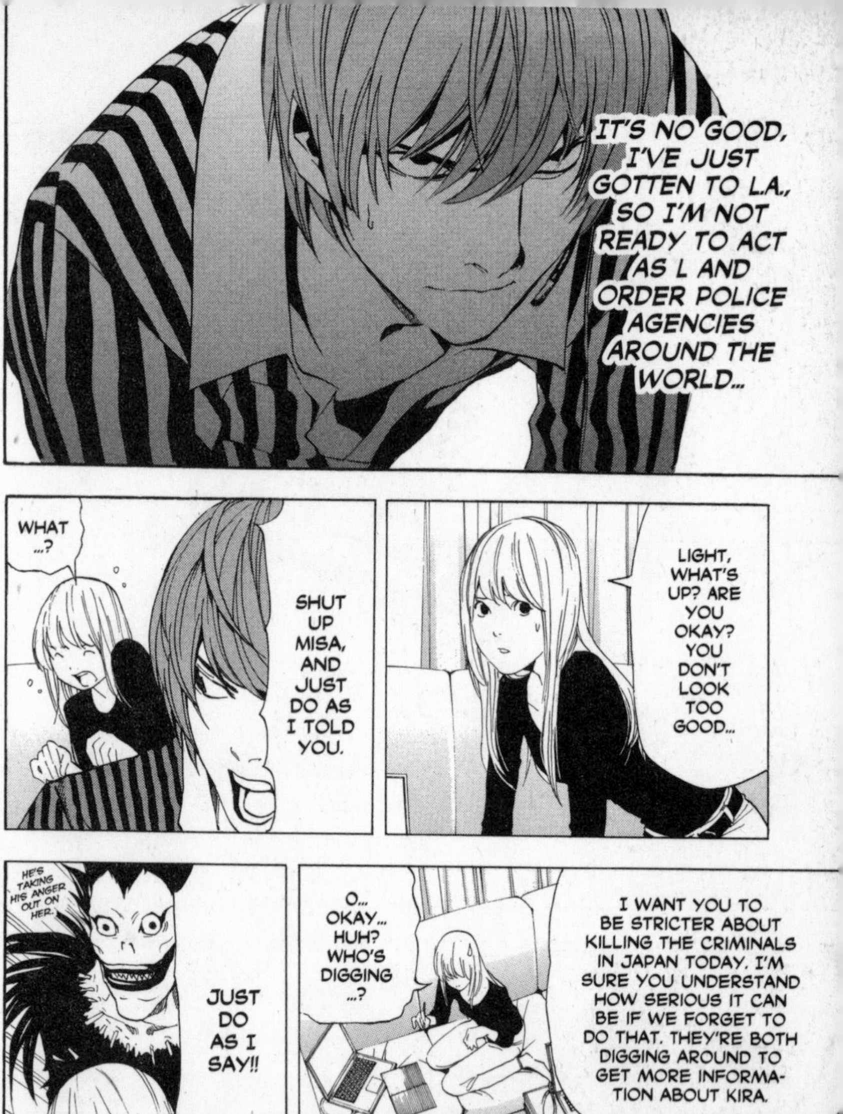
IT'S NO GOOD, I'VE JUST GOTTEN TO L.A., SO I'M NOT READY TO ACT AS L AND ORDER POLICE AGENCIES AROUND THE WORLD...
LIGHT, WHAT'S UP? ARE YOU OKAY? YOU DON'T LOOK TOO GOOD...
SHUT UP MISA, AND JUST DO AS I TOLD YOU.
WHAT ...?
I WANT YOU TO BE STRICTER ABOUT KILLING THE CRIMINALS IN JAPAN TODAY. I'M SURE YOU UNDERSTAND HOW SERIOUS IT CAN BE IF WE FORGET TO DO THAT. THEY'RE BOTH DIGGING AROUND TO GET MORE INFORMATION ABOUT KIRA.
O... OKAY... HUH? WHO'S DIGGING ...?
HE'S TAKING HIS ANGER OUT ON HER.
JUST DO AS I SAY!!
...

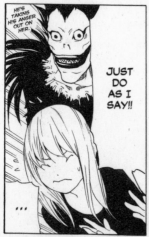

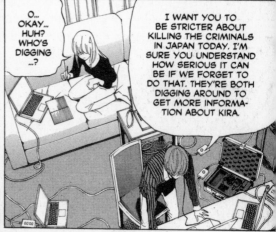

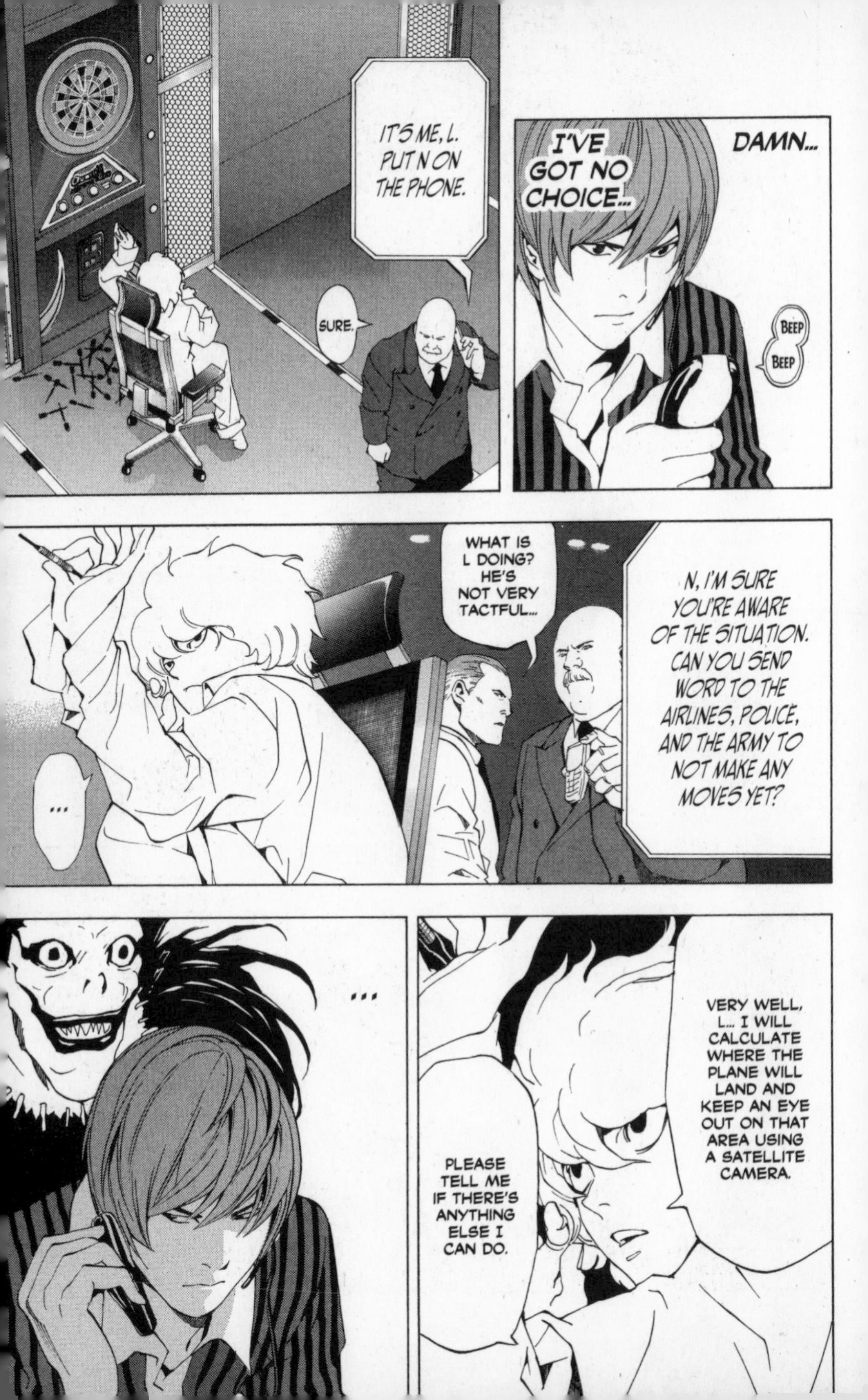
DAMN...
I'VE GOT NO CHOICE...
BEEP
BEEP
IT'S ME, L. PUT N ON THE PHONE.
SURE.
N, I'M SURE YOU'RE AWARE OF THE SITUATION. CAN YOU SEND WORD TO THE AIRLINES, POLICE, AND THE ARMY TO NOT MAKE ANY MOVES YET?
WHAT IS L DOING? HE'S NOT VERY TACTFUL...
...
VERY WELL, L... I WILL CALCULATE WHERE THE PLANE WILL LAND AND KEEP AN EYE OUT ON THAT AREA USING A SATELLITE CAMERA.
PLEASE TELL ME IF THERE'S ANYTHING ELSE I CAN DO.
...

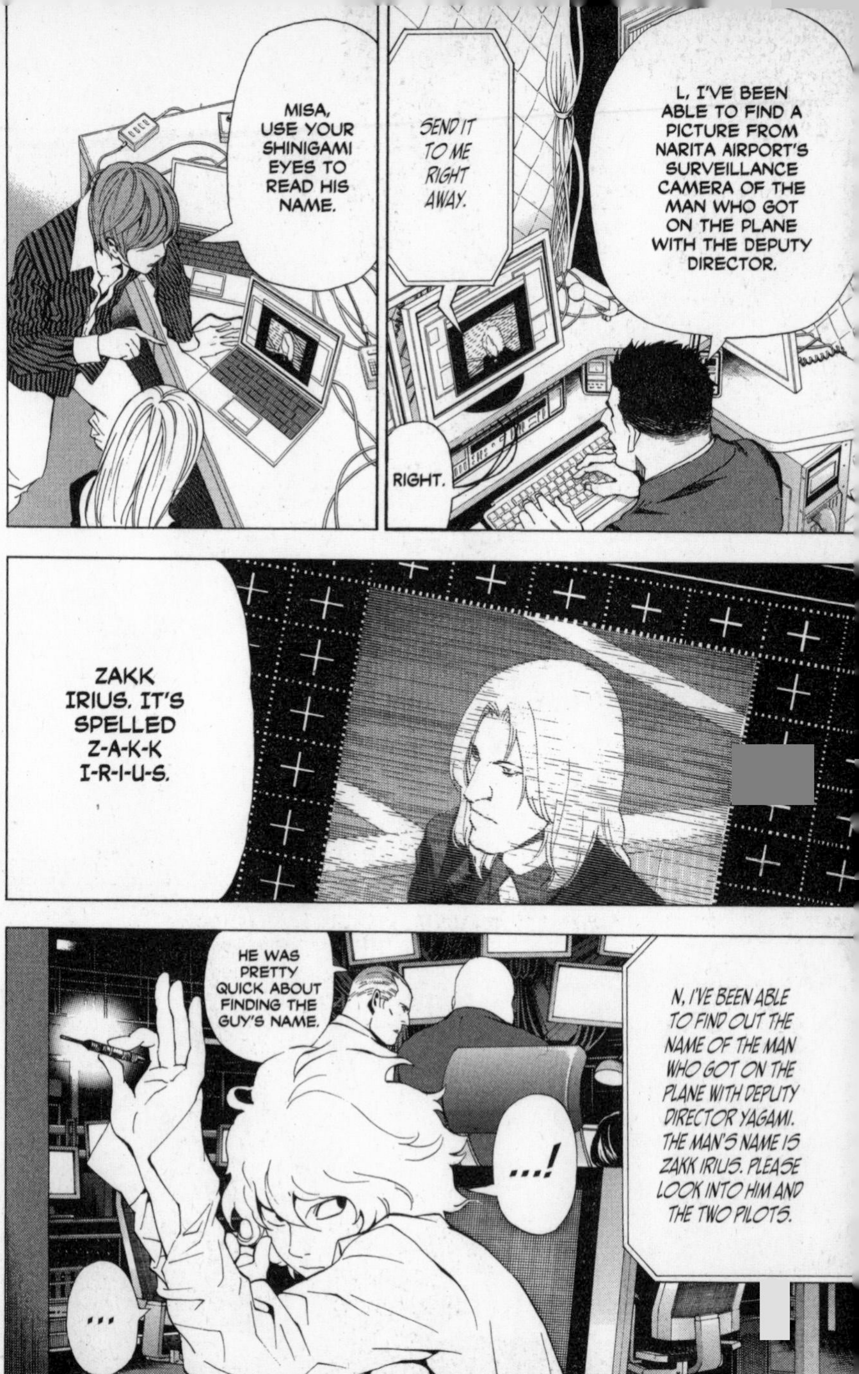
L, I'VE BEEN ABLE TO FIND A PICTURE FROM NARITA AIRPORT'S SURVEILLANCE CAMERA OF THE MAN WHO GOT ON THE PLANE WITH THE DEPUTY DIRECTOR.
SEND IT TO ME RIGHT AWAY.
RIGHT.
MISA, USE YOUR SHINIGAMI EYES TO READ HIS NAME.
ZAKK IRIUS. IT'S SPELLED Z-A-K-K I-R-I-U-S.
N, I'VE BEEN ABLE TO FIND OUT THE NAME OF THE MAN WHO GOT ON THE PLANE WITH DEPUTY DIRECTOR YAGAMI. THE MAN'S NAME IS ZAKK IRIUS. PLEASE LOOK INTO HIM AND THE TWO PILOTS.
HE WAS PRETTY QUICK ABOUT FINDING THE GUY'S NAME.
...!
...

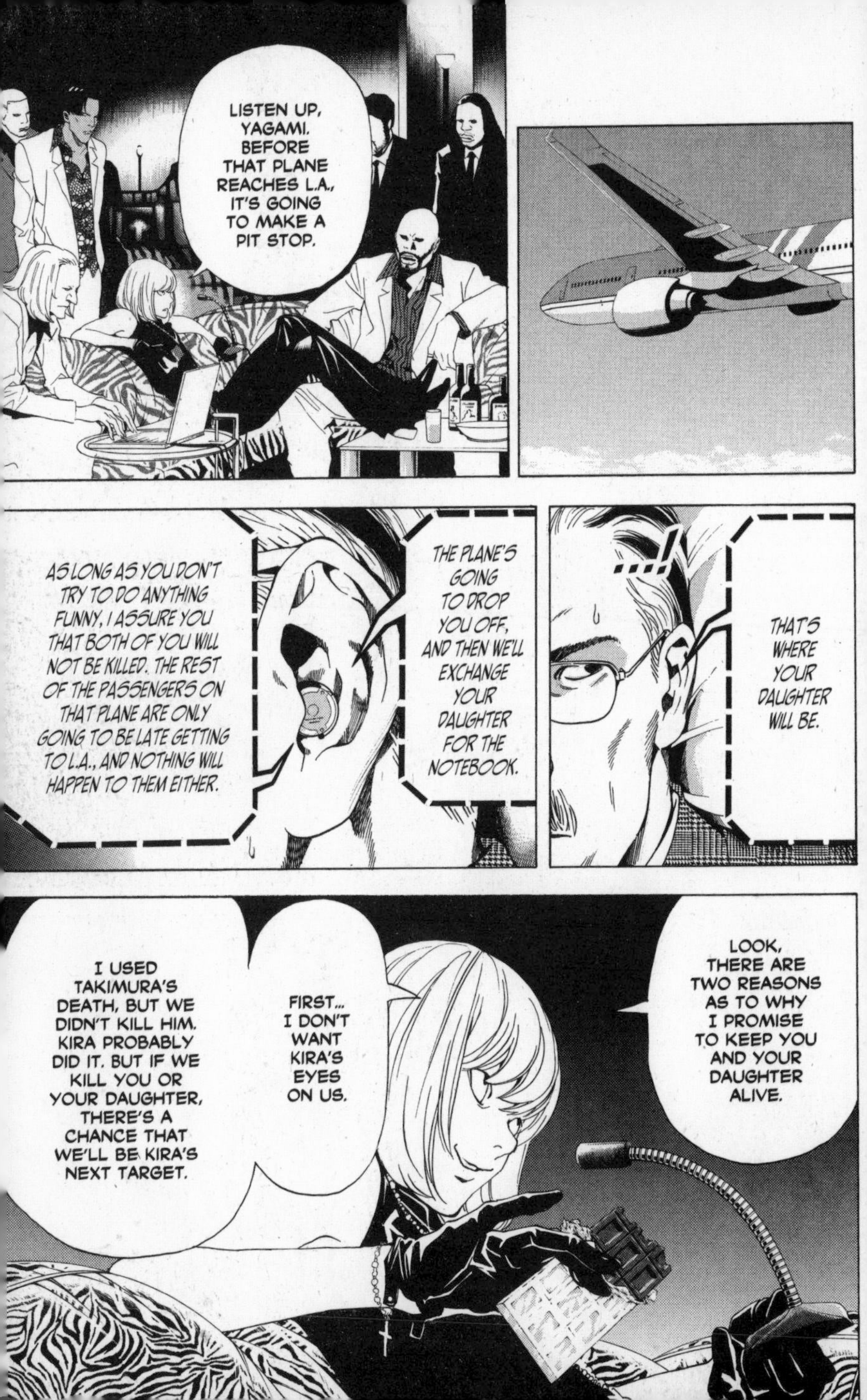
LISTEN UP, YAGAMI. BEFORE THAT PLANE REACHES L.A., IT'S GOING TO MAKE A PIT STOP.
THAT'S WHERE YOUR DAUGHTER WILL BE.
THE PLANE'S GOING TO DROP YOU OFF, AND THEN WE'LL EXCHANGE YOUR DAUGHTER FOR THE NOTEBOOK.
AS LONG AS YOU DON'T TRY TO DO ANYTHING FUNNY, I ASSURE YOU THAT BOTH OF YOU WILL NOT BE KILLED. THE REST OF THE PASSENGERS ON THAT PLANE ARE ONLY GOING TO BE LATE GETTING TO L.A., AND NOTHING WILL HAPPEN TO THEM EITHER.
LOOK, THERE ARE TWO REASONS AS TO WHY I PROMISE TO KEEP YOU AND YOUR DAUGHTER ALIVE.
FIRST... I DON'T WANT KIRA'S EYES ON US.
I USED TAKIMURA'S DEATH, BUT WE DIDN'T KILL HIM. KIRA PROBABLY DID IT. BUT IF WE KILL YOU OR YOUR DAUGHTER, THERE'S A CHANCE THAT WE'LL BE KIRA'S NEXT TARGET.

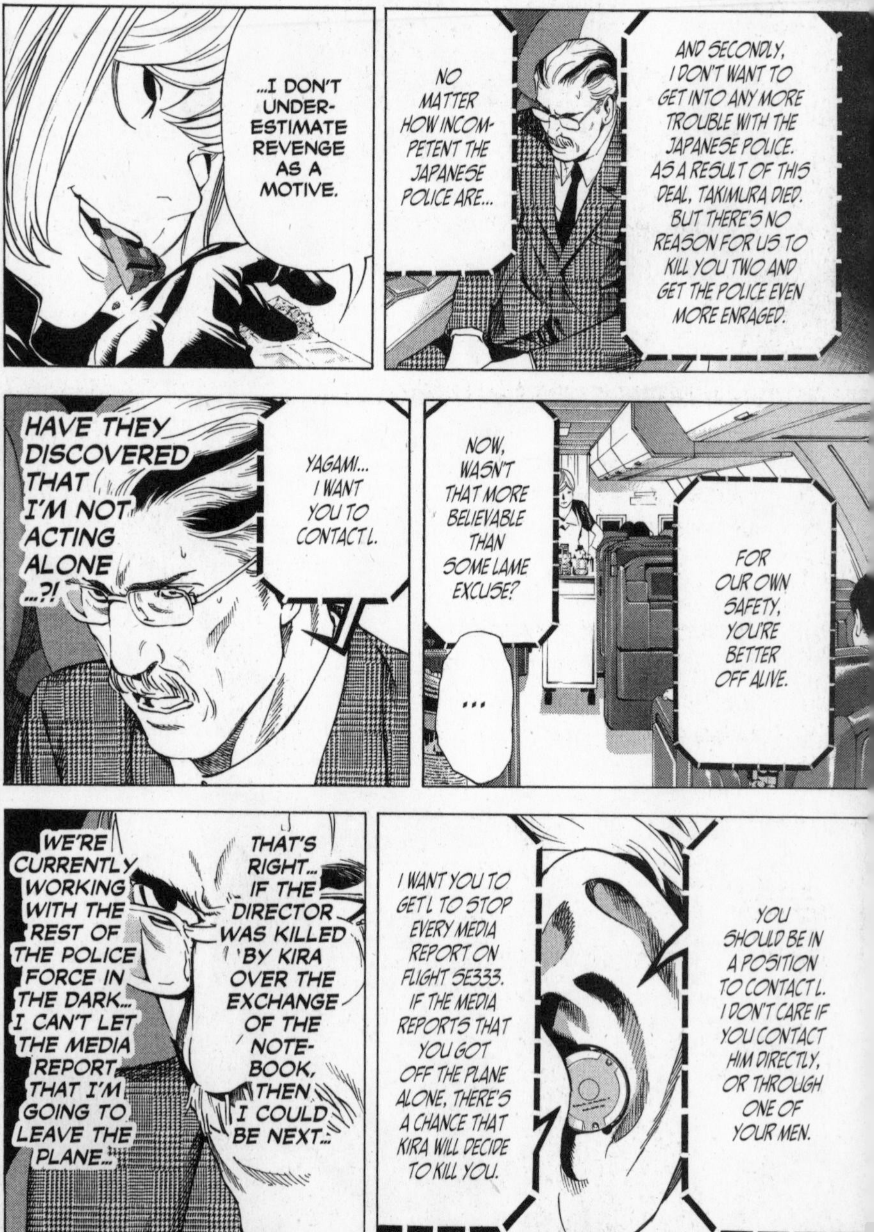
AND SECONDLY, I DON'T WANT TO GET INTO ANY MORE TROUBLE WITH THE JAPANESE POLICE. AS A RESULT OF THIS DEAL, TAKIMURA DIED. BUT THERE'S NO REASON FOR US TO KILL YOU TWO AND GET THE POLICE EVEN MORE ENRAGED.
NO MATTER HOW INCOMPETENT THE JAPANESE POLICE ARE...
...I DON'T UNDERESTIMATE REVENGE AS A MOTIVE.
FOR OUR OWN SAFETY, YOU'RE BETTER OFF ALIVE.
NOW, WASN'T THAT MORE BELIEVABLE THAN SOME LAME EXCUSE?
...
YAGAMI... I WANT YOU TO CONTACT L.
HAVE THEY DISCOVERED THAT I'M NOT ACTING ALONE ...?!
YOU SHOULD BE IN A POSITION TO CONTACT L. I DON'T CARE IF YOU CONTACT HIM DIRECTLY, OR THROUGH ONE OF YOUR MEN.
I WANT YOU TO GET L TO STOP EVERY MEDIA REPORT ON FLIGHT SE333. IF THE MEDIA REPORTS THAT YOU GOT OFF THE PLANE ALONE, THERE'S A CHANCE THAT KIRA WILL DECIDE TO KILL YOU.
THAT'S RIGHT... IF THE DIRECTOR WAS KILLED BY KIRA OVER THE EXCHANGE OF THE NOTEBOOK, THEN I COULD BE NEXT...
WE'RE CURRENTLY WORKING WITH THE REST OF THE POLICE FORCE IN THE DARK... I CAN'T LET THE MEDIA REPORT THAT I'M GOING TO LEAVE THE PLANE...

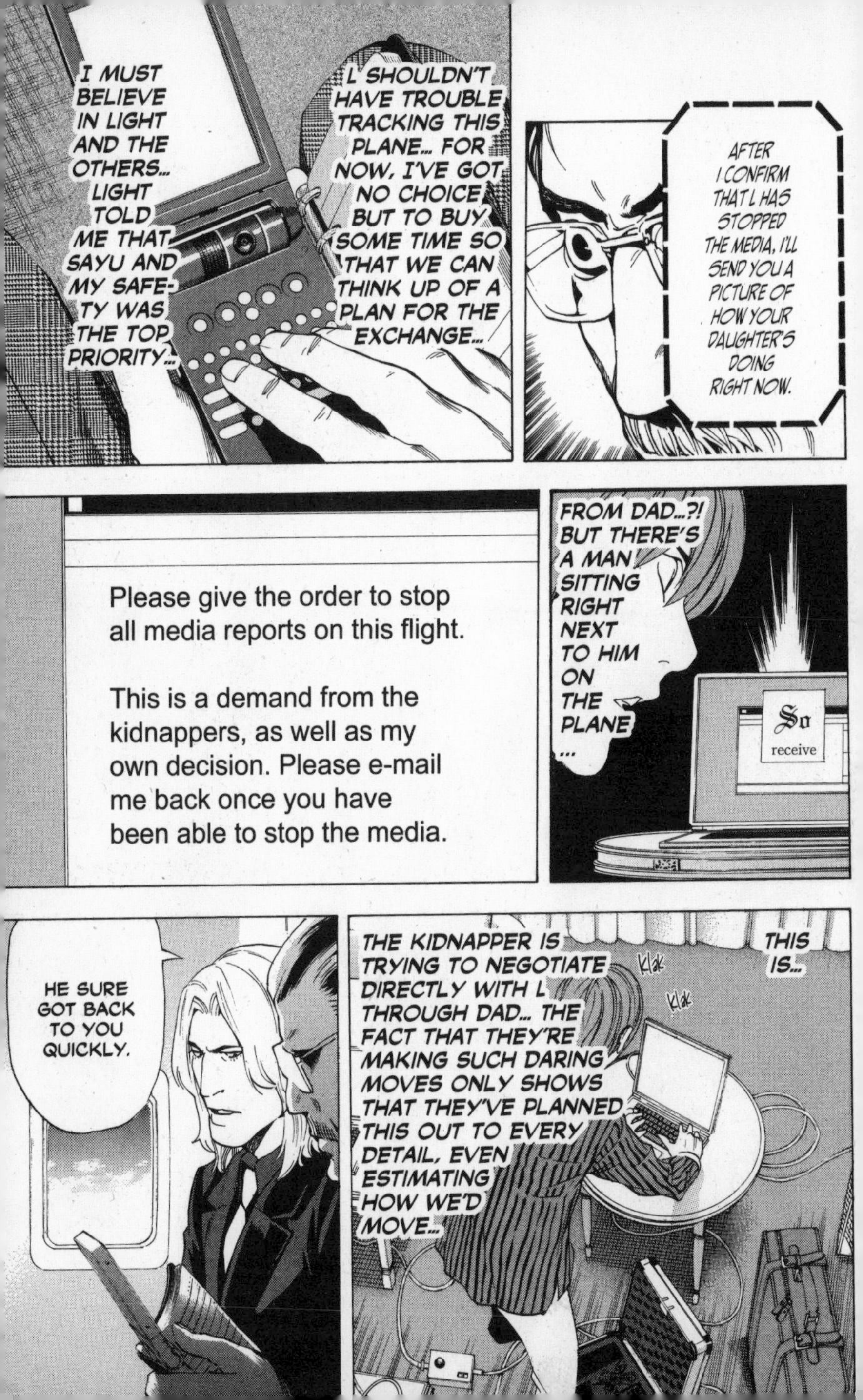
AFTER I CONFIRM THAT L HAS STOPPED THE MEDIA, I'LL SEND YOU A PICTURE OF HOW YOUR DAUGHTER'S DOING RIGHT NOW.
L SHOULDN'T HAVE TROUBLE TRACKING THIS PLANE... FOR NOW, I'VE GOT NO CHOICE BUT TO BUY SOME TIME SO THAT WE CAN THINK UP OF A PLAN FOR THE EXCHANGE...
I MUST BELIEVE IN LIGHT AND THE OTHERS... LIGHT TOLD ME THAT SAYU AND MY SAFETY WAS THE TOP PRIORITY...
FROM DAD...?! BUT THERE'S A MAN SITTING RIGHT NEXT TO HIM ON THE PLANE...
So
receive
Please give the order to stop all media reports on this flight.
This is a demand from the kidnappers, as well as my own decision. Please e-mail me back once you have been able to stop the media.
THIS IS...
KLAK
KLAK
THE KIDNAPPER IS TRYING TO NEGOTIATE DIRECTLY WITH L THROUGH DAD... THE FACT THAT THEY'RE MAKING SUCH DARING MOVES ONLY SHOWS THAT THEY'VE PLANNED THIS OUT TO EVERY DETAIL, EVEN ESTIMATING HOW WE'D MOVE...
HE SURE GOT BACK TO YOU QUICKLY.

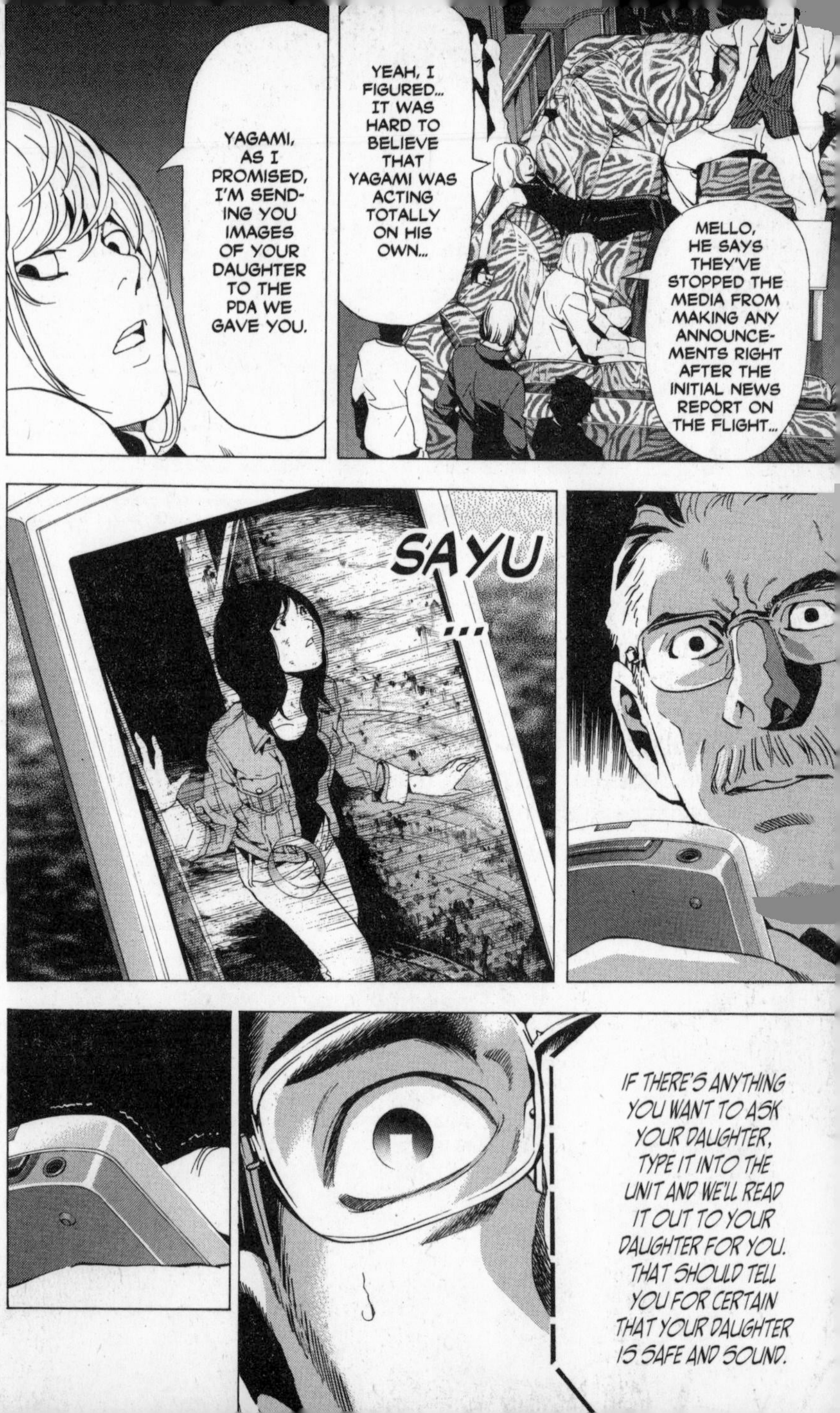
MELLO, HE SAYS THEY'VE STOPPED THE MEDIA FROM MAKING ANY ANNOUNCE-MENTS RIGHT AFTER THE INITIAL NEWS REPORT ON THE FLIGHT...
YEAH, I FIGURED... IT WAS HARD TO BELIEVE THAT YAGAMI WAS ACTING TOTALLY ON HIS OWN...
YAGAMI, AS I PROMISED, I'M SEND-ING YOU IMAGES OF YOUR DAUGHTER TO THE PDA WE GAVE YOU.
SAYU ...
IF THERE'S ANYTHING YOU WANT TO ASK YOUR DAUGHTER, TYPE IT INTO THE UNIT AND WE'LL READ IT OUT TO YOUR DAUGHTER FOR YOU. THAT SHOULD TELL YOU FOR CERTAIN THAT YOUR DAUGHTER IS SAFE AND SOUND.

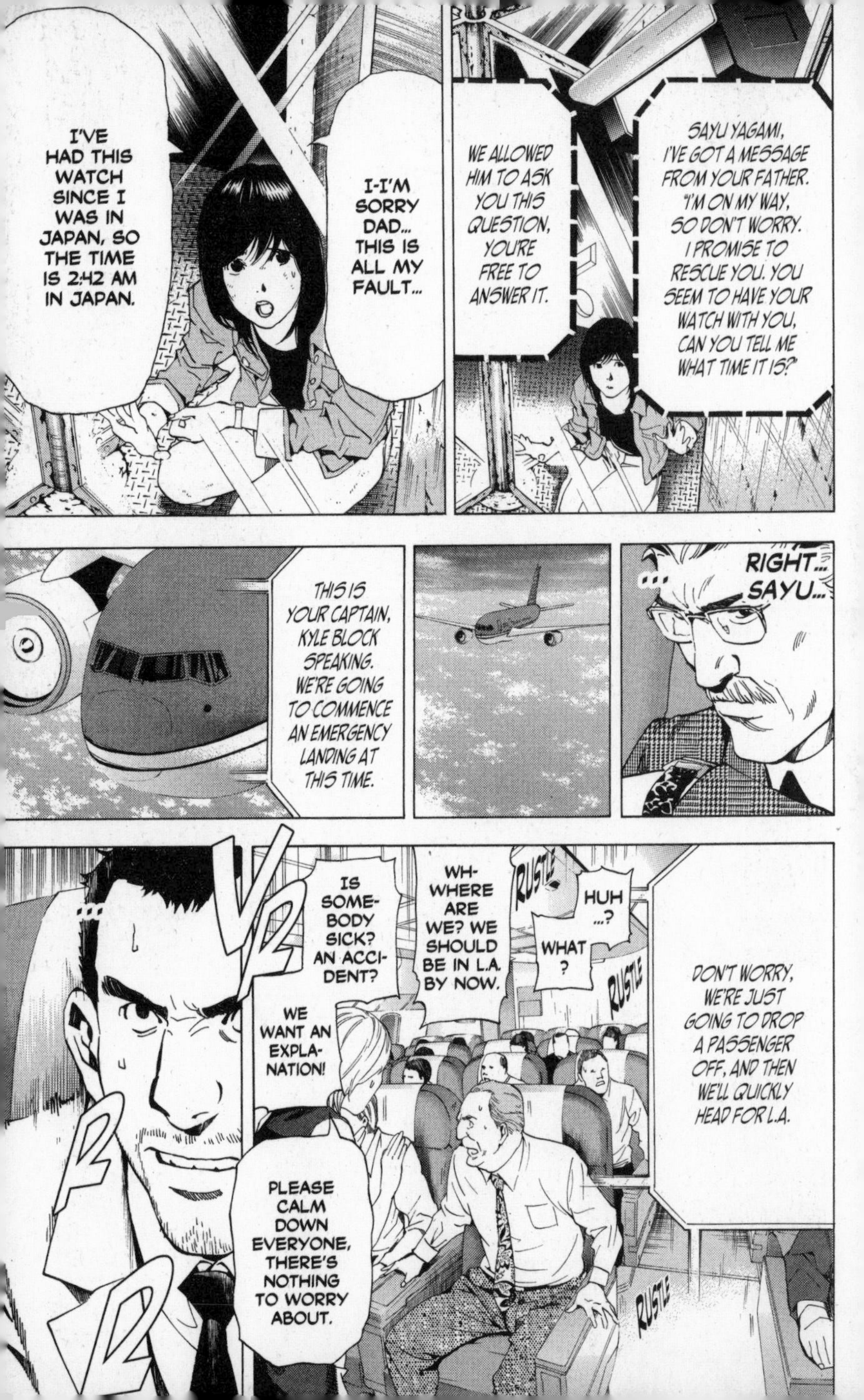
SAYU YAGAMI, I'VE GOT A MESSAGE FROM YOUR FATHER. "I'M ON MY WAY, SO DON'T WORRY. I PROMISE TO RESCUE YOU. YOU SEEM TO HAVE YOUR WATCH WITH YOU, CAN YOU TELL ME WHAT TIME IT IS?"
WE ALLOWED HIM TO ASK YOU THIS QUESTION, YOU'RE FREE TO ANSWER IT.
I-I'M SORRY DAD... THIS IS ALL MY FAULT...
I'VE HAD THIS WATCH SINCE I WAS IN JAPAN, SO THE TIME IS 2:42 AM IN JAPAN.
...
RIGHT... SAYU...
THIS IS YOUR CAPTAIN, KYLE BLOCK SPEAKING. WE'RE GOING TO COMMENCE AN EMERGENCY LANDING AT THIS TIME.
DON'T WORRY, WE'RE JUST GOING TO DROP A PASSENGER OFF, AND THEN WE'LL QUICKLY HEAD FOR L.A.
RUSTLE
HUH ...?
WHAT ?
RUSTLE
WH-WHERE ARE WE? WE SHOULD BE IN L.A. BY NOW.
IS SOME-BODY SICK? AN ACCI-DENT?
WE WANT AN EXPLA-NATION!
RUSTLE
...
PLEASE CALM DOWN EVERYONE, THERE'S NOTHING TO WORRY ABOUT.

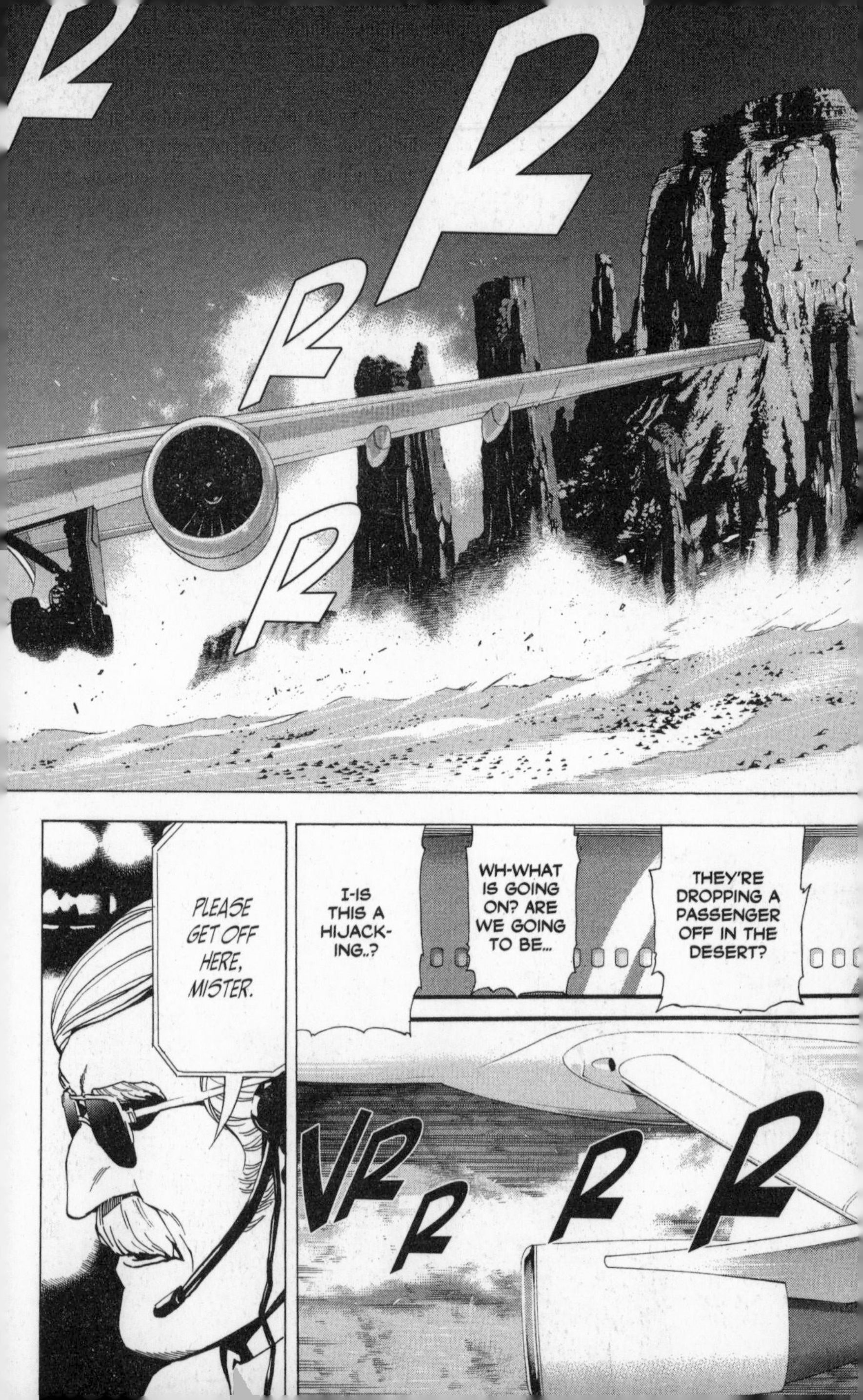
RRRRR
THEY'RE DROPPING A PASSENGER OFF IN THE DESERT?
WH-WHAT IS GOING ON? ARE WE GOING TO BE...
I-IS THIS A HIJACK-ING..?
VRRRR
PLEASE GET OFF HERE, MISTER.

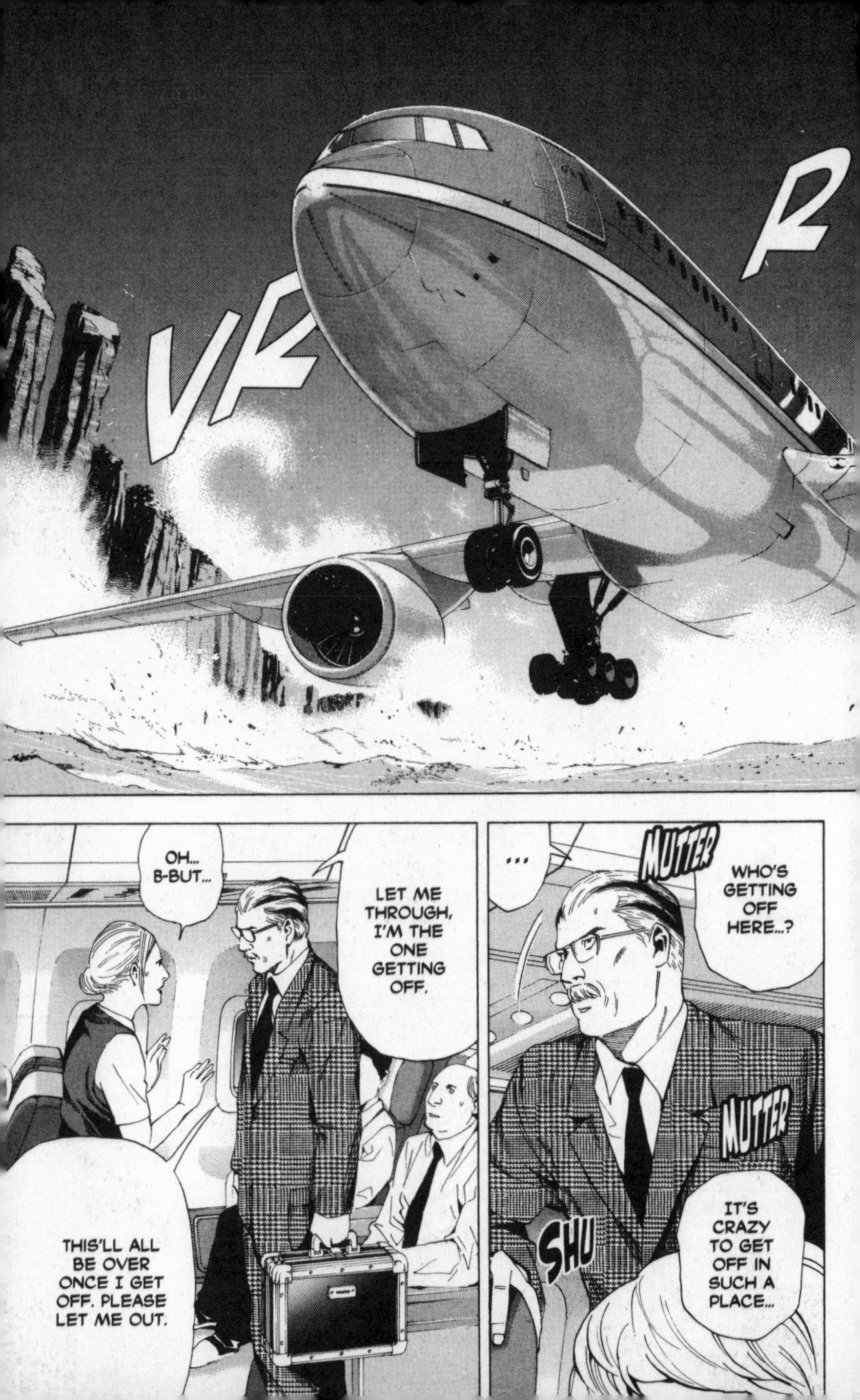
R
VR
MUTTER
WHO'S GETTING OFF HERE...?
...
MUTTER
IT'S CRAZY TO GET OFF IN SUCH A PLACE...
SHU
LET ME THROUGH, I'M THE ONE GETTING OFF.
OH... B-BUT...
THIS'LL ALL BE OVER ONCE I GET OFF. PLEASE LET ME OUT.

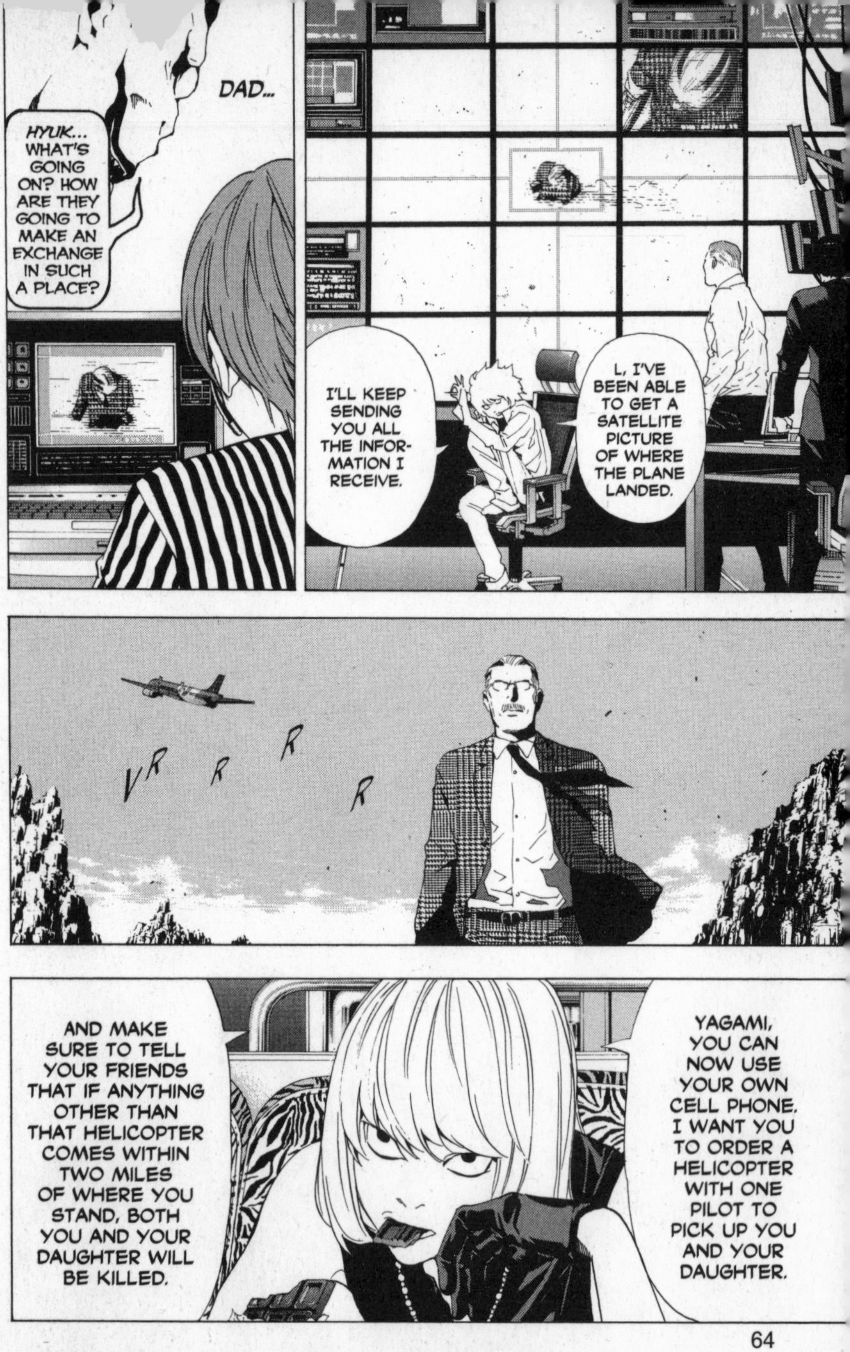
L, I'VE BEEN ABLE TO GET A SATELLITE PICTURE OF WHERE THE PLANE LANDED.
I'LL KEEP SENDING YOU ALL THE INFORMATION I RECEIVE.
DAD...
HYUK... WHAT'S GOING ON? HOW ARE THEY GOING TO MAKE AN EXCHANGE IN SUCH A PLACE?
VRRRR
YAGAMI, YOU CAN NOW USE YOUR OWN CELL PHONE. I WANT YOU TO ORDER A HELICOPTER WITH ONE PILOT TO PICK UP YOU AND YOUR DAUGHTER.
AND MAKE SURE TO TELL YOUR FRIENDS THAT IF ANYTHING OTHER THAN THAT HELICOPTER COMES WITHIN TWO MILES OF WHERE YOU STAND, BOTH YOU AND YOUR DAUGHTER WILL BE KILLED.

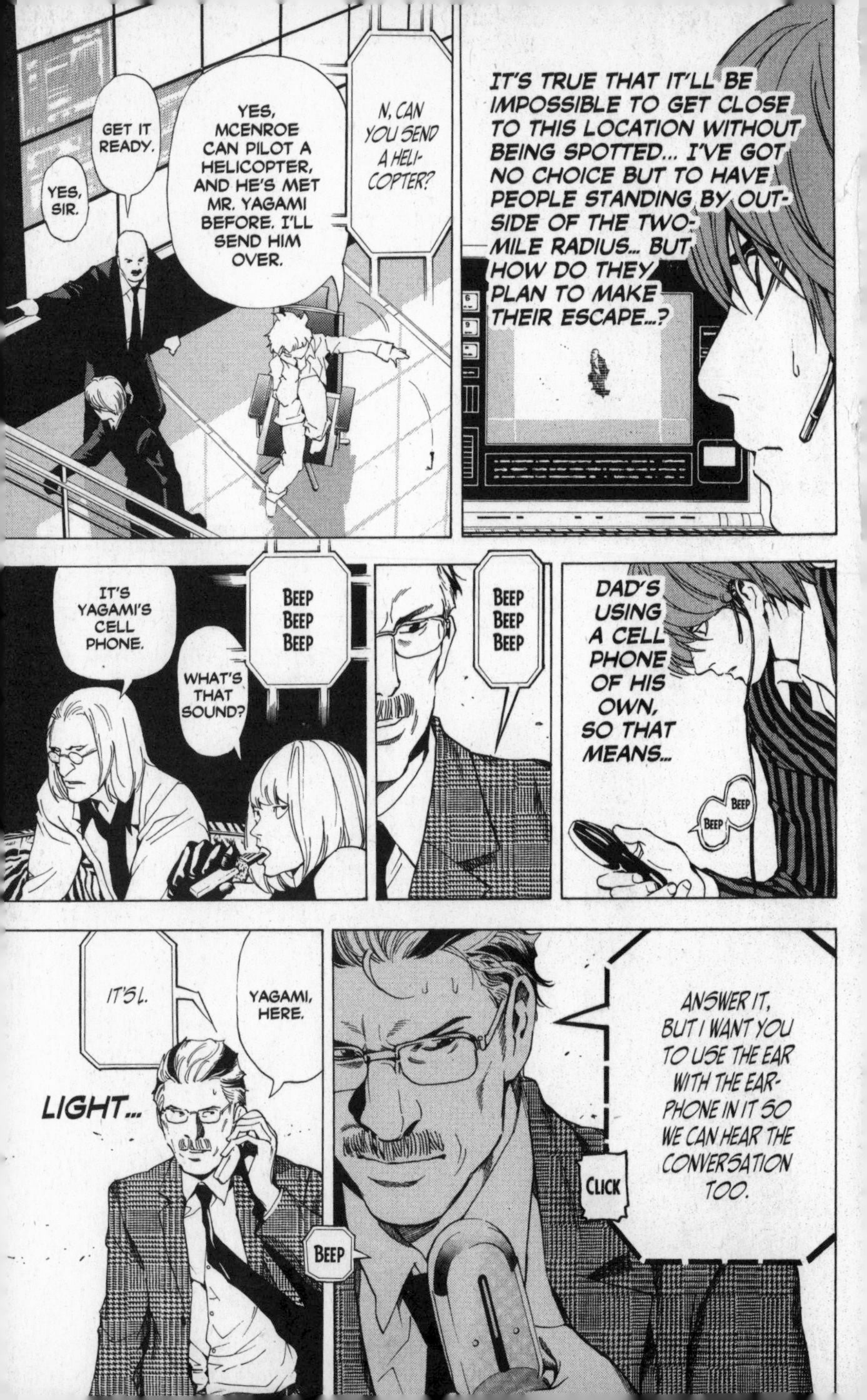
IT'S TRUE THAT IT'LL BE IMPOSSIBLE TO GET CLOSE TO THIS LOCATION WITHOUT BEING SPOTTED... I'VE GOT NO CHOICE BUT TO HAVE PEOPLE STANDING BY OUTSIDE OF THE TWO-MILE RADIUS... BUT HOW DO THEY PLAN TO MAKE THEIR ESCAPE...?
N, CAN YOU SEND A HELICOPTER?
YES, MCENROE CAN PILOT A HELICOPTER, AND HE'S MET MR. YAGAMI BEFORE. I'LL SEND HIM OVER.
GET IT READY.
YES, SIR.
DAD'S USING A CELL PHONE OF HIS OWN, SO THAT MEANS...
BEEP
BEEP
BEEP BEEP BEEP
BEEP BEEP BEEP
IT'S YAGAMI'S CELL PHONE.
WHAT'S THAT SOUND?
ANSWER IT, BUT I WANT YOU TO USE THE EAR WITH THE EARPHONE IN IT SO WE CAN HEAR THE CONVERSATION TOO.
CLICK
BEEP
YAGAMI, HERE.
IT'S L.
LIGHT...

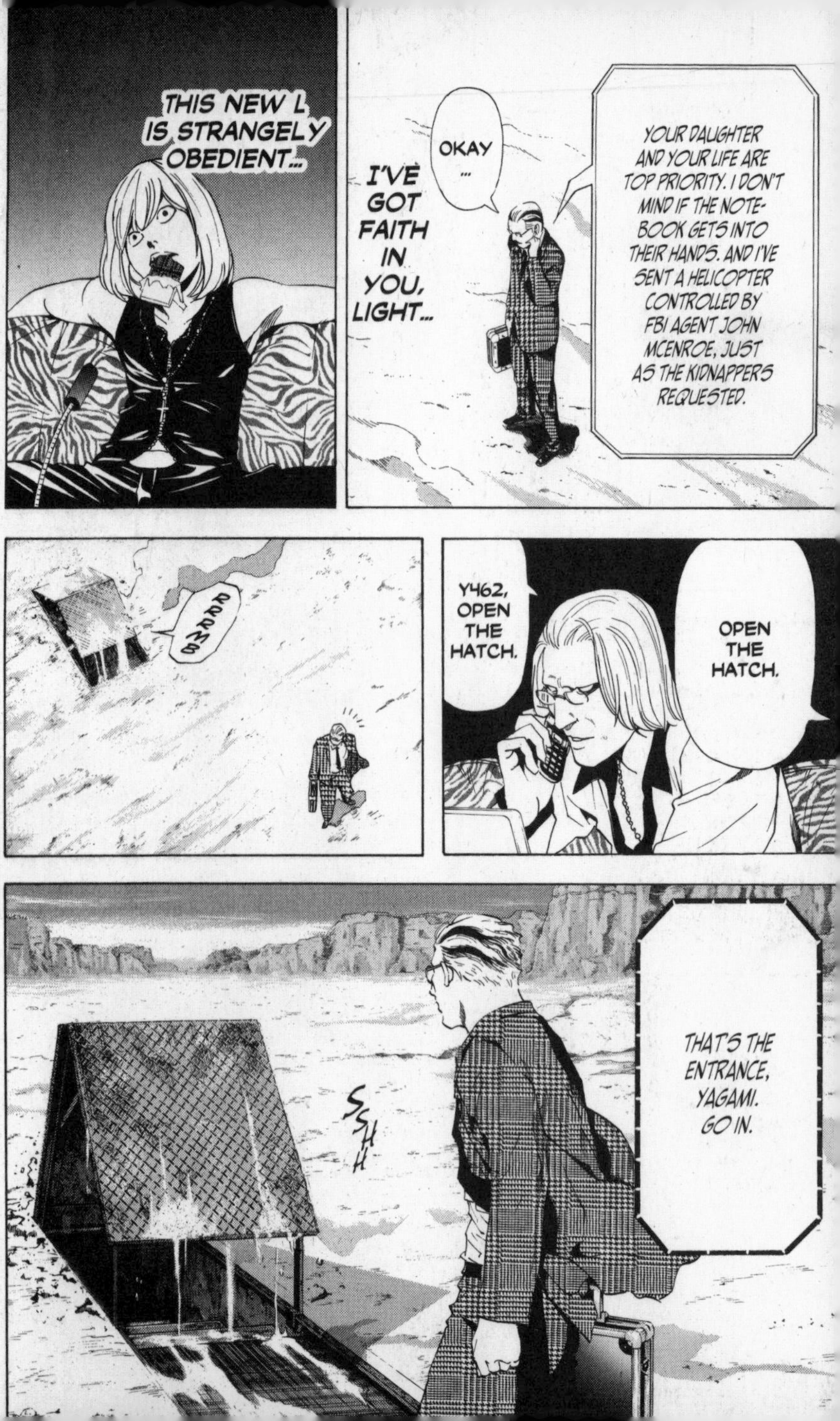
YOUR DAUGHTER AND YOUR LIFE ARE TOP PRIORITY. I DON'T MIND IF THE NOTE-BOOK GETS INTO THEIR HANDS. AND I'VE SENT A HELICOPTER CONTROLLED BY FBI AGENT JOHN MCENROE, JUST AS THE KIDNAPPERS REQUESTED.
OKAY ...
I'VE GOT FAITH IN YOU, LIGHT...
THIS NEW L IS STRANGELY OBEDIENT...
OPEN THE HATCH.
Y462, OPEN THE HATCH.
RRRMB
THAT'S THE ENTRANCE, YAGAMI. GO IN.
SSHH

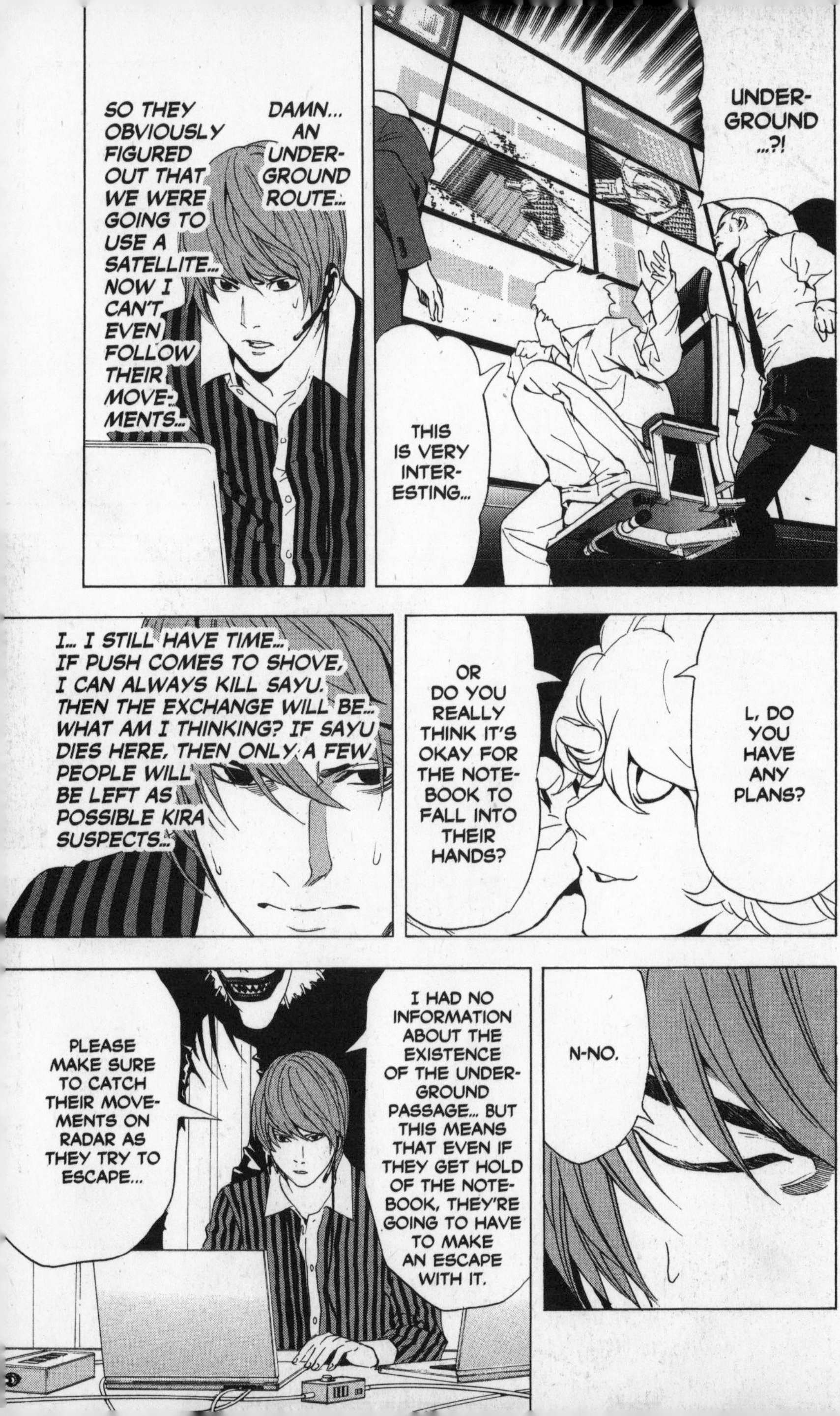
UNDER-GROUND ...?!
THIS IS VERY INTERESTING...
DAMN... AN UNDER-GROUND ROUTE...
SO THEY OBVIOUSLY FIGURED OUT THAT WE WERE GOING TO USE A SATELLITE... NOW I CAN'T EVEN FOLLOW THEIR MOVE-MENTS...
L, DO YOU HAVE ANY PLANS?
OR DO YOU REALLY THINK IT'S OKAY FOR THE NOTE-BOOK TO FALL INTO THEIR HANDS?
I... I STILL HAVE TIME... IF PUSH COMES TO SHOVE, I CAN ALWAYS KILL SAYU. THEN THE EXCHANGE WILL BE... WHAT AM I THINKING? IF SAYU DIES HERE, THEN ONLY A FEW PEOPLE WILL BE LEFT AS POSSIBLE KIRA SUSPECTS...
N-NO.
I HAD NO INFORMATION ABOUT THE EXISTENCE OF THE UNDER-GROUND PASSAGE... BUT THIS MEANS THAT EVEN IF THEY GET HOLD OF THE NOTE-BOOK, THEY'RE GOING TO HAVE TO MAKE AN ESCAPE WITH IT.
PLEASE MAKE SURE TO CATCH THEIR MOVE-MENTS ON RADAR AS THEY TRY TO ESCAPE...

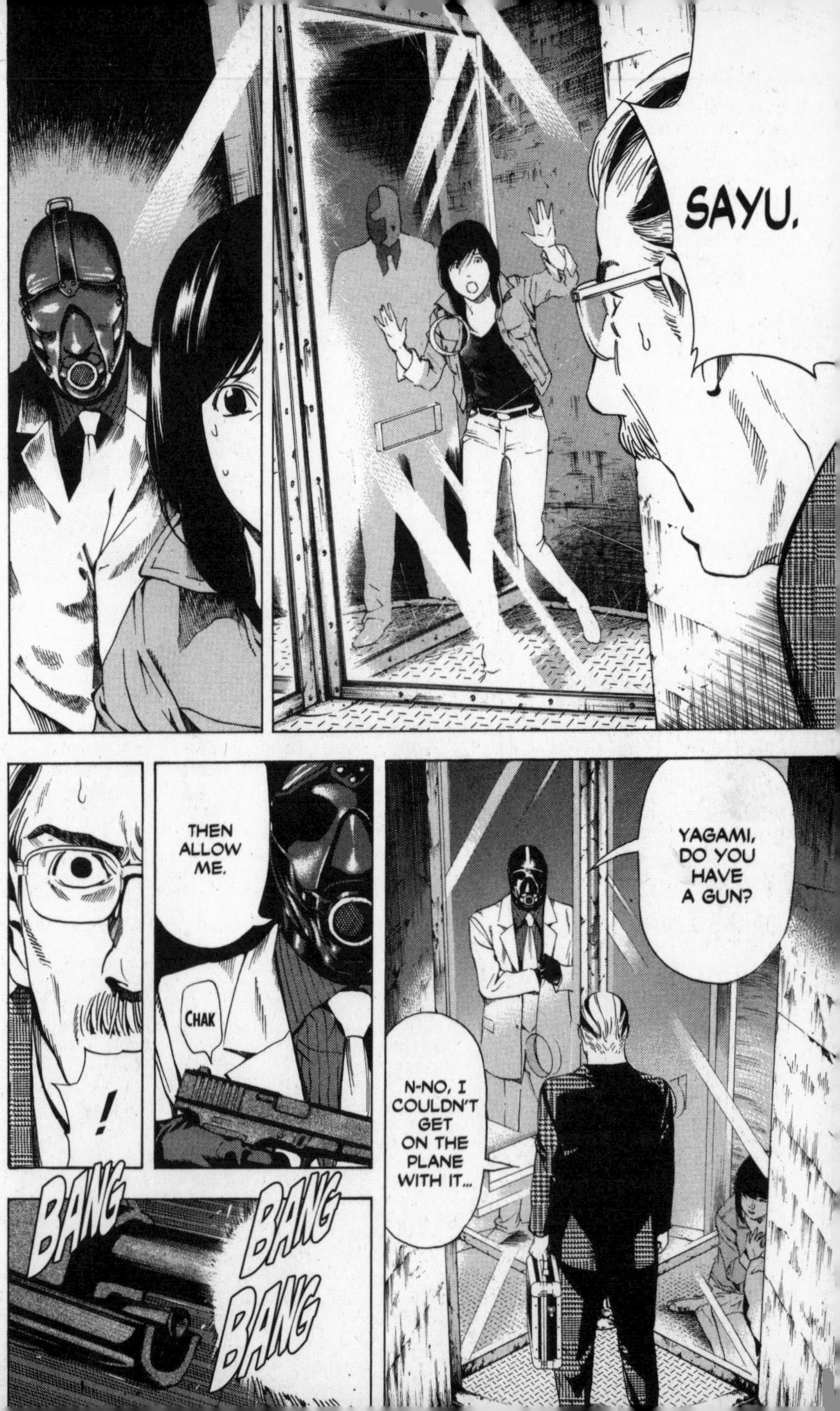
SAYU.
YAGAMI, DO YOU HAVE A GUN?
N-NO, I COULDN'T GET ON THE PLANE WITH IT...
THEN ALLOW ME.
CHAK
!
BANG
BANG
BANG

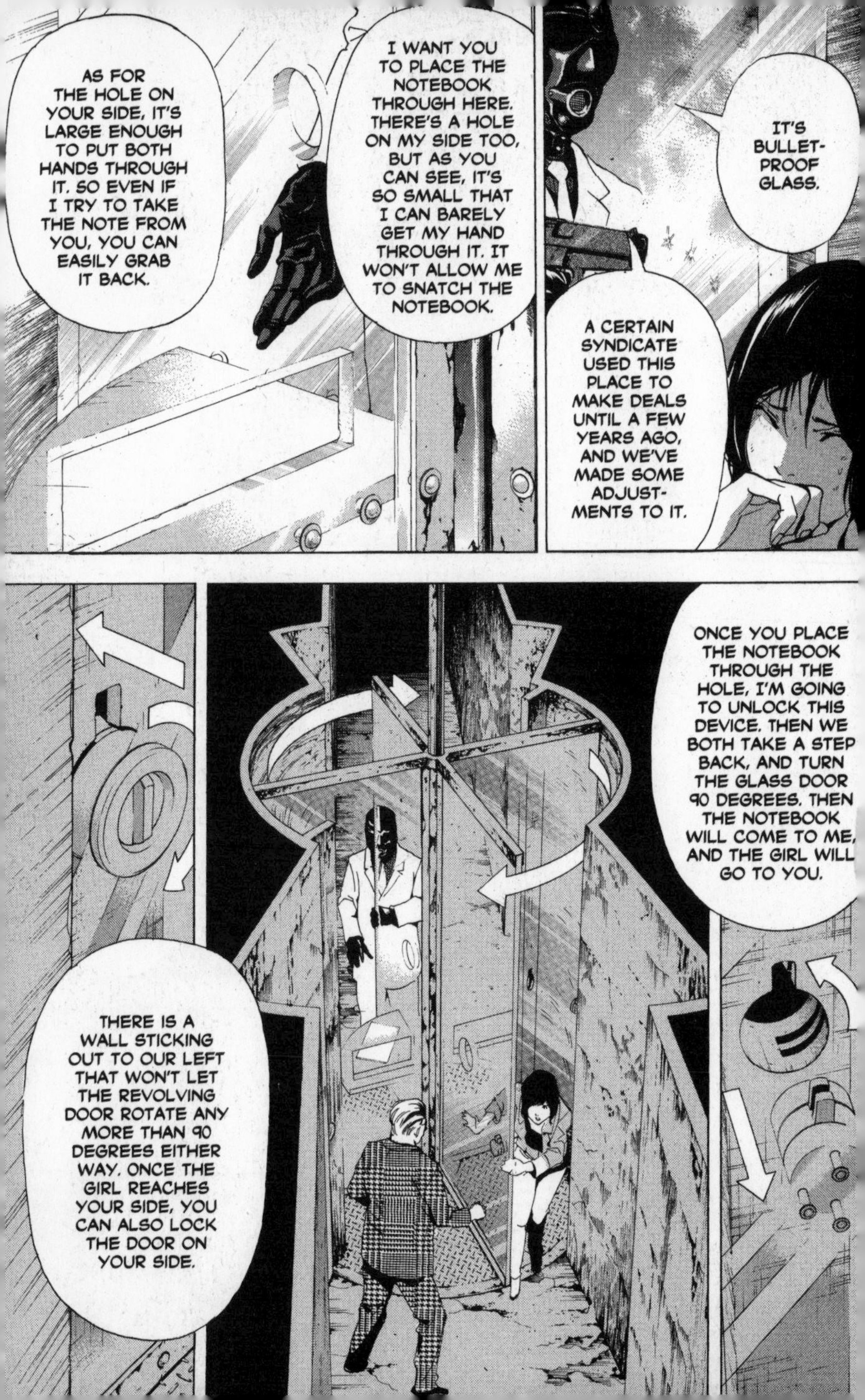
IT'S BULLET-PROOF GLASS.
A CERTAIN SYNDICATE USED THIS PLACE TO MAKE DEALS UNTIL A FEW YEARS AGO, AND WE'VE MADE SOME ADJUST-MENTS TO IT.
I WANT YOU TO PLACE THE NOTEBOOK THROUGH HERE. THERE'S A HOLE ON MY SIDE TOO, BUT AS YOU CAN SEE, IT'S SO SMALL THAT I CAN BARELY GET MY HAND THROUGH IT. IT WON'T ALLOW ME TO SNATCH THE NOTEBOOK.
AS FOR THE HOLE ON YOUR SIDE, IT'S LARGE ENOUGH TO PUT BOTH HANDS THROUGH IT. SO EVEN IF I TRY TO TAKE THE NOTE FROM YOU, YOU CAN EASILY GRAB IT BACK.
ONCE YOU PLACE THE NOTEBOOK THROUGH THE HOLE, I'M GOING TO UNLOCK THIS DEVICE. THEN WE BOTH TAKE A STEP BACK, AND TURN THE GLASS DOOR 90 DEGREES. THEN THE NOTEBOOK WILL COME TO ME, AND THE GIRL WILL GO TO YOU.
THERE IS A WALL STICKING OUT TO OUR LEFT THAT WON'T LET THE REVOLVING DOOR ROTATE ANY MORE THAN 90 DEGREES EITHER WAY. ONCE THE GIRL REACHES YOUR SIDE, YOU CAN ALSO LOCK THE DOOR ON YOUR SIDE.

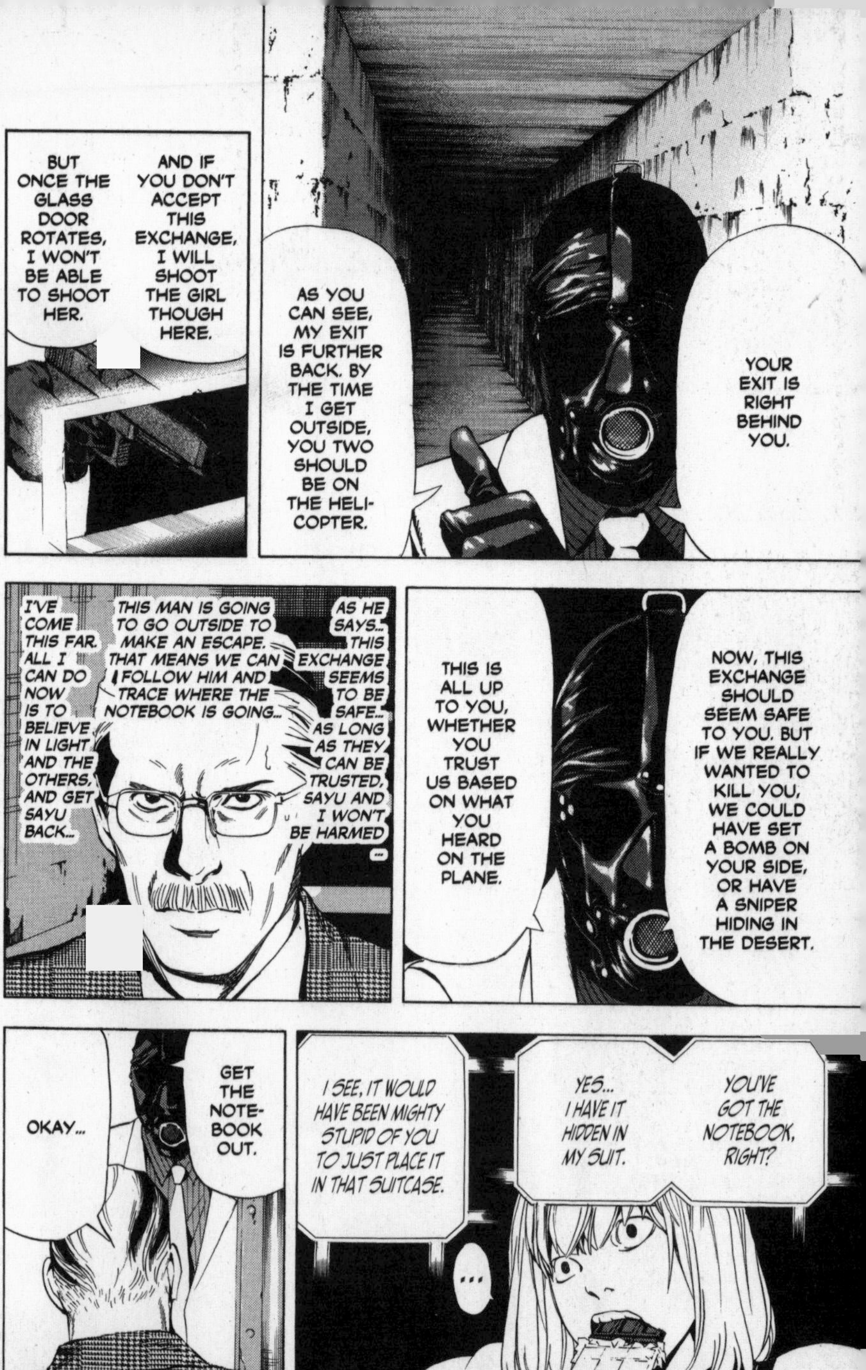
YOUR EXIT IS RIGHT BEHIND YOU.
AS YOU CAN SEE, MY EXIT IS FURTHER BACK. BY THE TIME I GET OUTSIDE, YOU TWO SHOULD BE ON THE HELI-COPTER.
AND IF YOU DON'T ACCEPT THIS EXCHANGE, I WILL SHOOT THE GIRL THOUGH HERE.
BUT ONCE THE GLASS DOOR ROTATES, I WON'T BE ABLE TO SHOOT HER.
NOW, THIS EXCHANGE SHOULD SEEM SAFE TO YOU. BUT IF WE REALLY WANTED TO KILL YOU, WE COULD HAVE SET A BOMB ON YOUR SIDE, OR HAVE A SNIPER HIDING IN THE DESERT.
THIS IS ALL UP TO YOU, WHETHER YOU TRUST US BASED ON WHAT YOU HEARD ON THE PLANE.
AS HE SAYS... THIS EXCHANGE SEEMS TO BE SAFE... AS LONG AS THEY CAN BE TRUSTED, SAYU AND I WON'T BE HARMED...
THIS MAN IS GOING TO GO OUTSIDE TO MAKE AN ESCAPE. THAT MEANS WE CAN FOLLOW HIM AND TRACE WHERE THE NOTEBOOK IS GOING...
I'VE COME THIS FAR. ALL I CAN DO NOW IS TO BELIEVE IN LIGHT AND THE OTHERS, AND GET SAYU BACK...
YOU'VE GOT THE NOTEBOOK, RIGHT?
YES... I HAVE IT HIDDEN IN MY SUIT.
I SEE, IT WOULD HAVE BEEN MIGHTY STUPID OF YOU TO JUST PLACE IT IN THAT SUITCASE.
...
GET THE NOTE-BOOK OUT.
OKAY...

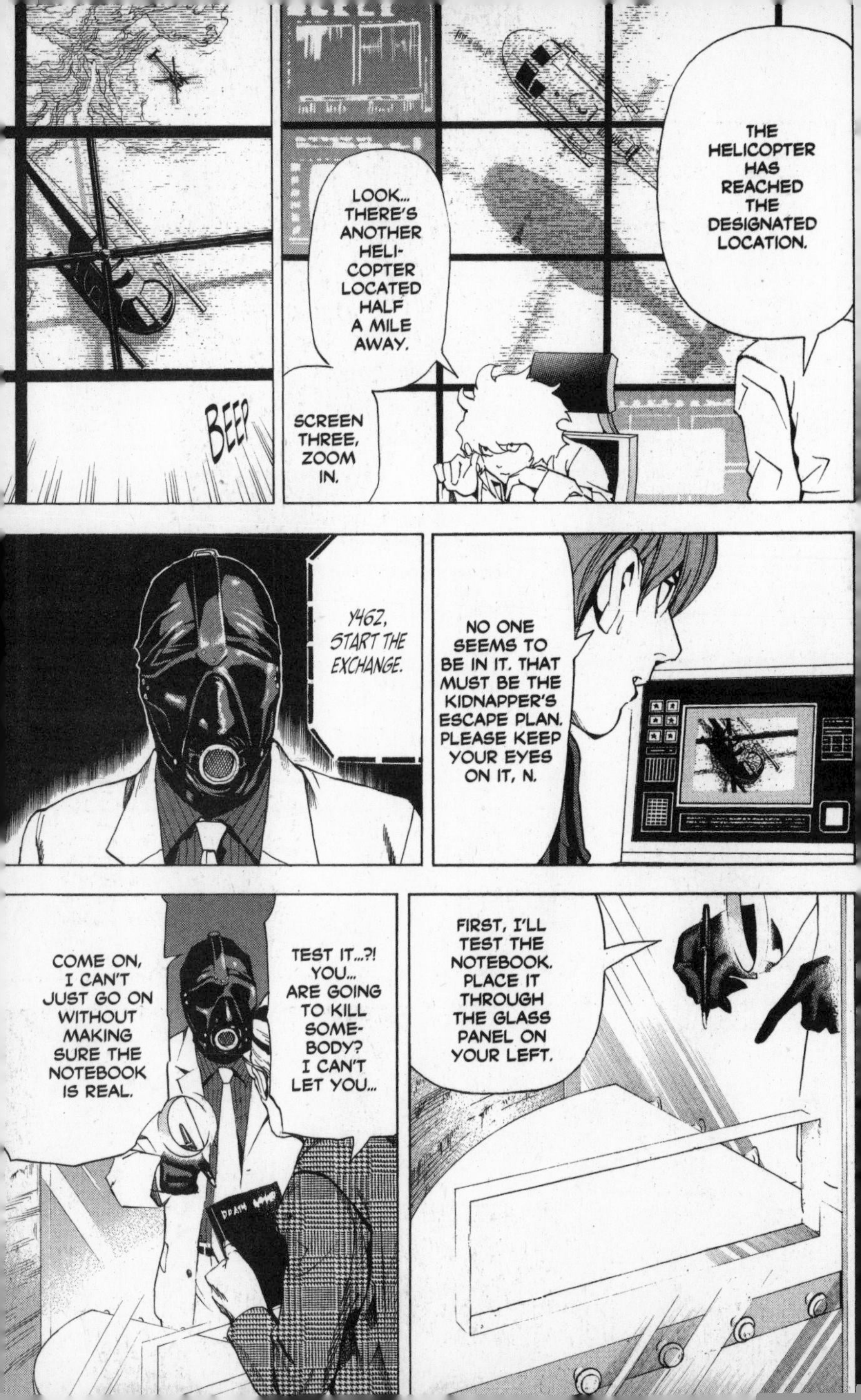
THE HELICOPTER HAS REACHED THE DESIGNATED LOCATION.
LOOK... THERE'S ANOTHER HELI-COPTER LOCATED HALF A MILE AWAY.
SCREEN THREE, ZOOM IN.
BEEP
NO ONE SEEMS TO BE IN IT. THAT MUST BE THE KIDNAPPER'S ESCAPE PLAN. PLEASE KEEP YOUR EYES ON IT, N.
Y462, START THE EXCHANGE.
FIRST, I'LL TEST THE NOTEBOOK. PLACE IT THROUGH THE GLASS PANEL ON YOUR LEFT.
TEST IT...?! YOU... ARE GOING TO KILL SOME-BODY? I CAN'T LET YOU...
COME ON, I CAN'T JUST GO ON WITHOUT MAKING SURE THE NOTEBOOK IS REAL.

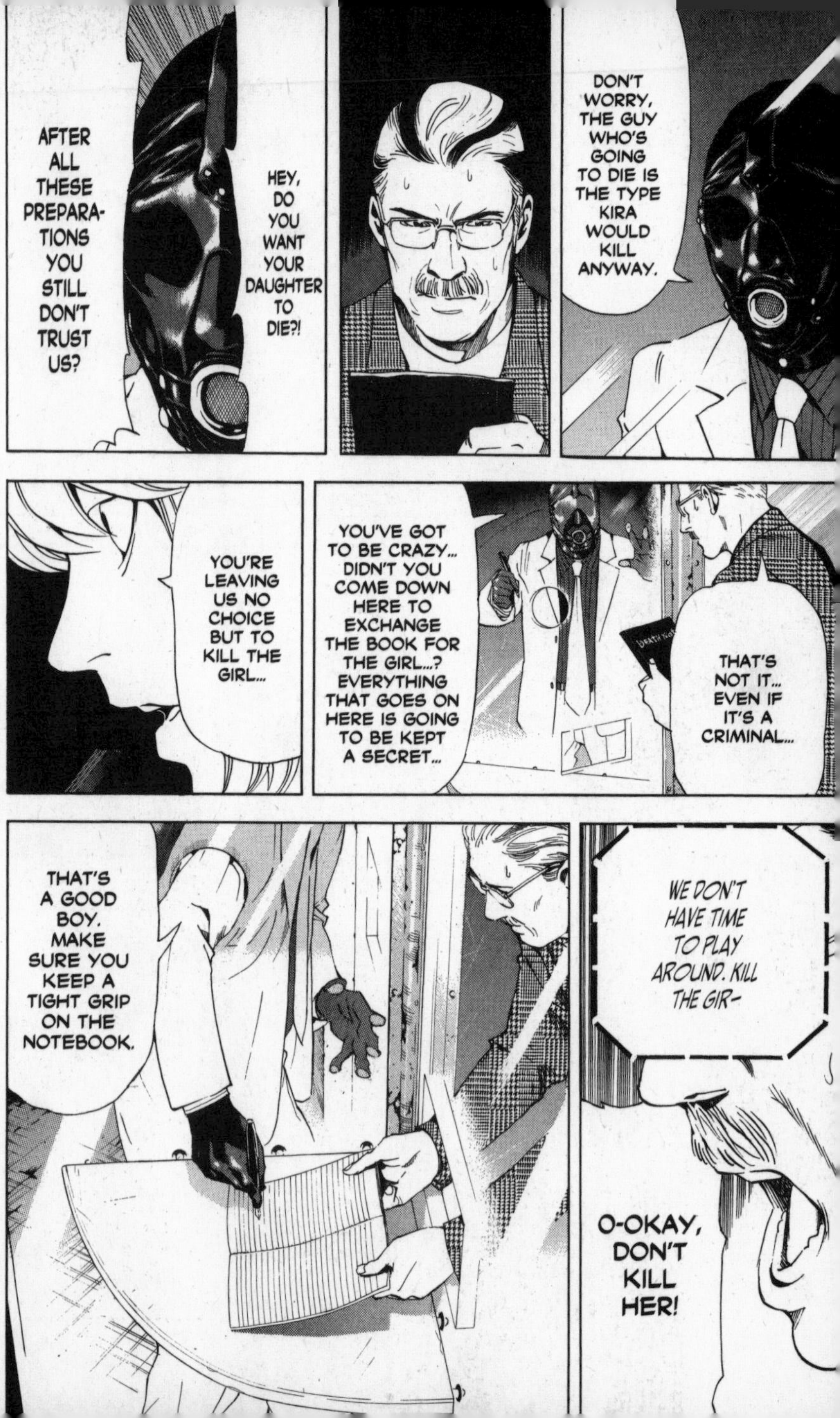
DON'T WORRY, THE GUY WHO'S GOING TO DIE IS THE TYPE KIRA WOULD KILL ANYWAY.
HEY, DO YOU WANT YOUR DAUGHTER TO DIE?!
AFTER ALL THESE PREPARATIONS YOU STILL DON'T TRUST US?
THAT'S NOT IT... EVEN IF IT'S A CRIMINAL...
YOU'VE GOT TO BE CRAZY... DIDN'T YOU COME DOWN HERE TO EXCHANGE THE BOOK FOR THE GIRL...? EVERYTHING THAT GOES ON HERE IS GOING TO BE KEPT A SECRET...
YOU'RE LEAVING US NO CHOICE BUT TO KILL THE GIRL...
WE DON'T HAVE TIME TO PLAY AROUND. KILL THE GIR-
O-OKAY, DON'T KILL HER!
THAT'S A GOOD BOY. MAKE SURE YOU KEEP A TIGHT GRIP ON THE NOTEBOOK.

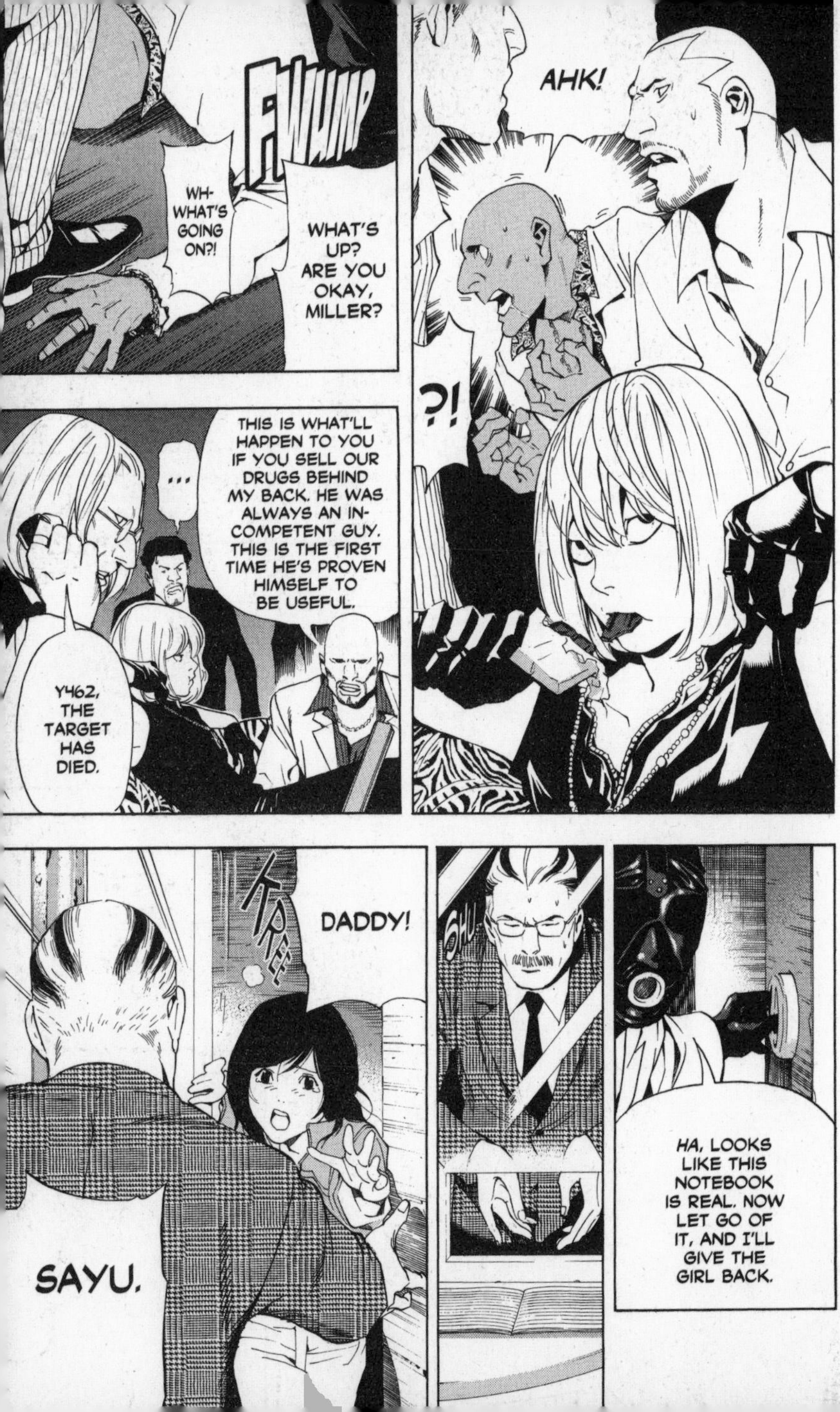
AHK!
?!
FWUMP
WHAT'S UP? ARE YOU OKAY, MILLER?
WH- WHAT'S GOING ON?!
THIS IS WHAT'LL HAPPEN TO YOU IF YOU SELL OUR DRUGS BEHIND MY BACK. HE WAS ALWAYS AN IN-COMPETENT GUY. THIS IS THE FIRST TIME HE'S PROVEN HIMSELF TO BE USEFUL.
...
Y462, THE TARGET HAS DIED.
HA, LOOKS LIKE THIS NOTEBOOK IS REAL. NOW LET GO OF IT, AND I'LL GIVE THE GIRL BACK.
SHU
KREE
DADDY!
SAYU.

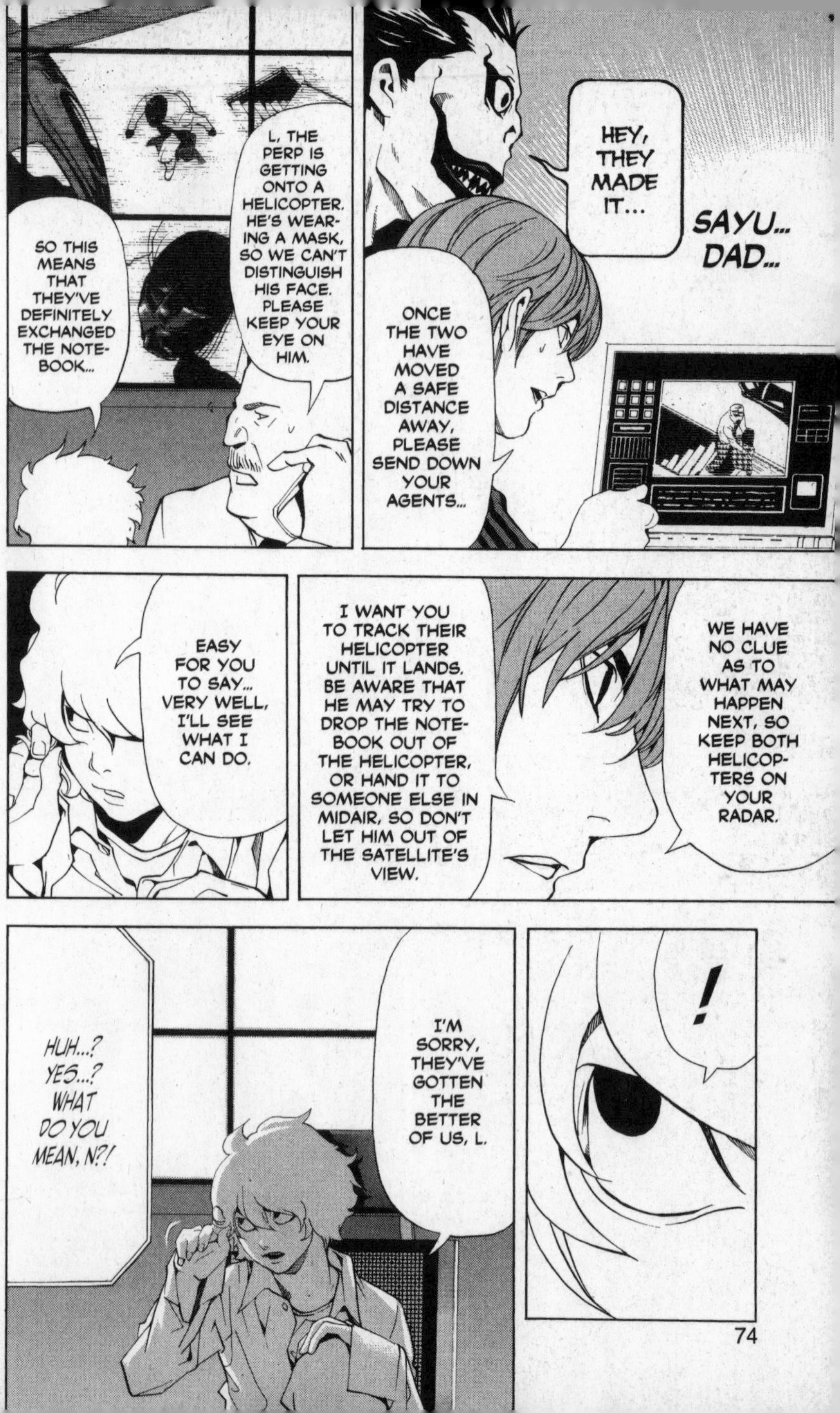
HEY, THEY MADE IT...
SAYU... DAD...
ONCE THE TWO HAVE MOVED A SAFE DISTANCE AWAY, PLEASE SEND DOWN YOUR AGENTS...
L, THE PERP IS GETTING ONTO A HELICOPTER. HE'S WEARING A MASK, SO WE CAN'T DISTINGUISH HIS FACE. PLEASE KEEP YOUR EYE ON HIM.
SO THIS MEANS THAT THEY'VE DEFINITELY EXCHANGED THE NOTEBOOK...
WE HAVE NO CLUE AS TO WHAT MAY HAPPEN NEXT, SO KEEP BOTH HELICOPTERS ON YOUR RADAR.
I WANT YOU TO TRACK THEIR HELICOPTER UNTIL IT LANDS. BE AWARE THAT HE MAY TRY TO DROP THE NOTEBOOK OUT OF THE HELICOPTER, OR HAND IT TO SOMEONE ELSE IN MIDAIR, SO DON'T LET HIM OUT OF THE SATELLITE'S VIEW.
EASY FOR YOU TO SAY... VERY WELL, I'LL SEE WHAT I CAN DO.
!
I'M SORRY, THEY'VE GOTTEN THE BETTER OF US, L.
HUH...? YES...? WHAT DO YOU MEAN, N?!

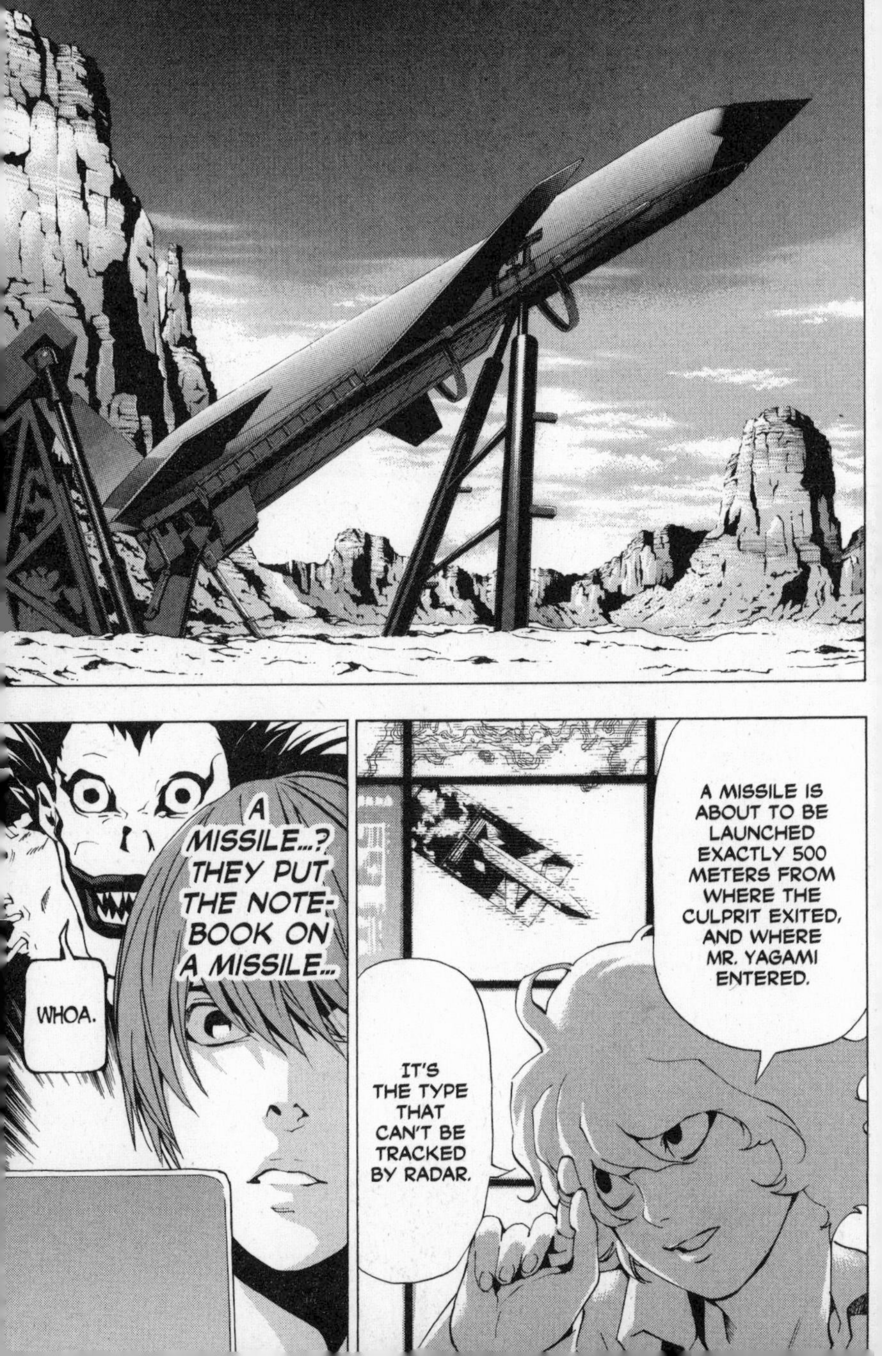
A MISSILE IS ABOUT TO BE LAUNCHED EXACTLY 500 METERS FROM WHERE THE CULPRIT EXITED, AND WHERE MR. YAGAMI ENTERED.
IT'S THE TYPE THAT CAN'T BE TRACKED BY RADAR.
A MISSILE...? THEY PUT THE NOTE-BOOK ON A MISSILE...
WHOA.

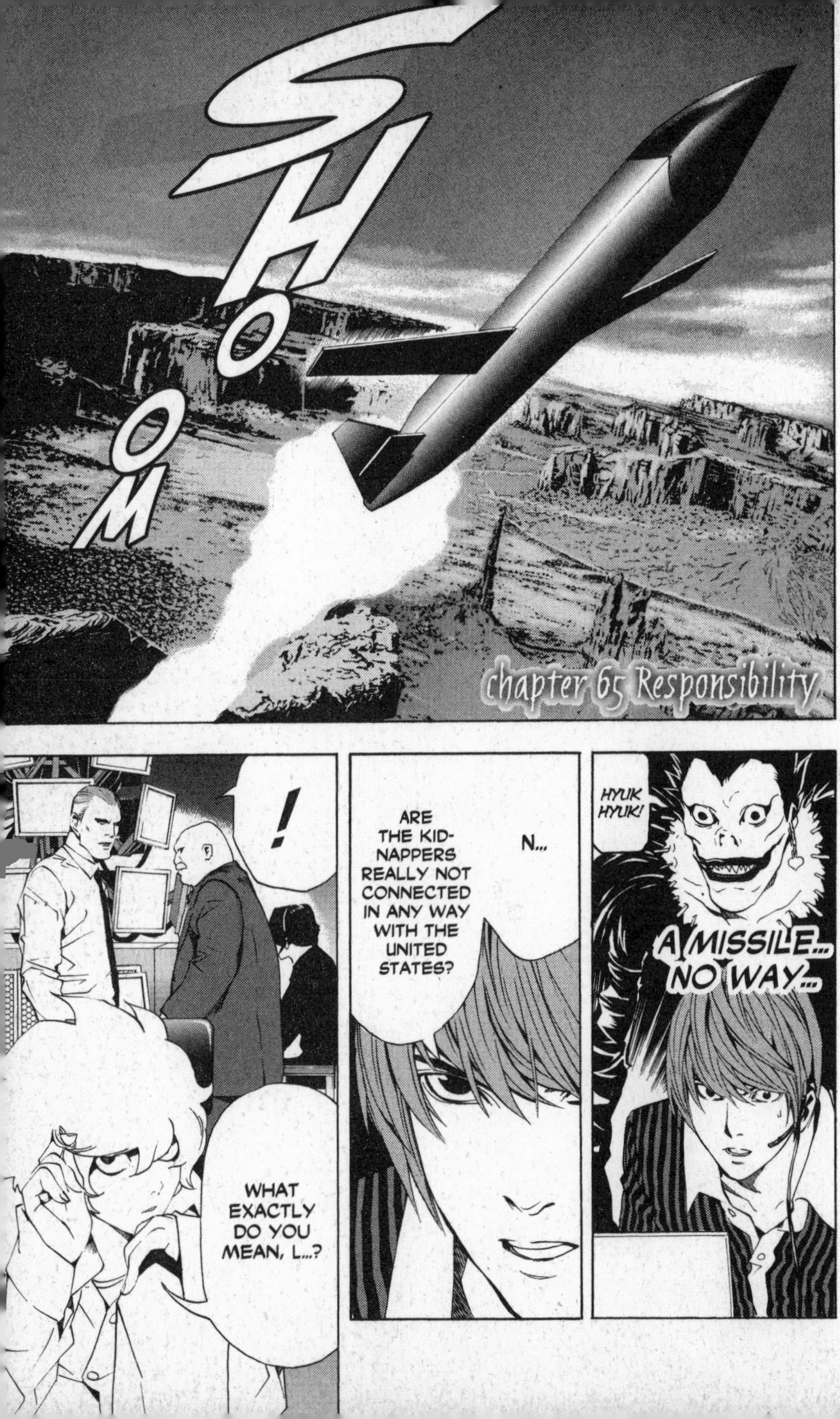
SHOOOM
chapter 65 Responsibility
HYUK HYUK!
A MISSILE... NO WAY...
N...
ARE THE KID-NAPPERS REALLY NOT CONNECTED IN ANY WAY WITH THE UNITED STATES?
!
WHAT EXACTLY DO YOU MEAN, L...?

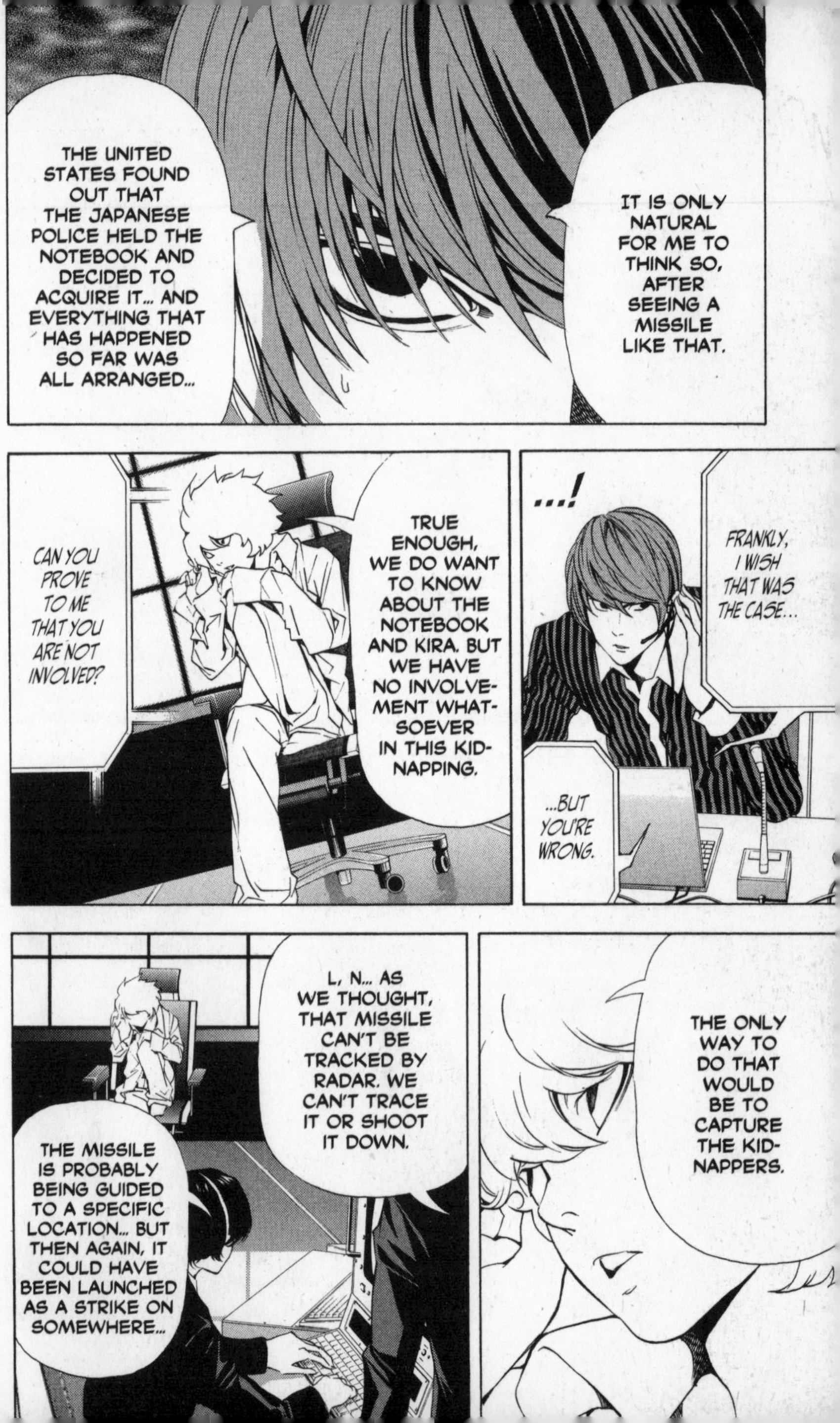
THE UNITED STATES FOUND OUT THAT THE JAPANESE POLICE HELD THE NOTEBOOK AND DECIDED TO ACQUIRE IT... AND EVERYTHING THAT HAS HAPPENED SO FAR WAS ALL ARRANGED...
IT IS ONLY NATURAL FOR ME TO THINK SO, AFTER SEEING A MISSILE LIKE THAT.
...!
FRANKLY, I WISH THAT WAS THE CASE...
...BUT YOU'RE WRONG.
TRUE ENOUGH, WE DO WANT TO KNOW ABOUT THE NOTEBOOK AND KIRA. BUT WE HAVE NO INVOLVEMENT WHATSOEVER IN THIS KIDNAPPING.
CAN YOU PROVE TO ME THAT YOU ARE NOT INVOLVED?
THE ONLY WAY TO DO THAT WOULD BE TO CAPTURE THE KIDNAPPERS.
L, N... AS WE THOUGHT, THAT MISSILE CAN'T BE TRACKED BY RADAR. WE CAN'T TRACE IT OR SHOOT IT DOWN.
THE MISSILE IS PROBABLY BEING GUIDED TO A SPECIFIC LOCATION... BUT THEN AGAIN, IT COULD HAVE BEEN LAUNCHED AS A STRIKE ON SOMEWHERE...

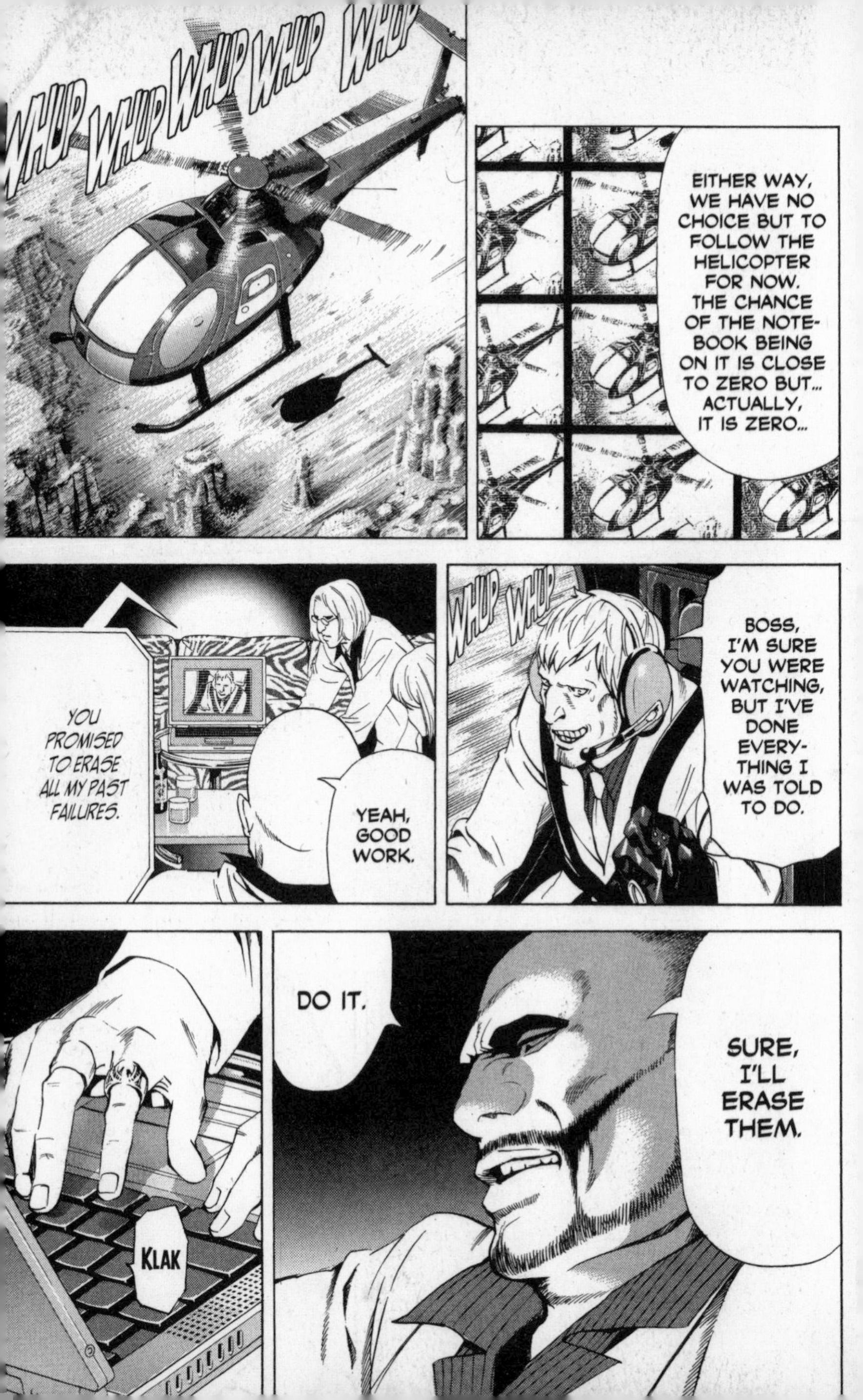

EITHER WAY, WE HAVE NO CHOICE BUT TO FOLLOW THE HELICOPTER FOR NOW. THE CHANCE OF THE NOTE-BOOK BEING ON IT IS CLOSE TO ZERO BUT... ACTUALLY, IT IS ZERO...
WHUP WHUP WHUP WHUP WHUP
WHUP WHUP
BOSS, I'M SURE YOU WERE WATCHING, BUT I'VE DONE EVERY-THING I WAS TOLD TO DO.
YOU PROMISED TO ERASE ALL MY PAST FAILURES.
YEAH, GOOD WORK.
SURE, I'LL ERASE THEM.
DO IT.
KLAK

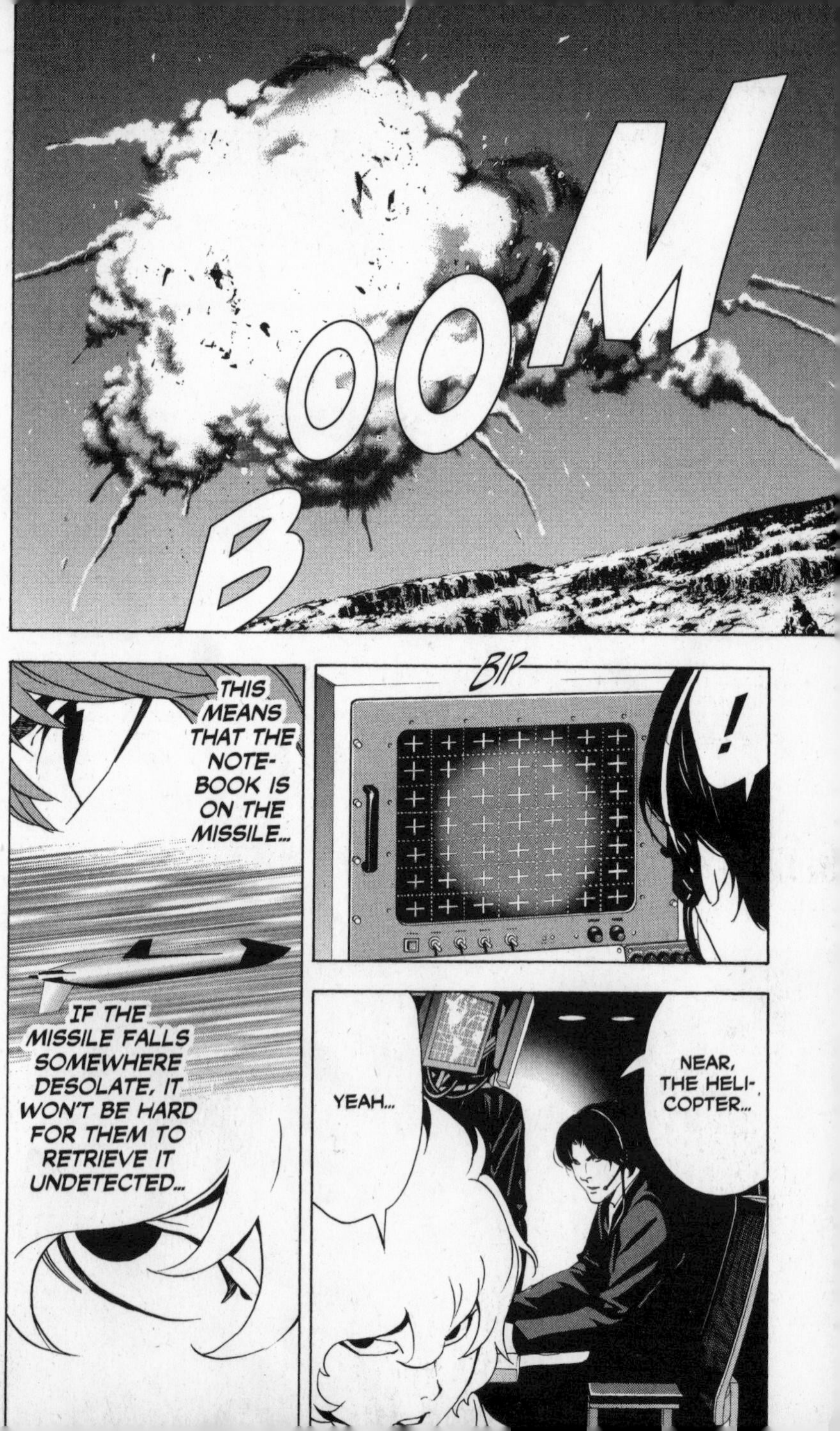
BOOM
BIP
!
NEAR, THE HELI-COPTER...
YEAH...
THIS MEANS THAT THE NOTE-BOOK IS ON THE MISSILE...
IF THE MISSILE FALLS SOMEWHERE DESOLATE, IT WON'T BE HARD FOR THEM TO RETRIEVE IT UNDETECTED...

READ THIS WAY

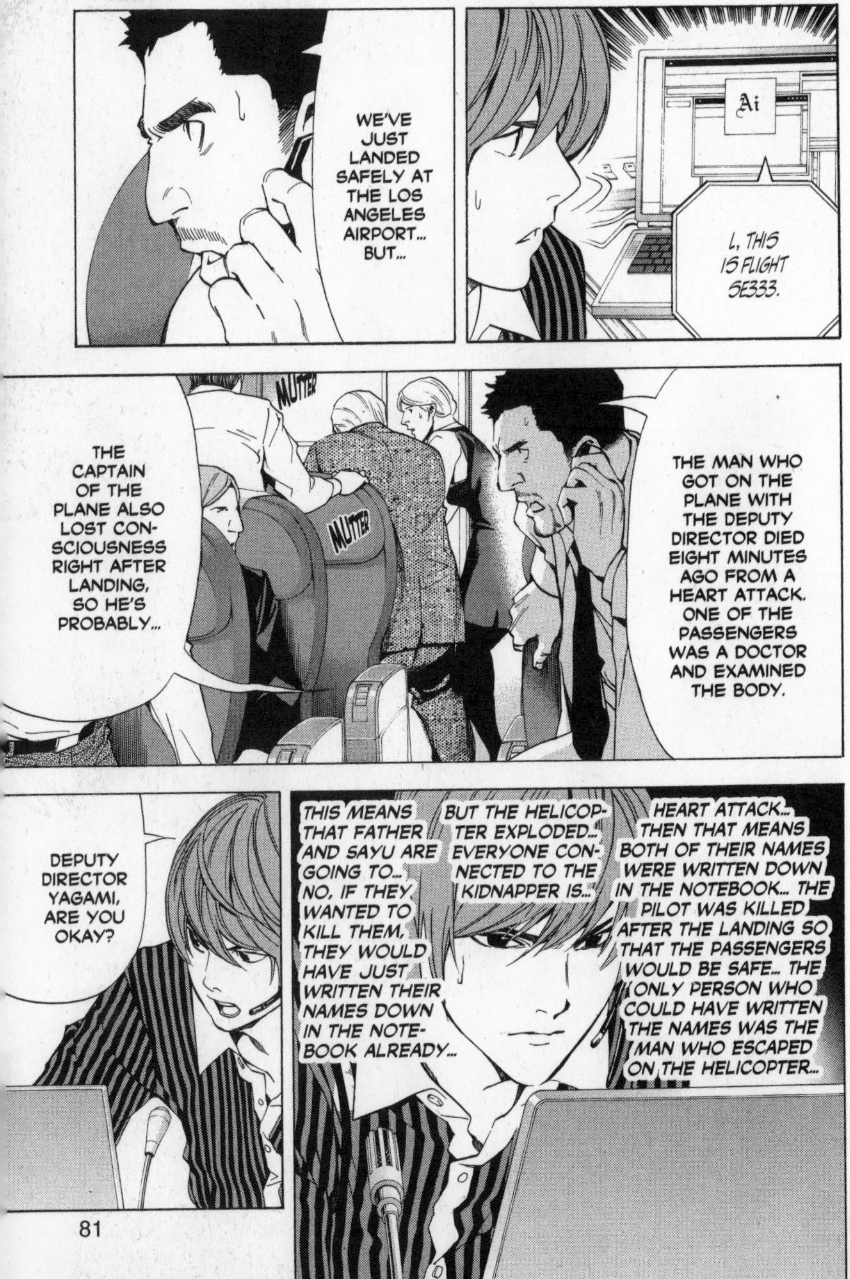

Ai
L, THIS IS FLIGHT SE333.
WE'VE JUST LANDED SAFELY AT THE LOS ANGELES AIRPORT... BUT...
THE MAN WHO GOT ON THE PLANE WITH THE DEPUTY DIRECTOR DIED EIGHT MINUTES AGO FROM A HEART ATTACK. ONE OF THE PASSENGERS WAS A DOCTOR AND EXAMINED THE BODY.
MUTTER
MUTTER
THE CAPTAIN OF THE PLANE ALSO LOST CONSCIOUSNESS RIGHT AFTER LANDING, SO HE'S PROBABLY...
HEART ATTACK... THEN THAT MEANS BOTH OF THEIR NAMES WERE WRITTEN DOWN IN THE NOTEBOOK... THE PILOT WAS KILLED AFTER THE LANDING SO THAT THE PASSENGERS WOULD BE SAFE... THE ONLY PERSON WHO COULD HAVE WRITTEN THE NAMES WAS THE MAN WHO ESCAPED ON THE HELICOPTER...
BUT THE HELICOPTER EXPLODED... EVERYONE CONNECTED TO THE KIDNAPPER IS...
THIS MEANS THAT FATHER AND SAYU ARE GOING TO... NO, IF THEY WANTED TO KILL THEM, THEY WOULD HAVE JUST WRITTEN THEIR NAMES DOWN IN THE NOTEBOOK ALREADY...
DEPUTY DIRECTOR YAGAMI, ARE YOU OKAY?

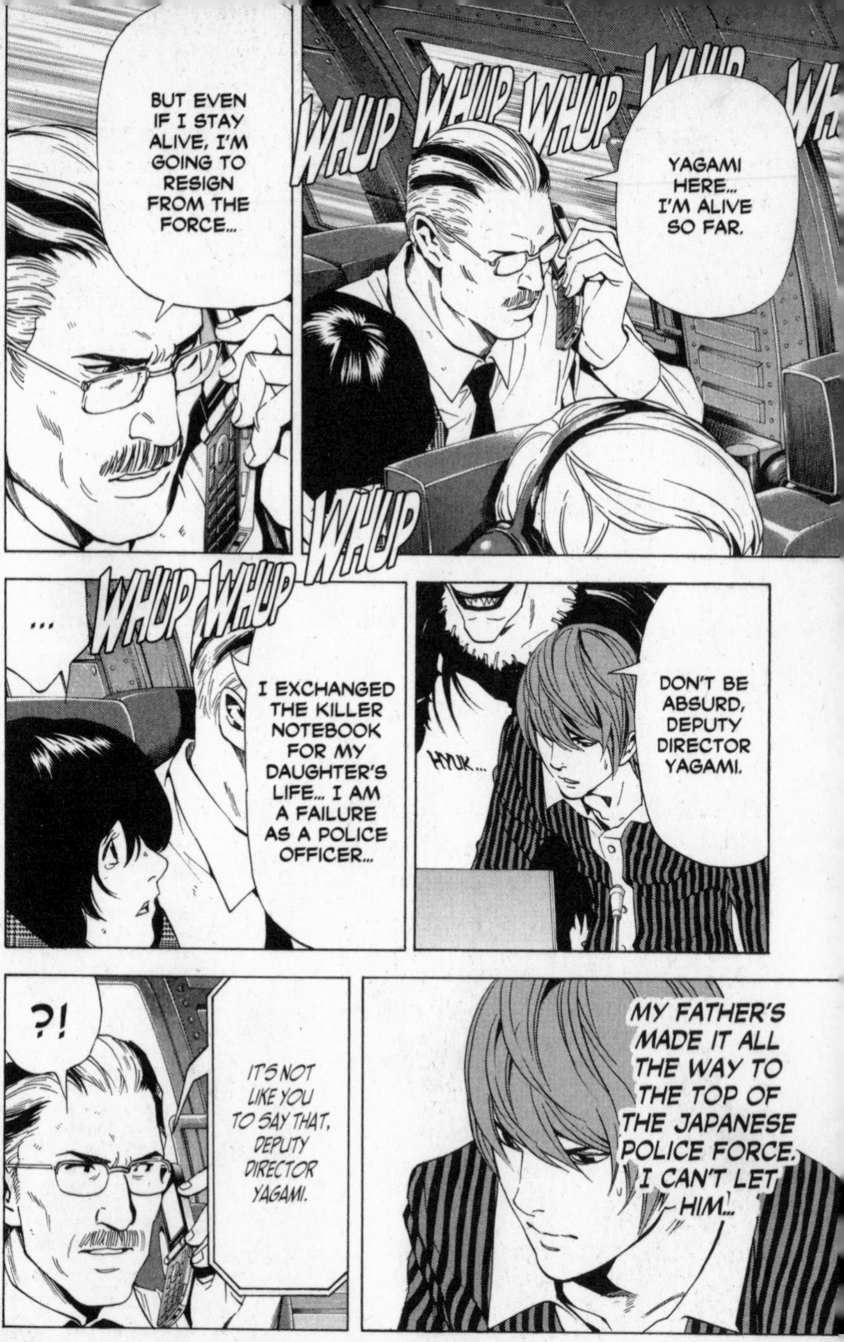
WHUP WHUP WHUP WHUP WH
YAGAMI HERE... I'M ALIVE SO FAR.
WHUP
BUT EVEN IF I STAY ALIVE, I'M GOING TO RESIGN FROM THE FORCE...
DON'T BE ABSURD, DEPUTY DIRECTOR YAGAMI.
HYUK...
WHUP WHUP
...
I EXCHANGED THE KILLER NOTEBOOK FOR MY DAUGHTER'S LIFE... I AM A FAILURE AS A POLICE OFFICER...
MY FATHER'S MADE IT ALL THE WAY TO THE TOP OF THE JAPANESE POLICE FORCE. I CAN'T LET HIM...
IT'S NOT LIKE YOU TO SAY THAT, DEPUTY DIRECTOR YAGAMI.
?!

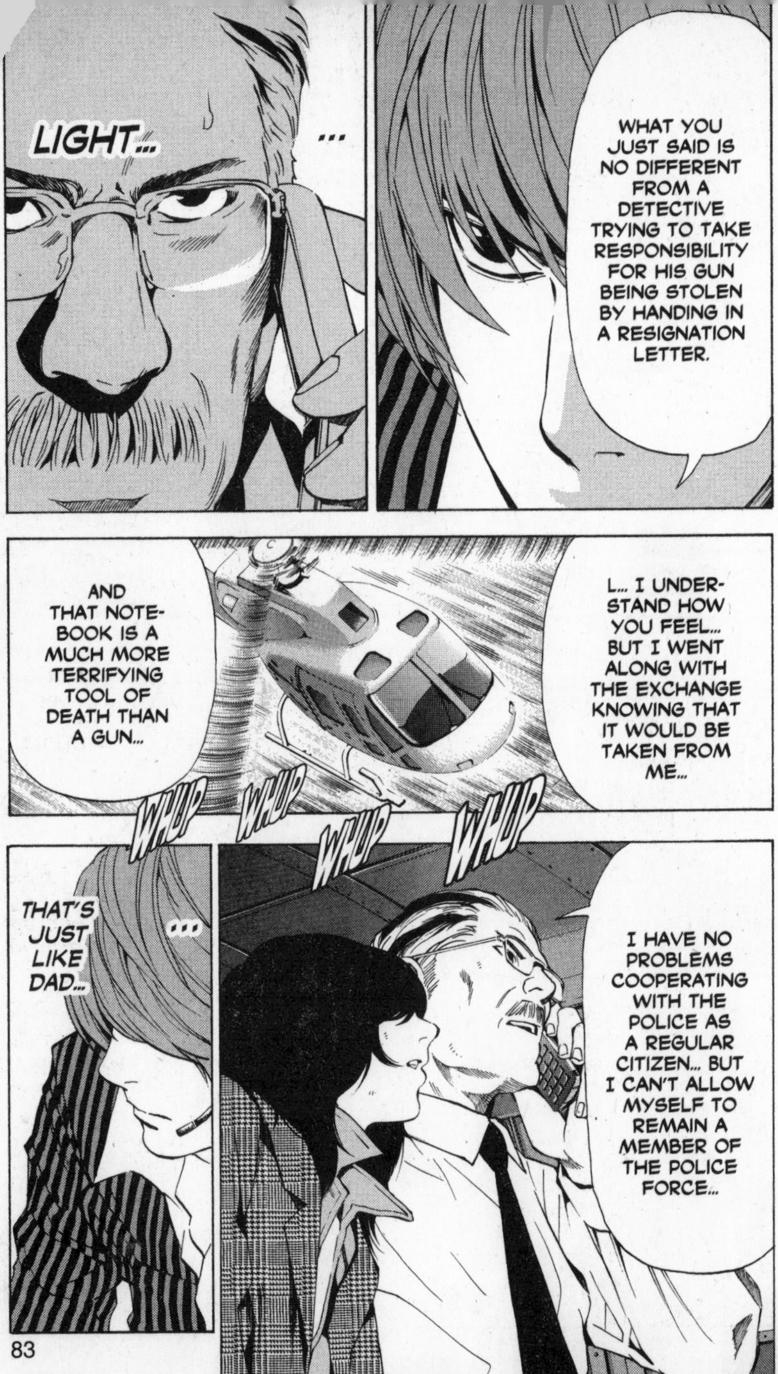
WHAT YOU JUST SAID IS NO DIFFERENT FROM A DETECTIVE TRYING TO TAKE RESPONSIBILITY FOR HIS GUN BEING STOLEN BY HANDING IN A RESIGNATION LETTER.
...
LIGHT...
L... I UNDERSTAND HOW YOU FEEL... BUT I WENT ALONG WITH THE EXCHANGE KNOWING THAT IT WOULD BE TAKEN FROM ME...
AND THAT NOTEBOOK IS A MUCH MORE TERRIFYING TOOL OF DEATH THAN A GUN...
WHUP
WHUP
WHUP
WHUP
I HAVE NO PROBLEMS COOPERATING WITH THE POLICE AS A REGULAR CITIZEN... BUT I CAN'T ALLOW MYSELF TO REMAIN A MEMBER OF THE POLICE FORCE...
...
THAT'S JUST LIKE DAD...

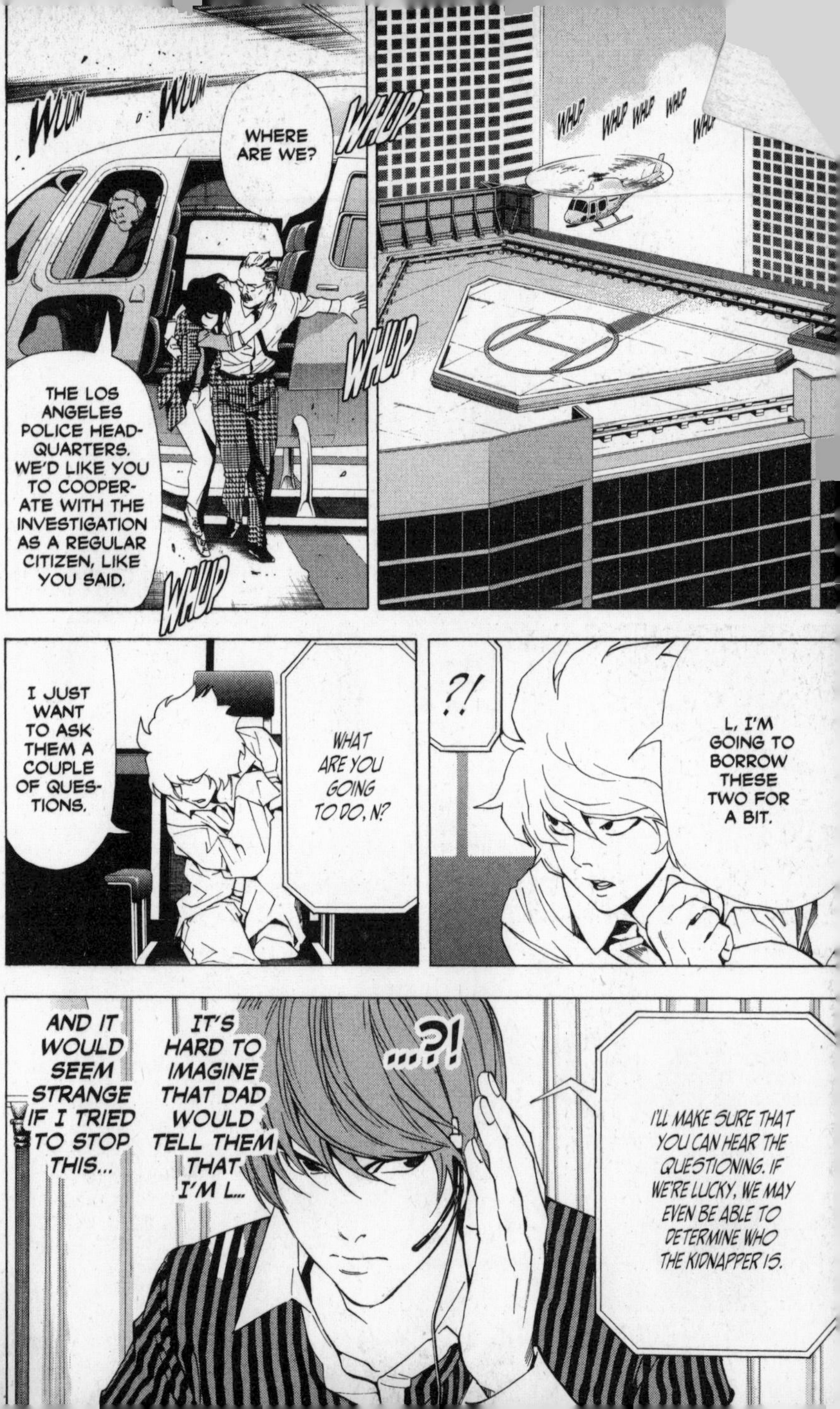
WHUP WHUP WHUP WHUP WHUP
WHUP
WHERE ARE WE?
WUUM WUUM
WHUP
THE LOS ANGELES POLICE HEAD-QUARTERS. WE'D LIKE YOU TO COOPER-ATE WITH THE INVESTIGATION AS A REGULAR CITIZEN, LIKE YOU SAID.
WHUP
L, I'M GOING TO BORROW THESE TWO FOR A BIT.
?!
WHAT ARE YOU GOING TO DO, N?
I JUST WANT TO ASK THEM A COUPLE OF QUES-TIONS.
I'LL MAKE SURE THAT YOU CAN HEAR THE QUESTIONING. IF WE'RE LUCKY, WE MAY EVEN BE ABLE TO DETERMINE WHO THE KIDNAPPER IS.
...?!
IT'S HARD TO IMAGINE THAT DAD WOULD TELL THEM THAT I'M L...
AND IT WOULD SEEM STRANGE IF I TRIED TO STOP THIS...

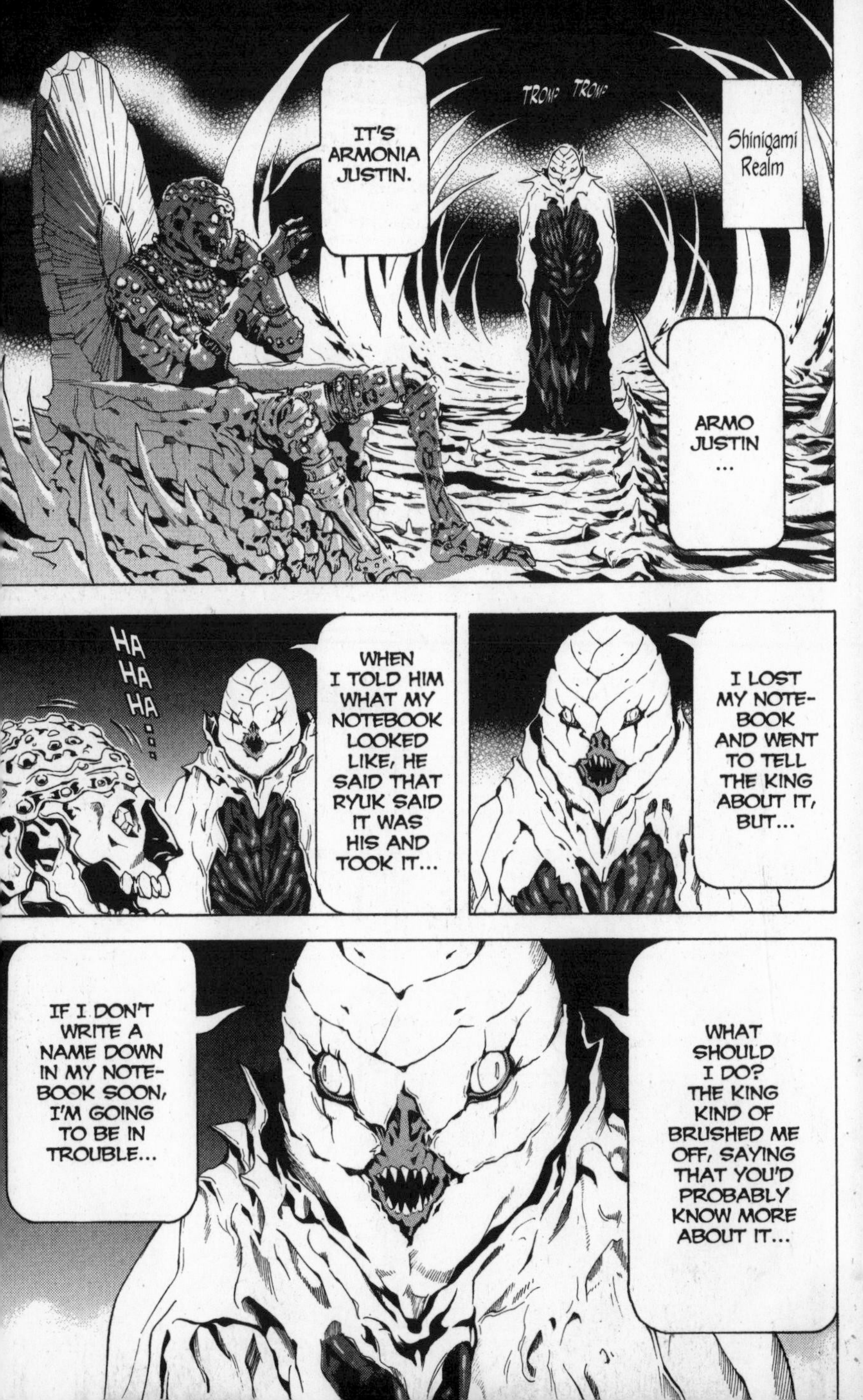
Shinigami Realm
ARMO JUSTIN ...
TROMP TROMP
IT'S ARMONIA JUSTIN.
I LOST MY NOTE-BOOK AND WENT TO TELL THE KING ABOUT IT, BUT...
WHEN I TOLD HIM WHAT MY NOTEBOOK LOOKED LIKE, HE SAID THAT RYUK SAID IT WAS HIS AND TOOK IT...
HA HA HA...
WHAT SHOULD I DO? THE KING KIND OF BRUSHED ME OFF, SAYING THAT YOU'D PROBABLY KNOW MORE ABOUT IT...
IF I DON'T WRITE A NAME DOWN IN MY NOTE-BOOK SOON, I'M GOING TO BE IN TROUBLE...

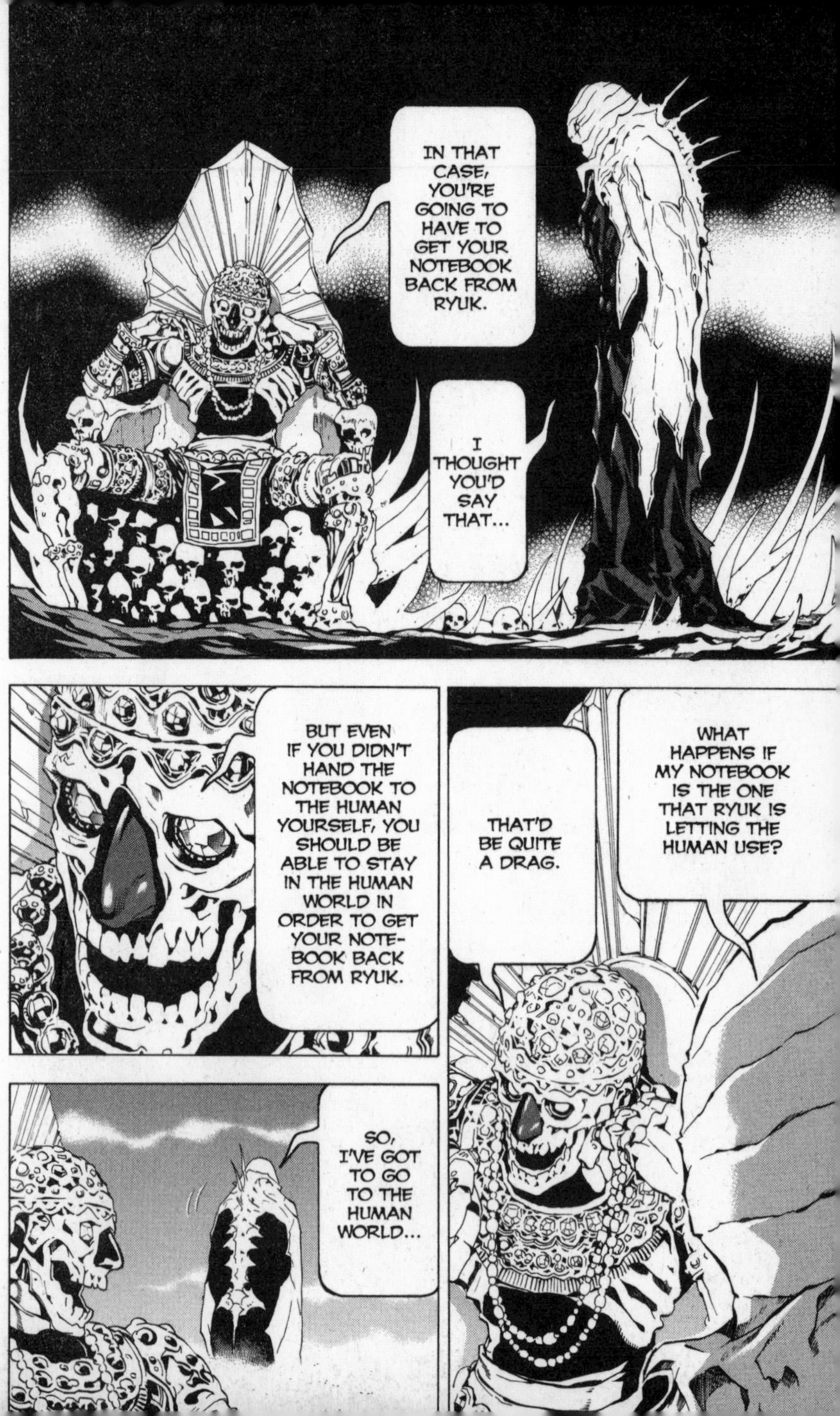
IN THAT CASE, YOU'RE GOING TO HAVE TO GET YOUR NOTEBOOK BACK FROM RYUK.
I THOUGHT YOU'D SAY THAT...
WHAT HAPPENS IF MY NOTEBOOK IS THE ONE THAT RYUK IS LETTING THE HUMAN USE?
THAT'D BE QUITE A DRAG.
BUT EVEN IF YOU DIDN'T HAND THE NOTEBOOK TO THE HUMAN YOURSELF, YOU SHOULD BE ABLE TO STAY IN THE HUMAN WORLD IN ORDER TO GET YOUR NOTE-BOOK BACK FROM RYUK.
SO, I'VE GOT TO GO TO THE HUMAN WORLD...

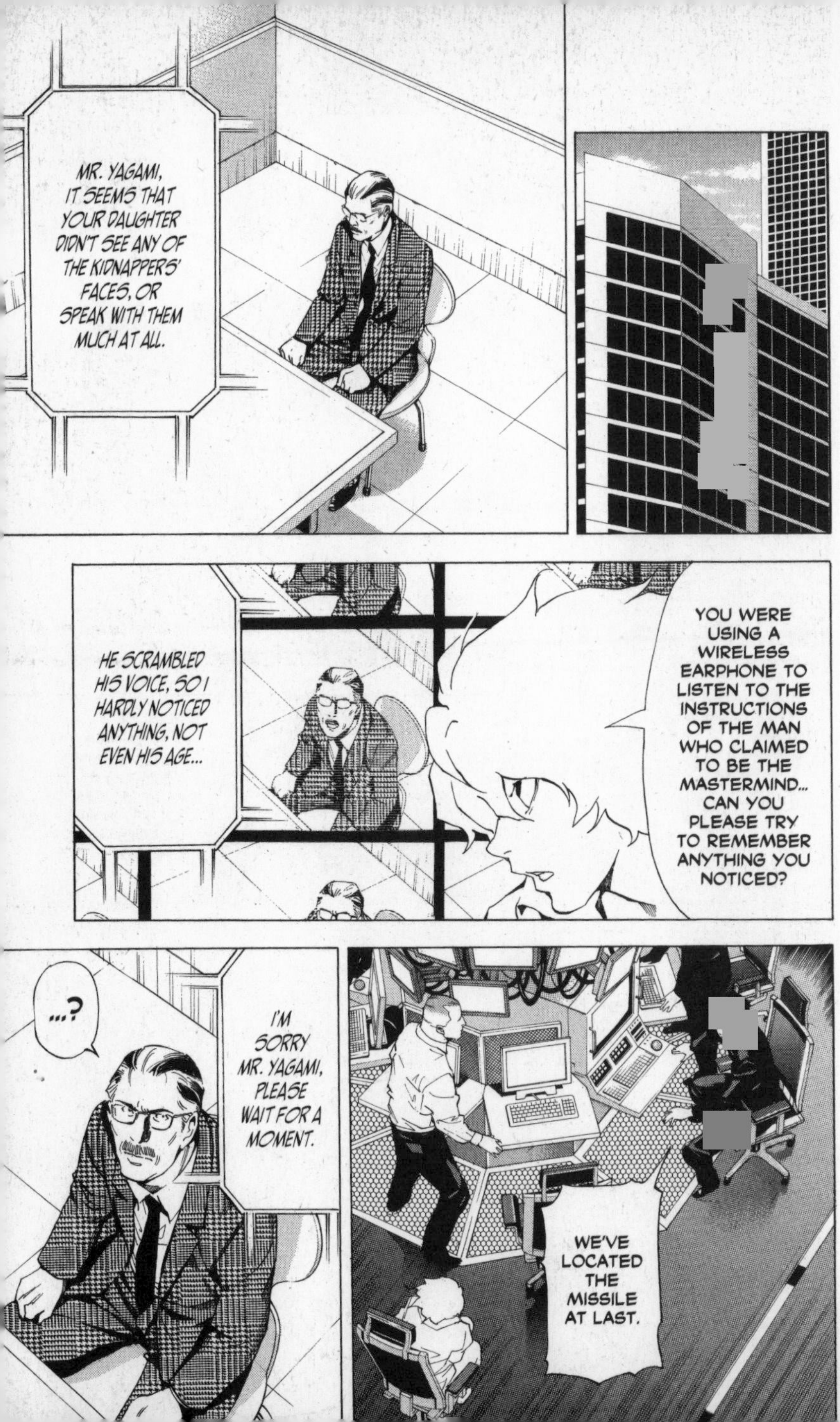
MR. YAGAMI, IT SEEMS THAT YOUR DAUGHTER DIDN'T SEE ANY OF THE KIDNAPPERS' FACES, OR SPEAK WITH THEM MUCH AT ALL.
YOU WERE USING A WIRELESS EARPHONE TO LISTEN TO THE INSTRUCTIONS OF THE MAN WHO CLAIMED TO BE THE MASTERMIND... CAN YOU PLEASE TRY TO REMEMBER ANYTHING YOU NOTICED?
HE SCRAMBLED HIS VOICE, SO I HARDLY NOTICED ANYTHING, NOT EVEN HIS AGE...
WE'VE LOCATED THE MISSILE AT LAST.
...?
I'M SORRY MR. YAGAMI, PLEASE WAIT FOR A MOMENT.

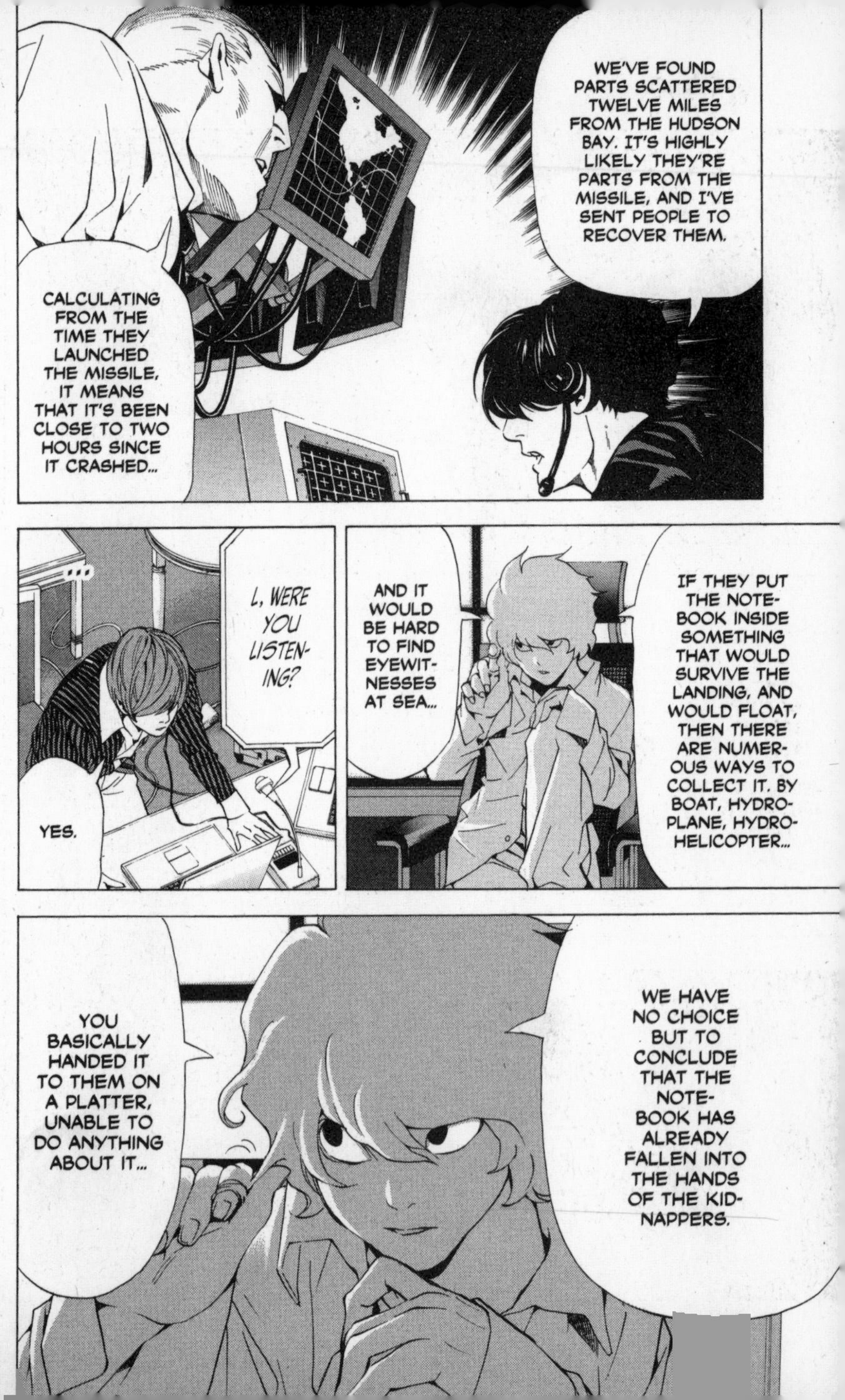
WE'VE FOUND PARTS SCATTERED TWELVE MILES FROM THE HUDSON BAY. IT'S HIGHLY LIKELY THEY'RE PARTS FROM THE MISSILE, AND I'VE SENT PEOPLE TO RECOVER THEM.
CALCULATING FROM THE TIME THEY LAUNCHED THE MISSILE, IT MEANS THAT IT'S BEEN CLOSE TO TWO HOURS SINCE IT CRASHED...
IF THEY PUT THE NOTE-BOOK INSIDE SOMETHING THAT WOULD SURVIVE THE LANDING, AND WOULD FLOAT, THEN THERE ARE NUMER-OUS WAYS TO COLLECT IT. BY BOAT, HYDRO-PLANE, HYDRO-HELICOPTER...
AND IT WOULD BE HARD TO FIND EYEWIT-NESSES AT SEA...
L, WERE YOU LISTEN-ING?
...
YES.
WE HAVE NO CHOICE BUT TO CONCLUDE THAT THE NOTE-BOOK HAS ALREADY FALLEN INTO THE HANDS OF THE KID-NAPPERS.
YOU BASICALLY HANDED IT TO THEM ON A PLATTER, UNABLE TO DO ANYTHING ABOUT IT...

READ THIS WAY

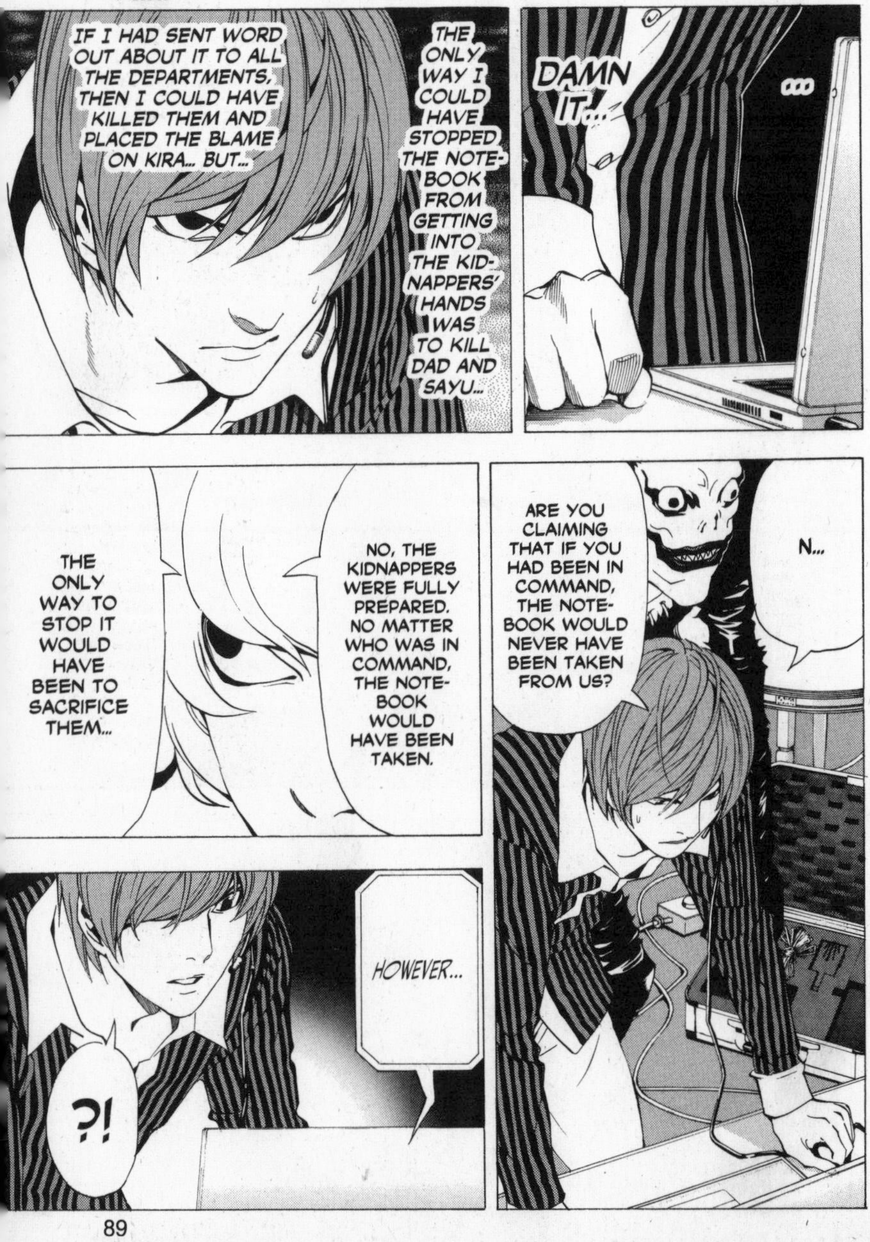
...
DAMN IT...
THE ONLY WAY I COULD HAVE STOPPED THE NOTE-BOOK FROM GETTING INTO THE KID-NAPPERS' HANDS WAS TO KILL DAD AND SAYU...
IF I HAD SENT WORD OUT ABOUT IT TO ALL THE DEPARTMENTS, THEN I COULD HAVE KILLED THEM AND PLACED THE BLAME ON KIRA... BUT...
ARE YOU CLAIMING THAT IF YOU HAD BEEN IN COMMAND, THE NOTE-BOOK WOULD NEVER HAVE BEEN TAKEN FROM US?
N...
NO, THE KIDNAPPERS WERE FULLY PREPARED. NO MATTER WHO WAS IN COMMAND, THE NOTE-BOOK WOULD HAVE BEEN TAKEN.
THE ONLY WAY TO STOP IT WOULD HAVE BEEN TO SACRIFICE THEM...
HOWEVER...
?!

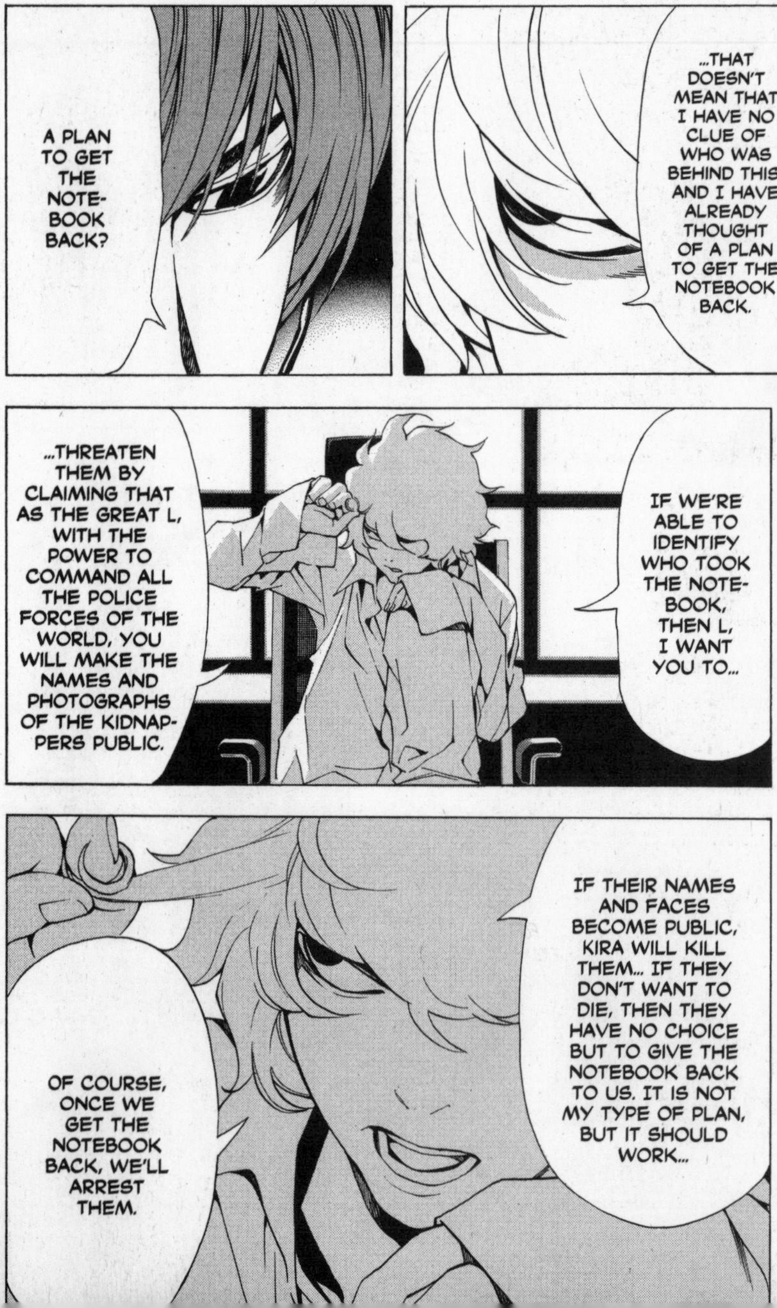
...THAT DOESN'T MEAN THAT I HAVE NO CLUE OF WHO WAS BEHIND THIS, AND I HAVE ALREADY THOUGHT OF A PLAN TO GET THE NOTEBOOK BACK.
A PLAN TO GET THE NOTE-BOOK BACK?
IF WE'RE ABLE TO IDENTIFY WHO TOOK THE NOTE-BOOK, THEN L, I WANT YOU TO...
...THREATEN THEM BY CLAIMING THAT AS THE GREAT L, WITH THE POWER TO COMMAND ALL THE POLICE FORCES OF THE WORLD, YOU WILL MAKE THE NAMES AND PHOTOGRAPHS OF THE KIDNAP-PERS PUBLIC.
IF THEIR NAMES AND FACES BECOME PUBLIC, KIRA WILL KILL THEM... IF THEY DON'T WANT TO DIE, THEN THEY HAVE NO CHOICE BUT TO GIVE THE NOTEBOOK BACK TO US. IT IS NOT MY TYPE OF PLAN, BUT IT SHOULD WORK...
OF COURSE, ONCE WE GET THE NOTEBOOK BACK, WE'LL ARREST THEM.

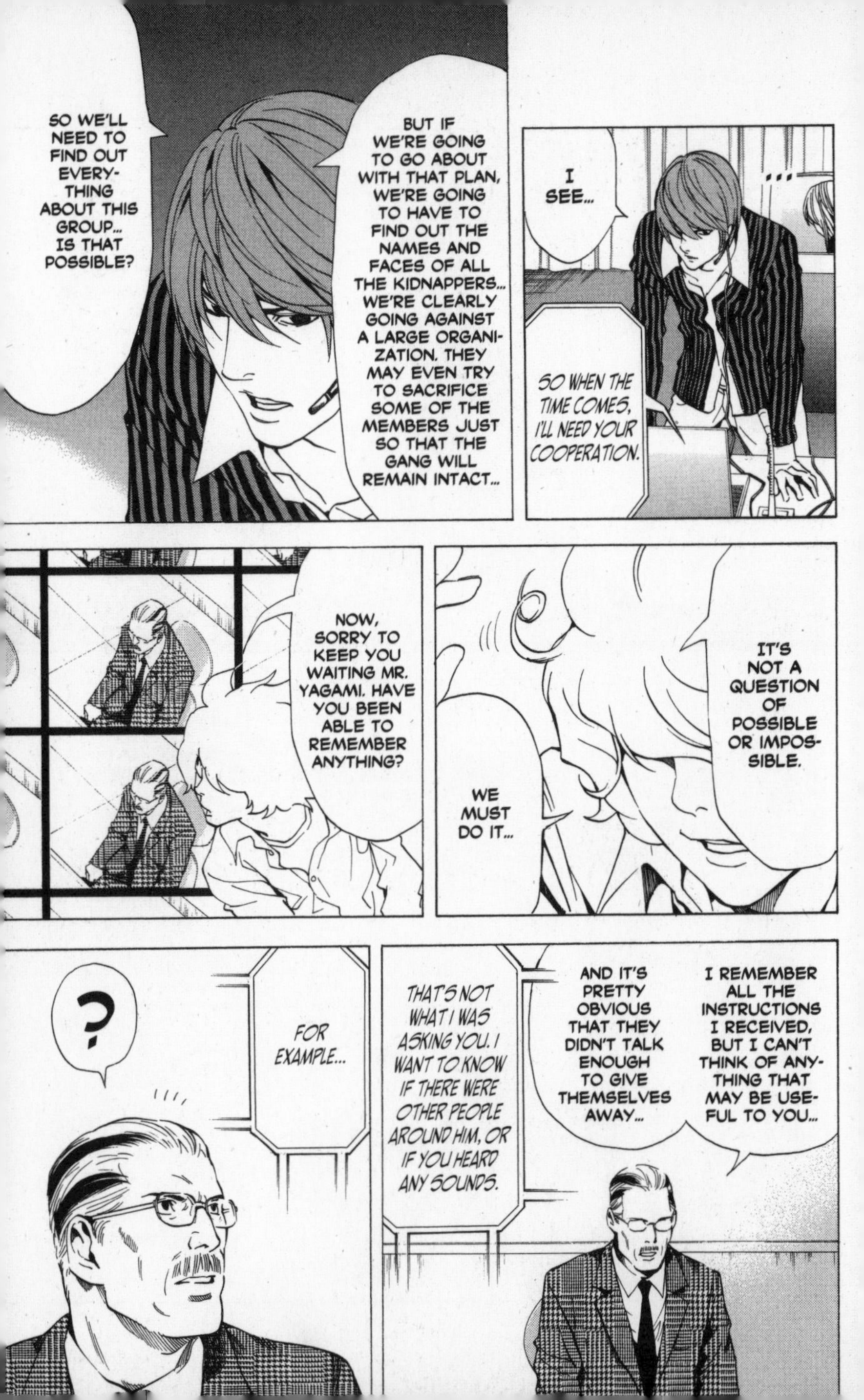
...
I SEE...
SO WHEN THE TIME COMES, I'LL NEED YOUR COOPERATION.
BUT IF WE'RE GOING TO GO ABOUT WITH THAT PLAN, WE'RE GOING TO HAVE TO FIND OUT THE NAMES AND FACES OF ALL THE KIDNAPPERS... WE'RE CLEARLY GOING AGAINST A LARGE ORGANIZATION. THEY MAY EVEN TRY TO SACRIFICE SOME OF THE MEMBERS JUST SO THAT THE GANG WILL REMAIN INTACT...
SO WE'LL NEED TO FIND OUT EVERYTHING ABOUT THIS GROUP... IS THAT POSSIBLE?
IT'S NOT A QUESTION OF POSSIBLE OR IMPOSSIBLE.
WE MUST DO IT...
NOW, SORRY TO KEEP YOU WAITING MR. YAGAMI. HAVE YOU BEEN ABLE TO REMEMBER ANYTHING?
I REMEMBER ALL THE INSTRUCTIONS I RECEIVED, BUT I CAN'T THINK OF ANYTHING THAT MAY BE USEFUL TO YOU...
AND IT'S PRETTY OBVIOUS THAT THEY DIDN'T TALK ENOUGH TO GIVE THEMSELVES AWAY...
THAT'S NOT WHAT I WAS ASKING YOU. I WANT TO KNOW IF THERE WERE OTHER PEOPLE AROUND HIM, OR IF YOU HEARD ANY SOUNDS.
FOR EXAMPLE...
?

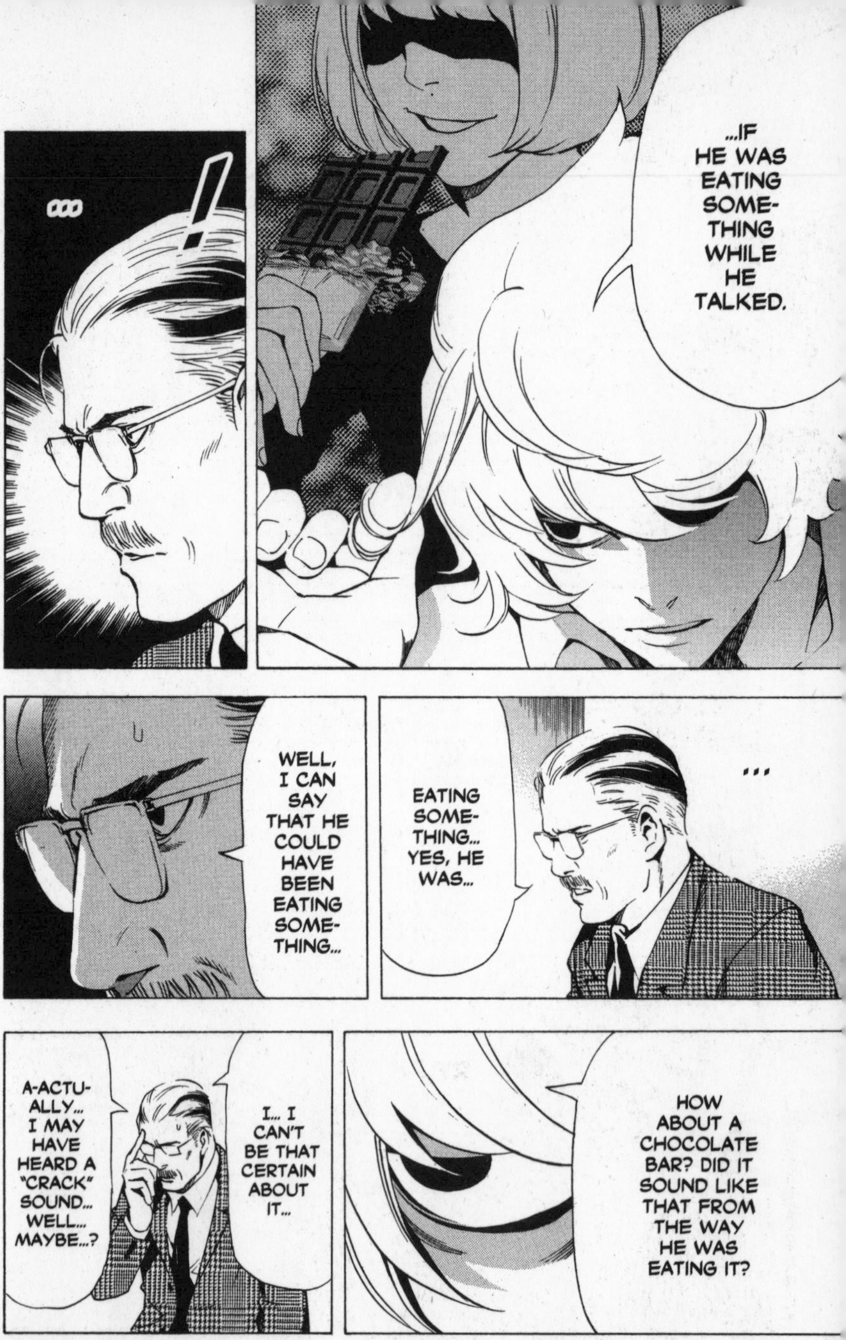
...IF HE WAS EATING SOMETHING WHILE HE TALKED.
...
EATING SOMETHING... YES, HE WAS...
WELL, I CAN SAY THAT HE COULD HAVE BEEN EATING SOMETHING...
HOW ABOUT A CHOCOLATE BAR? DID IT SOUND LIKE THAT FROM THE WAY HE WAS EATING IT?
I... I CAN'T BE THAT CERTAIN ABOUT IT...
A-ACTUALLY... I MAY HAVE HEARD A "CRACK" SOUND... WELL... MAYBE...?

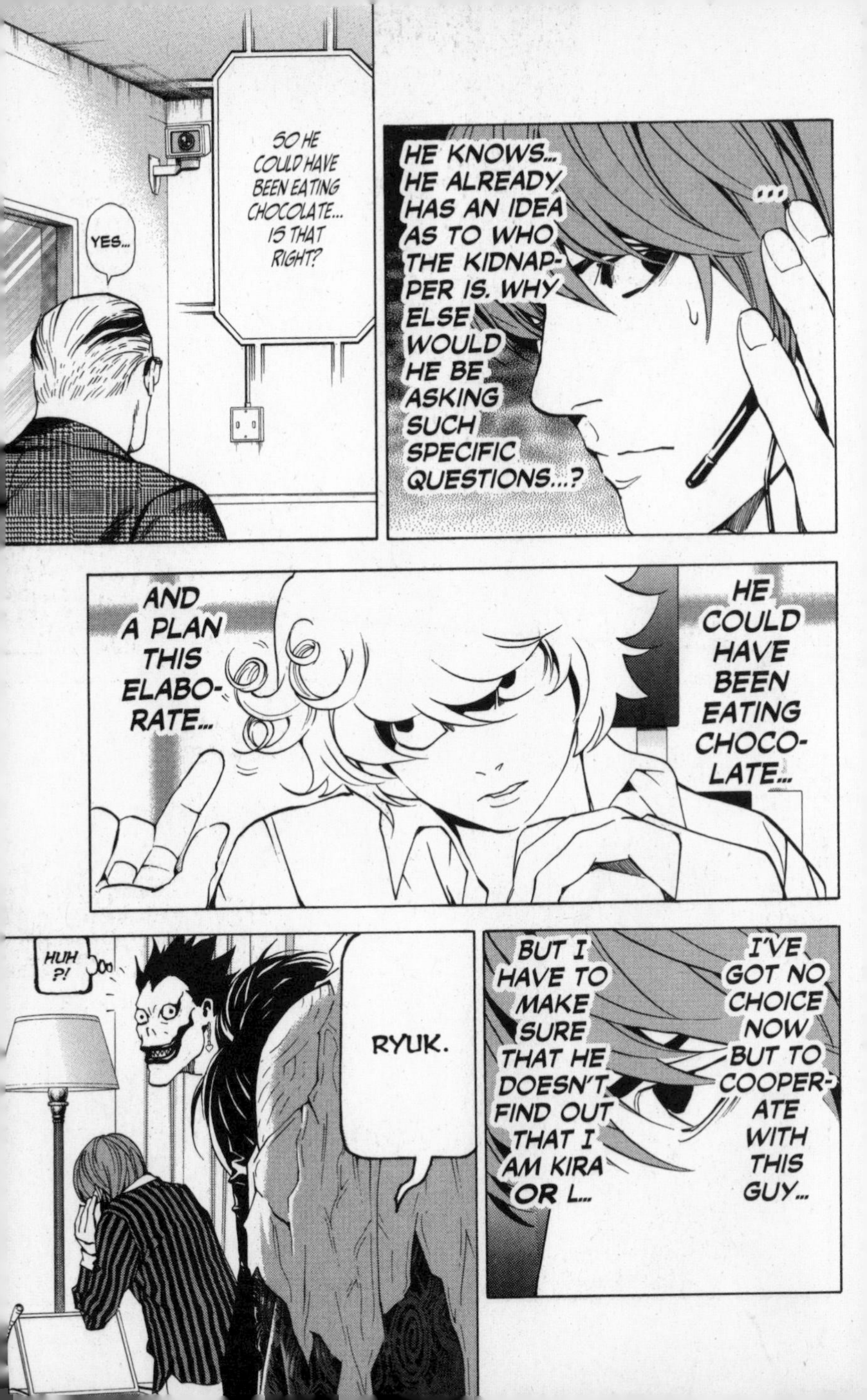
...
HE KNOWS... HE ALREADY HAS AN IDEA AS TO WHO THE KIDNAPPER IS. WHY ELSE WOULD HE BE ASKING SUCH SPECIFIC QUESTIONS...?
SO HE COULD HAVE BEEN EATING CHOCOLATE... IS THAT RIGHT?
YES...
HE COULD HAVE BEEN EATING CHOCOLATE...
AND A PLAN THIS ELABORATE...
I'VE GOT NO CHOICE NOW BUT TO COOPERATE WITH THIS GUY...
BUT I HAVE TO MAKE SURE THAT HE DOESN'T FIND OUT THAT I AM KIRA OR L...
RYUK.
HUH?!

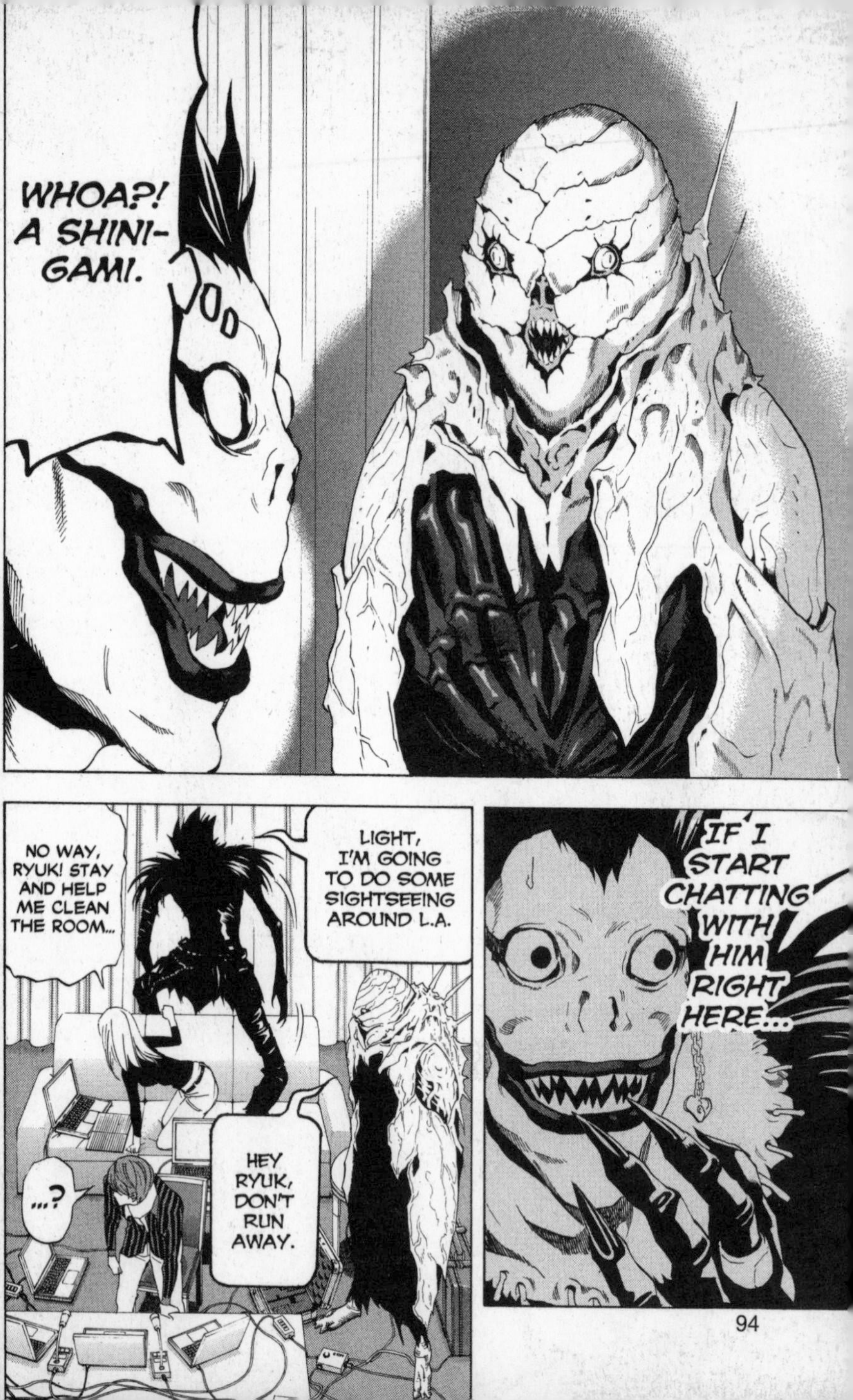
WHOA?! A SHINI-GAMI.
IF I START CHATTING WITH HIM RIGHT HERE...
LIGHT, I'M GOING TO DO SOME SIGHTSEEING AROUND L.A.
NO WAY, RYUK! STAY AND HELP ME CLEAN THE ROOM...
HEY RYUK, DON'T RUN AWAY.
...?

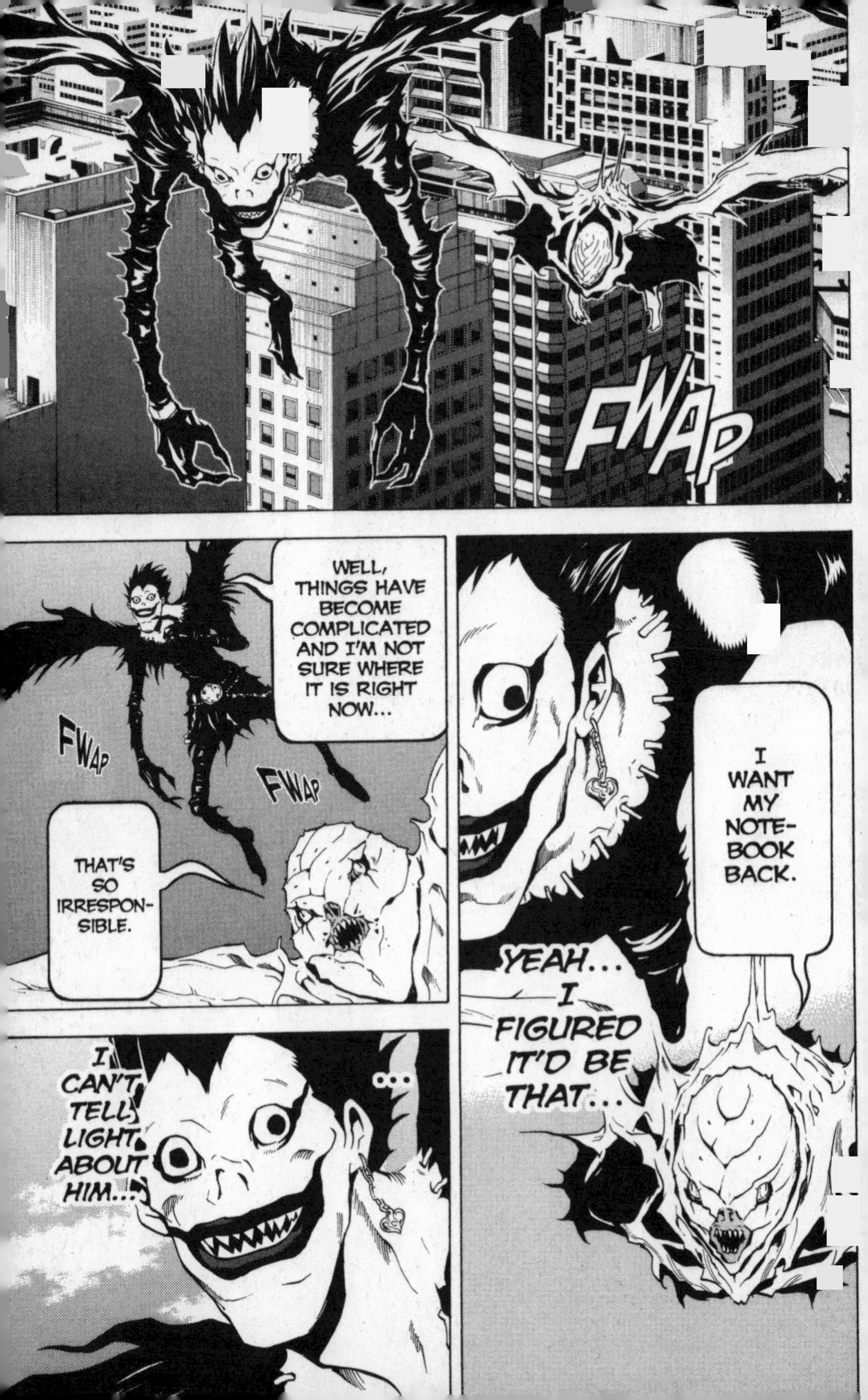
FWAP
I WANT MY NOTE-BOOK BACK.
YEAH... I FIGURED IT'D BE THAT...
WELL, THINGS HAVE BECOME COMPLICATED AND I'M NOT SURE WHERE IT IS RIGHT NOW...
FWAP
FWAP
THAT'S SO IRRESPON-SIBLE.
...
I CAN'T TELL LIGHT ABOUT HIM...

DEATH NOTE
How to use it
XLIII

- If a DEATH NOTE is owned in the human world against the god of death's will, that god of death is permitted to stay in the human world in order to retrieve it.

死神が自分の所有すべきデスノートを
不本意に人間界のものにされている場合、
そのノートを取り戻す目的で人間界に居る事は許される。

- In that case, if there are other DEATH NOTES in the human world, the gods of death are not allowed to reveal to humans that DEATH NOTE'S owner or its location.

その時、人間界に他にもノートが存在していた場合、
人間にそのノートのある場所や所有者を教えてはならない。

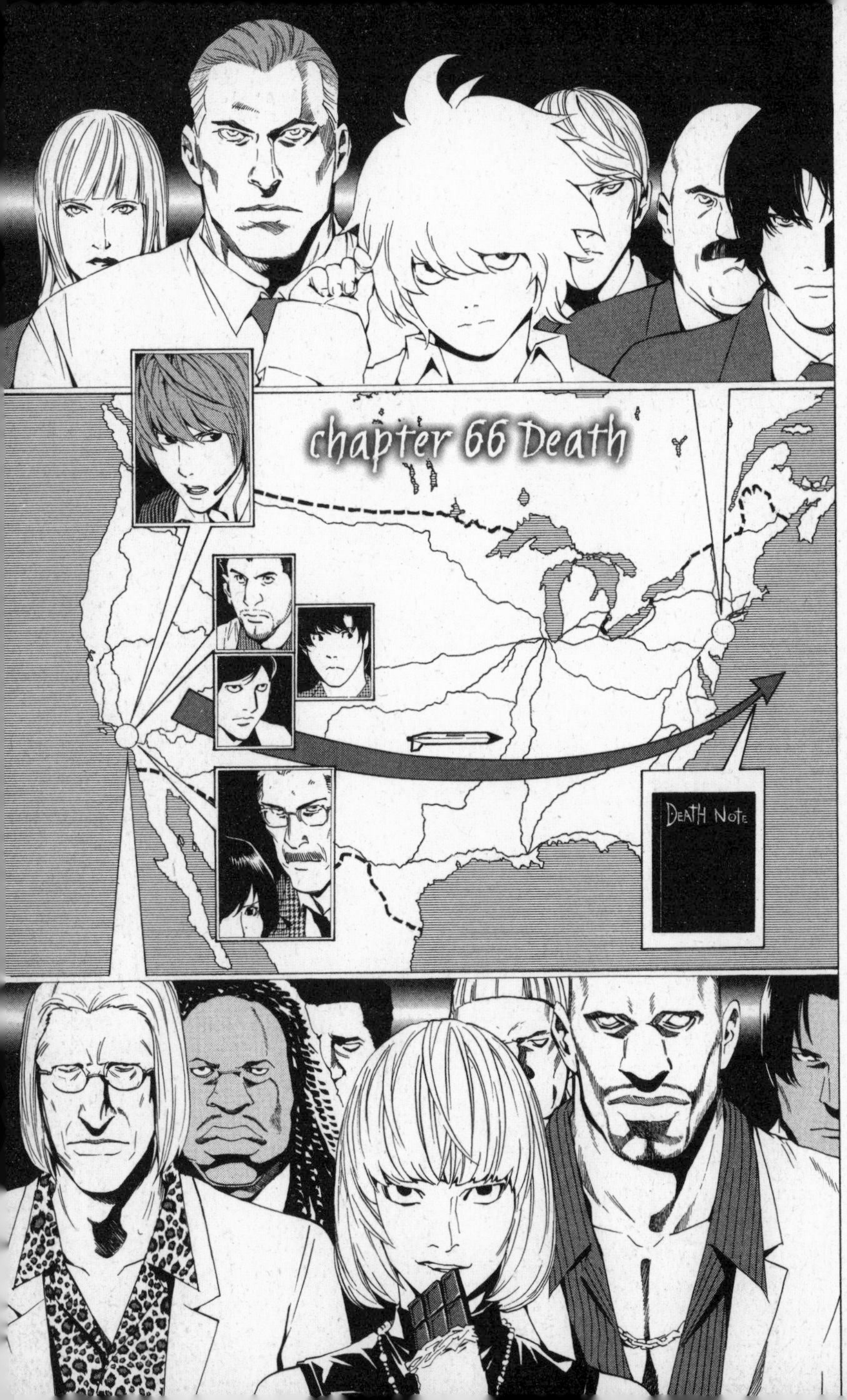
chapter 66 Death
DEATH NOTE

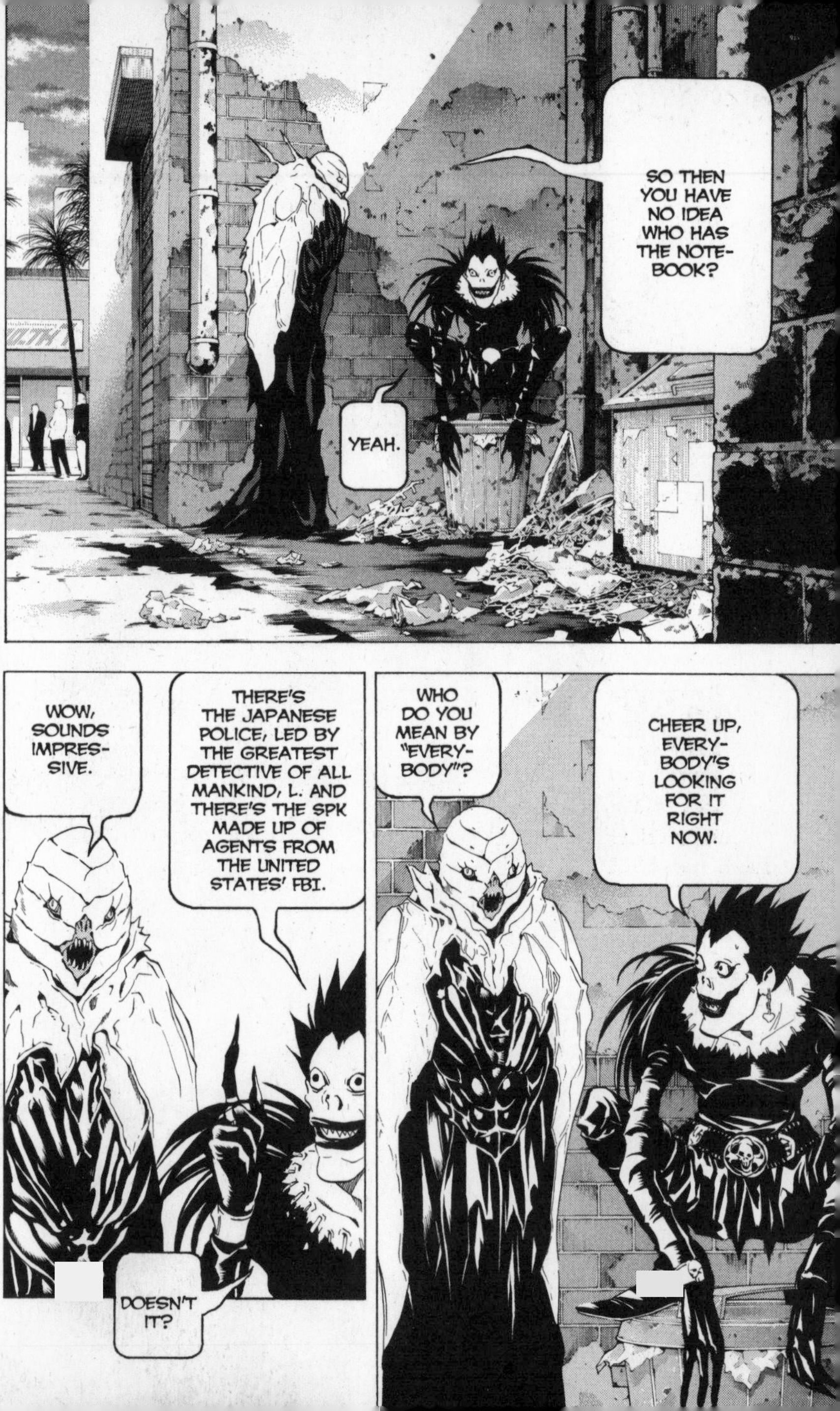
SO THEN YOU HAVE NO IDEA WHO HAS THE NOTE-BOOK?
YEAH.
CHEER UP, EVERY-BODY'S LOOKING FOR IT RIGHT NOW.
WHO DO YOU MEAN BY "EVERY-BODY"?
THERE'S THE JAPANESE POLICE, LED BY THE GREATEST DETECTIVE OF ALL MANKIND, L. AND THERE'S THE SPK MADE UP OF AGENTS FROM THE UNITED STATES' FBI.
WOW, SOUNDS IMPRES-SIVE.
DOESN'T IT?

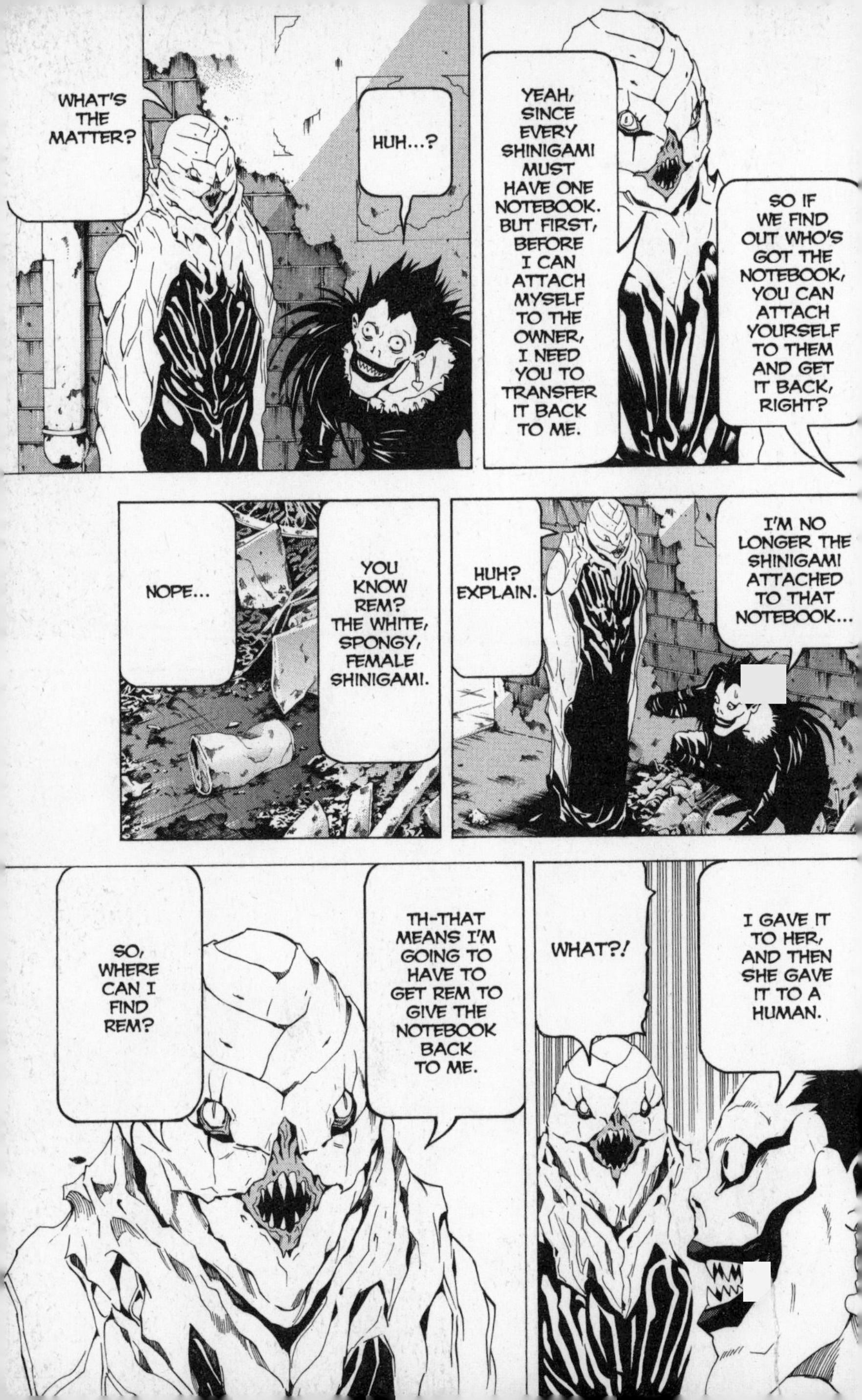
SO IF WE FIND OUT WHO'S GOT THE NOTEBOOK, YOU CAN ATTACH YOURSELF TO THEM AND GET IT BACK, RIGHT?
YEAH, SINCE EVERY SHINIGAMI MUST HAVE ONE NOTEBOOK. BUT FIRST, BEFORE I CAN ATTACH MYSELF TO THE OWNER, I NEED YOU TO TRANSFER IT BACK TO ME.
HUH...?
WHAT'S THE MATTER?
I'M NO LONGER THE SHINIGAMI ATTACHED TO THAT NOTEBOOK...
HUH? EXPLAIN.
YOU KNOW REM? THE WHITE, SPONGY, FEMALE SHINIGAMI.
NOPE...
I GAVE IT TO HER, AND THEN SHE GAVE IT TO A HUMAN.
WHAT?!
TH-THAT MEANS I'M GOING TO HAVE TO GET REM TO GIVE THE NOTEBOOK BACK TO ME.
SO, WHERE CAN I FIND REM?

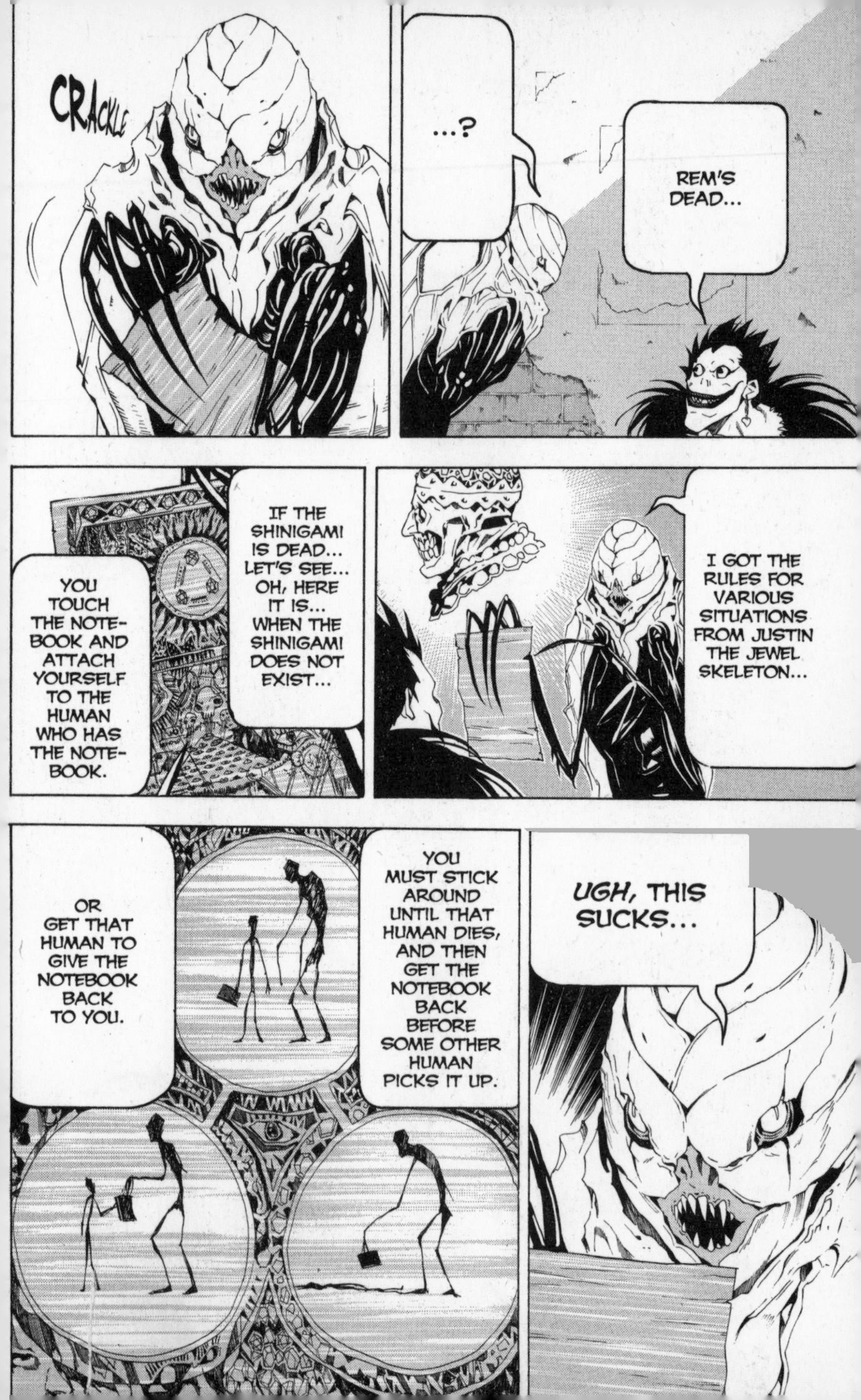
REM'S DEAD...
...?
CRACKLE
I GOT THE RULES FOR VARIOUS SITUATIONS FROM JUSTIN THE JEWEL SKELETON...
IF THE SHINIGAMI IS DEAD... LET'S SEE... OH, HERE IT IS... WHEN THE SHINIGAMI DOES NOT EXIST...
YOU TOUCH THE NOTE-BOOK AND ATTACH YOURSELF TO THE HUMAN WHO HAS THE NOTE-BOOK.
UGH, THIS SUCKS...
YOU MUST STICK AROUND UNTIL THAT HUMAN DIES, AND THEN GET THE NOTEBOOK BACK BEFORE SOME OTHER HUMAN PICKS IT UP.
OR GET THAT HUMAN TO GIVE THE NOTEBOOK BACK TO YOU.

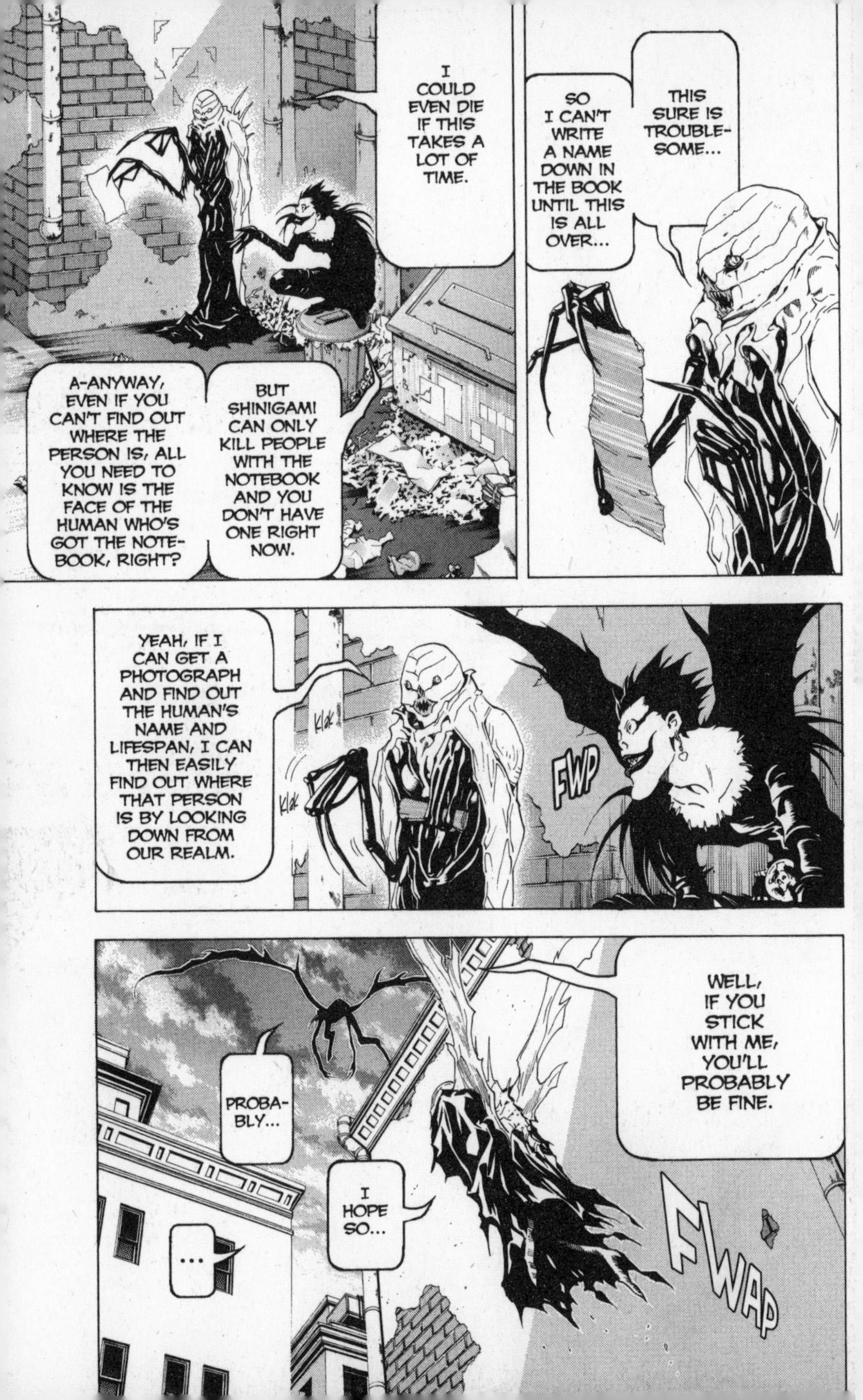
THIS SURE IS TROUBLE-SOME...
SO I CAN'T WRITE A NAME DOWN IN THE BOOK UNTIL THIS IS ALL OVER...
I COULD EVEN DIE IF THIS TAKES A LOT OF TIME.
BUT SHINIGAMI CAN ONLY KILL PEOPLE WITH THE NOTEBOOK AND YOU DON'T HAVE ONE RIGHT NOW.
A-ANYWAY, EVEN IF YOU CAN'T FIND OUT WHERE THE PERSON IS, ALL YOU NEED TO KNOW IS THE FACE OF THE HUMAN WHO'S GOT THE NOTE-BOOK, RIGHT?
FWP
YEAH, IF I CAN GET A PHOTOGRAPH AND FIND OUT THE HUMAN'S NAME AND LIFESPAN, I CAN THEN EASILY FIND OUT WHERE THAT PERSON IS BY LOOKING DOWN FROM OUR REALM.
Klak
Klak
WELL, IF YOU STICK WITH ME, YOU'LL PROBABLY BE FINE.
FWAP
PROBA-BLY...
I HOPE SO...
...

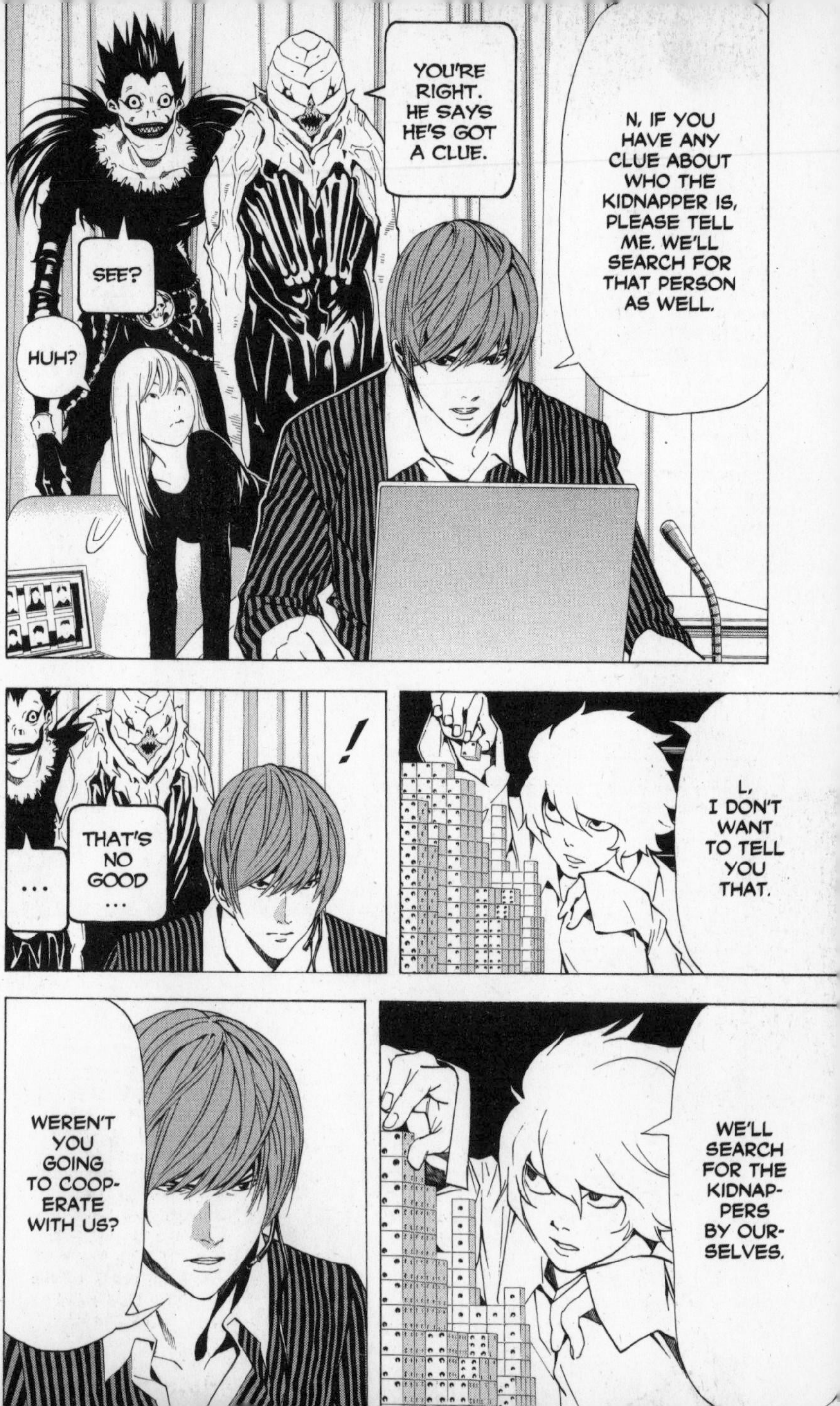
N, IF YOU HAVE ANY CLUE ABOUT WHO THE KIDNAPPER IS, PLEASE TELL ME. WE'LL SEARCH FOR THAT PERSON AS WELL.
YOU'RE RIGHT. HE SAYS HE'S GOT A CLUE.
SEE?
HUH?
L, I DON'T WANT TO TELL YOU THAT.
!
THAT'S NO GOOD ...
...
WE'LL SEARCH FOR THE KIDNAPPERS BY OURSELVES.
WEREN'T YOU GOING TO COOPERATE WITH US?

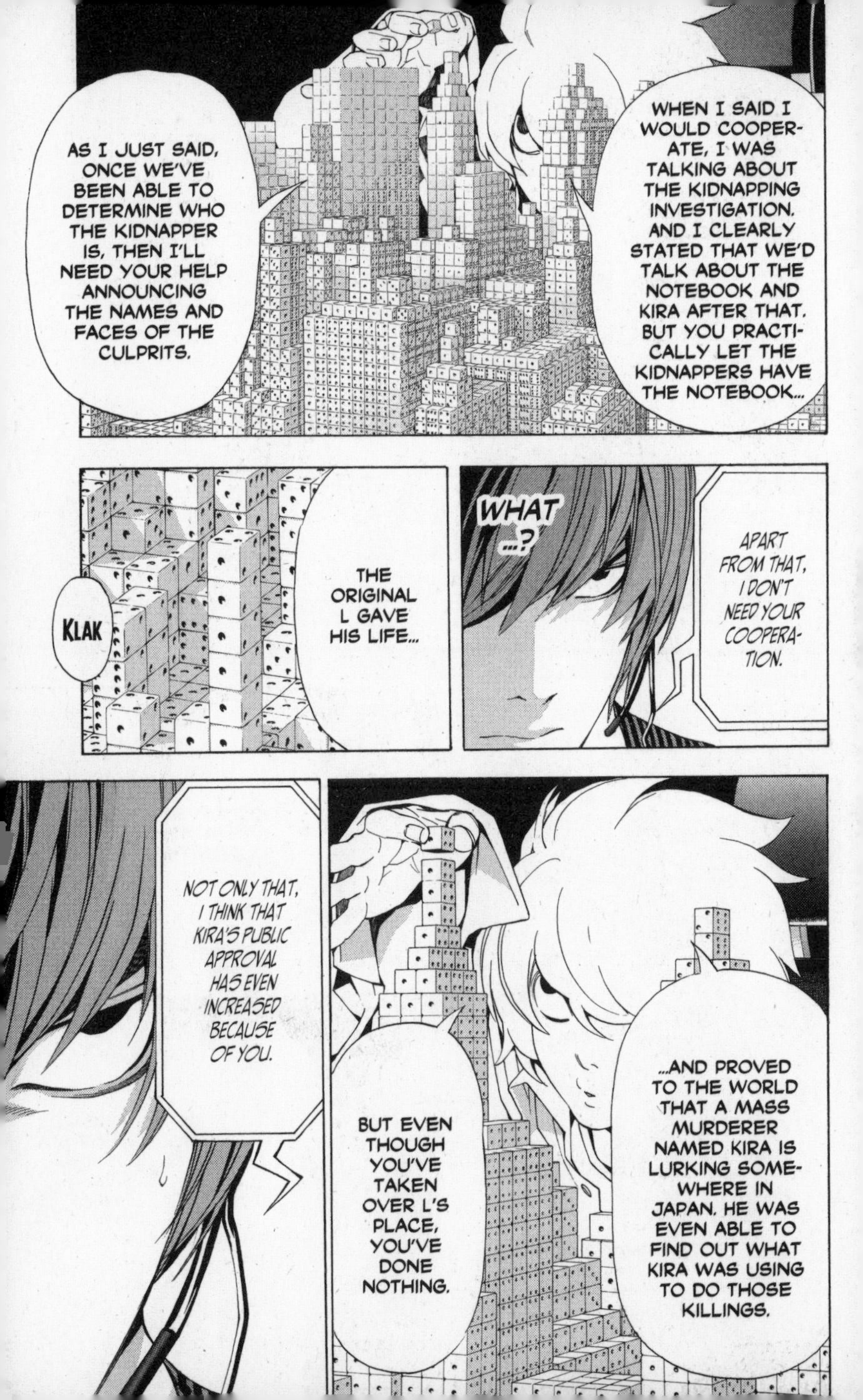

WHEN I SAID I WOULD COOPERATE, I WAS TALKING ABOUT THE KIDNAPPING INVESTIGATION. AND I CLEARLY STATED THAT WE'D TALK ABOUT THE NOTEBOOK AND KIRA AFTER THAT. BUT YOU PRACTICALLY LET THE KIDNAPPERS HAVE THE NOTEBOOK...
AS I JUST SAID, ONCE WE'VE BEEN ABLE TO DETERMINE WHO THE KIDNAPPER IS, THEN I'LL NEED YOUR HELP ANNOUNCING THE NAMES AND FACES OF THE CULPRITS.
APART FROM THAT, I DON'T NEED YOUR COOPERATION.
WHAT ...?
THE ORIGINAL L GAVE HIS LIFE...
KLAK
...AND PROVED TO THE WORLD THAT A MASS MURDERER NAMED KIRA IS LURKING SOMEWHERE IN JAPAN. HE WAS EVEN ABLE TO FIND OUT WHAT KIRA WAS USING TO DO THOSE KILLINGS.
BUT EVEN THOUGH YOU'VE TAKEN OVER L'S PLACE, YOU'VE DONE NOTHING.
NOT ONLY THAT, I THINK THAT KIRA'S PUBLIC APPROVAL HAS EVEN INCREASED BECAUSE OF YOU.

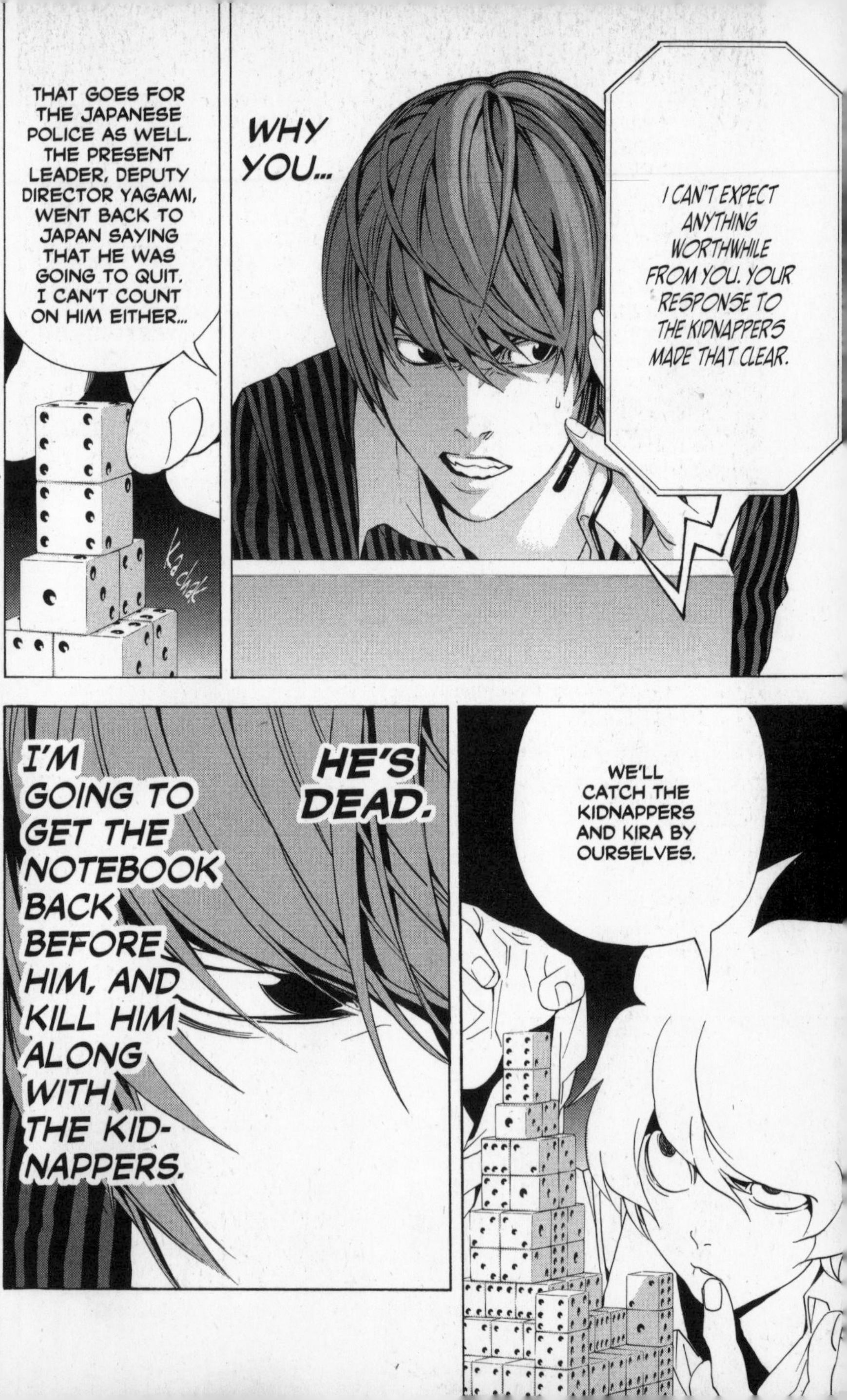
I CAN'T EXPECT ANYTHING WORTHWHILE FROM YOU. YOUR RESPONSE TO THE KIDNAPPERS MADE THAT CLEAR.
WHY YOU...
THAT GOES FOR THE JAPANESE POLICE AS WELL. THE PRESENT LEADER, DEPUTY DIRECTOR YAGAMI, WENT BACK TO JAPAN SAYING THAT HE WAS GOING TO QUIT. I CAN'T COUNT ON HIM EITHER...
ka chak
WE'LL CATCH THE KIDNAPPERS AND KIRA BY OURSELVES.
HE'S DEAD.
I'M GOING TO GET THE NOTEBOOK BACK BEFORE HIM, AND KILL HIM ALONG WITH THE KID-NAPPERS.

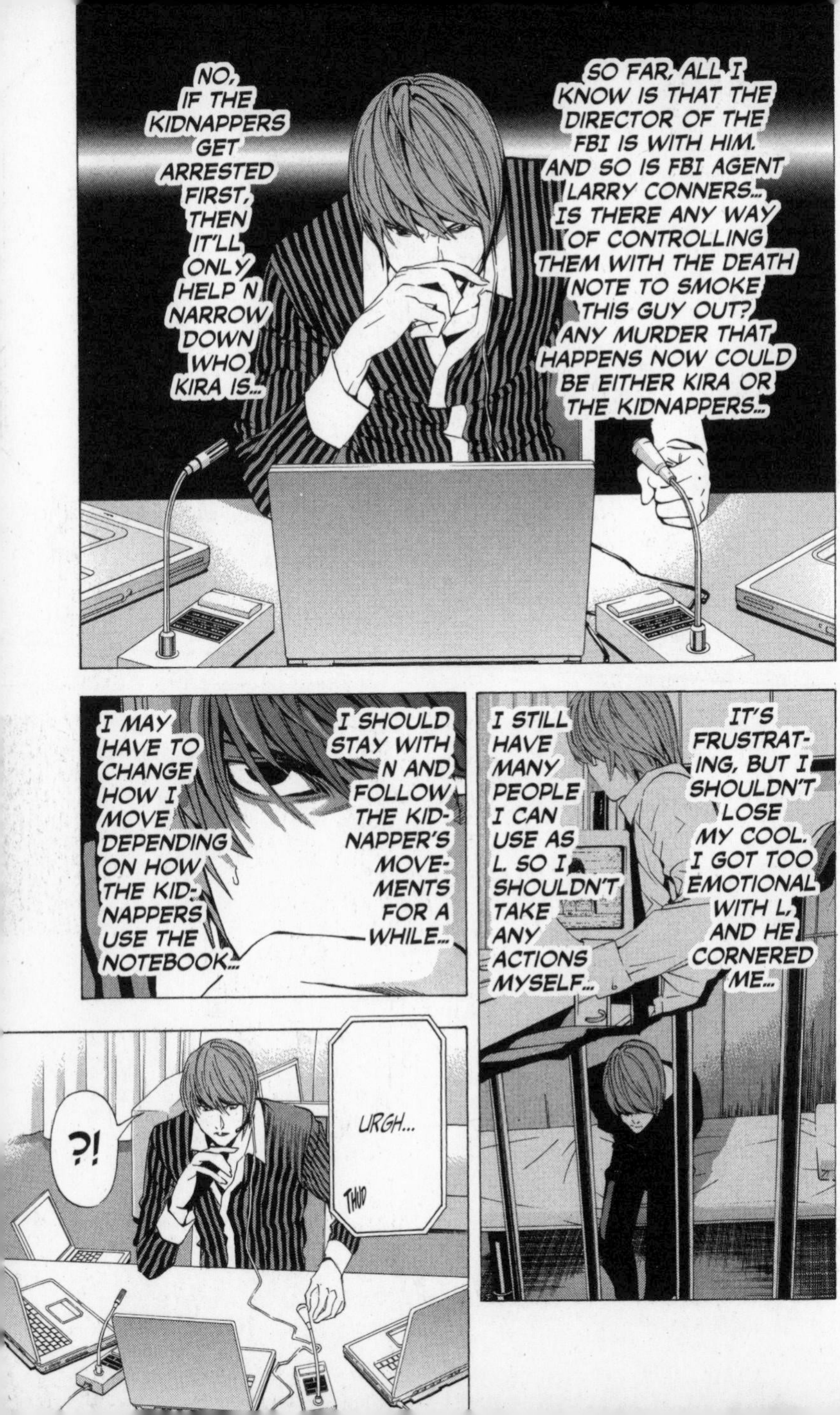
SO FAR, ALL I KNOW IS THAT THE DIRECTOR OF THE FBI IS WITH HIM. AND SO IS FBI AGENT LARRY CONNERS... IS THERE ANY WAY OF CONTROLLING THEM WITH THE DEATH NOTE TO SMOKE THIS GUY OUT? ANY MURDER THAT HAPPENS NOW COULD BE EITHER KIRA OR THE KIDNAPPERS...
NO, IF THE KIDNAPPERS GET ARRESTED FIRST, THEN IT'LL ONLY HELP N NARROW DOWN WHO KIRA IS...
IT'S FRUSTRATING, BUT I SHOULDN'T LOSE MY COOL. I GOT TOO EMOTIONAL WITH L, AND HE CORNERED ME...
I STILL HAVE MANY PEOPLE I CAN USE AS L. SO I SHOULDN'T TAKE ANY ACTIONS MYSELF...
I SHOULD STAY WITH N AND FOLLOW THE KIDNAPPER'S MOVEMENTS FOR A WHILE...
I MAY HAVE TO CHANGE HOW I MOVE DEPENDING ON HOW THE KIDNAPPERS USE THE NOTEBOOK...
URGH...
THUD
?!

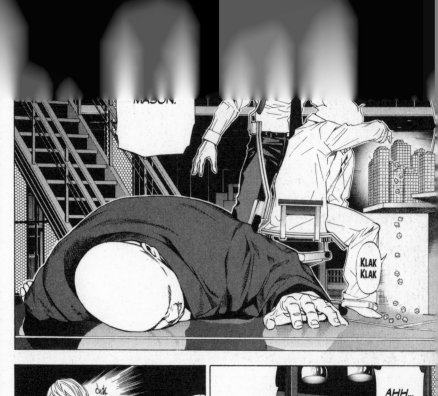

MASON.

KLAK
KLAK

crak

RATT?!

GARDNER.

AHH...

CLICK

BANG

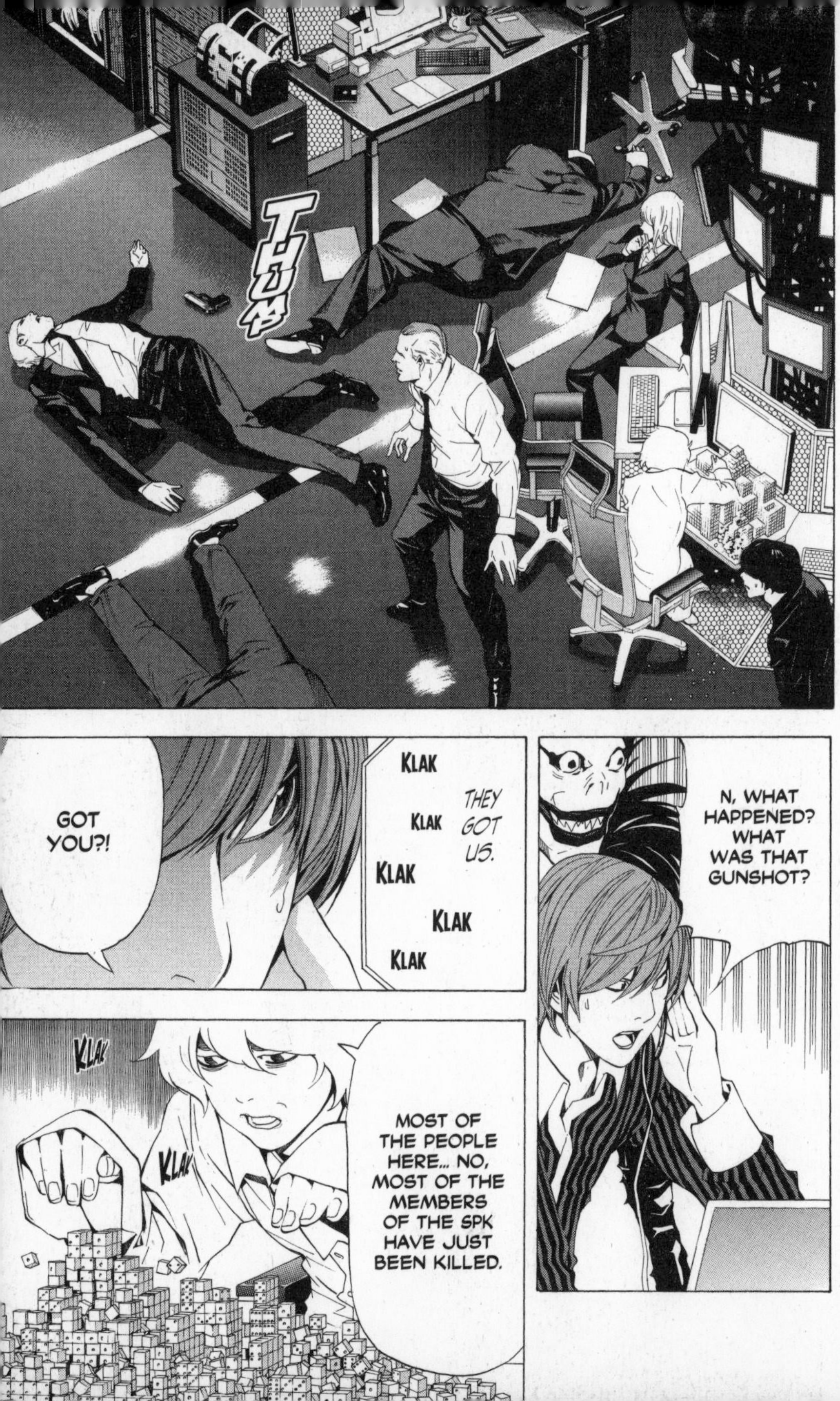
THUMP
N, WHAT HAPPENED? WHAT WAS THAT GUNSHOT?
KLAK
KLAK
THEY GOT US.
KLAK
KLAK
KLAK
GOT YOU?!
KLAK
KLAK
MOST OF THE PEOPLE HERE... NO, MOST OF THE MEMBERS OF THE SPK HAVE JUST BEEN KILLED.

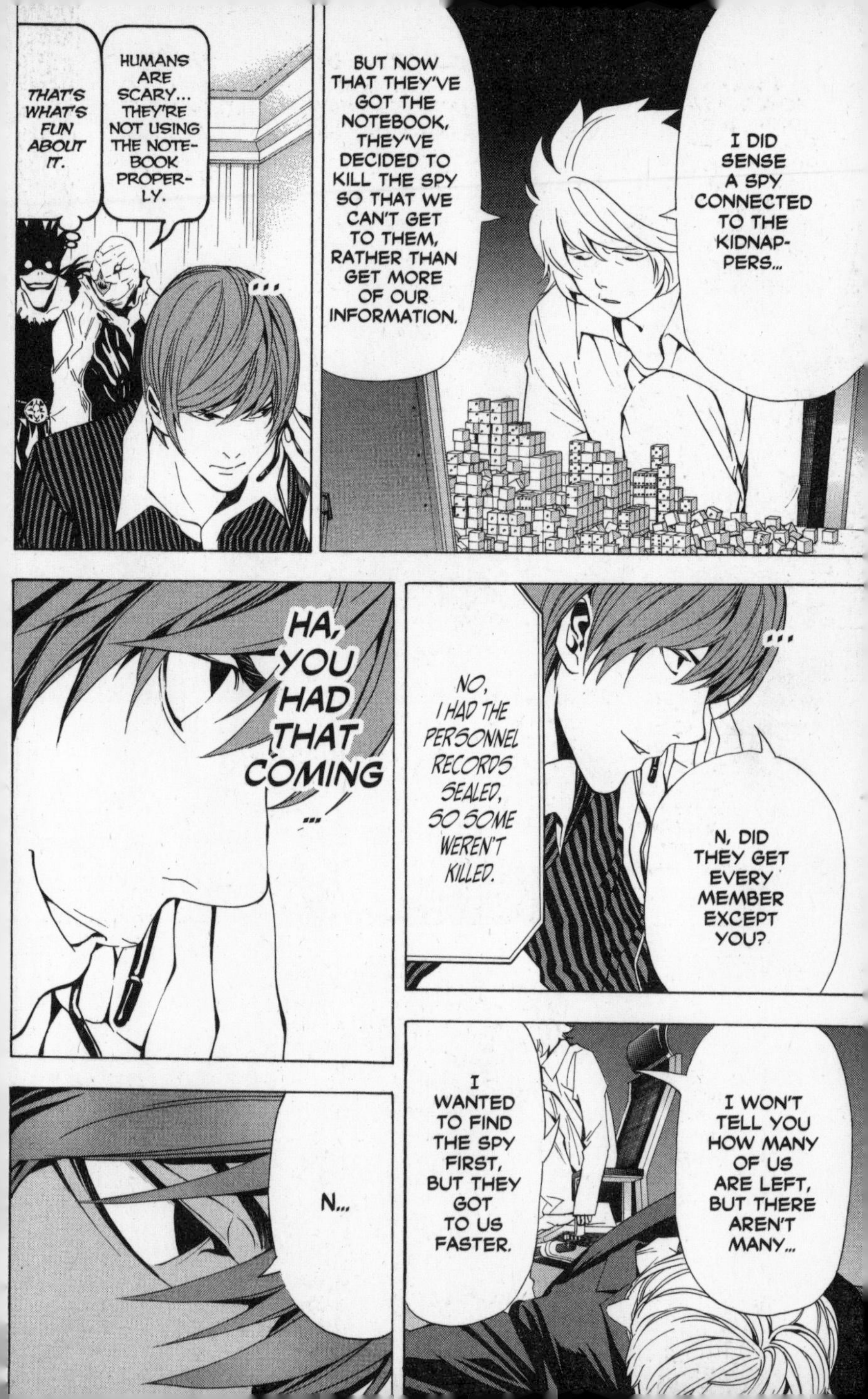
I DID SENSE A SPY CONNECTED TO THE KIDNAPPERS...
BUT NOW THAT THEY'VE GOT THE NOTEBOOK, THEY'VE DECIDED TO KILL THE SPY SO THAT WE CAN'T GET TO THEM, RATHER THAN GET MORE OF OUR INFORMATION.
HUMANS ARE SCARY... THEY'RE NOT USING THE NOTEBOOK PROPERLY.
THAT'S WHAT'S FUN ABOUT IT.
...
...
N, DID THEY GET EVERY MEMBER EXCEPT YOU?
NO, I HAD THE PERSONNEL RECORDS SEALED, SO SOME WEREN'T KILLED.
HA, YOU HAD THAT COMING...
I WON'T TELL YOU HOW MANY OF US ARE LEFT, BUT THERE AREN'T MANY...
I WANTED TO FIND THE SPY FIRST, BUT THEY GOT TO US FASTER.
N...

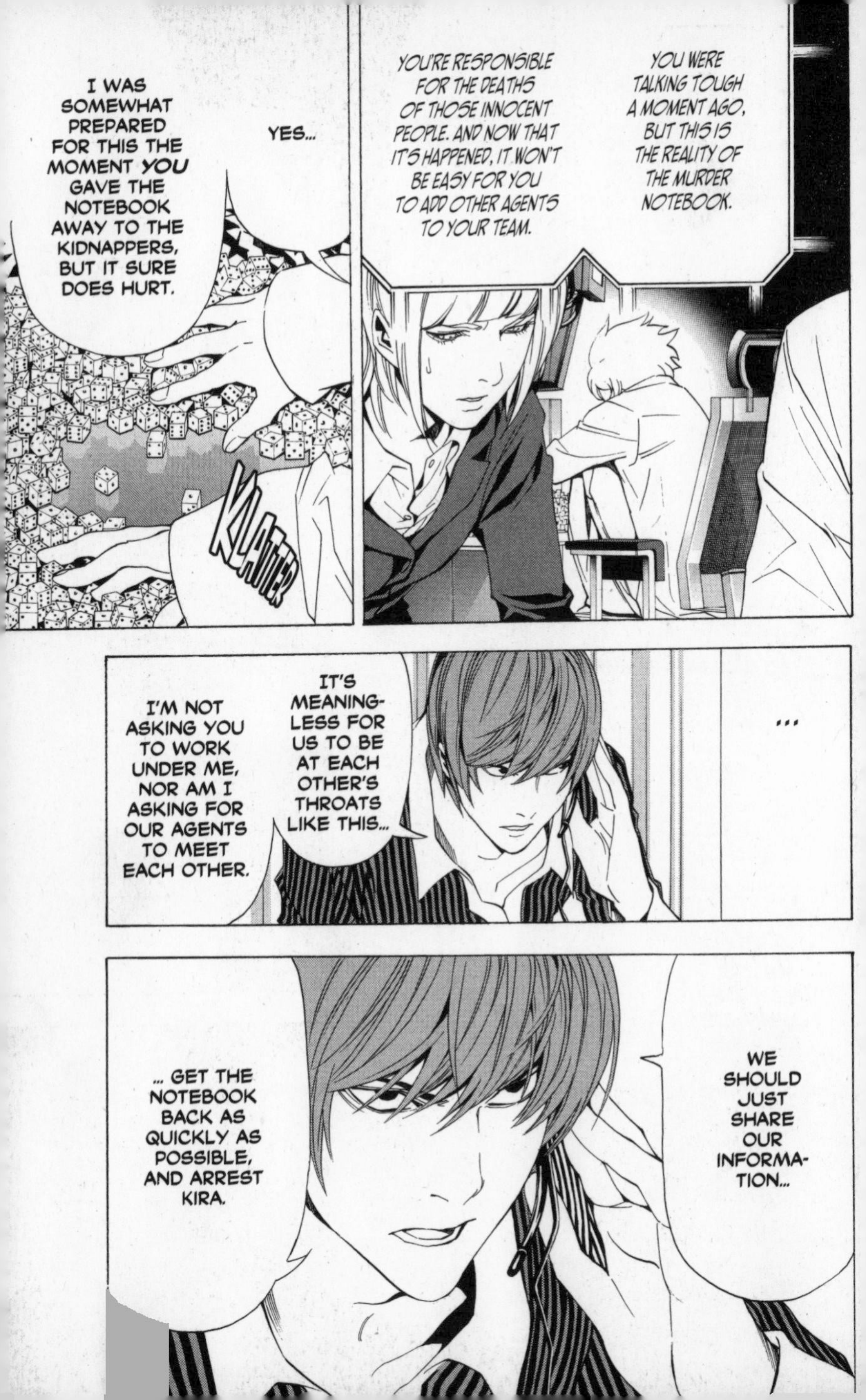
YOU WERE TALKING TOUGH A MOMENT AGO, BUT THIS IS THE REALITY OF THE MURDER NOTEBOOK.
YOU'RE RESPONSIBLE FOR THE DEATHS OF THOSE INNOCENT PEOPLE. AND NOW THAT IT'S HAPPENED, IT WON'T BE EASY FOR YOU TO ADD OTHER AGENTS TO YOUR TEAM.
YES...
I WAS SOMEWHAT PREPARED FOR THIS THE MOMENT YOU GAVE THE NOTEBOOK AWAY TO THE KIDNAPPERS, BUT IT SURE DOES HURT.
KLATTER
...
IT'S MEANING-LESS FOR US TO BE AT EACH OTHER'S THROATS LIKE THIS...
I'M NOT ASKING YOU TO WORK UNDER ME, NOR AM I ASKING FOR OUR AGENTS TO MEET EACH OTHER.
WE SHOULD JUST SHARE OUR INFORMA-TION...
... GET THE NOTEBOOK BACK AS QUICKLY AS POSSIBLE, AND ARREST KIRA.

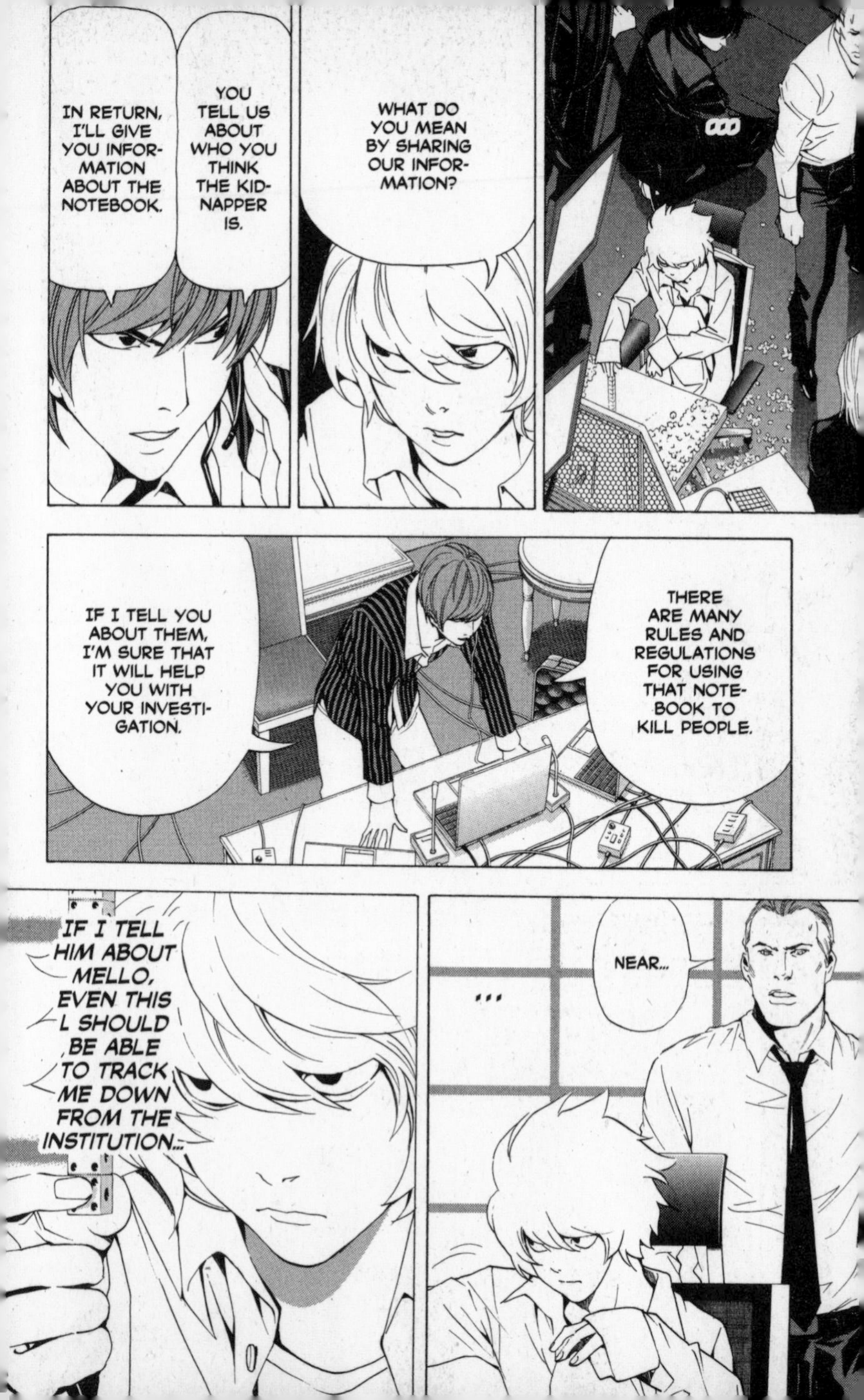
WHAT DO YOU MEAN BY SHARING OUR INFORMATION?
YOU TELL US ABOUT WHO YOU THINK THE KIDNAPPER IS.
IN RETURN, I'LL GIVE YOU INFORMATION ABOUT THE NOTEBOOK.
THERE ARE MANY RULES AND REGULATIONS FOR USING THAT NOTEBOOK TO KILL PEOPLE.
IF I TELL YOU ABOUT THEM, I'M SURE THAT IT WILL HELP YOU WITH YOUR INVESTIGATION.
NEAR...
...
IF I TELL HIM ABOUT MELLO, EVEN THIS L SHOULD BE ABLE TO TRACK ME DOWN FROM THE INSTITUTION...

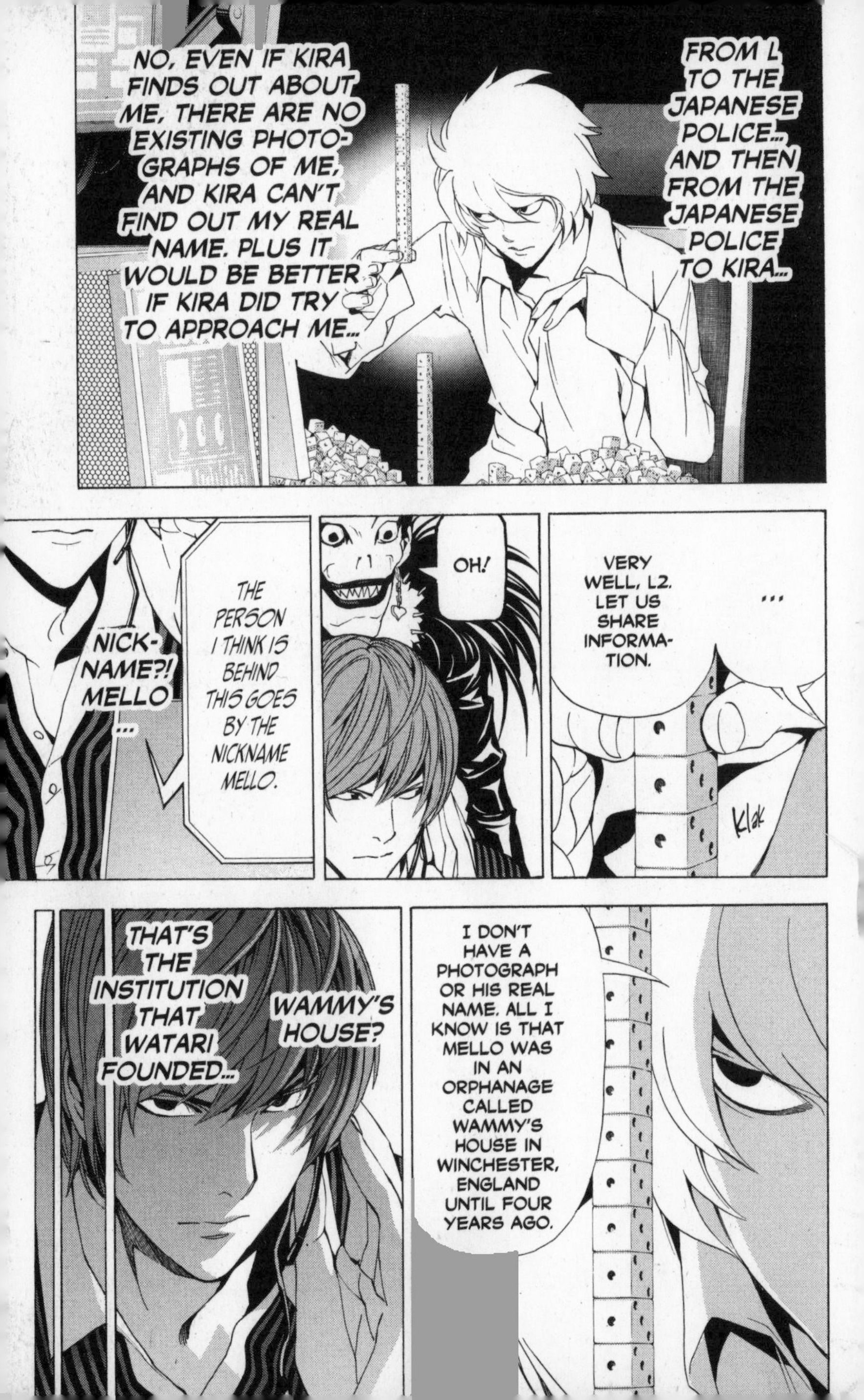
FROM L TO THE JAPANESE POLICE... AND THEN FROM THE JAPANESE POLICE TO KIRA...
NO, EVEN IF KIRA FINDS OUT ABOUT ME, THERE ARE NO EXISTING PHOTOGRAPHS OF ME, AND KIRA CAN'T FIND OUT MY REAL NAME. PLUS IT WOULD BE BETTER IF KIRA DID TRY TO APPROACH ME...
...
VERY WELL, L2. LET US SHARE INFORMATION.
Klak
OH!
THE PERSON I THINK IS BEHIND THIS GOES BY THE NICKNAME MELLO.
NICKNAME?! MELLO...
I DON'T HAVE A PHOTOGRAPH OR HIS REAL NAME. ALL I KNOW IS THAT MELLO WAS IN AN ORPHANAGE CALLED WAMMY'S HOUSE IN WINCHESTER, ENGLAND UNTIL FOUR YEARS AGO.
WAMMY'S HOUSE?
THAT'S THE INSTITUTION THAT WATARI FOUNDED...

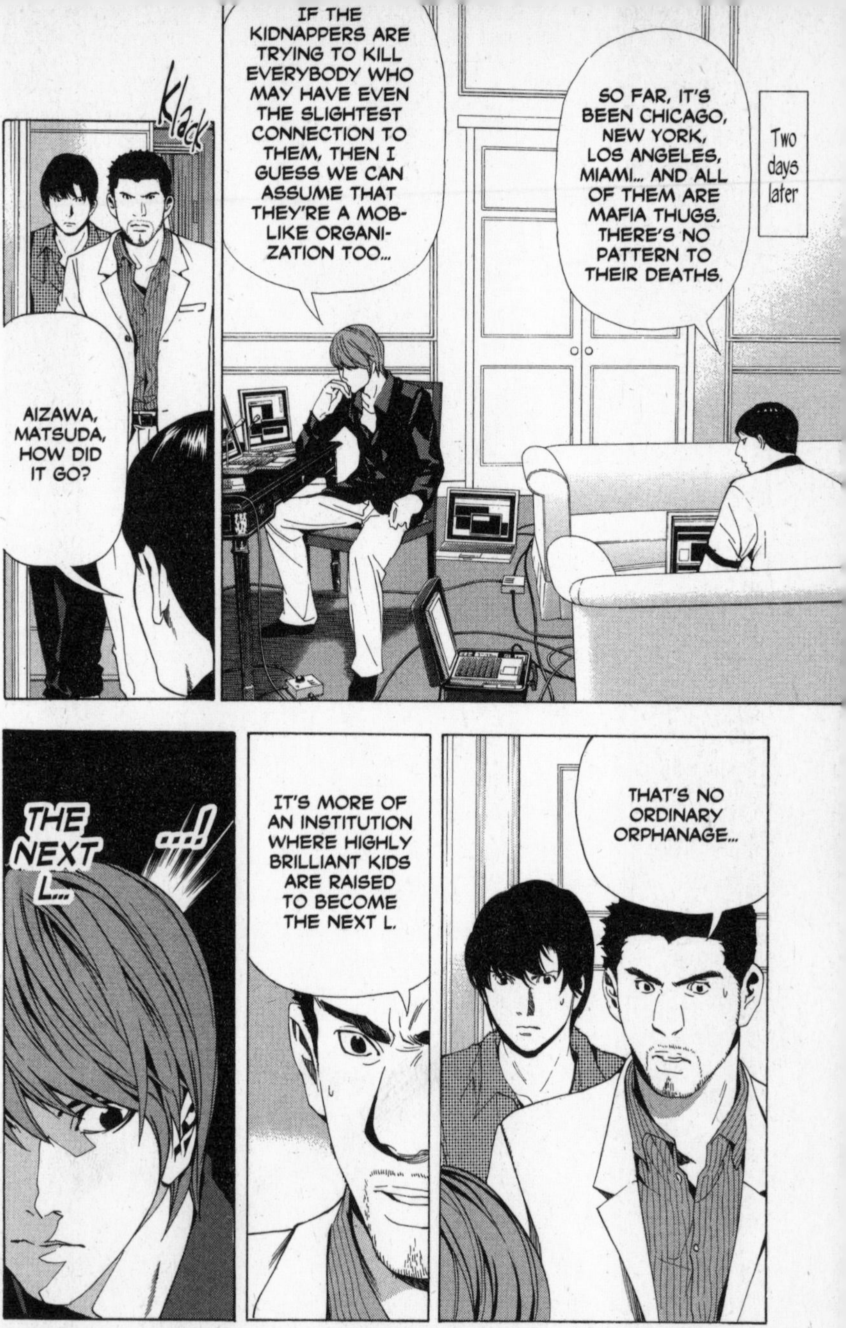
Two days later
SO FAR, IT'S BEEN CHICAGO, NEW YORK, LOS ANGELES, MIAMI... AND ALL OF THEM ARE MAFIA THUGS. THERE'S NO PATTERN TO THEIR DEATHS.
IF THE KIDNAPPERS ARE TRYING TO KILL EVERYBODY WHO MAY HAVE EVEN THE SLIGHTEST CONNECTION TO THEM, THEN I GUESS WE CAN ASSUME THAT THEY'RE A MOB-LIKE ORGANIZATION TOO...
Klack
AIZAWA, MATSUDA, HOW DID IT GO?
THAT'S NO ORDINARY ORPHANAGE...
IT'S MORE OF AN INSTITUTION WHERE HIGHLY BRILLIANT KIDS ARE RAISED TO BECOME THE NEXT L.
...!
THE NEXT L...

READ THIS WAY

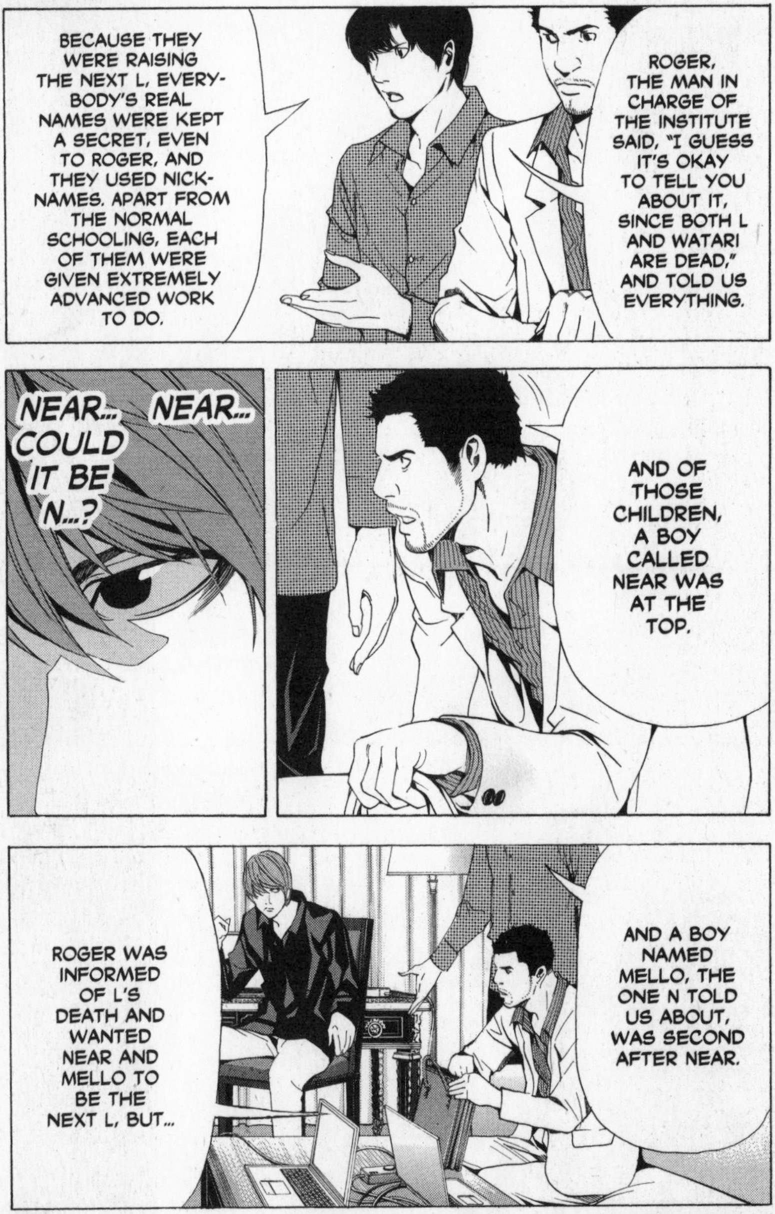
ROGER, THE MAN IN CHARGE OF THE INSTITUTE SAID, "I GUESS IT'S OKAY TO TELL YOU ABOUT IT, SINCE BOTH L AND WATARI ARE DEAD," AND TOLD US EVERYTHING.
BECAUSE THEY WERE RAISING THE NEXT L, EVERYBODY'S REAL NAMES WERE KEPT A SECRET, EVEN TO ROGER, AND THEY USED NICKNAMES. APART FROM THE NORMAL SCHOOLING, EACH OF THEM WERE GIVEN EXTREMELY ADVANCED WORK TO DO.
AND OF THOSE CHILDREN, A BOY CALLED NEAR WAS AT THE TOP.
NEAR...
NEAR... COULD IT BE N...?
AND A BOY NAMED MELLO, THE ONE N TOLD US ABOUT, WAS SECOND AFTER NEAR.
ROGER WAS INFORMED OF L'S DEATH AND WANTED NEAR AND MELLO TO BE THE NEXT L, BUT...

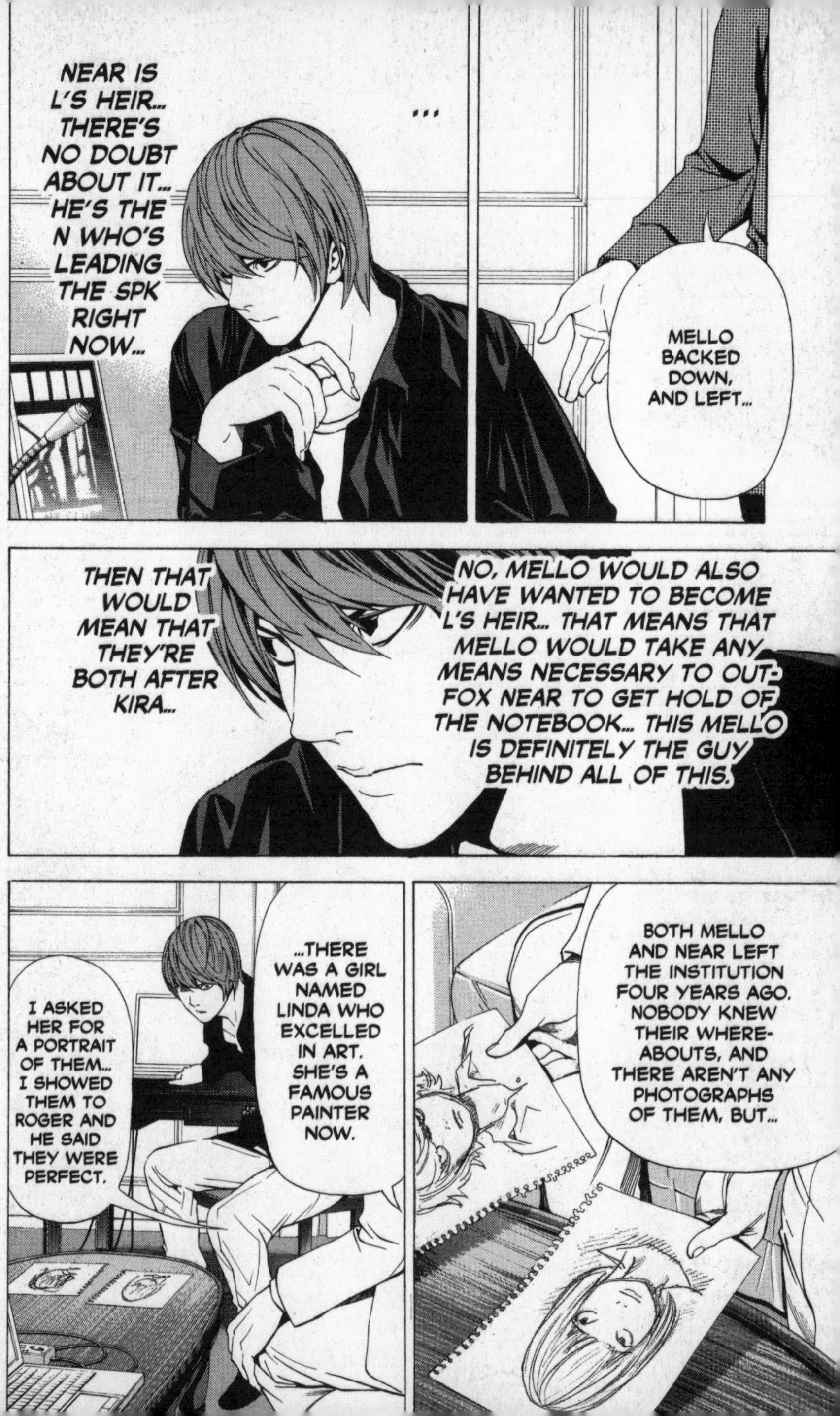
MELLO BACKED DOWN, AND LEFT...
...
NEAR IS L'S HEIR... THERE'S NO DOUBT ABOUT IT... HE'S THE N WHO'S LEADING THE SPK RIGHT NOW...
NO, MELLO WOULD ALSO HAVE WANTED TO BECOME L'S HEIR... THAT MEANS THAT MELLO WOULD TAKE ANY MEANS NECESSARY TO OUT-FOX NEAR TO GET HOLD OF THE NOTEBOOK... THIS MELLO IS DEFINITELY THE GUY BEHIND ALL OF THIS.
THEN THAT WOULD MEAN THAT THEY'RE BOTH AFTER KIRA...
BOTH MELLO AND NEAR LEFT THE INSTITUTION FOUR YEARS AGO. NOBODY KNEW THEIR WHERE-ABOUTS, AND THERE AREN'T ANY PHOTOGRAPHS OF THEM, BUT...
...THERE WAS A GIRL NAMED LINDA WHO EXCELLED IN ART. SHE'S A FAMOUS PAINTER NOW.
I ASKED HER FOR A PORTRAIT OF THEM... I SHOWED THEM TO ROGER AND HE SAID THEY WERE PERFECT.

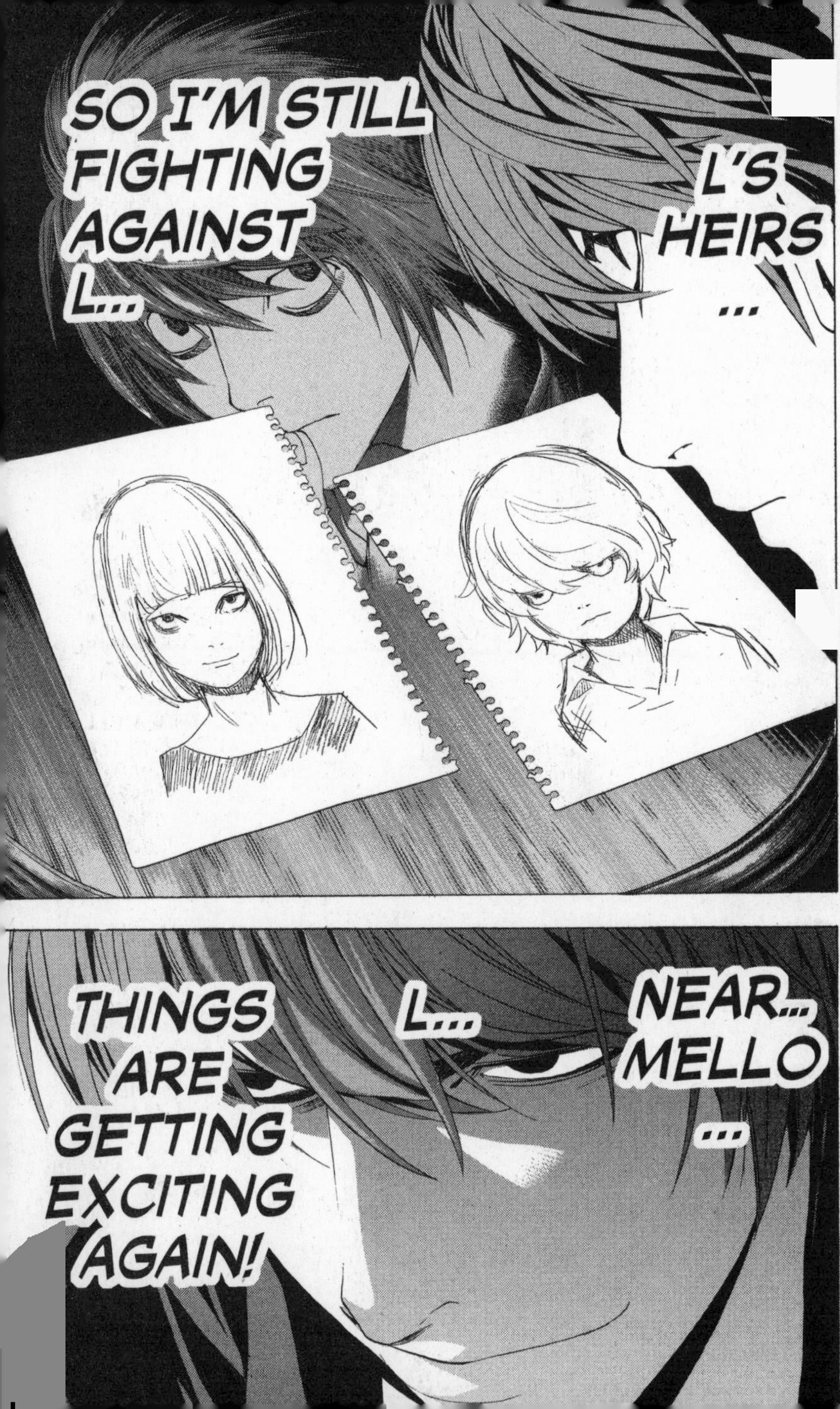
L'S HEIRS ...
SO I'M STILL FIGHTING AGAINST L...
NEAR... MELLO ...
L...
THINGS ARE GETTING EXCITING AGAIN!

DEATH NOTE
How to use it
XLIV

- If the DEATH NOTE that the god of death owns is taken away; by being cheated by other gods of death and so forth, it can only be retrieved from the god of death who is possessing it at the time. If there is no god of death, but a human possessing it, the only way that the god of death can retrieve it will be to first touch the DEATH NOTE and become the god of death that haunts that human.

- Then wait until that human dies to take it away before any other human touches it or whenever the human shows a will to let go of it.

死神が自分の所有すべきデスノートを
他の死神に騙し取られた等で失った場合、
その時ノートに憑く死神から返してもらうしかない。
憑く死神がいない状態で人間が持っている場合は、
一度ノートに触りその人間に憑く死神となり、
その人間の最期を見届け他の人間が触る前に取り上げるか、
その人間に返してもらわなければならない。

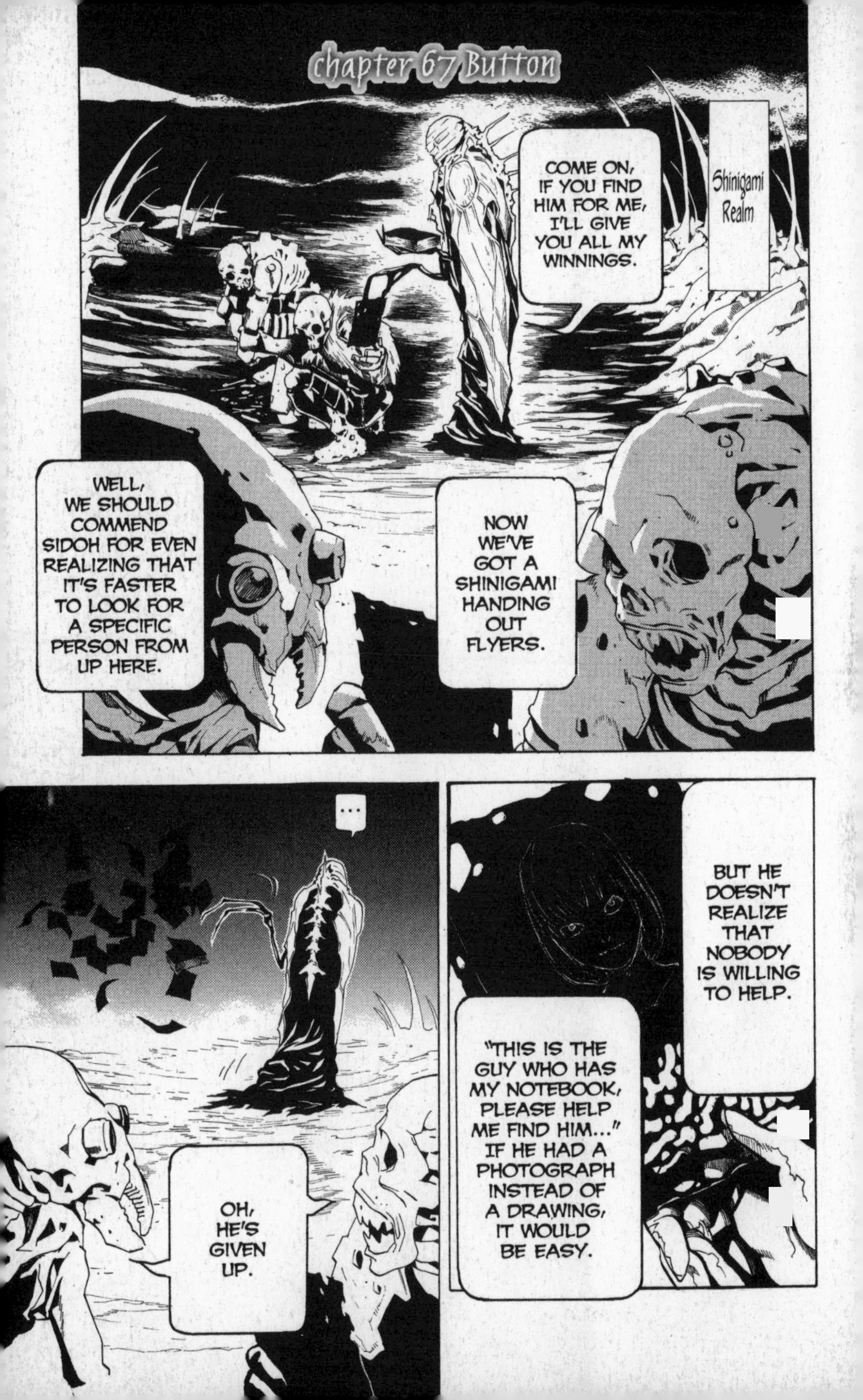
chapter 67 Button
Shinigami Realm
COME ON, IF YOU FIND HIM FOR ME, I'LL GIVE YOU ALL MY WINNINGS.
NOW WE'VE GOT A SHINIGAMI HANDING OUT FLYERS.
WELL, WE SHOULD COMMEND SIDOH FOR EVEN REALIZING THAT IT'S FASTER TO LOOK FOR A SPECIFIC PERSON FROM UP HERE.
BUT HE DOESN'T REALIZE THAT NOBODY IS WILLING TO HELP.
"THIS IS THE GUY WHO HAS MY NOTEBOOK, PLEASE HELP ME FIND HIM..." IF HE HAD A PHOTOGRAPH INSTEAD OF A DRAWING, IT WOULD BE EASY.
...
OH, HE'S GIVEN UP.

chapter 67 Button

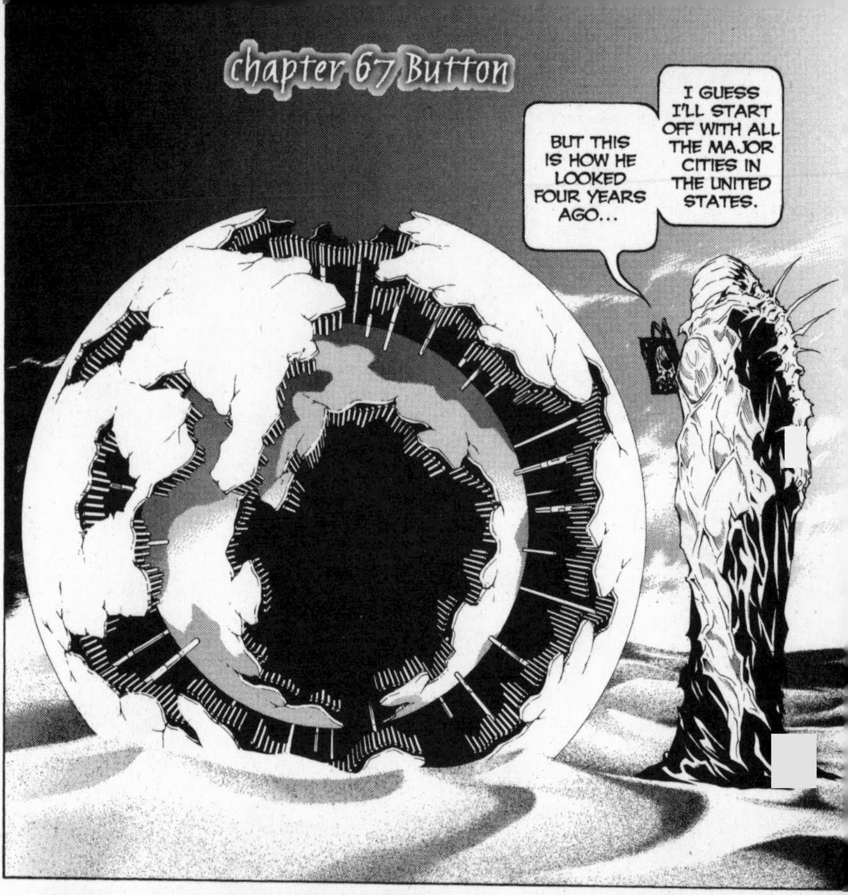
I GUESS I'LL START OFF WITH ALL THE MAJOR CITIES IN THE UNITED STATES.
BUT THIS IS HOW HE LOOKED FOUR YEARS AGO...

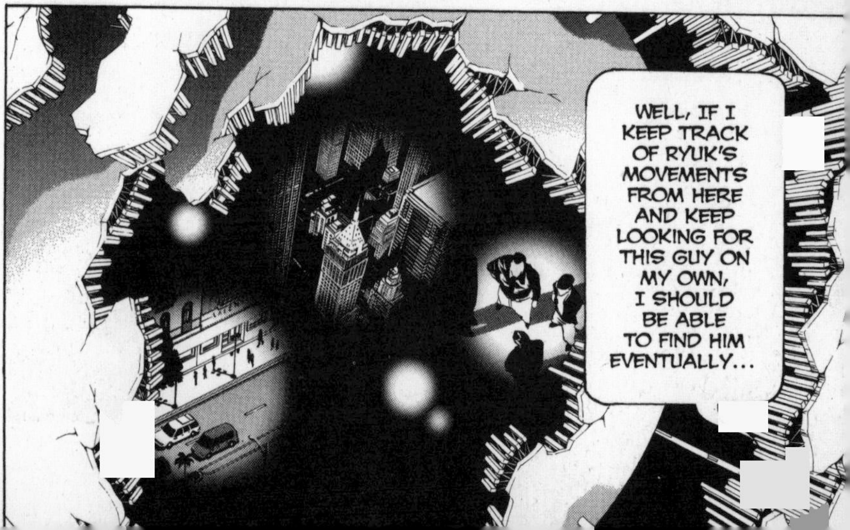
WELL, IF I KEEP TRACK OF RYUK'S MOVEMENTS FROM HERE AND KEEP LOOKING FOR THIS GUY ON MY OWN, I SHOULD BE ABLE TO FIND HIM EVENTUALLY...

YAGAMI
BEEP BEEP BEEP
BEEP BEEP BEEP
BEEP BEEP BEEP
BIP
YAGAMI HERE.

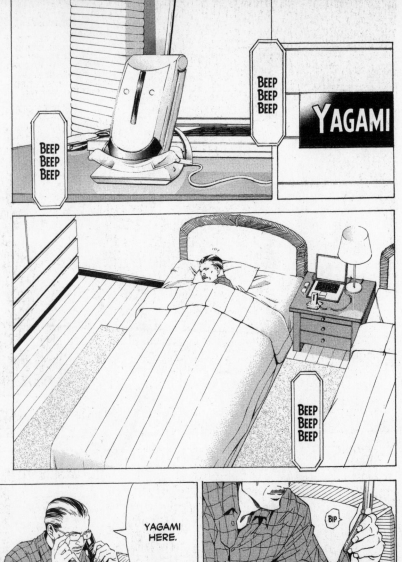

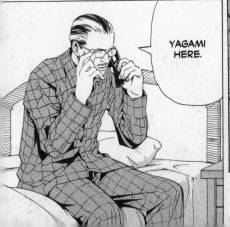

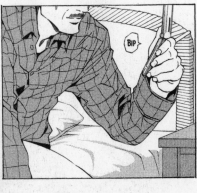

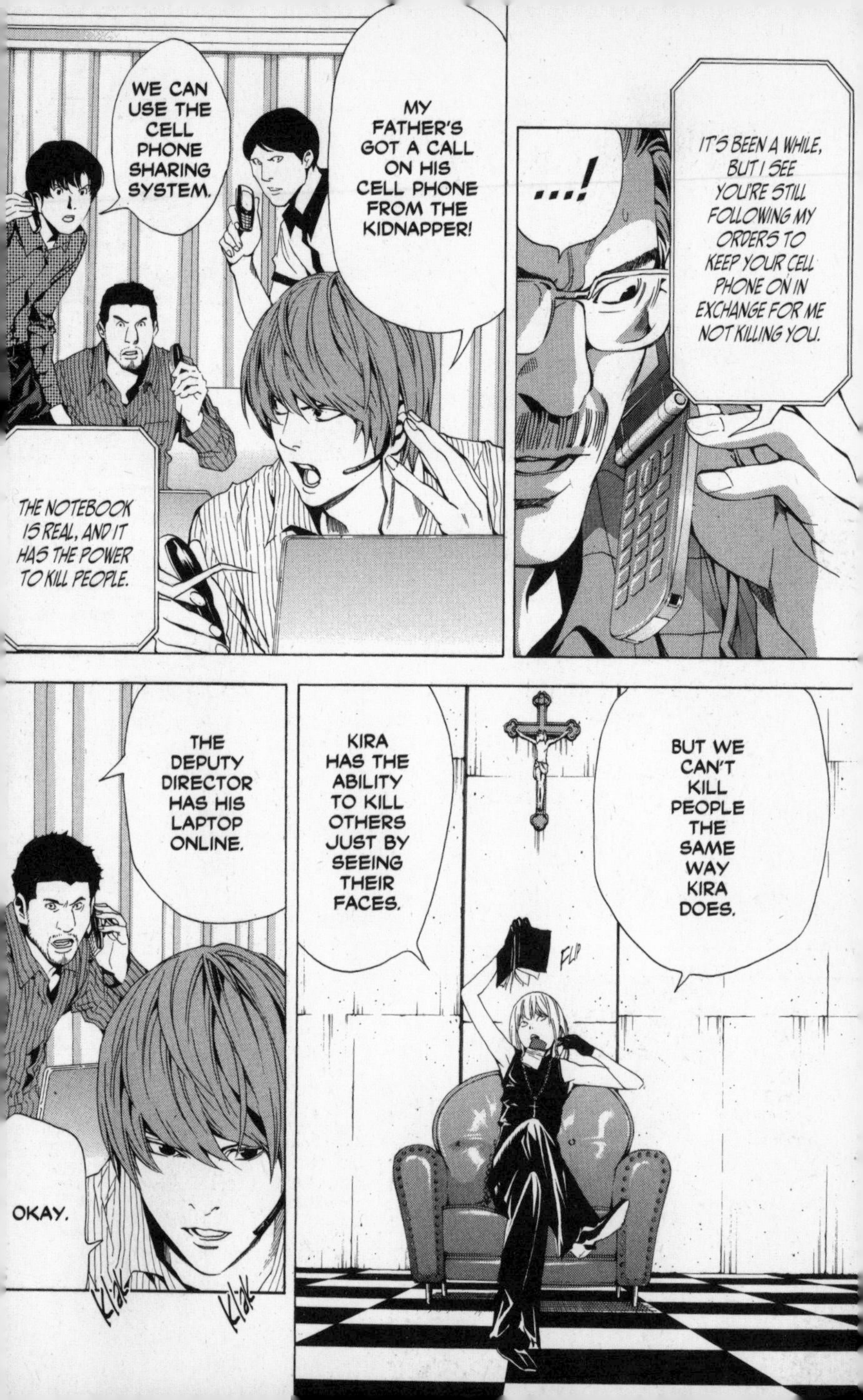
IT'S BEEN A WHILE, BUT I SEE YOU'RE STILL FOLLOWING MY ORDERS TO KEEP YOUR CELL PHONE ON IN EXCHANGE FOR ME NOT KILLING YOU.
...!
MY FATHER'S GOT A CALL ON HIS CELL PHONE FROM THE KIDNAPPER!
WE CAN USE THE CELL PHONE SHARING SYSTEM.
THE NOTEBOOK IS REAL, AND IT HAS THE POWER TO KILL PEOPLE.
BUT WE CAN'T KILL PEOPLE THE SAME WAY KIRA DOES.
FLIP
KIRA HAS THE ABILITY TO KILL OTHERS JUST BY SEEING THEIR FACES.
THE DEPUTY DIRECTOR HAS HIS LAPTOP ONLINE.
OKAY.
KLAK
KLAK

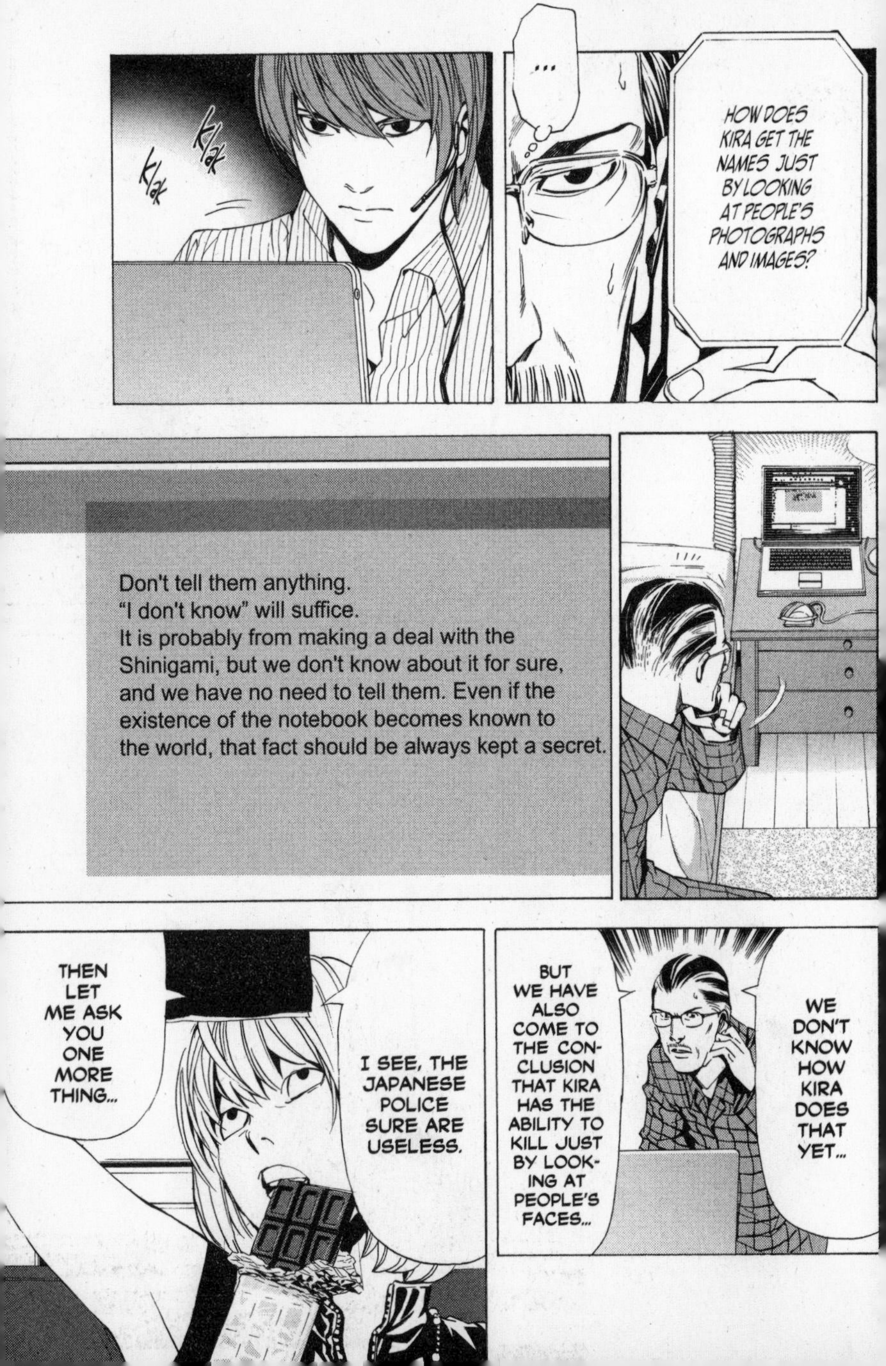
HOW DOES KIRA GET THE NAMES JUST BY LOOKING AT PEOPLE'S PHOTOGRAPHS AND IMAGES?
...
Klak
Klak
Don't tell them anything.
"I don't know" will suffice.
It is probably from making a deal with the Shinigami, but we don't know about it for sure, and we have no need to tell them. Even if the existence of the notebook becomes known to the world, that fact should be always kept a secret.
WE DON'T KNOW HOW KIRA DOES THAT YET...
BUT WE HAVE ALSO COME TO THE CONCLUSION THAT KIRA HAS THE ABILITY TO KILL JUST BY LOOKING AT PEOPLE'S FACES...
I SEE, THE JAPANESE POLICE SURE ARE USELESS.
THEN LET ME ASK YOU ONE MORE THING...

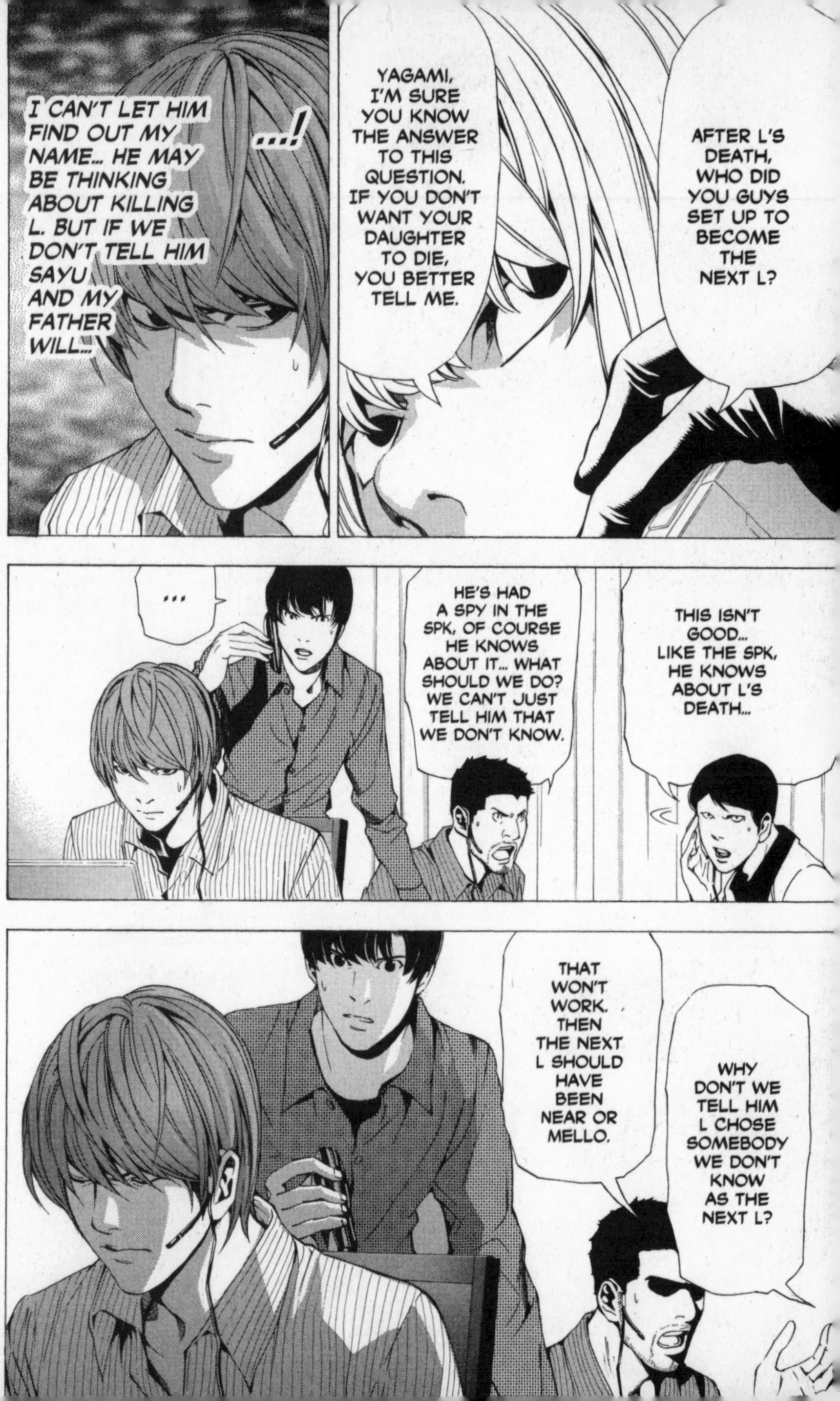
AFTER L'S DEATH, WHO DID YOU GUYS SET UP TO BECOME THE NEXT L?
YAGAMI, I'M SURE YOU KNOW THE ANSWER TO THIS QUESTION. IF YOU DON'T WANT YOUR DAUGHTER TO DIE, YOU BETTER TELL ME.
...!
I CAN'T LET HIM FIND OUT MY NAME... HE MAY BE THINKING ABOUT KILLING L. BUT IF WE DON'T TELL HIM SAYU AND MY FATHER WILL...
THIS ISN'T GOOD... LIKE THE SPK, HE KNOWS ABOUT L'S DEATH...
HE'S HAD A SPY IN THE SPK, OF COURSE HE KNOWS ABOUT IT... WHAT SHOULD WE DO? WE CAN'T JUST TELL HIM THAT WE DON'T KNOW.
...
WHY DON'T WE TELL HIM L CHOSE SOMEBODY WE DON'T KNOW AS THE NEXT L?
THAT WON'T WORK. THEN THE NEXT L SHOULD HAVE BEEN NEAR OR MELLO.

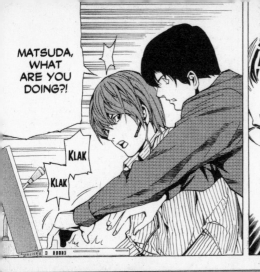

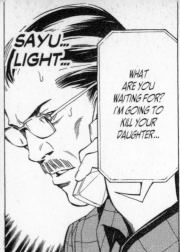

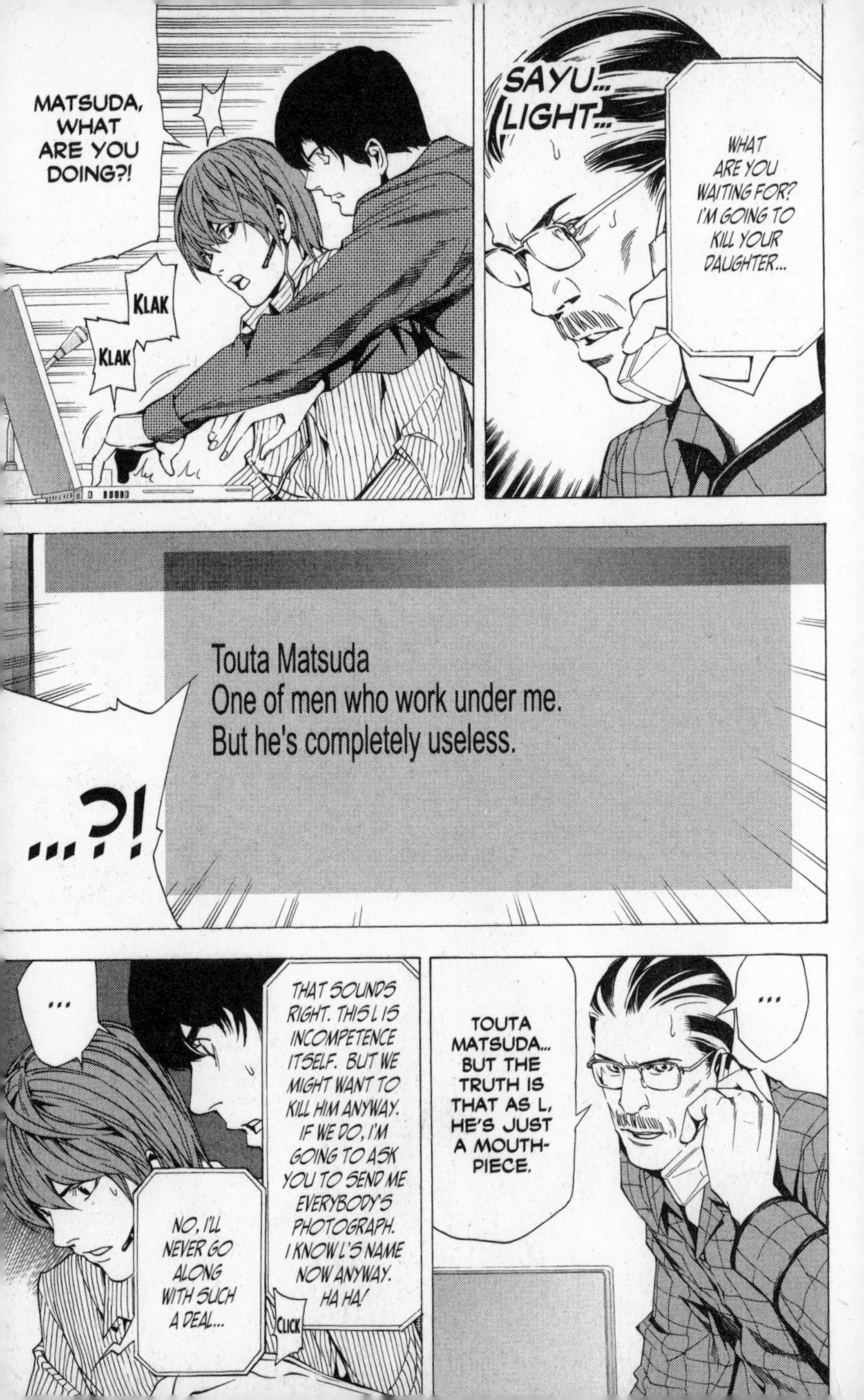
SAYU... LIGHT...
WHAT ARE YOU WAITING FOR? I'M GOING TO KILL YOUR DAUGHTER...
MATSUDA, WHAT ARE YOU DOING?!
KLAK
KLAK
Touta Matsuda
One of men who work under me.
But he's completely useless.
...?!
...
TOUTA MATSUDA... BUT THE TRUTH IS THAT AS L, HE'S JUST A MOUTH-PIECE.
THAT SOUNDS RIGHT. THIS L IS INCOMPETENCE ITSELF. BUT WE MIGHT WANT TO KILL HIM ANYWAY. IF WE DO, I'M GOING TO ASK YOU TO SEND ME EVERYBODY'S PHOTOGRAPH. I KNOW L'S NAME NOW ANYWAY. HA HA!
...
NO, I'LL NEVER GO ALONG WITH SUCH A DEAL...
CLICK

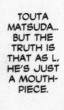

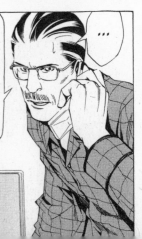

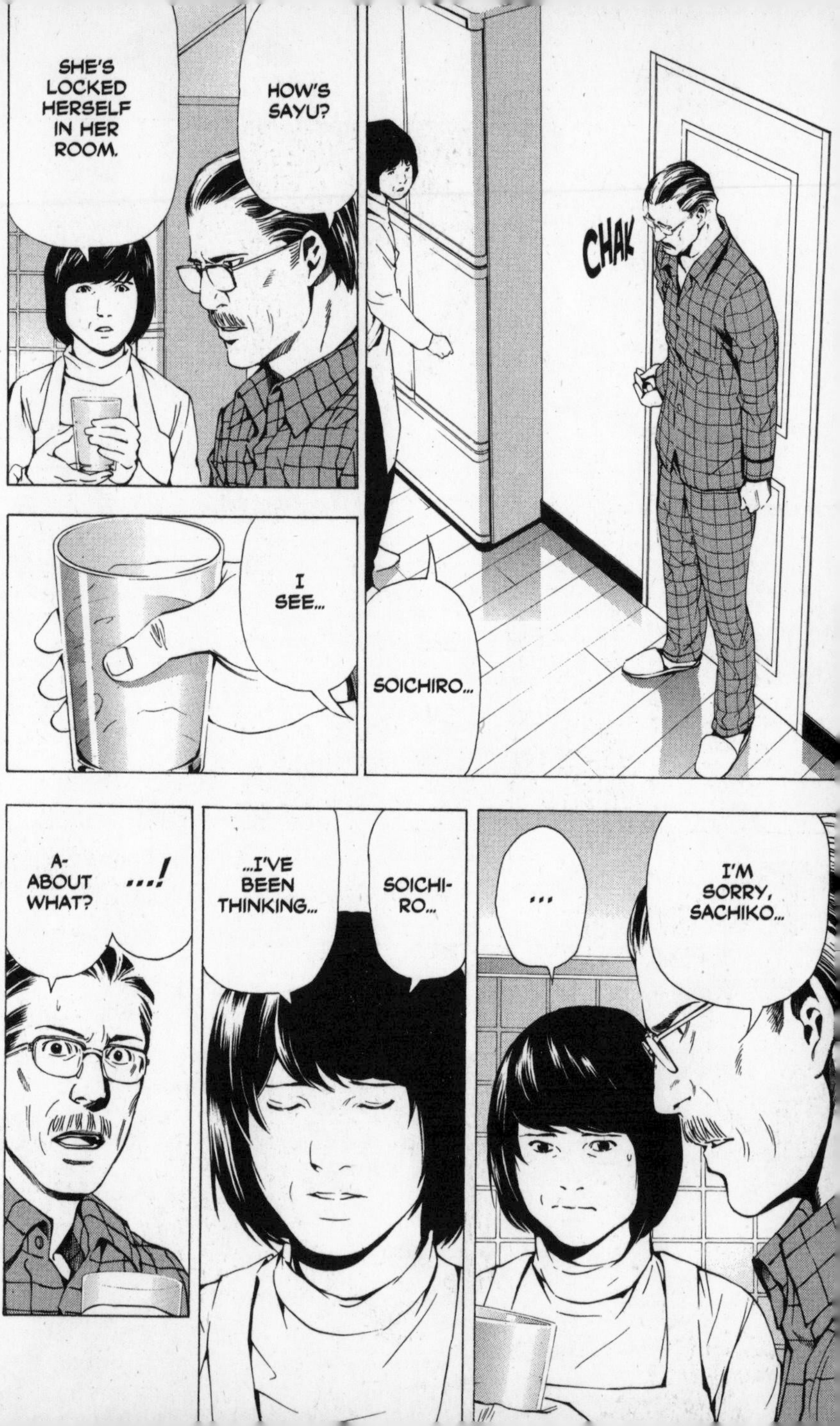
CHAK
SOICHIRO...
HOW'S SAYU?
SHE'S LOCKED HERSELF IN HER ROOM.
I SEE...
I'M SORRY, SACHIKO...
...
SOICHI-RO...
...I'VE BEEN THINKING...
...!
A- ABOUT WHAT?

READ THIS WAY

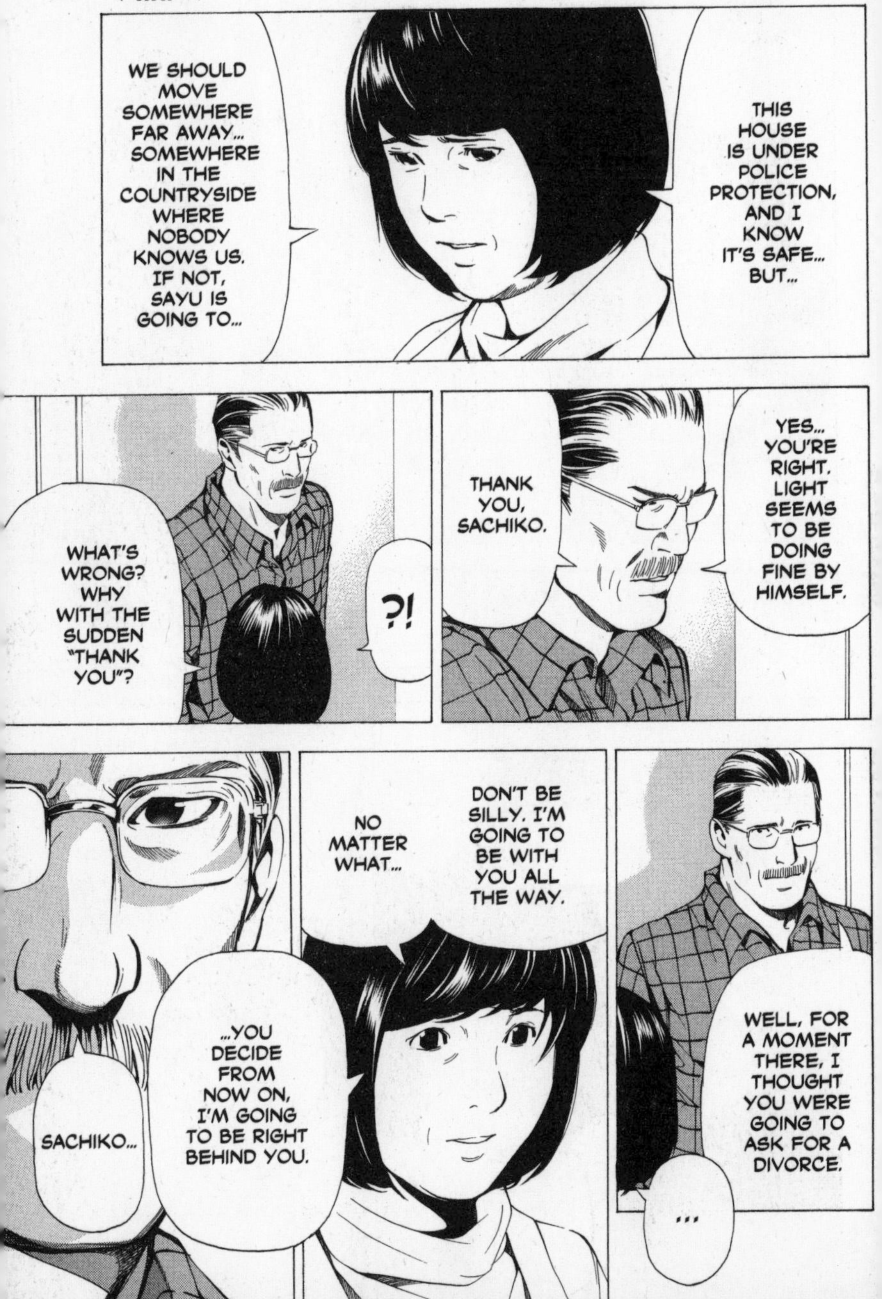
THIS HOUSE IS UNDER POLICE PROTECTION, AND I KNOW IT'S SAFE... BUT...
WE SHOULD MOVE SOMEWHERE FAR AWAY... SOMEWHERE IN THE COUNTRYSIDE WHERE NOBODY KNOWS US. IF NOT, SAYU IS GOING TO...
YES... YOU'RE RIGHT. LIGHT SEEMS TO BE DOING FINE BY HIMSELF.
THANK YOU, SACHIKO.
?!
WHAT'S WRONG? WHY WITH THE SUDDEN "THANK YOU"?
WELL, FOR A MOMENT THERE, I THOUGHT YOU WERE GOING TO ASK FOR A DIVORCE.
...
DON'T BE SILLY. I'M GOING TO BE WITH YOU ALL THE WAY.
NO MATTER WHAT...
...YOU DECIDE FROM NOW ON, I'M GOING TO BE RIGHT BEHIND YOU.
SACHIKO...

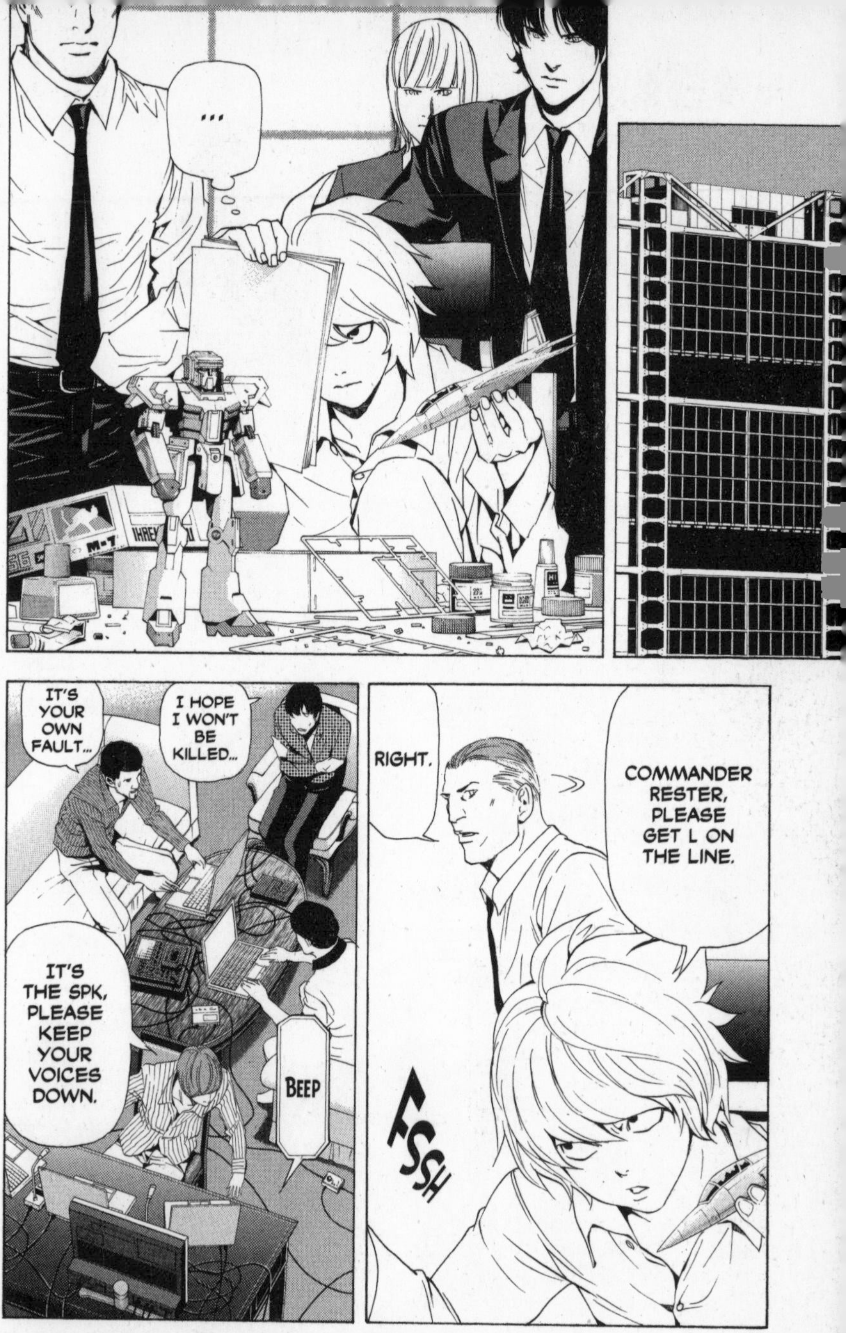
...
COMMANDER RESTER, PLEASE GET L ON THE LINE.
RIGHT.
FSSH
I HOPE I WON'T BE KILLED...
IT'S YOUR OWN FAULT...
IT'S THE SPK, PLEASE KEEP YOUR VOICES DOWN.
BEEP

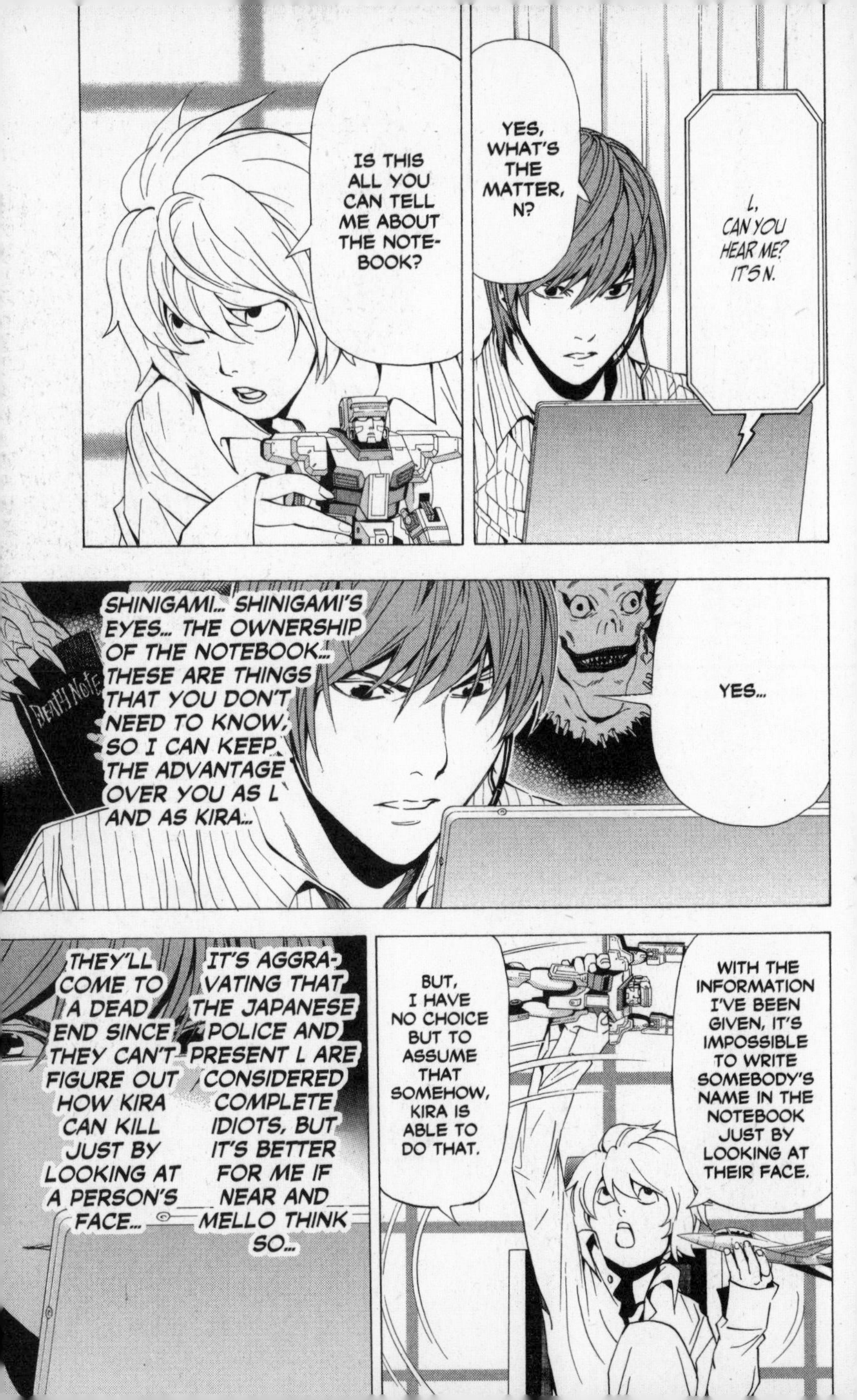
L, CAN YOU HEAR ME? IT'S N.
YES, WHAT'S THE MATTER, N?
IS THIS ALL YOU CAN TELL ME ABOUT THE NOTE-BOOK?
YES...
SHINIGAMI... SHINIGAMI'S EYES... THE OWNERSHIP OF THE NOTEBOOK... THESE ARE THINGS THAT YOU DON'T NEED TO KNOW, SO I CAN KEEP THE ADVANTAGE OVER YOU AS L AND AS KIRA...
DEATH NOTE
WITH THE INFORMATION I'VE BEEN GIVEN, IT'S IMPOSSIBLE TO WRITE SOMEBODY'S NAME IN THE NOTEBOOK JUST BY LOOKING AT THEIR FACE.
BUT, I HAVE NO CHOICE BUT TO ASSUME THAT SOMEHOW, KIRA IS ABLE TO DO THAT.
IT'S AGGRA-VATING THAT THE JAPANESE POLICE AND PRESENT L ARE CONSIDERED COMPLETE IDIOTS, BUT IT'S BETTER FOR ME IF NEAR AND MELLO THINK SO...
THEY'LL COME TO A DEAD END SINCE THEY CAN'T FIGURE OUT HOW KIRA CAN KILL JUST BY LOOKING AT A PERSON'S FACE...

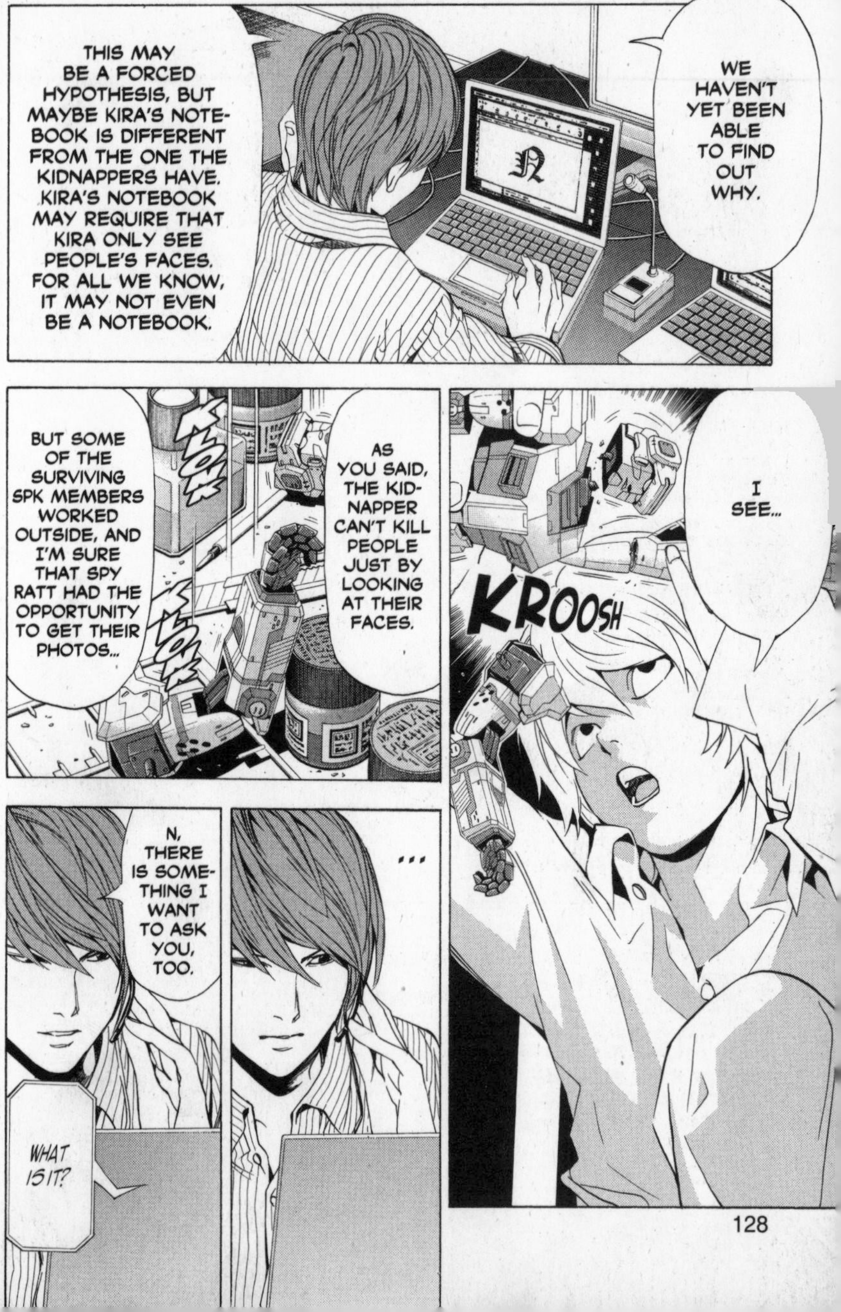
WE HAVEN'T YET BEEN ABLE TO FIND OUT WHY.
THIS MAY BE A FORCED HYPOTHESIS, BUT MAYBE KIRA'S NOTE-BOOK IS DIFFERENT FROM THE ONE THE KIDNAPPERS HAVE. KIRA'S NOTEBOOK MAY REQUIRE THAT KIRA ONLY SEE PEOPLE'S FACES. FOR ALL WE KNOW, IT MAY NOT EVEN BE A NOTEBOOK.
I SEE...
KROOSH
AS YOU SAID, THE KID-NAPPER CAN'T KILL PEOPLE JUST BY LOOKING AT THEIR FACES.
KLONK
BUT SOME OF THE SURVIVING SPK MEMBERS WORKED OUTSIDE, AND I'M SURE THAT SPY RATT HAD THE OPPORTUNITY TO GET THEIR PHOTOS...
KLONK
...
N, THERE IS SOME-THING I WANT TO ASK YOU, TOO.
WHAT IS IT?

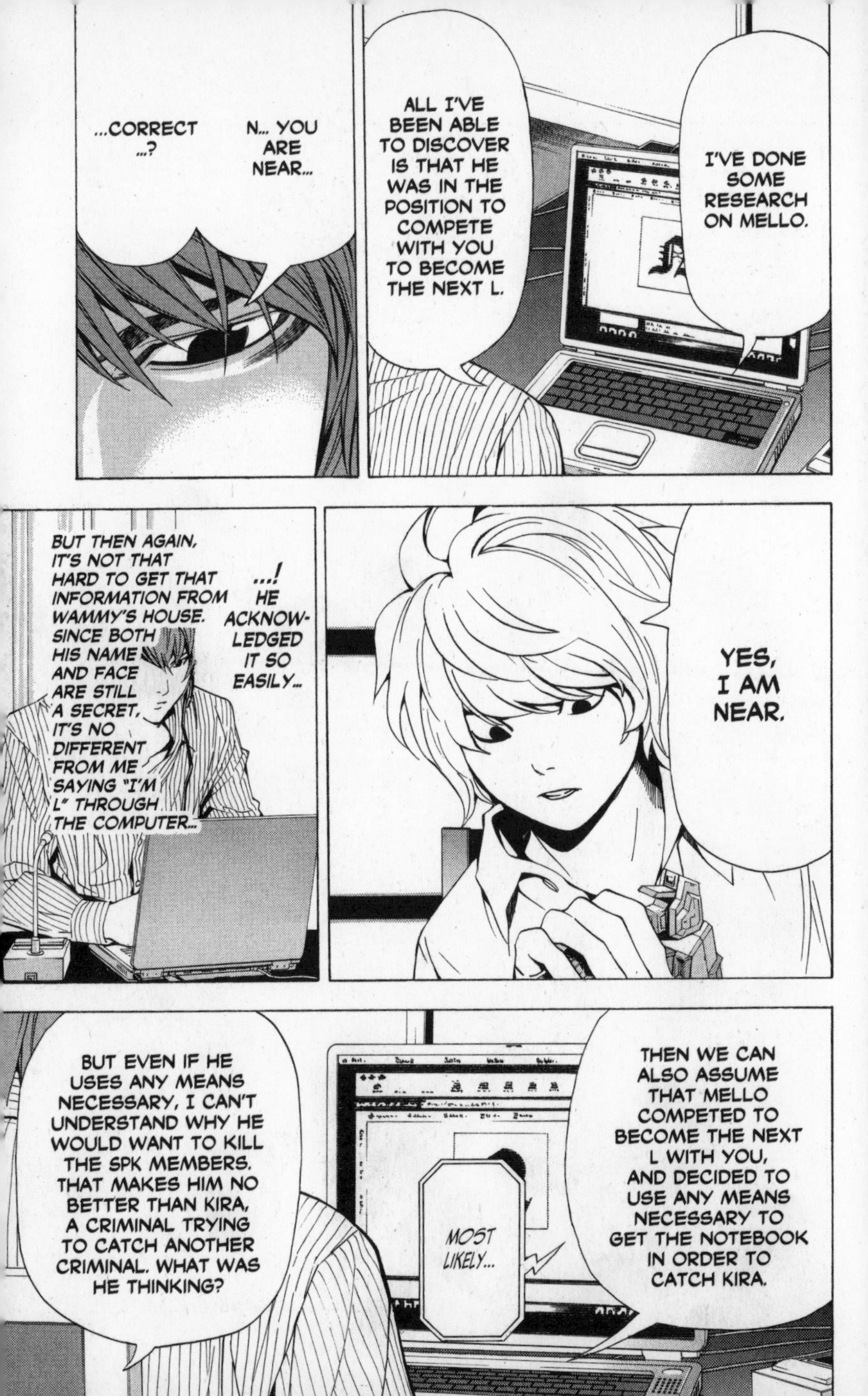
I'VE DONE SOME RESEARCH ON MELLO.
ALL I'VE BEEN ABLE TO DISCOVER IS THAT HE WAS IN THE POSITION TO COMPETE WITH YOU TO BECOME THE NEXT L.
N... YOU ARE NEAR...
...CORRECT ...?
YES, I AM NEAR.
...! HE ACKNOWLEDGED IT SO EASILY...
BUT THEN AGAIN, IT'S NOT THAT HARD TO GET THAT INFORMATION FROM WAMMY'S HOUSE. SINCE BOTH HIS NAME AND FACE ARE STILL A SECRET, IT'S NO DIFFERENT FROM ME SAYING "I'M L" THROUGH THE COMPUTER...
THEN WE CAN ALSO ASSUME THAT MELLO COMPETED TO BECOME THE NEXT L WITH YOU, AND DECIDED TO USE ANY MEANS NECESSARY TO GET THE NOTEBOOK IN ORDER TO CATCH KIRA.
MOST LIKELY...
BUT EVEN IF HE USES ANY MEANS NECESSARY, I CAN'T UNDERSTAND WHY HE WOULD WANT TO KILL THE SPK MEMBERS. THAT MAKES HIM NO BETTER THAN KIRA, A CRIMINAL TRYING TO CATCH ANOTHER CRIMINAL. WHAT WAS HE THINKING?

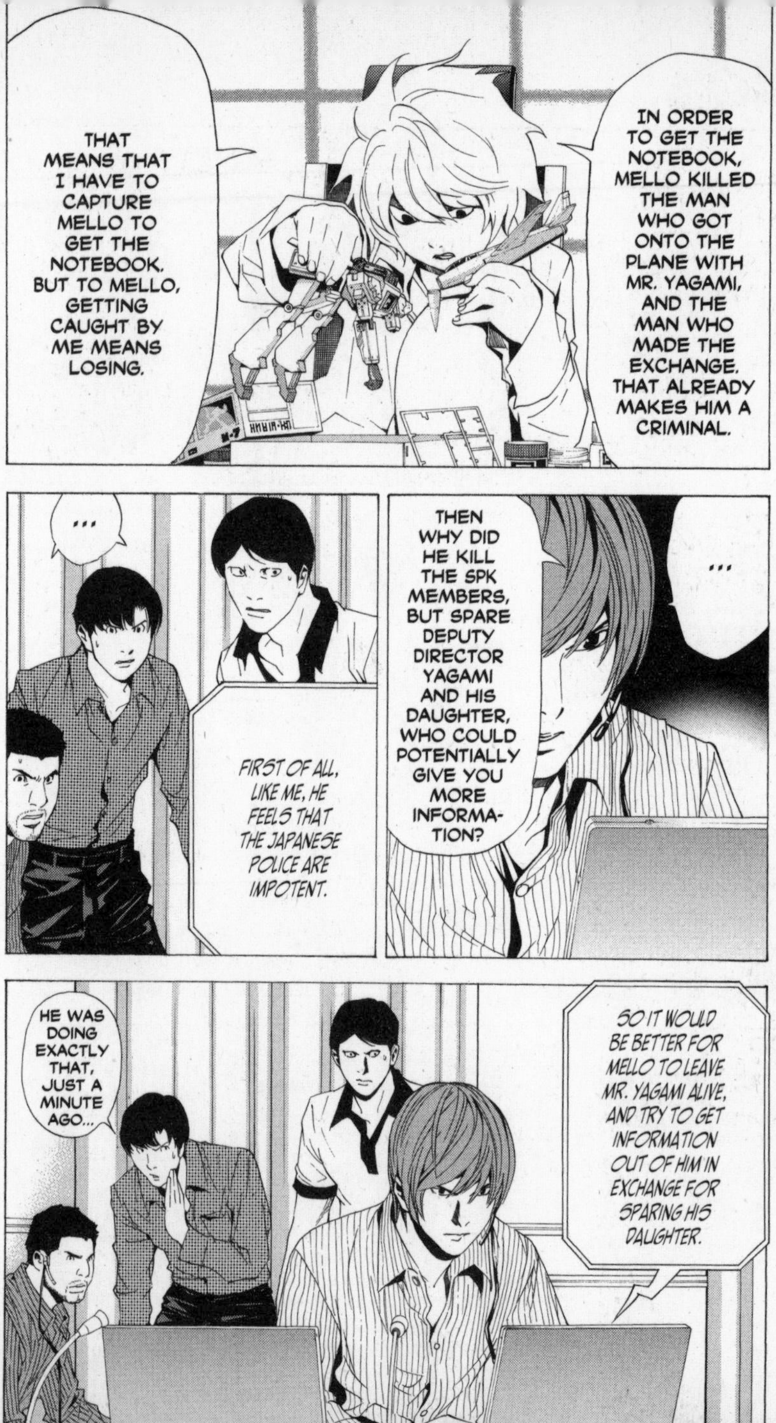
IN ORDER TO GET THE NOTEBOOK, MELLO KILLED THE MAN WHO GOT ONTO THE PLANE WITH MR. YAGAMI, AND THE MAN WHO MADE THE EXCHANGE. THAT ALREADY MAKES HIM A CRIMINAL.
THAT MEANS THAT I HAVE TO CAPTURE MELLO TO GET THE NOTEBOOK. BUT TO MELLO, GETTING CAUGHT BY ME MEANS LOSING.
THEN WHY DID HE KILL THE SPK MEMBERS, BUT SPARE DEPUTY DIRECTOR YAGAMI AND HIS DAUGHTER, WHO COULD POTENTIALLY GIVE YOU MORE INFORMATION?
...
...
FIRST OF ALL, LIKE ME, HE FEELS THAT THE JAPANESE POLICE ARE IMPOTENT.
SO IT WOULD BE BETTER FOR MELLO TO LEAVE MR. YAGAMI ALIVE, AND TRY TO GET INFORMATION OUT OF HIM IN EXCHANGE FOR SPARING HIS DAUGHTER.
HE WAS DOING EXACTLY THAT, JUST A MINUTE AGO...

READ THIS WAY

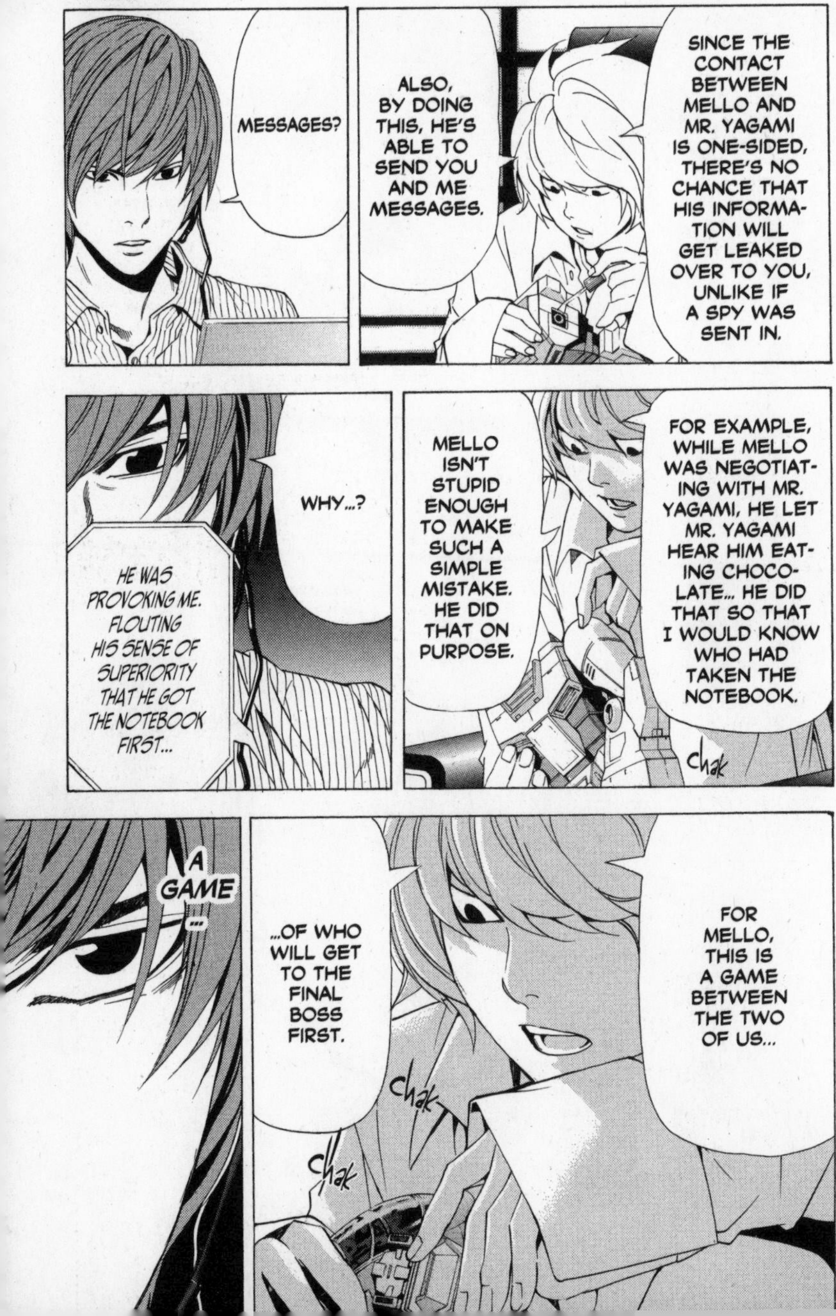
SINCE THE CONTACT BETWEEN MELLO AND MR. YAGAMI IS ONE-SIDED, THERE'S NO CHANCE THAT HIS INFORMATION WILL GET LEAKED OVER TO YOU, UNLIKE IF A SPY WAS SENT IN.
ALSO, BY DOING THIS, HE'S ABLE TO SEND YOU AND ME MESSAGES.
MESSAGES?
FOR EXAMPLE, WHILE MELLO WAS NEGOTIATING WITH MR. YAGAMI, HE LET MR. YAGAMI HEAR HIM EATING CHOCOLATE... HE DID THAT SO THAT I WOULD KNOW WHO HAD TAKEN THE NOTEBOOK.
MELLO ISN'T STUPID ENOUGH TO MAKE SUCH A SIMPLE MISTAKE. HE DID THAT ON PURPOSE.
Chak
WHY...?
HE WAS PROVOKING ME. FLOUTING HIS SENSE OF SUPERIORITY THAT HE GOT THE NOTEBOOK FIRST...
FOR MELLO, THIS IS A GAME BETWEEN THE TWO OF US...
...OF WHO WILL GET TO THE FINAL BOSS FIRST.
Chak
Chak
A GAME ...

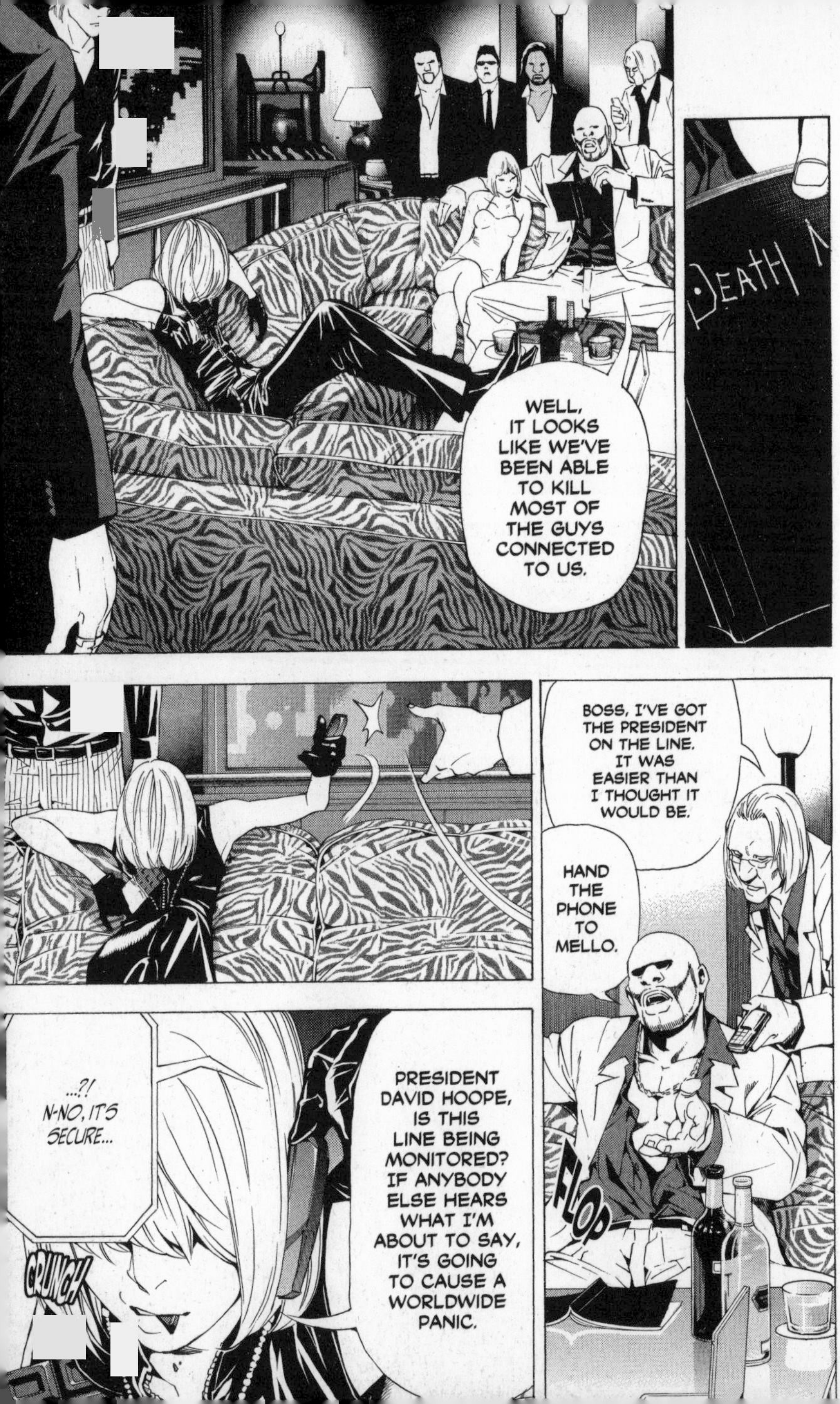
DEATH
WELL, IT LOOKS LIKE WE'VE BEEN ABLE TO KILL MOST OF THE GUYS CONNECTED TO US.
BOSS, I'VE GOT THE PRESIDENT ON THE LINE. IT WAS EASIER THAN I THOUGHT IT WOULD BE.
HAND THE PHONE TO MELLO.
FLOP
PRESIDENT DAVID HOOPE, IS THIS LINE BEING MONITORED? IF ANYBODY ELSE HEARS WHAT I'M ABOUT TO SAY, IT'S GOING TO CAUSE A WORLDWIDE PANIC.
...?! N-NO, IT'S SECURE...
CRUNCH

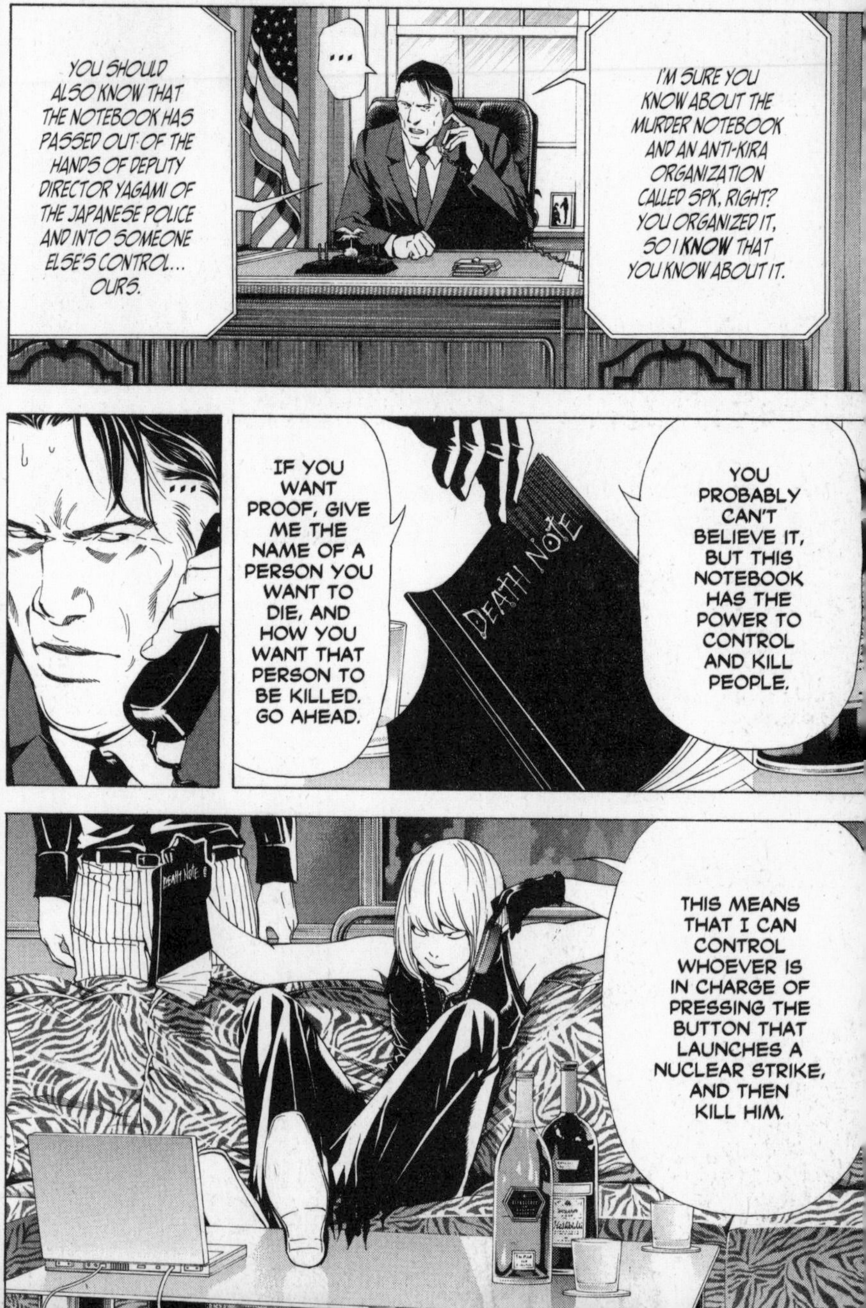
I'M SURE YOU KNOW ABOUT THE MURDER NOTEBOOK AND AN ANTI-KIRA ORGANIZATION CALLED SPK, RIGHT? YOU ORGANIZED IT, SO I **KNOW** THAT YOU KNOW ABOUT IT.
...
YOU SHOULD ALSO KNOW THAT THE NOTEBOOK HAS PASSED OUT OF THE HANDS OF DEPUTY DIRECTOR YAGAMI OF THE JAPANESE POLICE AND INTO SOMEONE ELSE'S CONTROL... OURS.
YOU PROBABLY CAN'T BELIEVE IT, BUT THIS NOTEBOOK HAS THE POWER TO CONTROL AND KILL PEOPLE.
DEATH NOTE
IF YOU WANT PROOF, GIVE ME THE NAME OF A PERSON YOU WANT TO DIE, AND HOW YOU WANT THAT PERSON TO BE KILLED. GO AHEAD.
...
THIS MEANS THAT I CAN CONTROL WHOEVER IS IN CHARGE OF PRESSING THE BUTTON THAT LAUNCHES A NUCLEAR STRIKE, AND THEN KILL HIM.

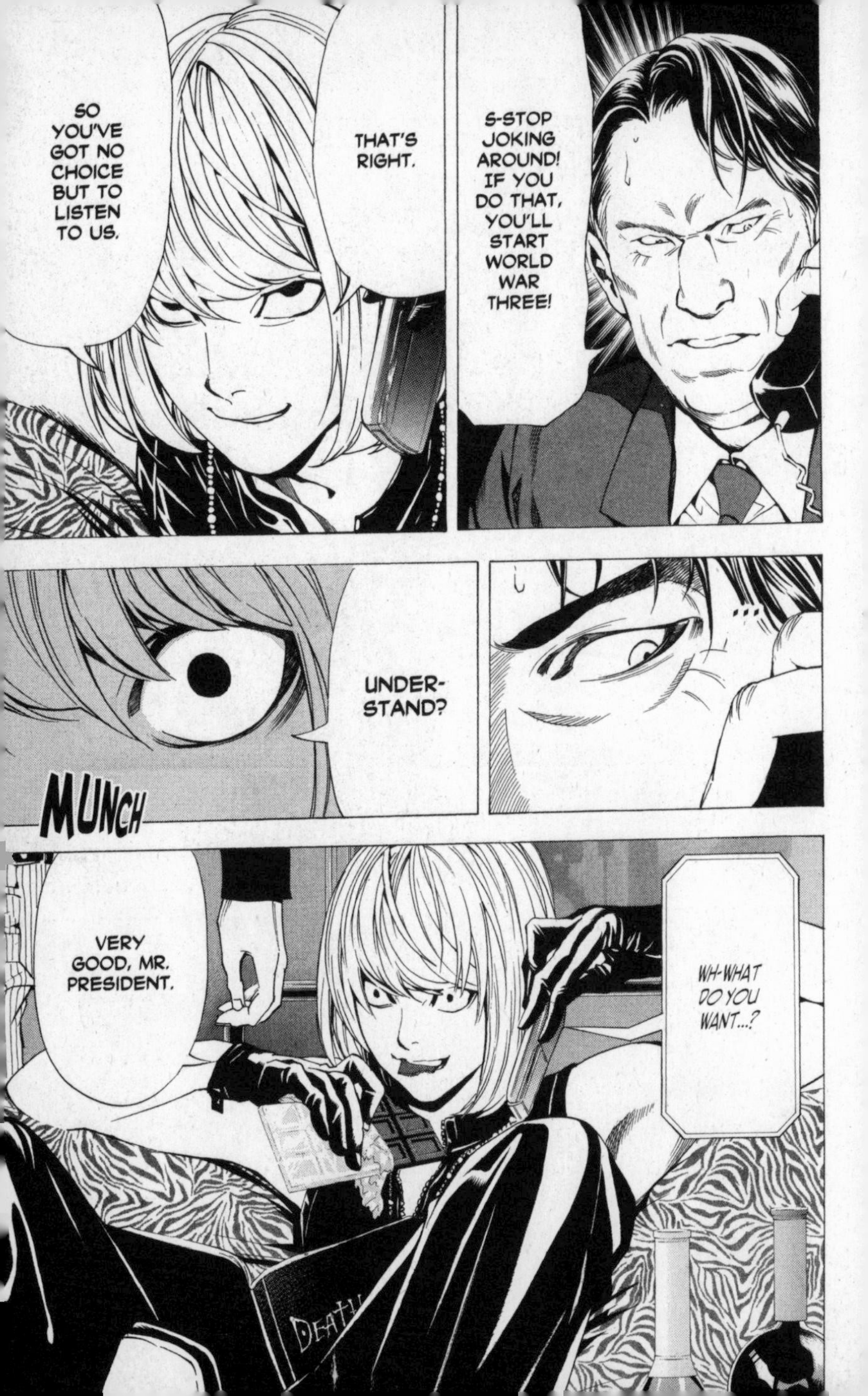
S-STOP JOKING AROUND! IF YOU DO THAT, YOU'LL START WORLD WAR THREE!
THAT'S RIGHT.
SO YOU'VE GOT NO CHOICE BUT TO LISTEN TO US.
...
UNDER-STAND?
MUNCH
WH-WHAT DO YOU WANT...?
VERY GOOD, MR. PRESIDENT.

DEATH NOTE
How to use it
XLV

- As long as the god of death has at least once seen a human and knows his/her name and life-span, the god of death is capable of finding that human from a hole in the world of the gods of death.

死神は、一度でも顔を見て名前と寿命がわかっている人間ならば、死神界の穴からその人間の居場所を知る事ができる。

chapter 68 Discovery

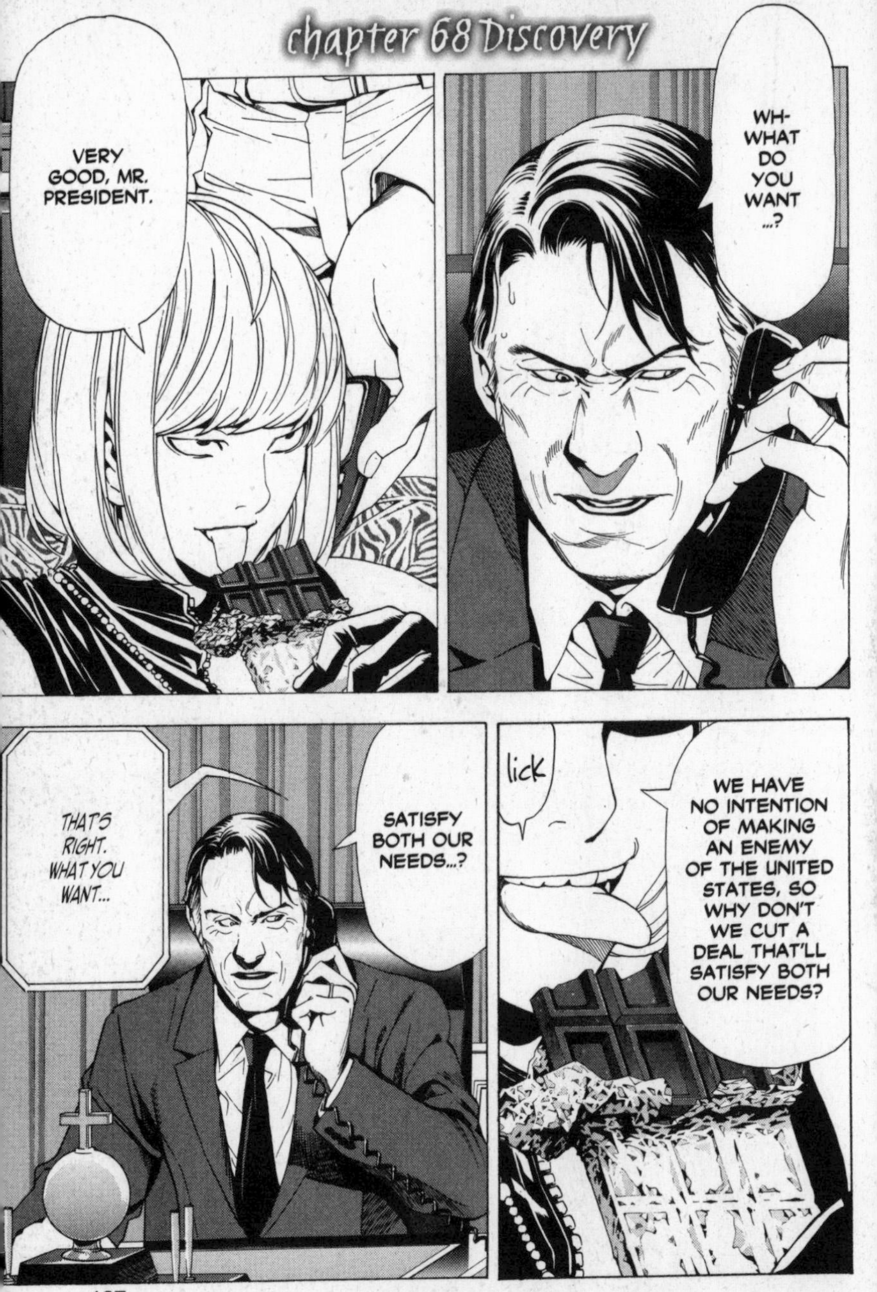
WH- WHAT DO YOU WANT ...?
VERY GOOD, MR. PRESIDENT.
WE HAVE NO INTENTION OF MAKING AN ENEMY OF THE UNITED STATES, SO WHY DON'T WE CUT A DEAL THAT'LL SATISFY BOTH OUR NEEDS?
lick
SATISFY BOTH OUR NEEDS...?
THAT'S RIGHT. WHAT YOU WANT...

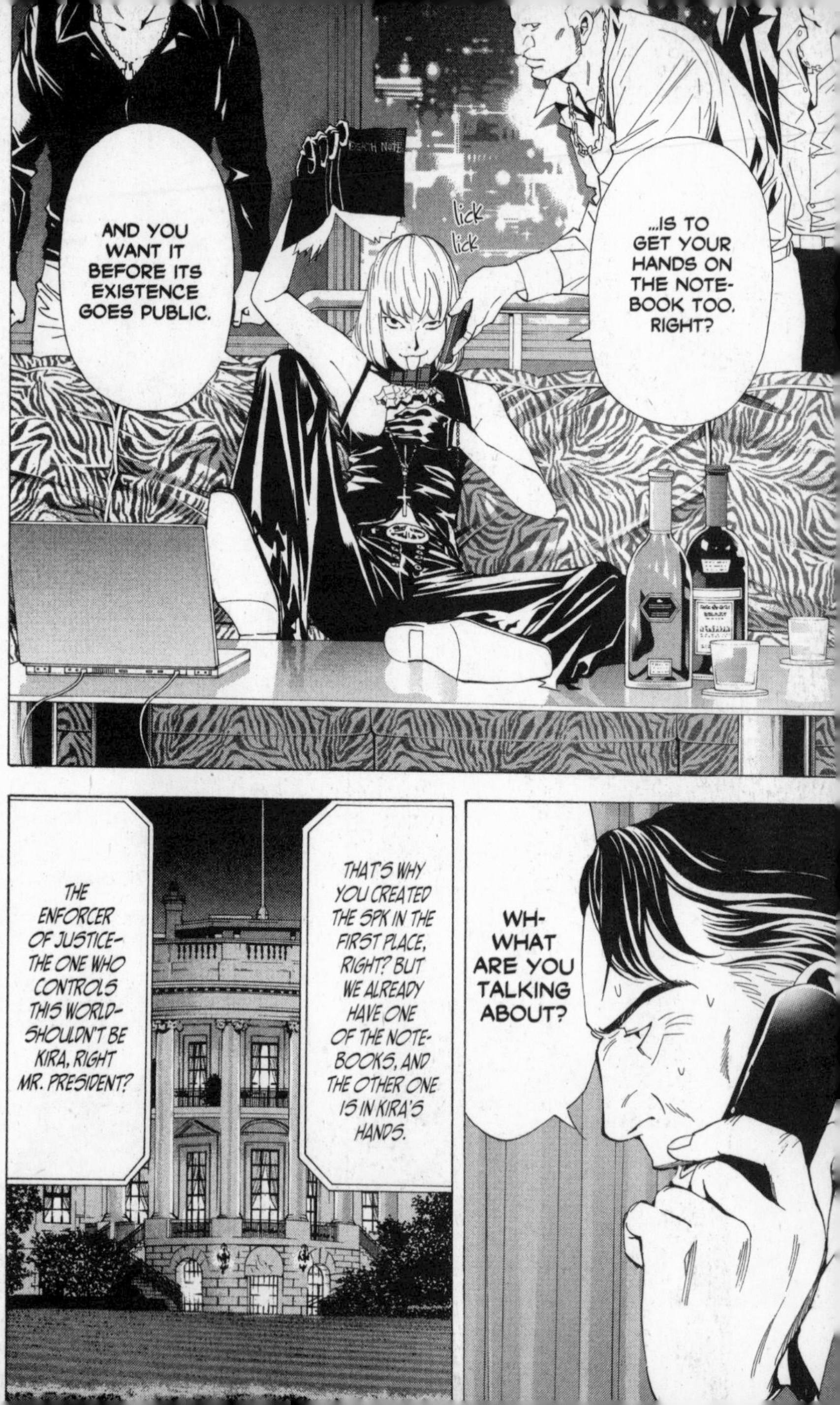
...IS TO GET YOUR HANDS ON THE NOTE-BOOK TOO, RIGHT?
DEATH NOTE
lick lick
AND YOU WANT IT BEFORE ITS EXISTENCE GOES PUBLIC.
WH-WHAT ARE YOU TALKING ABOUT?
THAT'S WHY YOU CREATED THE SPK IN THE FIRST PLACE, RIGHT? BUT WE ALREADY HAVE ONE OF THE NOTE-BOOKS, AND THE OTHER ONE IS IN KIRA'S HANDS.
THE ENFORCER OF JUSTICE-THE ONE WHO CONTROLS THIS WORLD-SHOULDN'T BE KIRA, RIGHT MR. PRESIDENT?

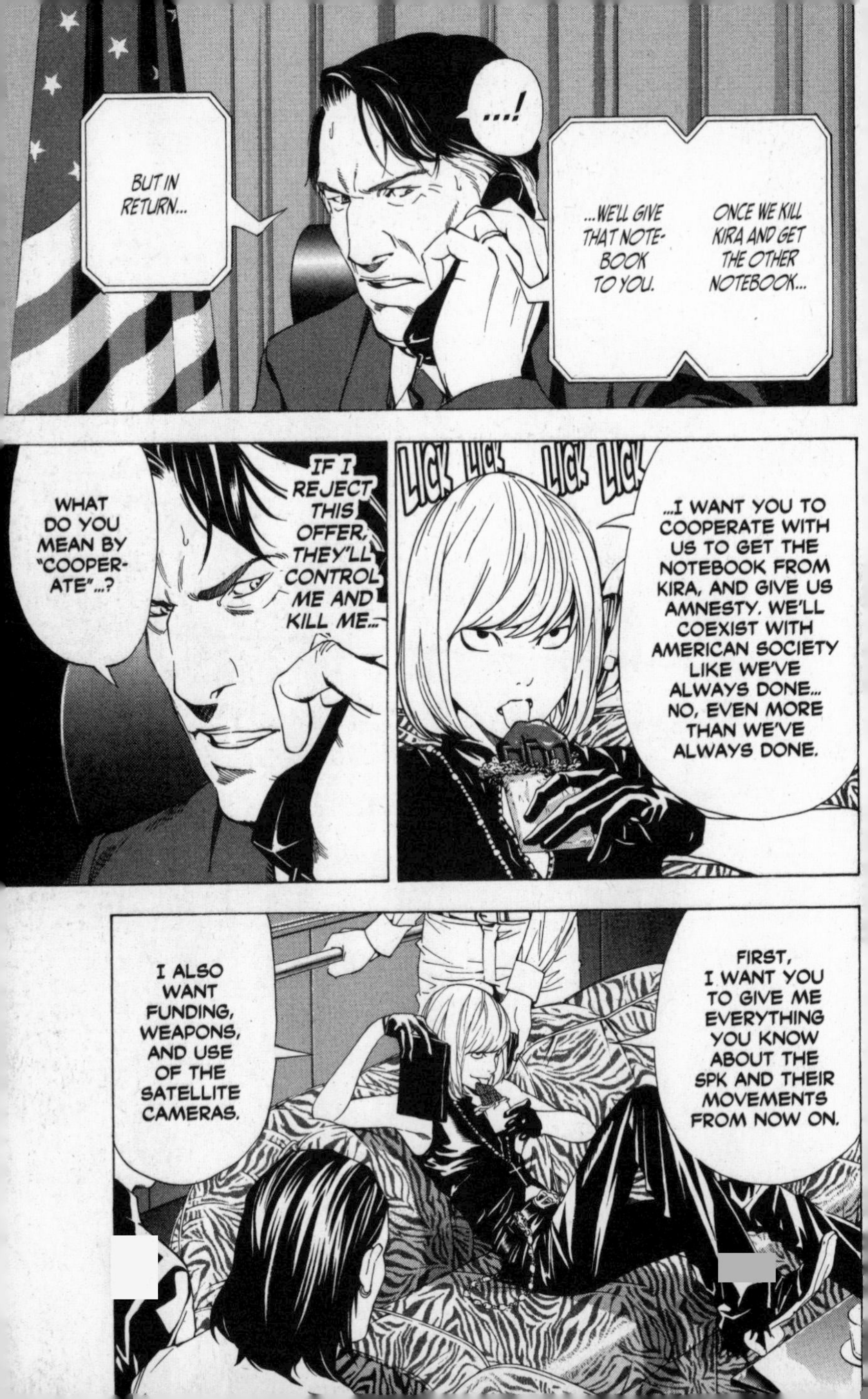
ONCE WE KILL KIRA AND GET THE OTHER NOTEBOOK...
...WE'LL GIVE THAT NOTE-BOOK TO YOU.
...!
BUT IN RETURN...
LICK LICK LICK LICK
...I WANT YOU TO COOPERATE WITH US TO GET THE NOTEBOOK FROM KIRA, AND GIVE US AMNESTY. WE'LL COEXIST WITH AMERICAN SOCIETY LIKE WE'VE ALWAYS DONE... NO, EVEN MORE THAN WE'VE ALWAYS DONE.
IF I REJECT THIS OFFER, THEY'LL CONTROL ME AND KILL ME...
WHAT DO YOU MEAN BY "COOPER-ATE"...?
FIRST, I WANT YOU TO GIVE ME EVERYTHING YOU KNOW ABOUT THE SPK AND THEIR MOVEMENTS FROM NOW ON.
I ALSO WANT FUNDING, WEAPONS, AND USE OF THE SATELLITE CAMERAS.

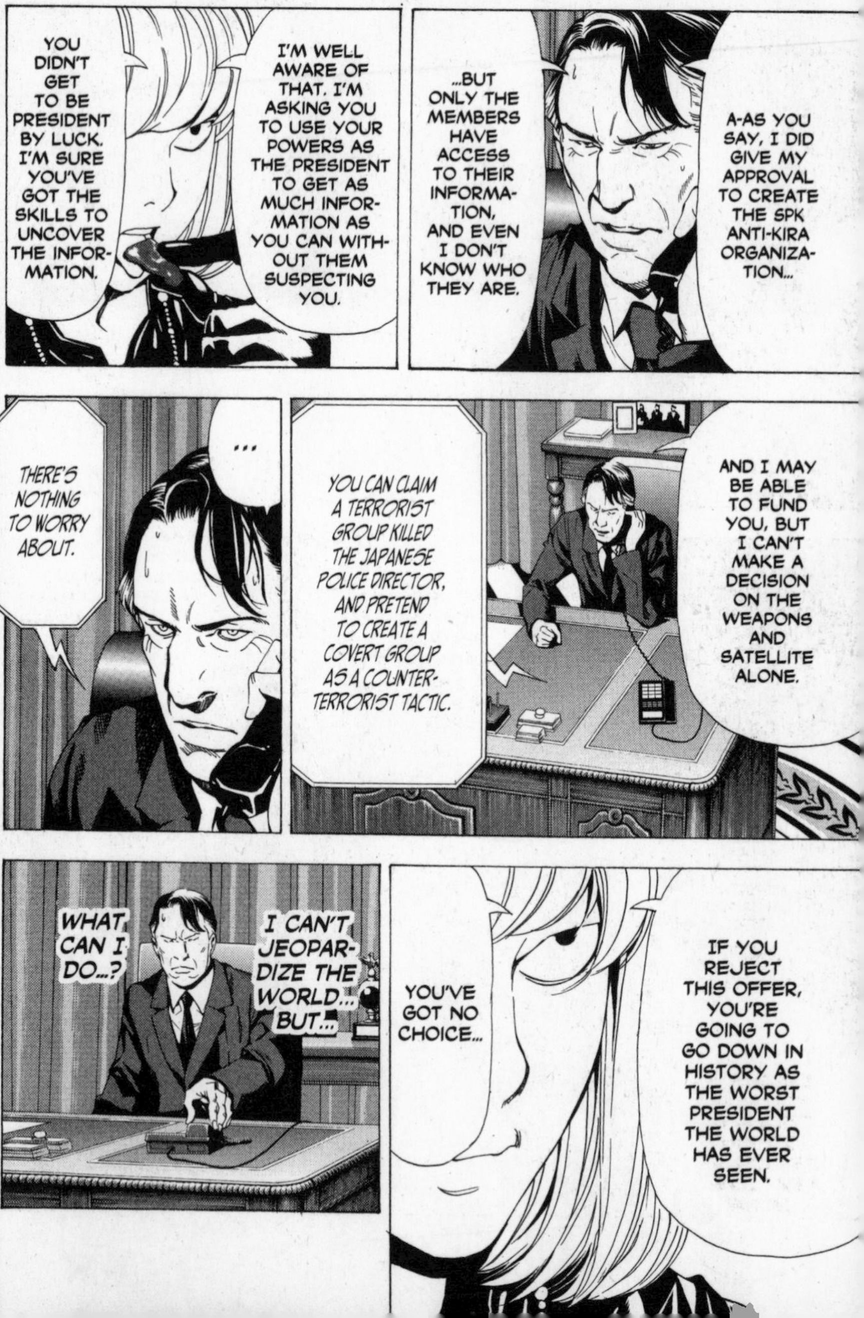
A-AS YOU SAY, I DID GIVE MY APPROVAL TO CREATE THE SPK ANTI-KIRA ORGANIZATION...
...BUT ONLY THE MEMBERS HAVE ACCESS TO THEIR INFORMATION, AND EVEN I DON'T KNOW WHO THEY ARE.
I'M WELL AWARE OF THAT. I'M ASKING YOU TO USE YOUR POWERS AS THE PRESIDENT TO GET AS MUCH INFORMATION AS YOU CAN WITHOUT THEM SUSPECTING YOU.
YOU DIDN'T GET TO BE PRESIDENT BY LUCK. I'M SURE YOU'VE GOT THE SKILLS TO UNCOVER THE INFORMATION.
AND I MAY BE ABLE TO FUND YOU, BUT I CAN'T MAKE A DECISION ON THE WEAPONS AND SATELLITE ALONE.
YOU CAN CLAIM A TERRORIST GROUP KILLED THE JAPANESE POLICE DIRECTOR, AND PRETEND TO CREATE A COVERT GROUP AS A COUNTER-TERRORIST TACTIC.
...
THERE'S NOTHING TO WORRY ABOUT.
IF YOU REJECT THIS OFFER, YOU'RE GOING TO GO DOWN IN HISTORY AS THE WORST PRESIDENT THE WORLD HAS EVER SEEN.
YOU'VE GOT NO CHOICE...
I CAN'T JEOPARDIZE THE WORLD... BUT...
WHAT CAN I DO...?

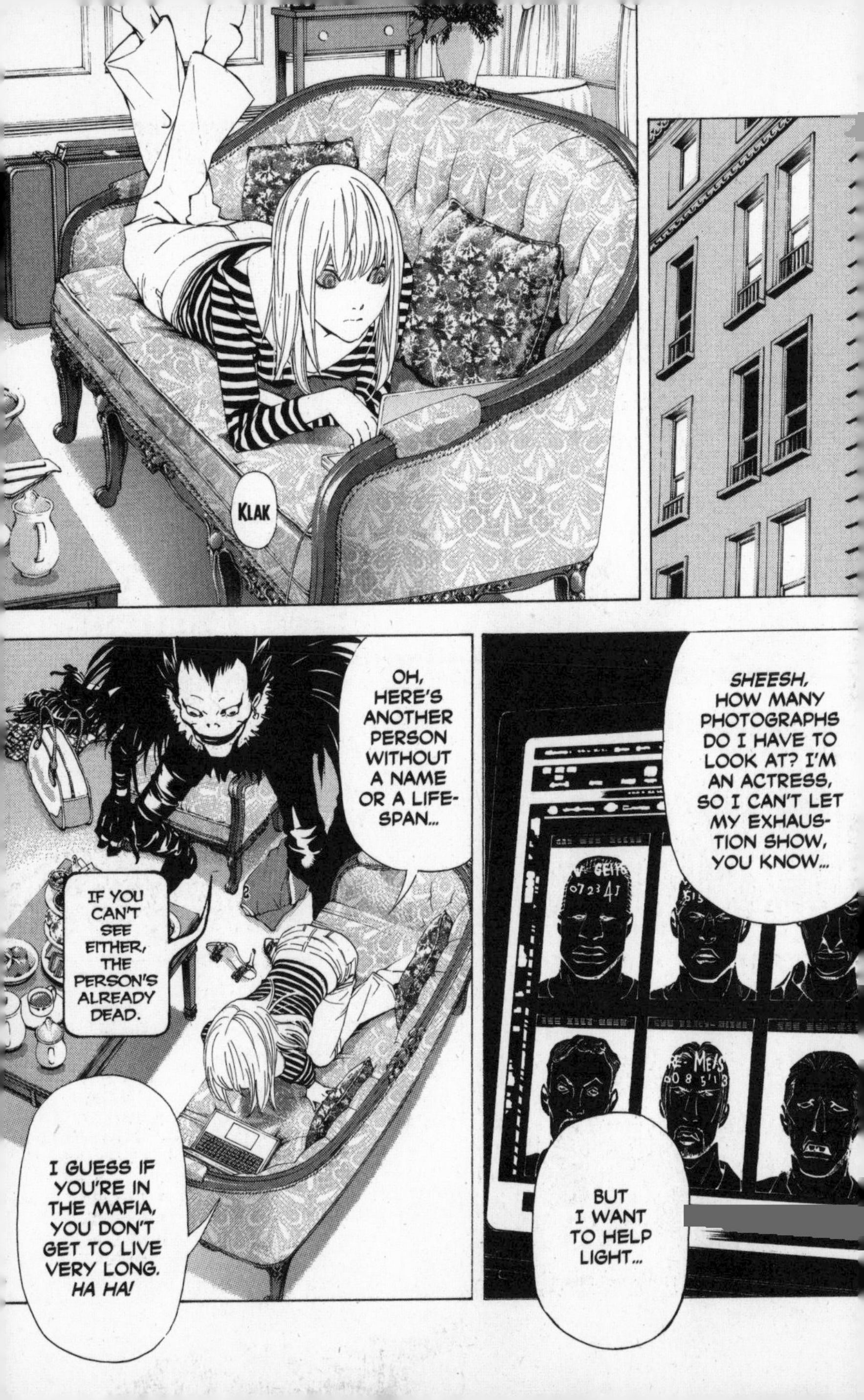
KLAK
SHEESH, HOW MANY PHOTOGRAPHS DO I HAVE TO LOOK AT? I'M AN ACTRESS, SO I CAN'T LET MY EXHAUSTION SHOW, YOU KNOW...
BUT I WANT TO HELP LIGHT...
OH, HERE'S ANOTHER PERSON WITHOUT A NAME OR A LIFE-SPAN...
IF YOU CAN'T SEE EITHER, THE PERSON'S ALREADY DEAD.
I GUESS IF YOU'RE IN THE MAFIA, YOU DON'T GET TO LIVE VERY LONG. *HA HA!*

BUT IF THEY CATCH THE KIDNAPPERS FIRST, THEN THE UNITED STATES WILL HAVE POSSESSION OF THE NOTEBOOK.

AS LONG AS THEY'RE CAUGHT, DOES IT MATTER WHO GETS THEM—THE SPK OR US?

NEAR SAID THAT THEY'VE NARROWED DOWN THE WHEREABOUTS OF THE KIDNAPPERS...

I MUST PROTECT THE PEACE OF THE NEW WORLD THAT IS BEGINNING TO BLOOM.

BUT I HAVE TO GET RID OF NEAR AND MELLO, WHATEVER IT TAKES.

AND IF THE UNITED STATES POLICE GIVE N'S ORDERS PRIORITY OVER L'S...

DAMN IT... WE HAVEN'T BEEN ABLE TO FIND OUT ANYTHING OTHER THAN THE FACT THAT MELLO EXISTS. IF NEAR REALLY IS GETTING CLOSE TO CATCHING THE KIDNAPPERS...

142

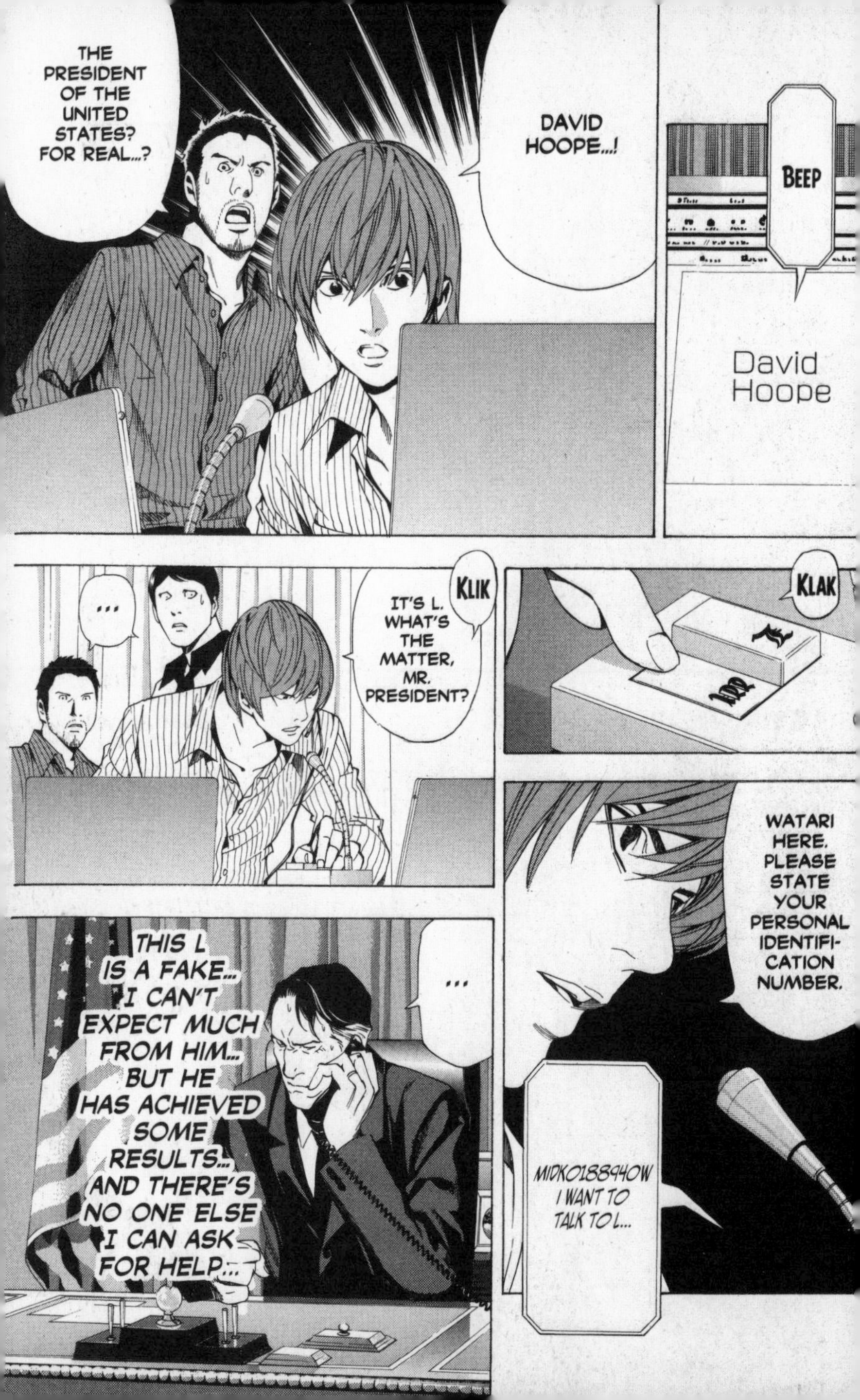
BEEP
David Hoope
DAVID HOOPE...!
THE PRESIDENT OF THE UNITED STATES? FOR REAL...?
KLAK
KLIK
IT'S L. WHAT'S THE MATTER, MR. PRESIDENT?
...
WATARI HERE. PLEASE STATE YOUR PERSONAL IDENTIFI-CATION NUMBER.
MIDKO188940W I WANT TO TALK TO L...
...
THIS L IS A FAKE... I CAN'T EXPECT MUCH FROM HIM... BUT HE HAS ACHIEVED SOME RESULTS... AND THERE'S NO ONE ELSE I CAN ASK FOR HELP...

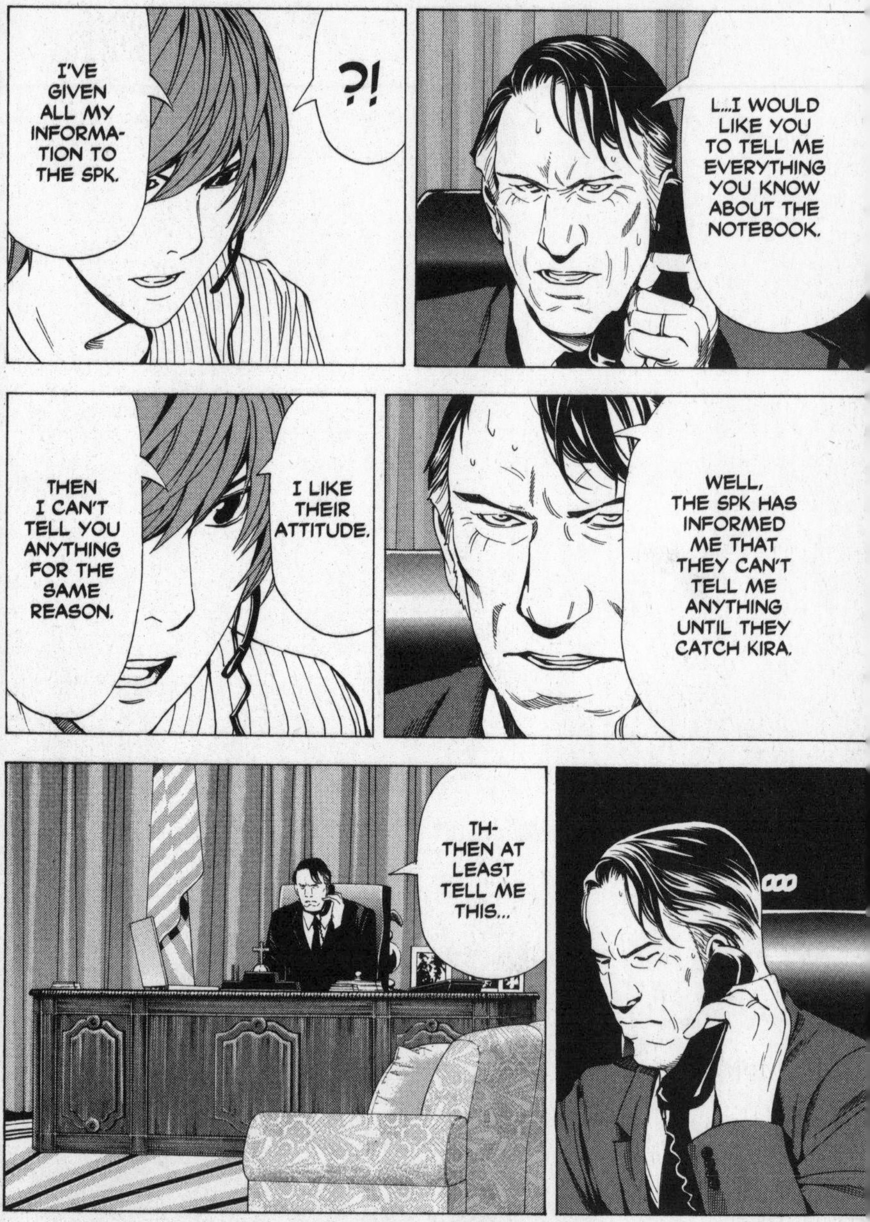
L...I WOULD LIKE YOU TO TELL ME EVERYTHING YOU KNOW ABOUT THE NOTEBOOK.
?!
I'VE GIVEN ALL MY INFORMATION TO THE SPK.
WELL, THE SPK HAS INFORMED ME THAT THEY CAN'T TELL ME ANYTHING UNTIL THEY CATCH KIRA.
I LIKE THEIR ATTITUDE.
THEN I CAN'T TELL YOU ANYTHING FOR THE SAME REASON.
TH- THEN AT LEAST TELL ME THIS...

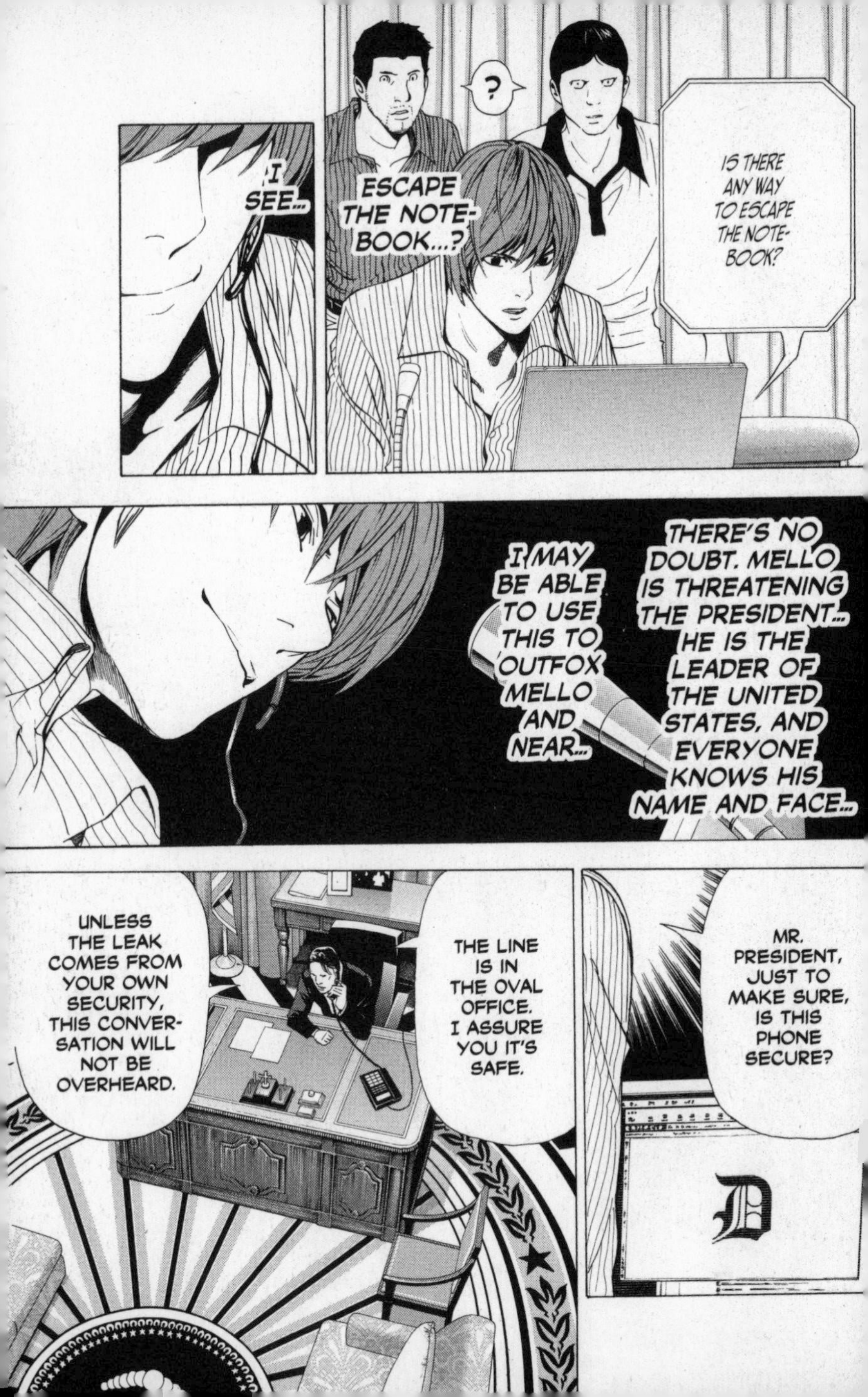
IS THERE ANY WAY TO ESCAPE THE NOTEBOOK?
?
ESCAPE THE NOTEBOOK...?
I SEE...
THERE'S NO DOUBT. MELLO IS THREATENING THE PRESIDENT... HE IS THE LEADER OF THE UNITED STATES, AND EVERYONE KNOWS HIS NAME AND FACE...
I MAY BE ABLE TO USE THIS TO OUTFOX MELLO AND NEAR...
MR. PRESIDENT, JUST TO MAKE SURE, IS THIS PHONE SECURE?
THE LINE IS IN THE OVAL OFFICE. I ASSURE YOU IT'S SAFE.
UNLESS THE LEAK COMES FROM YOUR OWN SECURITY, THIS CONVERSATION WILL NOT BE OVERHEARD.

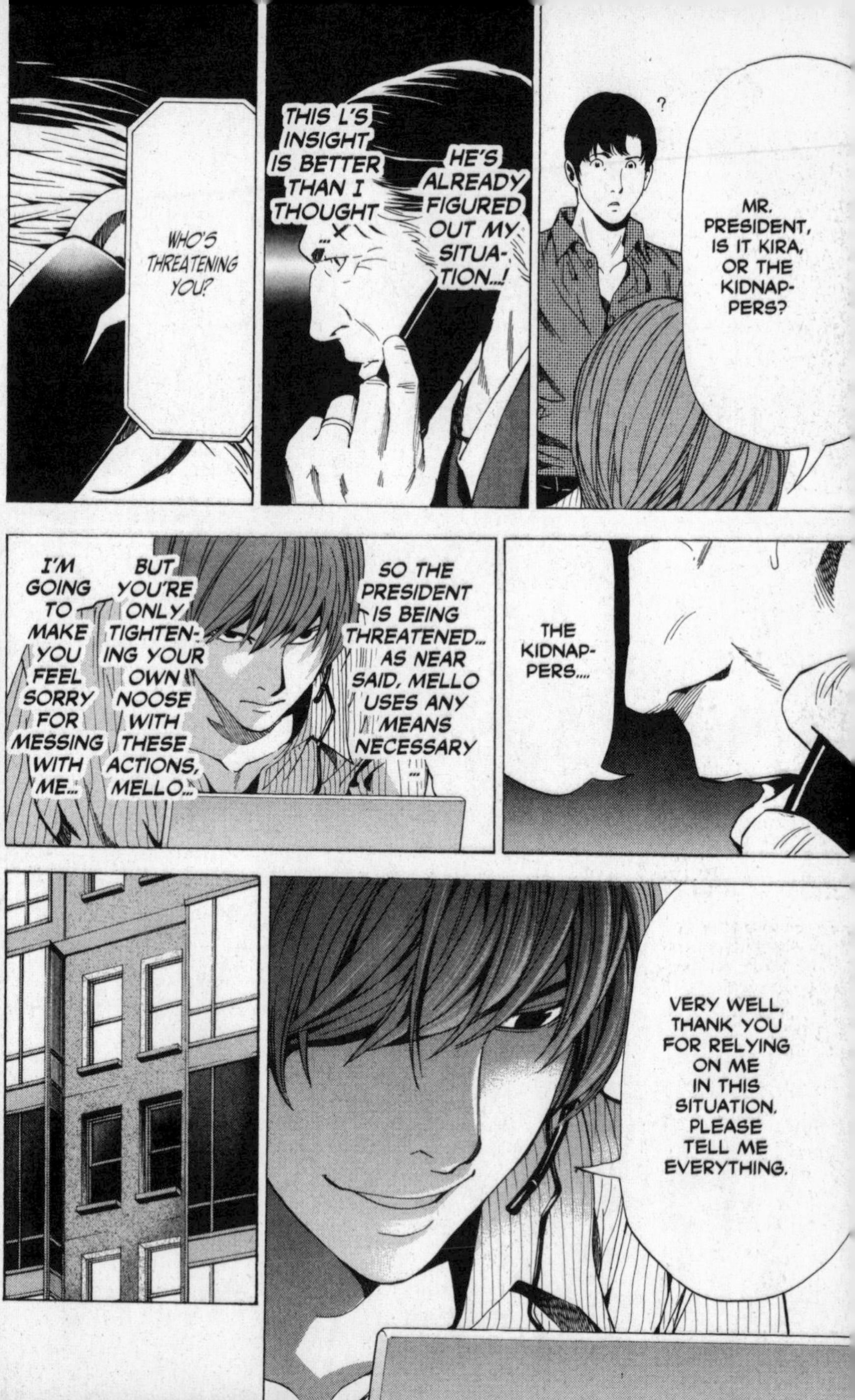
?
MR. PRESIDENT, IS IT KIRA, OR THE KIDNAPPERS?
THIS L'S INSIGHT IS BETTER THAN I THOUGHT...
HE'S ALREADY FIGURED OUT MY SITUATION...!
WHO'S THREATENING YOU?
THE KIDNAPPERS....
SO THE PRESIDENT IS BEING THREATENED... AS NEAR SAID, MELLO USES ANY MEANS NECESSARY...
BUT YOU'RE ONLY TIGHTENING YOUR OWN NOOSE WITH THESE ACTIONS, MELLO...
I'M GOING TO MAKE YOU FEEL SORRY FOR MESSING WITH ME...
VERY WELL. THANK YOU FOR RELYING ON ME IN THIS SITUATION. PLEASE TELL ME EVERYTHING.

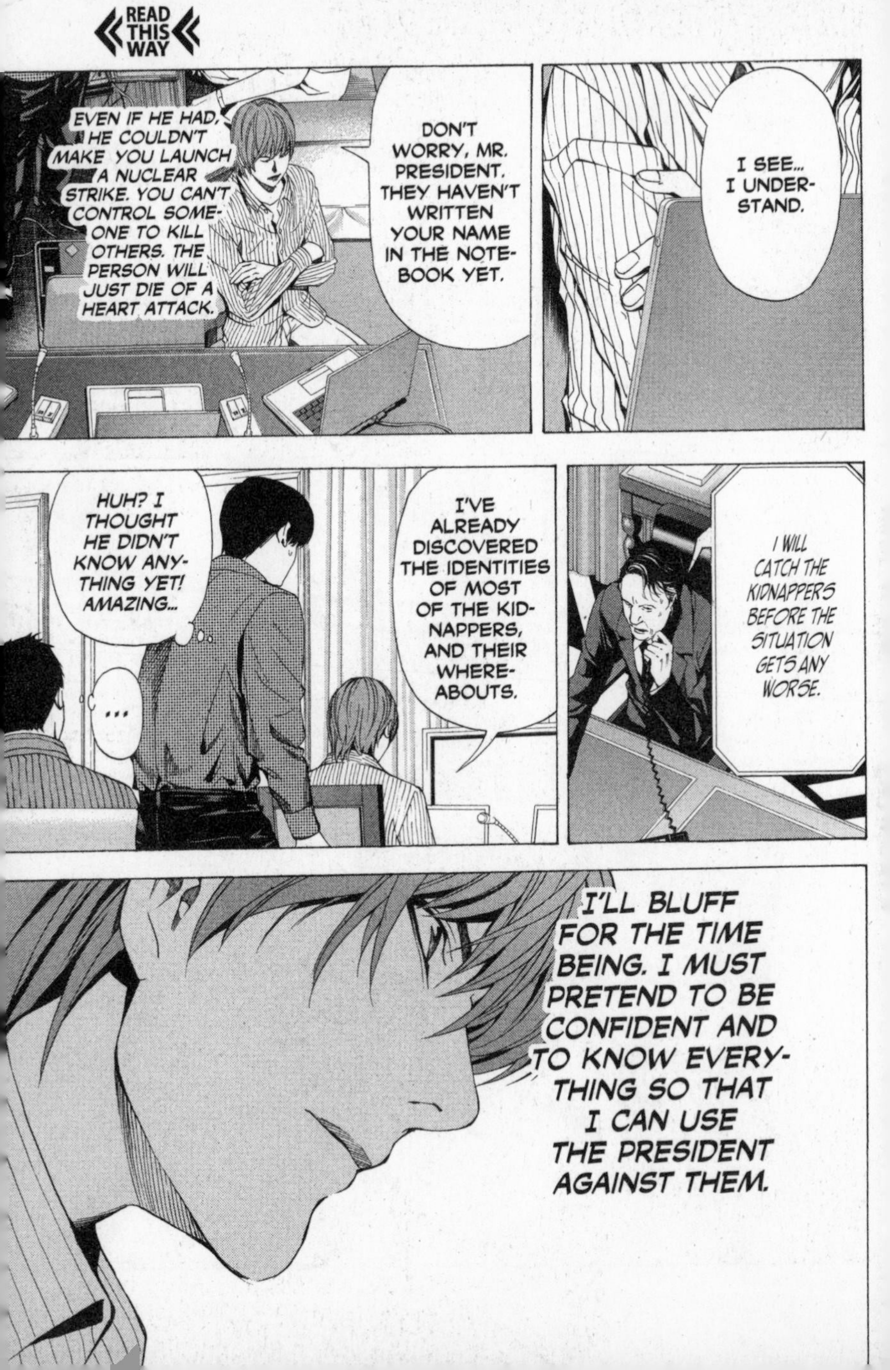
READ THIS WAY
I SEE... I UNDERSTAND.
DON'T WORRY, MR. PRESIDENT. THEY HAVEN'T WRITTEN YOUR NAME IN THE NOTEBOOK YET.
EVEN IF HE HAD, HE COULDN'T MAKE YOU LAUNCH A NUCLEAR STRIKE. YOU CAN'T CONTROL SOMEONE TO KILL OTHERS. THE PERSON WILL JUST DIE OF A HEART ATTACK.
I WILL CATCH THE KIDNAPPERS BEFORE THE SITUATION GETS ANY WORSE.
I'VE ALREADY DISCOVERED THE IDENTITIES OF MOST OF THE KIDNAPPERS, AND THEIR WHEREABOUTS.
HUH? I THOUGHT HE DIDN'T KNOW ANYTHING YET! AMAZING...
...
I'LL BLUFF FOR THE TIME BEING. I MUST PRETEND TO BE CONFIDENT AND TO KNOW EVERYTHING SO THAT I CAN USE THE PRESIDENT AGAINST THEM.

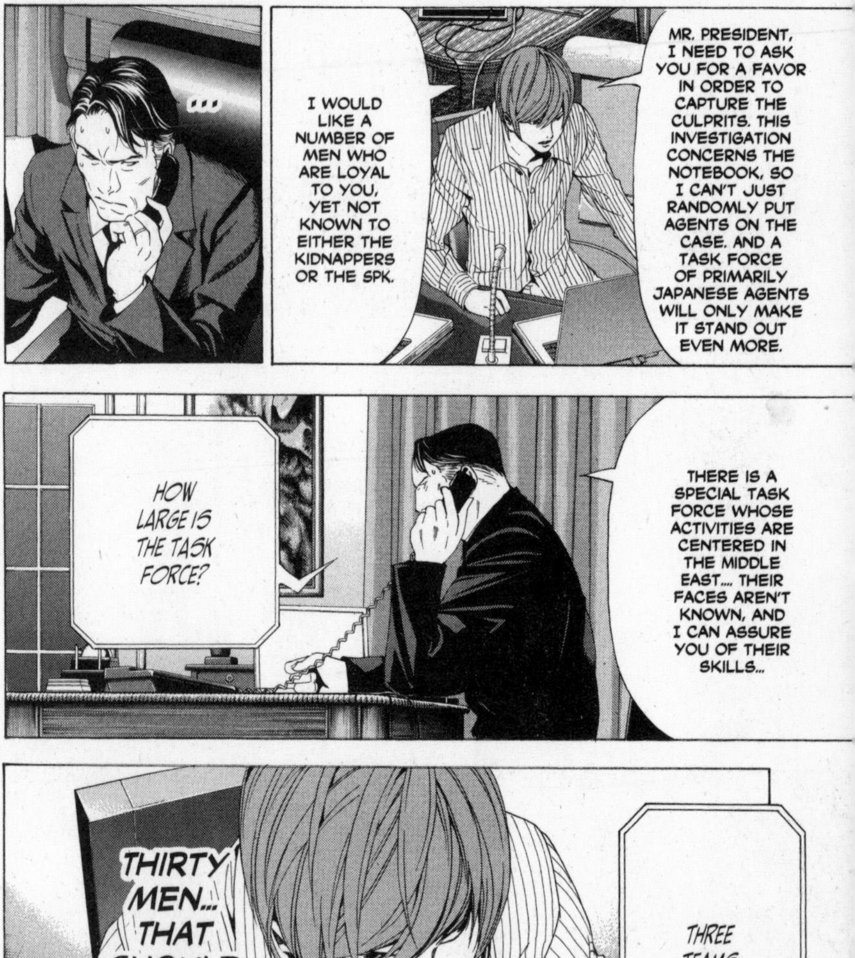
MR. PRESIDENT, I NEED TO ASK YOU FOR A FAVOR IN ORDER TO CAPTURE THE CULPRITS. THIS INVESTIGATION CONCERNS THE NOTEBOOK, SO I CAN'T JUST RANDOMLY PUT AGENTS ON THE CASE. AND A TASK FORCE OF PRIMARILY JAPANESE AGENTS WILL ONLY MAKE IT STAND OUT EVEN MORE.
I WOULD LIKE A NUMBER OF MEN WHO ARE LOYAL TO YOU, YET NOT KNOWN TO EITHER THE KIDNAPPERS OR THE SPK.
...
THERE IS A SPECIAL TASK FORCE WHOSE ACTIVITIES ARE CENTERED IN THE MIDDLE EAST.... THEIR FACES AREN'T KNOWN, AND I CAN ASSURE YOU OF THEIR SKILLS...
HOW LARGE IS THE TASK FORCE?
THREE TEAMS OF 10.
THIRTY MEN... THAT SHOULD BE ENOUGH.

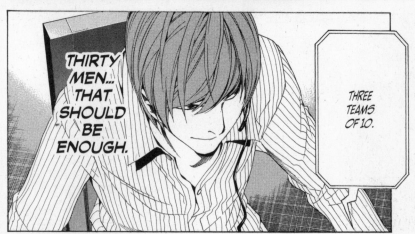

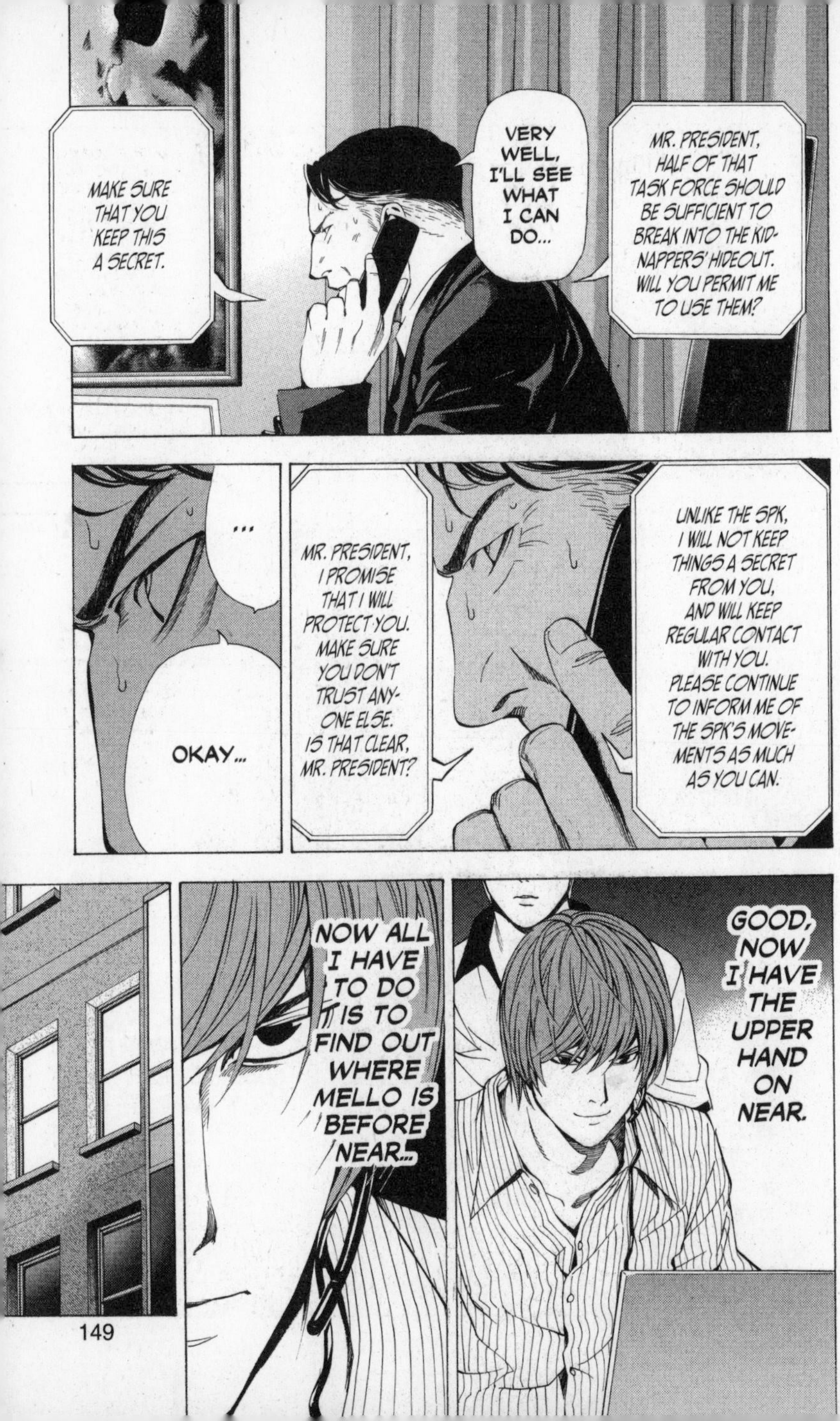
MR. PRESIDENT, HALF OF THAT TASK FORCE SHOULD BE SUFFICIENT TO BREAK INTO THE KID-NAPPERS' HIDEOUT. WILL YOU PERMIT ME TO USE THEM?
VERY WELL, I'LL SEE WHAT I CAN DO...
MAKE SURE THAT YOU KEEP THIS A SECRET.
UNLIKE THE SPK, I WILL NOT KEEP THINGS A SECRET FROM YOU, AND WILL KEEP REGULAR CONTACT WITH YOU. PLEASE CONTINUE TO INFORM ME OF THE SPK'S MOVE-MENTS AS MUCH AS YOU CAN.
MR. PRESIDENT, I PROMISE THAT I WILL PROTECT YOU. MAKE SURE YOU DON'T TRUST ANY-ONE ELSE. IS THAT CLEAR, MR. PRESIDENT?
...
OKAY...
GOOD, NOW I HAVE THE UPPER HAND ON NEAR.
NOW ALL I HAVE TO DO IS TO FIND OUT WHERE MELLO IS BEFORE NEAR...

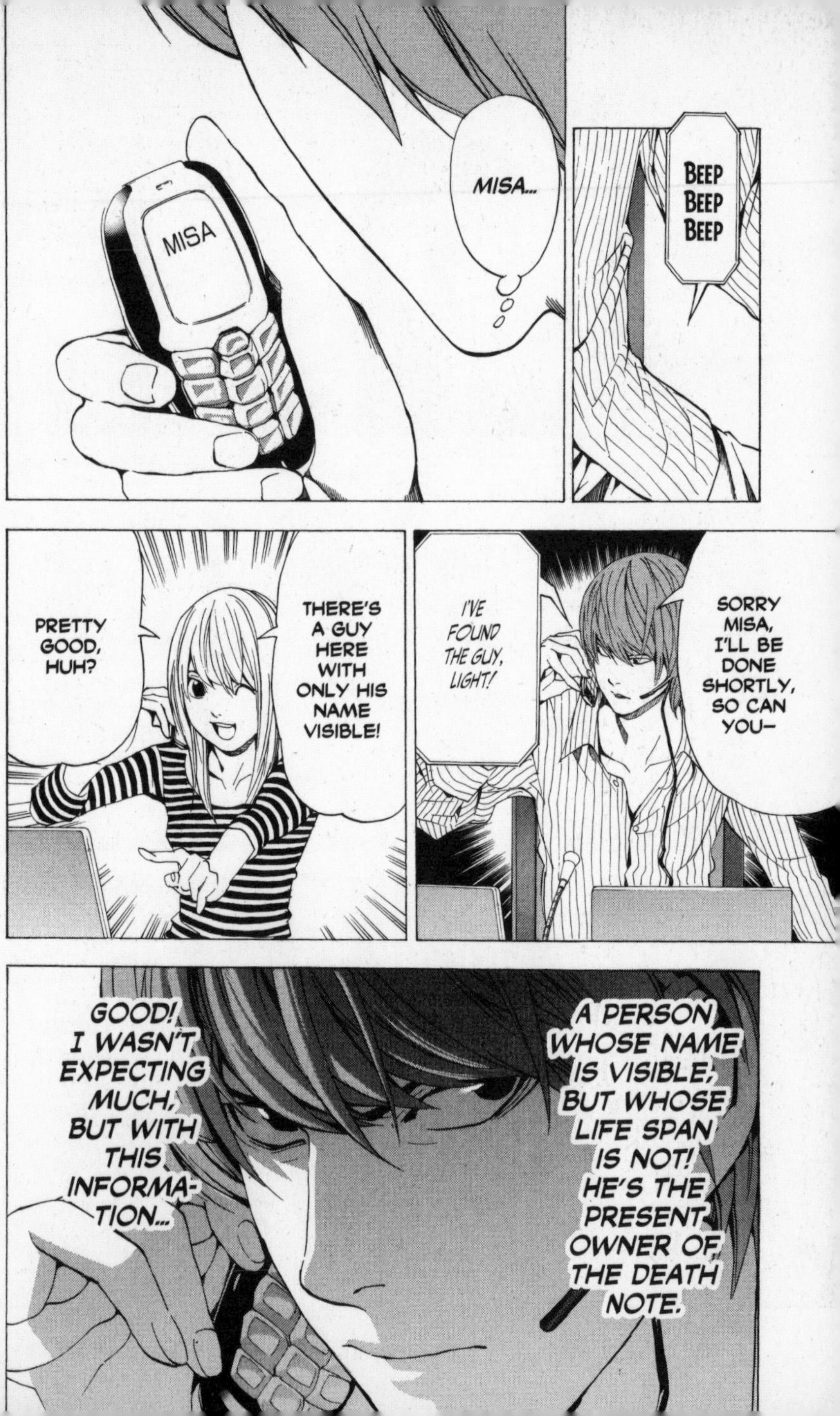
BEEP BEEP BEEP
MISA...
MISA
SORRY MISA, I'LL BE DONE SHORTLY, SO CAN YOU—
I'VE FOUND THE GUY, LIGHT!
THERE'S A GUY HERE WITH ONLY HIS NAME VISIBLE!
PRETTY GOOD, HUH?
A PERSON WHOSE NAME IS VISIBLE, BUT WHOSE LIFE SPAN IS NOT! HE'S THE PRESENT OWNER OF THE DEATH NOTE.
GOOD! I WASN'T EXPECTING MUCH, BUT WITH THIS INFORMATION...

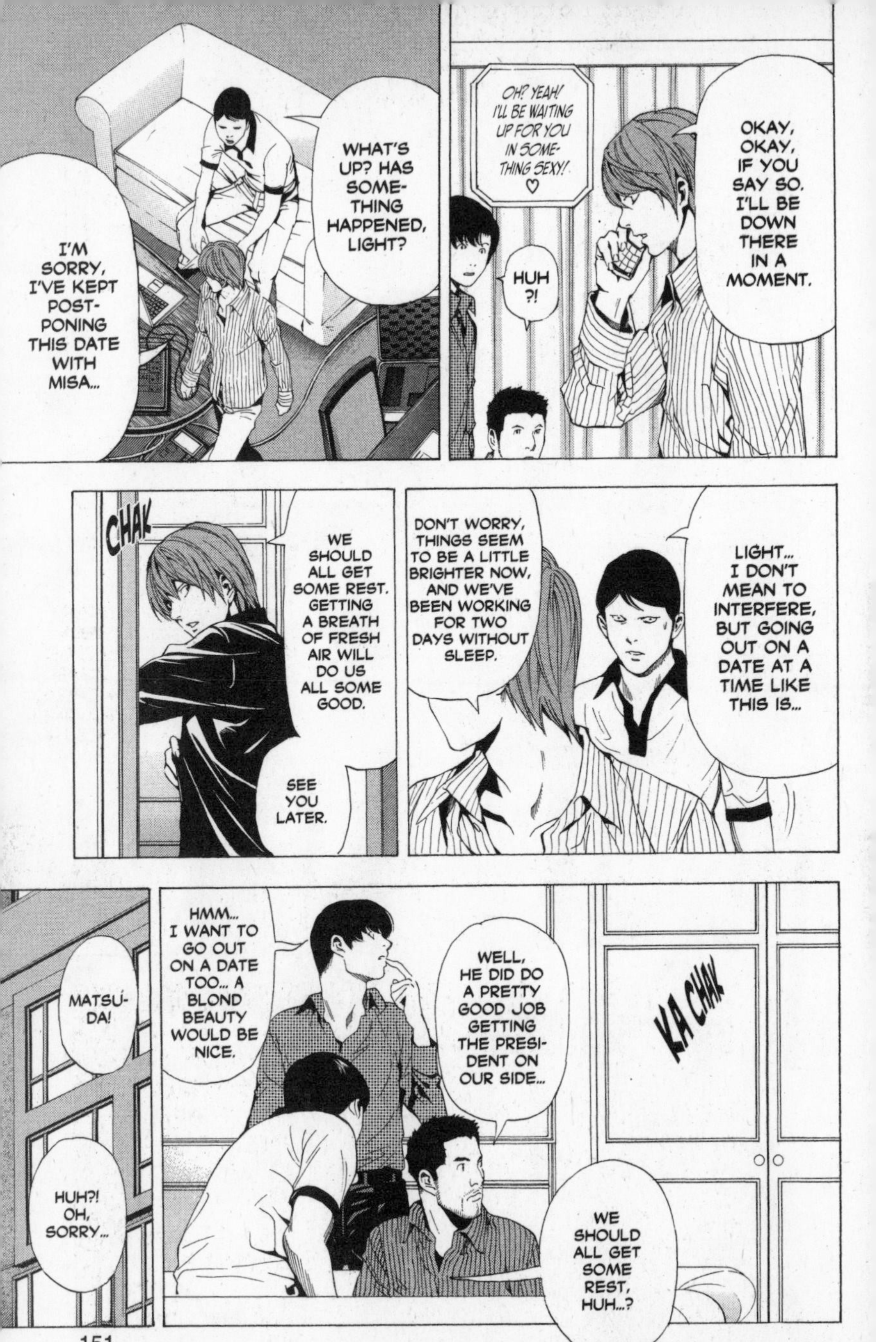
OKAY, OKAY, IF YOU SAY SO. I'LL BE DOWN THERE IN A MOMENT.
OH? YEAH! I'LL BE WAITING UP FOR YOU IN SOMETHING SEXY! ♡
HUH ?!
WHAT'S UP? HAS SOMETHING HAPPENED, LIGHT?
I'M SORRY, I'VE KEPT POSTPONING THIS DATE WITH MISA...
LIGHT... I DON'T MEAN TO INTERFERE, BUT GOING OUT ON A DATE AT A TIME LIKE THIS IS...
DON'T WORRY, THINGS SEEM TO BE A LITTLE BRIGHTER NOW, AND WE'VE BEEN WORKING FOR TWO DAYS WITHOUT SLEEP.
WE SHOULD ALL GET SOME REST. GETTING A BREATH OF FRESH AIR WILL DO US ALL SOME GOOD.
CHAK
SEE YOU LATER.
KA CHAK
WELL, HE DID DO A PRETTY GOOD JOB GETTING THE PRESIDENT ON OUR SIDE...
HMM... I WANT TO GO OUT ON A DATE TOO... A BLOND BEAUTY WOULD BE NICE.
WE SHOULD ALL GET SOME REST, HUH...?
MATSUDA!
HUH?! OH, SORRY...

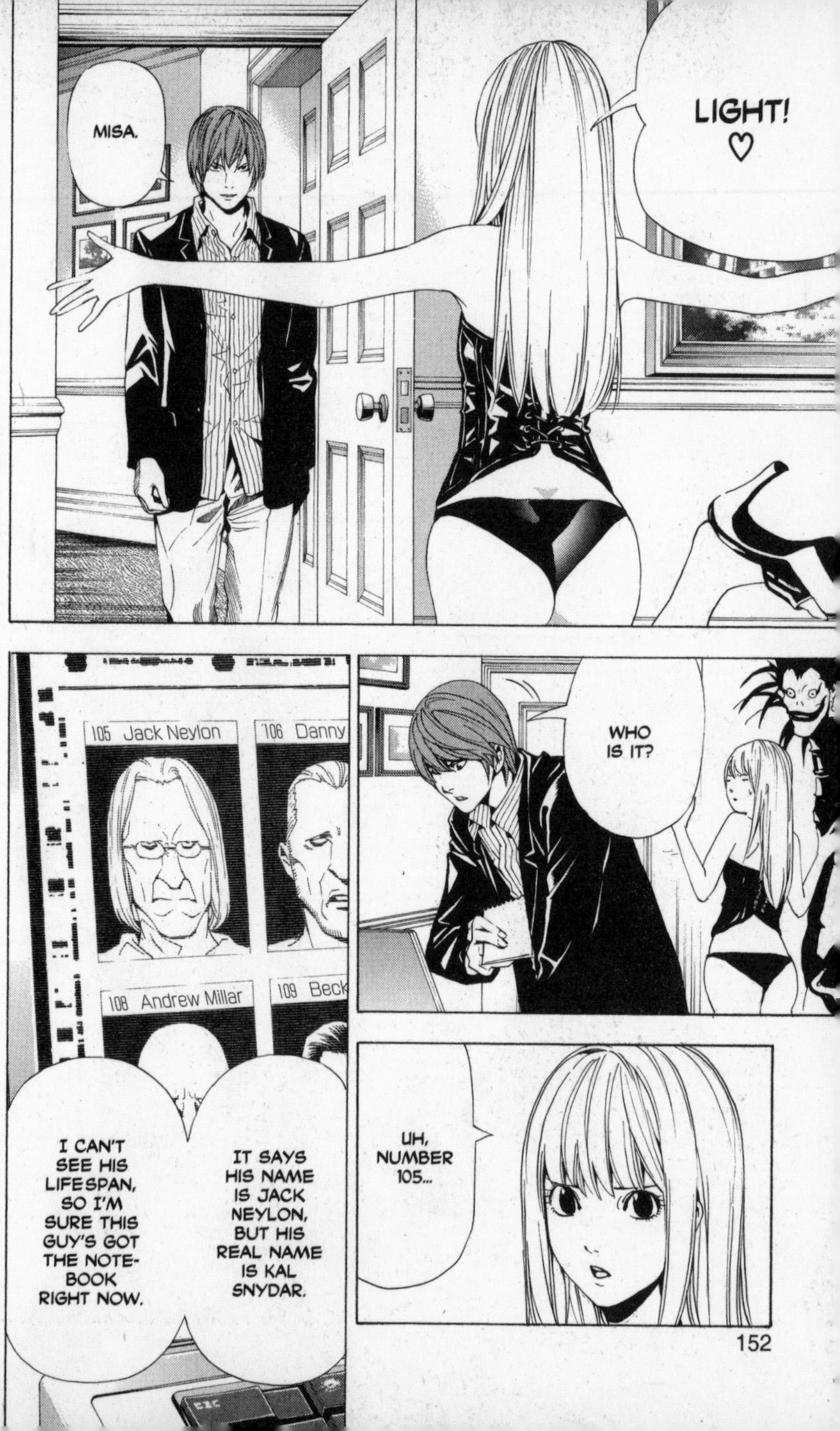
LIGHT! ♡
MISA.
WHO IS IT?
UH, NUMBER 105...
105 Jack Neylon
106 Danny
108 Andrew Millar
109 Beck
IT SAYS HIS NAME IS JACK NEYLON, BUT HIS REAL NAME IS KAL SNYDAR.
I CAN'T SEE HIS LIFESPAN, SO I'M SURE THIS GUY'S GOT THE NOTE-BOOK RIGHT NOW.

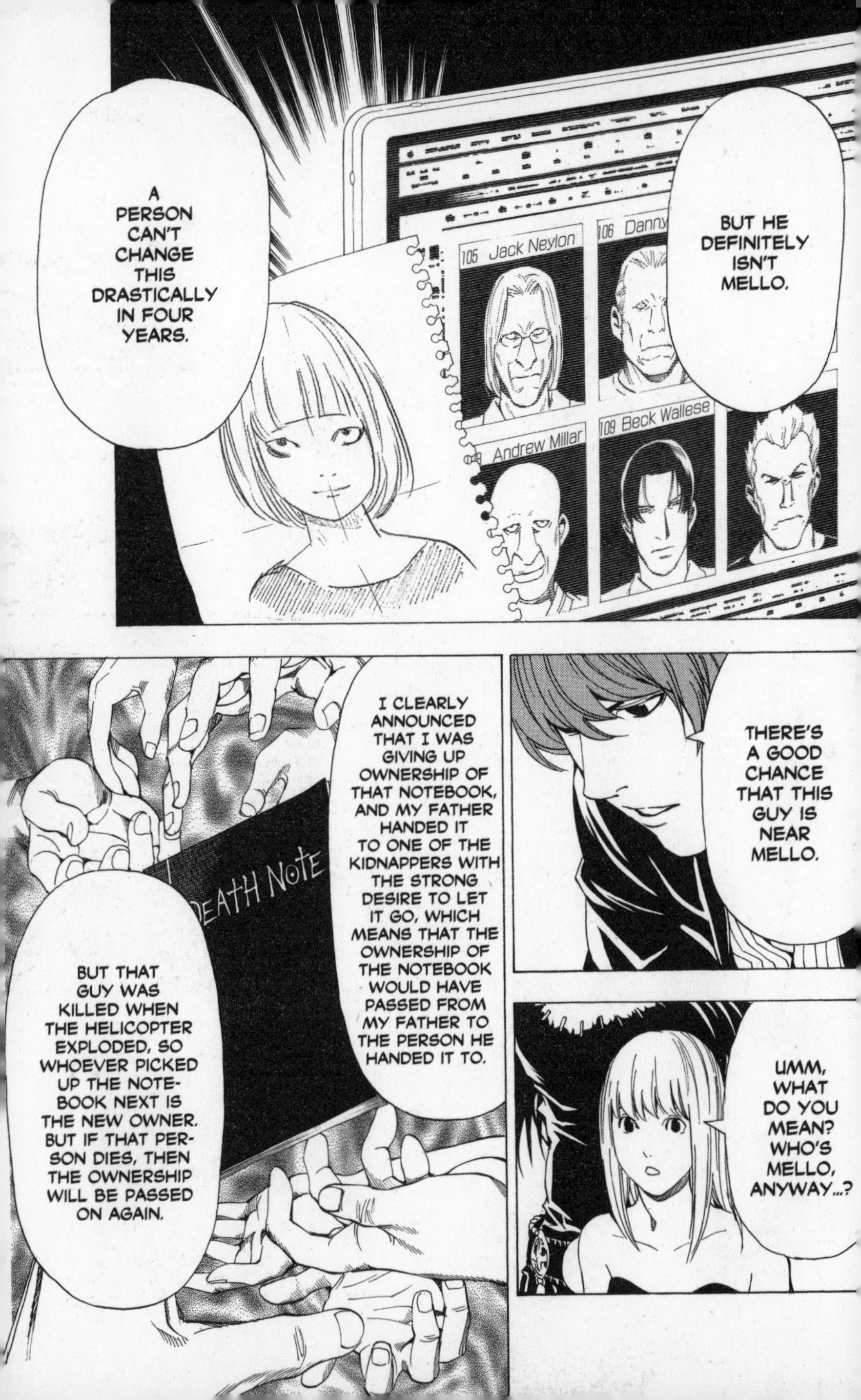
BUT HE DEFINITELY ISN'T MELLO.
105 Jack Neylon
106 Danny
Andrew Millar
109 Beck Wallese
A PERSON CAN'T CHANGE THIS DRASTICALLY IN FOUR YEARS.
THERE'S A GOOD CHANCE THAT THIS GUY IS NEAR MELLO.
UMM, WHAT DO YOU MEAN? WHO'S MELLO, ANYWAY...?
I CLEARLY ANNOUNCED THAT I WAS GIVING UP OWNERSHIP OF THAT NOTEBOOK, AND MY FATHER HANDED IT TO ONE OF THE KIDNAPPERS WITH THE STRONG DESIRE TO LET IT GO, WHICH MEANS THAT THE OWNERSHIP OF THE NOTEBOOK WOULD HAVE PASSED FROM MY FATHER TO THE PERSON HE HANDED IT TO.
DEATH NOTE
BUT THAT GUY WAS KILLED WHEN THE HELICOPTER EXPLODED, SO WHOEVER PICKED UP THE NOTE-BOOK NEXT IS THE NEW OWNER. BUT IF THAT PER-SON DIES, THEN THE OWNERSHIP WILL BE PASSED ON AGAIN.

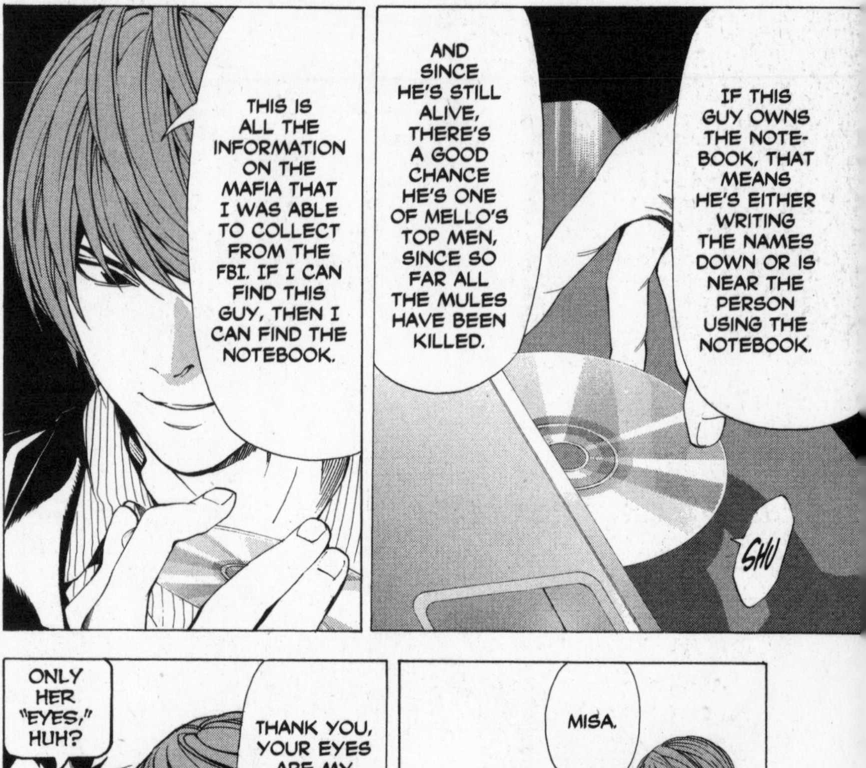
IF THIS GUY OWNS THE NOTE-BOOK, THAT MEANS HE'S EITHER WRITING THE NAMES DOWN OR IS NEAR THE PERSON USING THE NOTEBOOK.
AND SINCE HE'S STILL ALIVE, THERE'S A GOOD CHANCE HE'S ONE OF MELLO'S TOP MEN, SINCE SO FAR ALL THE MULES HAVE BEEN KILLED.
SHU
THIS IS ALL THE INFORMATION ON THE MAFIA THAT I WAS ABLE TO COLLECT FROM THE FBI. IF I CAN FIND THIS GUY, THEN I CAN FIND THE NOTEBOOK.
MISA.
THANK YOU, YOUR EYES ARE MY TREASURES... NO, THEY'RE TREASURES OF THE NEW WORLD!
ONLY HER "EYES," HUH?
OH, LIGHT...

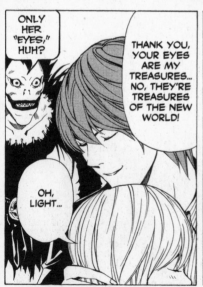

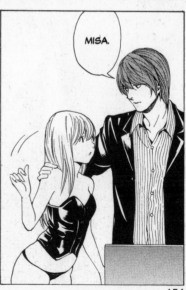

READ THIS WAY

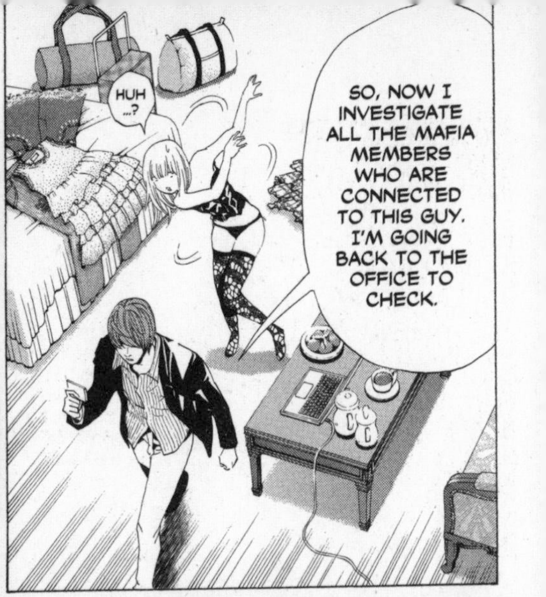
SO, NOW I INVESTIGATE ALL THE MAFIA MEMBERS WHO ARE CONNECTED TO THIS GUY. I'M GOING BACK TO THE OFFICE TO CHECK.
HUH ...?

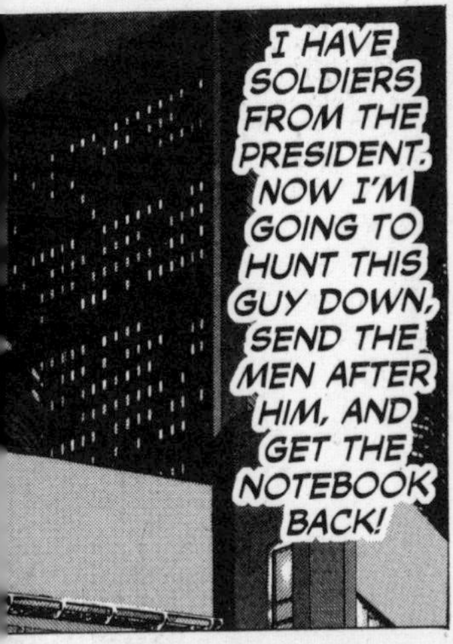
I HAVE SOLDIERS FROM THE PRESIDENT. NOW I'M GOING TO HUNT THIS GUY DOWN, SEND THE MEN AFTER HIM, AND GET THE NOTEBOOK BACK!

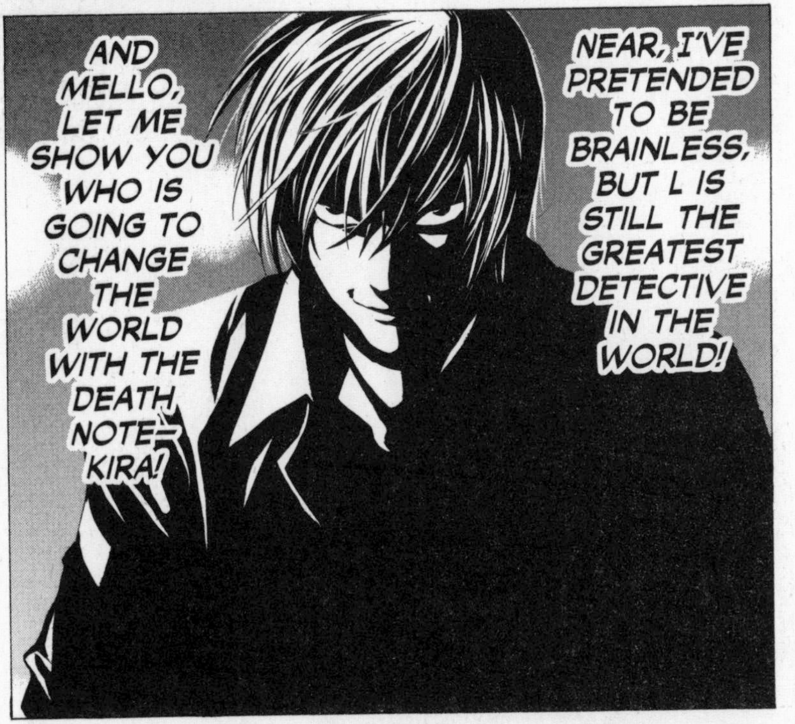
NEAR, I'VE PRETENDED TO BE BRAINLESS, BUT L IS STILL THE GREATEST DETECTIVE IN THE WORLD!
AND MELLO, LET ME SHOW YOU WHO IS GOING TO CHANGE THE WORLD WITH THE DEATH NOTE— KIRA!

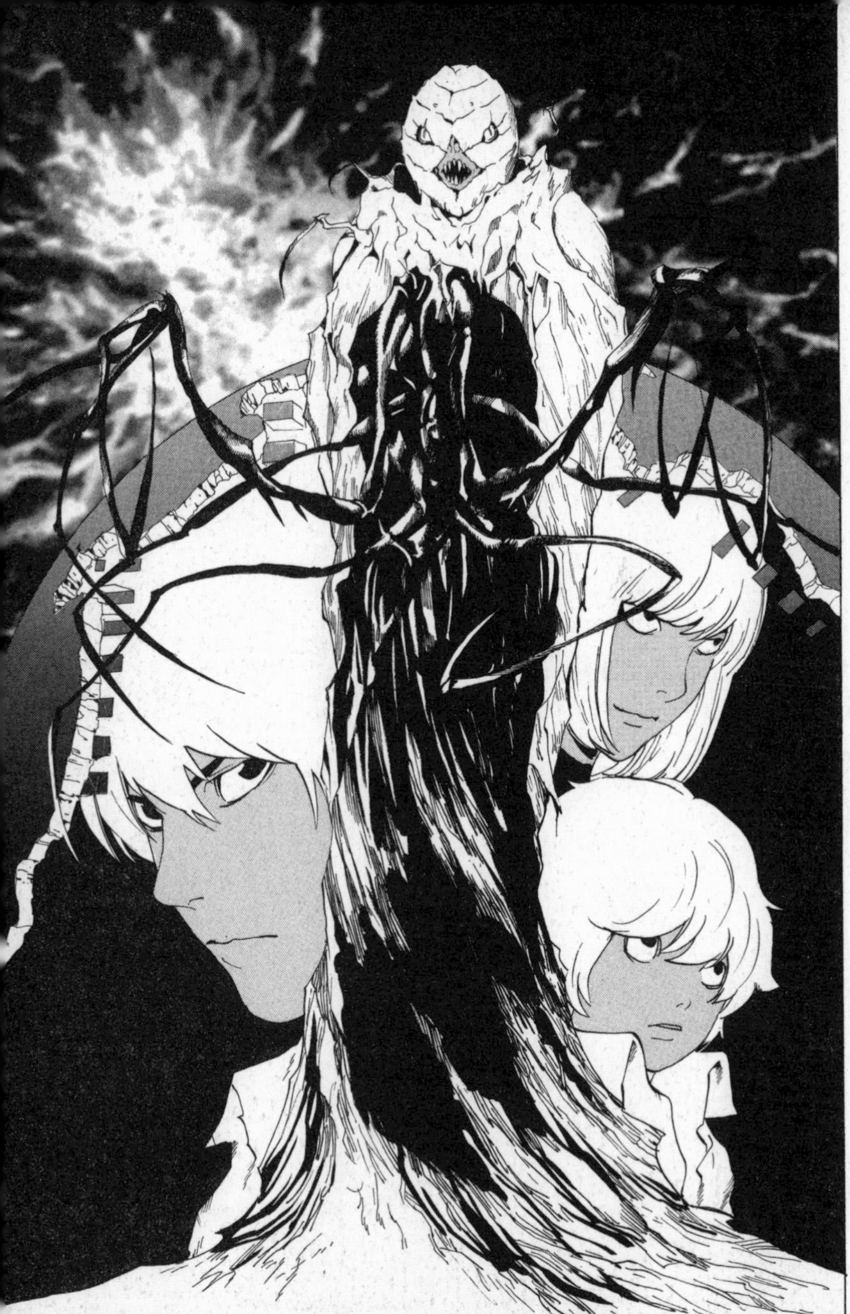

chapter 69 Flight

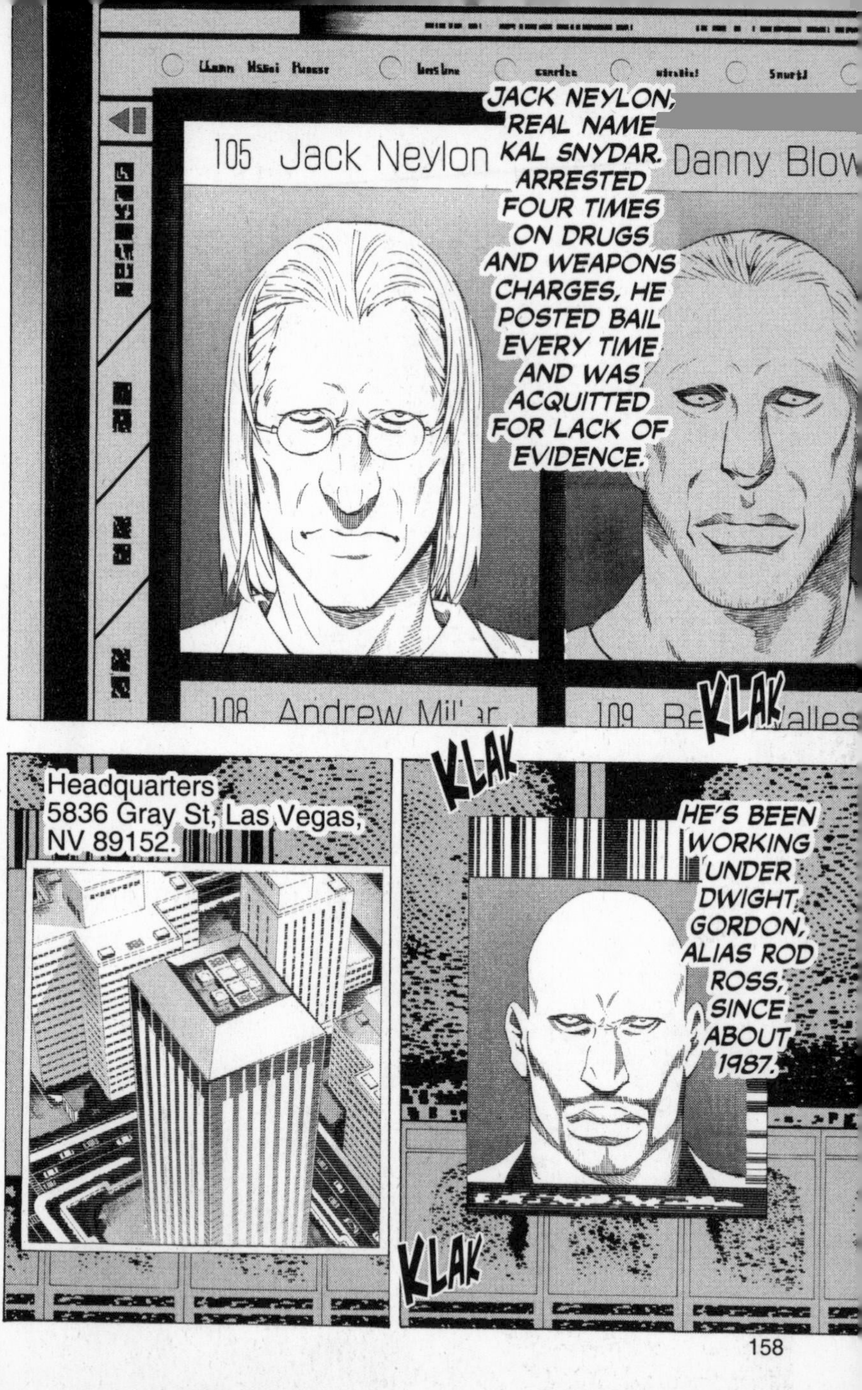
105 Jack Neylon
JACK NEYLON, REAL NAME KAL SNYDAR. ARRESTED FOUR TIMES ON DRUGS AND WEAPONS CHARGES, HE POSTED BAIL EVERY TIME AND WAS ACQUITTED FOR LACK OF EVIDENCE.
KLAK
KLAK
HE'S BEEN WORKING UNDER DWIGHT GORDON, ALIAS ROD ROSS, SINCE ABOUT 1987.
KLAK
Headquarters
5836 Gray St, Las Vegas, NV 89152.

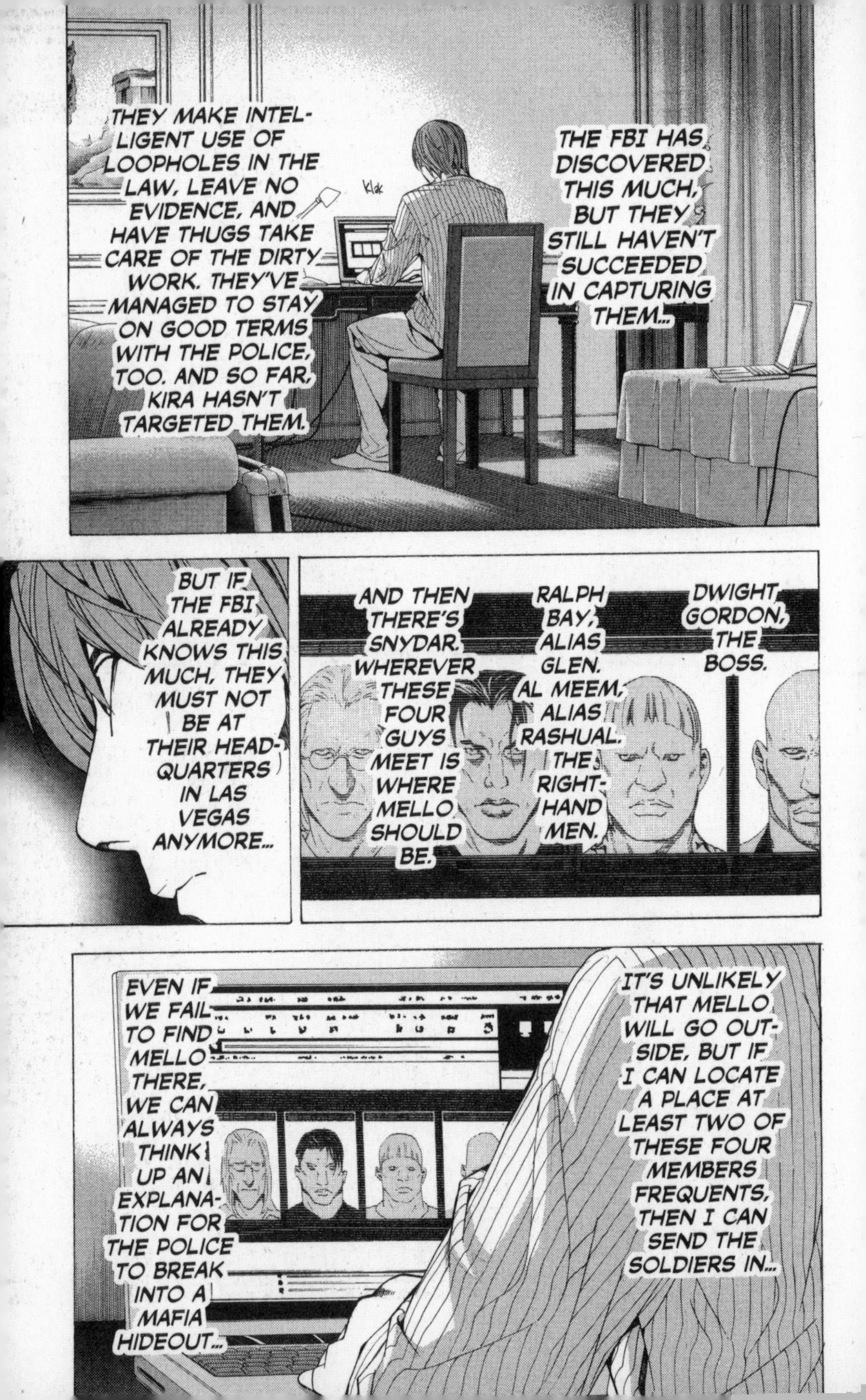
THE FBI HAS DISCOVERED THIS MUCH, BUT THEY STILL HAVEN'T SUCCEEDED IN CAPTURING THEM...
Klak
THEY MAKE INTELLIGENT USE OF LOOPHOLES IN THE LAW, LEAVE NO EVIDENCE, AND HAVE THUGS TAKE CARE OF THE DIRTY WORK. THEY'VE MANAGED TO STAY ON GOOD TERMS WITH THE POLICE, TOO. AND SO FAR, KIRA HASN'T TARGETED THEM.
DWIGHT GORDON, THE BOSS.
RALPH BAY, ALIAS GLEN. AL MEEM, ALIAS RASHUAL. THE RIGHT-HAND MEN.
AND THEN THERE'S SNYDAR. WHEREVER THESE FOUR GUYS MEET IS WHERE MELLO SHOULD BE.
BUT IF THE FBI ALREADY KNOWS THIS MUCH, THEY MUST NOT BE AT THEIR HEADQUARTERS IN LAS VEGAS ANYMORE...
IT'S UNLIKELY THAT MELLO WILL GO OUTSIDE, BUT IF I CAN LOCATE A PLACE AT LEAST TWO OF THESE FOUR MEMBERS FREQUENTS, THEN I CAN SEND THE SOLDIERS IN...
EVEN IF WE FAIL TO FIND MELLO THERE, WE CAN ALWAYS THINK UP AN EXPLANATION FOR THE POLICE TO BREAK INTO A MAFIA HIDEOUT...

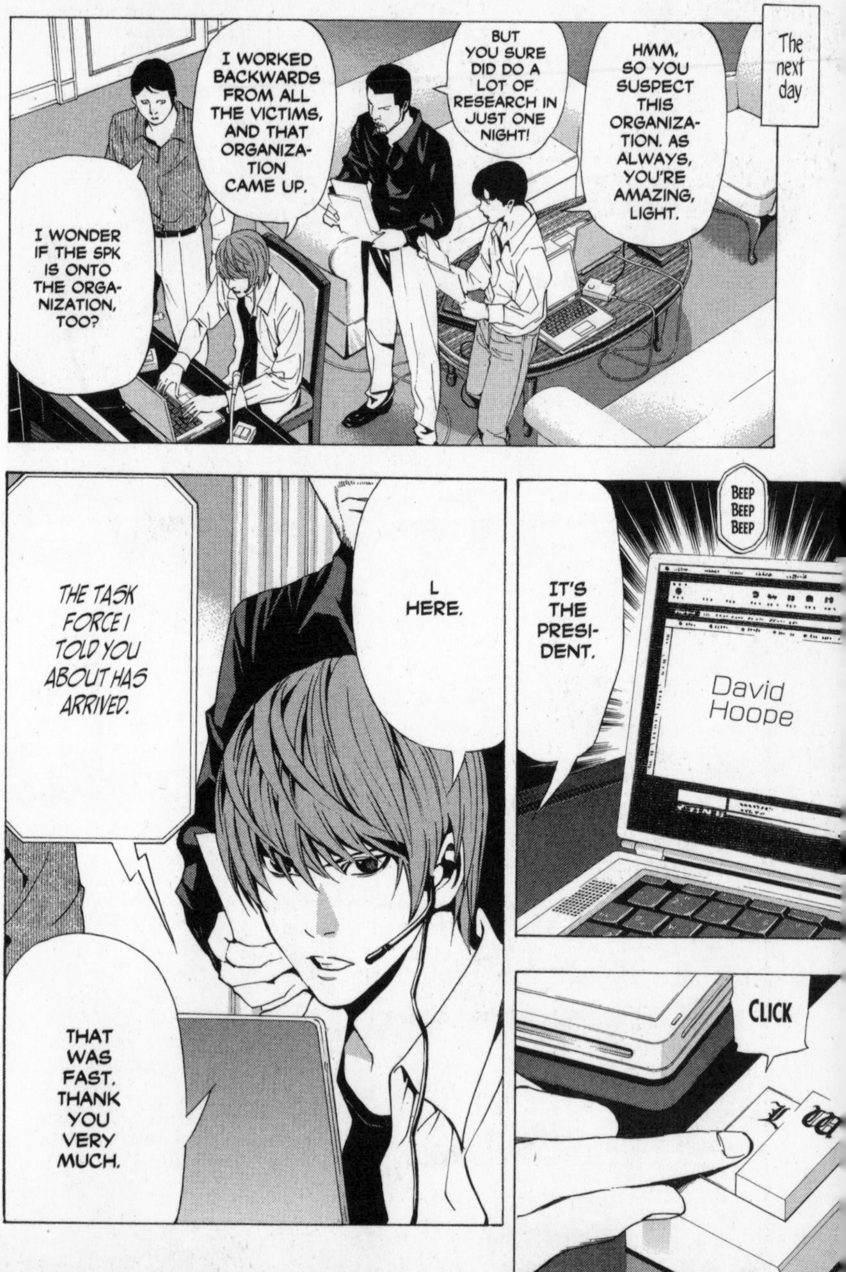
The next day
HMM, SO YOU SUSPECT THIS ORGANIZATION. AS ALWAYS, YOU'RE AMAZING, LIGHT.
BUT YOU SURE DID DO A LOT OF RESEARCH IN JUST ONE NIGHT!
I WORKED BACKWARDS FROM ALL THE VICTIMS, AND THAT ORGANIZATION CAME UP.
I WONDER IF THE SPK IS ONTO THE ORGANIZATION, TOO?
BEEP BEEP BEEP
David Hoope
IT'S THE PRESIDENT.
CLICK
L HERE.
THE TASK FORCE I TOLD YOU ABOUT HAS ARRIVED.
THAT WAS FAST. THANK YOU VERY MUCH.

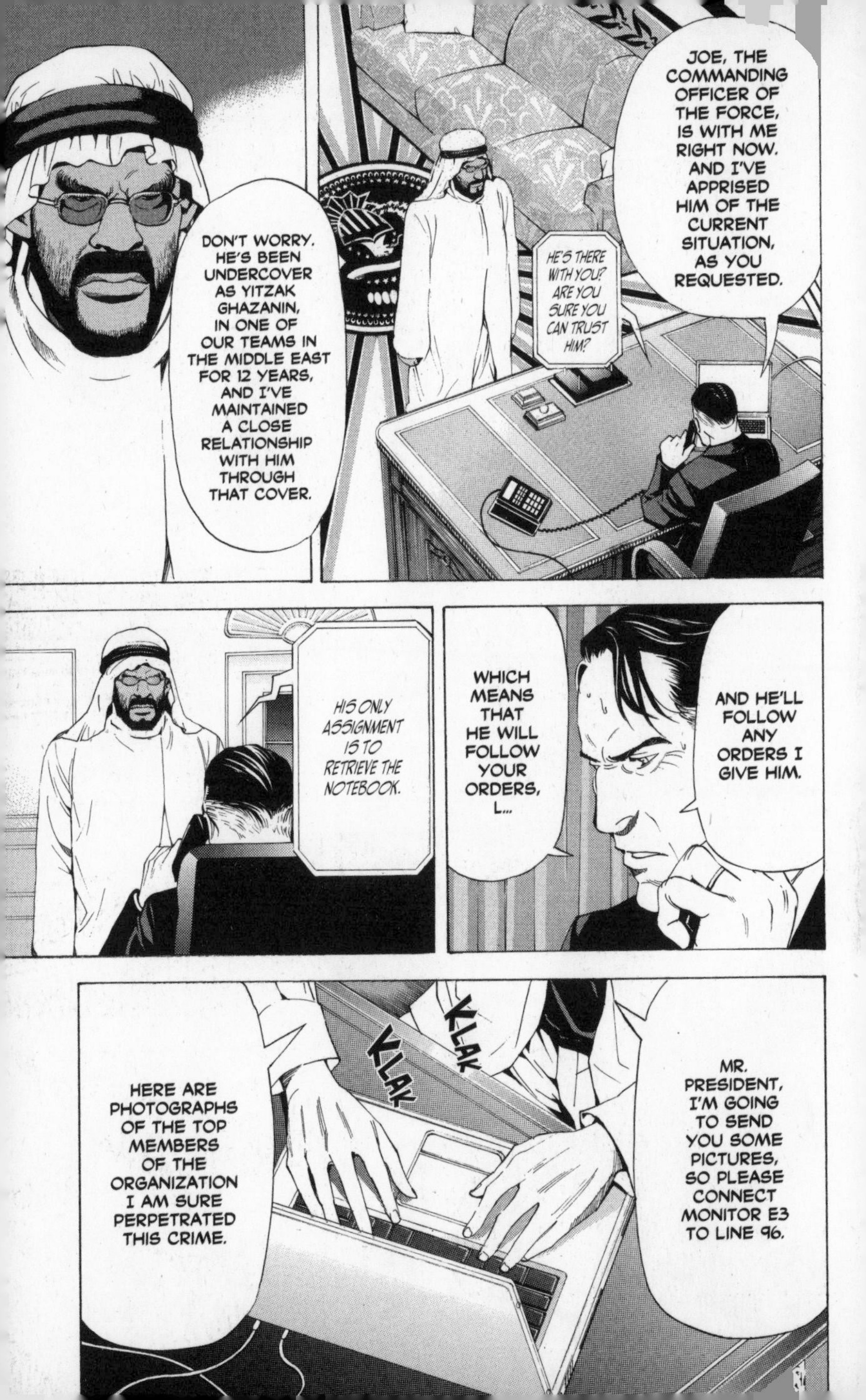
JOE, THE COMMANDING OFFICER OF THE FORCE, IS WITH ME RIGHT NOW. AND I'VE APPRISED HIM OF THE CURRENT SITUATION, AS YOU REQUESTED.
HE'S THERE WITH YOU? ARE YOU SURE YOU CAN TRUST HIM?
DON'T WORRY. HE'S BEEN UNDERCOVER AS YITZAK GHAZANIN, IN ONE OF OUR TEAMS IN THE MIDDLE EAST FOR 12 YEARS, AND I'VE MAINTAINED A CLOSE RELATIONSHIP WITH HIM THROUGH THAT COVER.
AND HE'LL FOLLOW ANY ORDERS I GIVE HIM.
WHICH MEANS THAT HE WILL FOLLOW YOUR ORDERS, L...
HIS ONLY ASSIGNMENT IS TO RETRIEVE THE NOTEBOOK.
MR. PRESIDENT, I'M GOING TO SEND YOU SOME PICTURES, SO PLEASE CONNECT MONITOR E3 TO LINE 96.
KLAK
KLAK
HERE ARE PHOTOGRAPHS OF THE TOP MEMBERS OF THE ORGANIZATION I AM SURE PERPETRATED THIS CRIME.

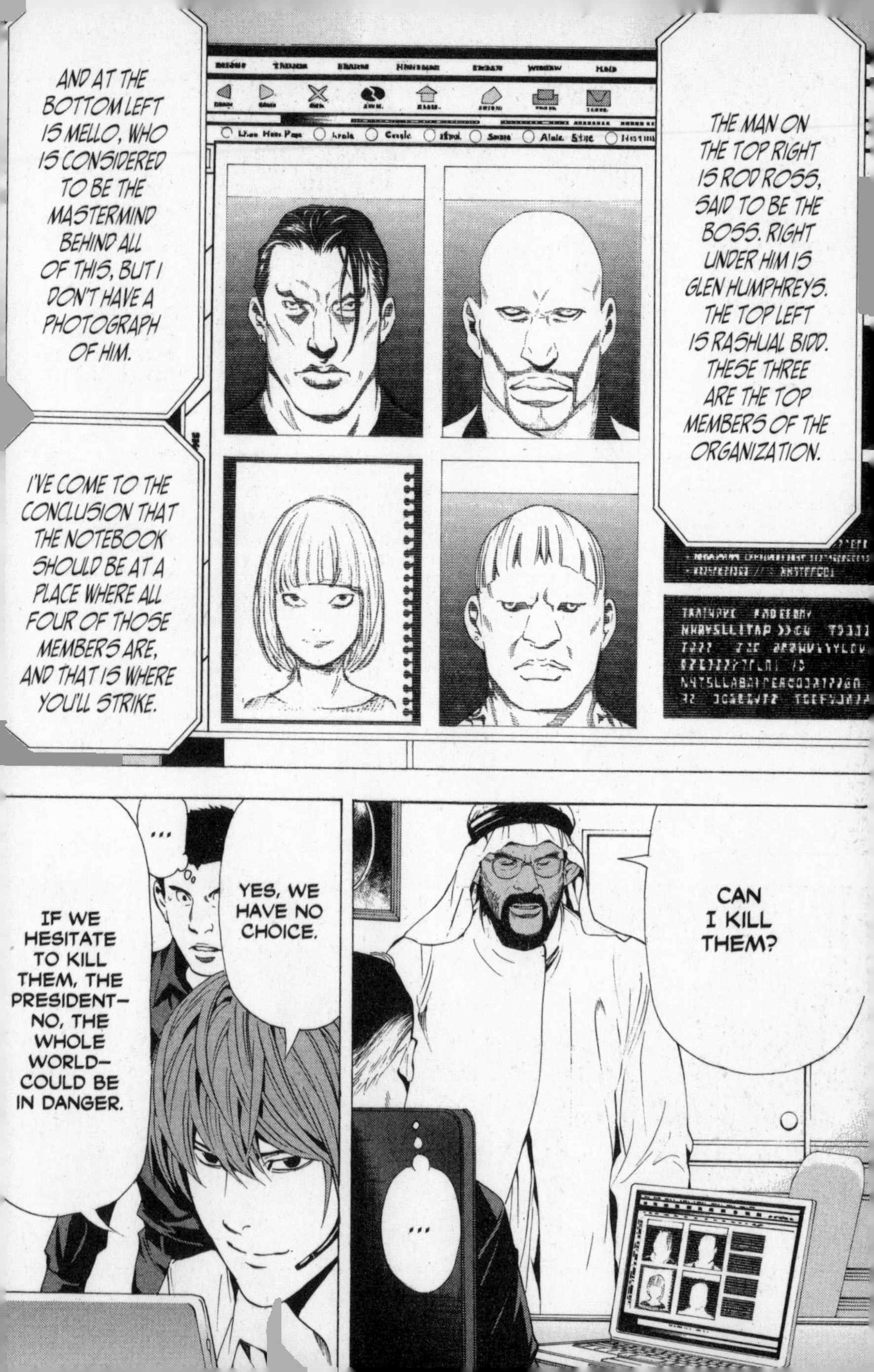
THE MAN ON THE TOP RIGHT IS ROD ROSS, SAID TO BE THE BOSS. RIGHT UNDER HIM IS GLEN HUMPHREYS. THE TOP LEFT IS RASHUAL BIDD. THESE THREE ARE THE TOP MEMBERS OF THE ORGANIZATION.
AND AT THE BOTTOM LEFT IS MELLO, WHO IS CONSIDERED TO BE THE MASTERMIND BEHIND ALL OF THIS, BUT I DON'T HAVE A PHOTOGRAPH OF HIM.
I'VE COME TO THE CONCLUSION THAT THE NOTEBOOK SHOULD BE AT A PLACE WHERE ALL FOUR OF THOSE MEMBERS ARE, AND THAT IS WHERE YOU'LL STRIKE.
CAN I KILL THEM?
...
...
YES, WE HAVE NO CHOICE.
IF WE HESITATE TO KILL THEM, THE PRESIDENT— NO, THE WHOLE WORLD— COULD BE IN DANGER.

WE'LL BE FULLY EQUIPPED AND OUR FACES WILL BE HIDDEN. THAT NOTEBOOK WILL BE USELESS AGAINST US. EVEN IF THERE ARE A HUNDRED OF THEM, WE'LL STILL BE ABLE TO DEFEAT THEM.

IF WE CAN KILL, THIS JOB WILL BE EASY.

THEY'VE GOT THE KILLER NOTEBOOK, BUT AS LONG AS YOU DON'T GIVE THEM THE CHANCE TO WRITE IN IT, YOU'LL HAVE NOTHING TO WORRY ABOUT.

VERY WELL, I'LL GET JOE TO TIE ME UP AND LOCK ME INSIDE A SAFE OR SOMETHING.

...

THE NOTEBOOK CAN'T KILL PEOPLE IN A WAY THAT INVOLVES OTHERS. THIS WILL MAKE THINGS EASIER FOR ME.

MR. PRESIDENT, I'M SURE THAT THERE'S NOTHING TO WORRY ABOUT, BUT I'D LIKE YOU TO TAKE PRECAUTIONS TO MAKE SURE THAT YOU WILL NOT BE ABLE TO PRESS THAT BUTTON.

OKAY.

KLAK

MR. PRESIDENT, CAN YOU SEND ME IMAGES FROM THE SATELLITE THAT THE SPK AND THE KIDNAPPERS ARE USING?

GOOD, NOW...

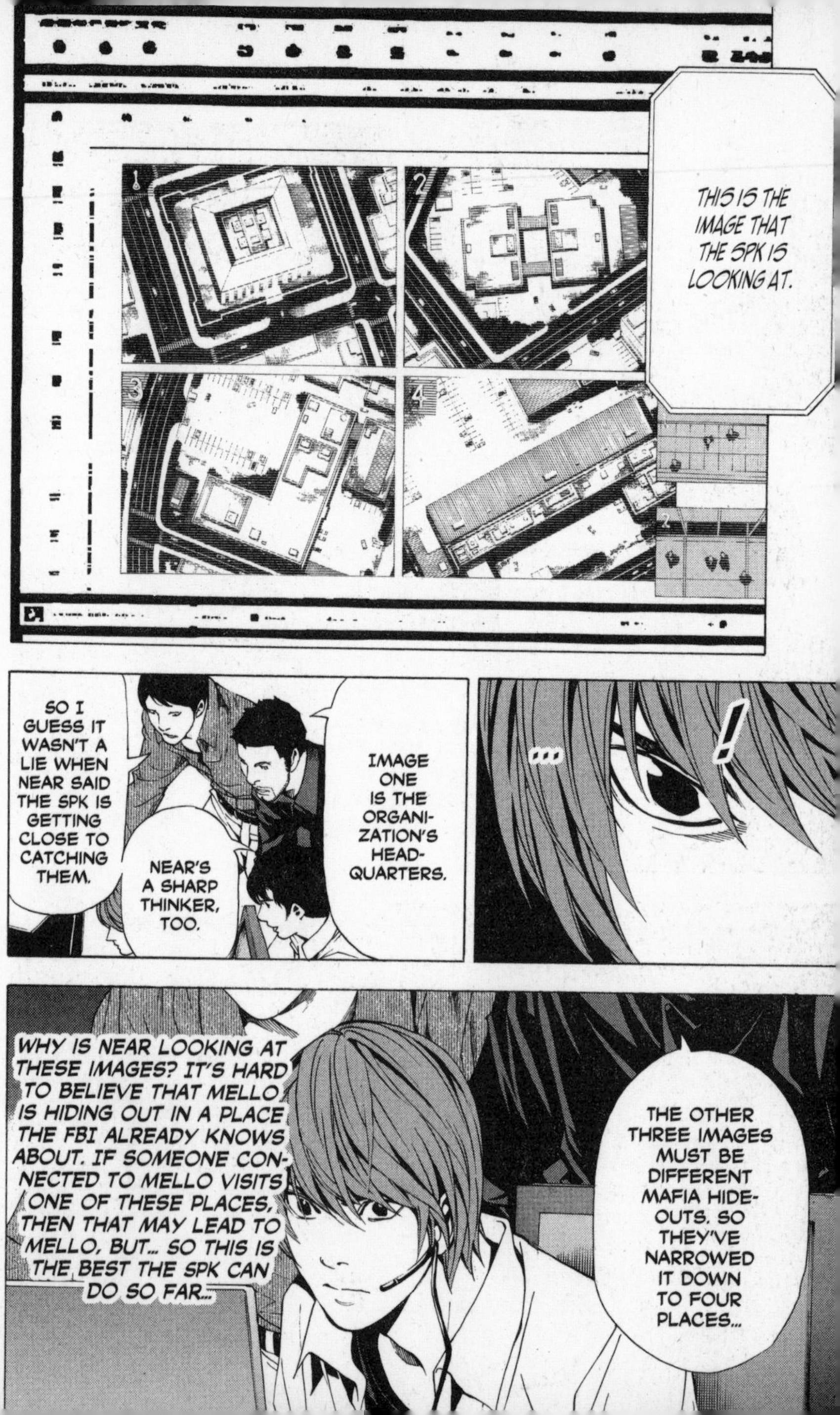
THIS IS THE IMAGE THAT THE SPK IS LOOKING AT.
...
!
IMAGE ONE IS THE ORGANIZATION'S HEADQUARTERS.
SO I GUESS IT WASN'T A LIE WHEN NEAR SAID THE SPK IS GETTING CLOSE TO CATCHING THEM.
NEAR'S A SHARP THINKER, TOO.
THE OTHER THREE IMAGES MUST BE DIFFERENT MAFIA HIDE-OUTS. SO THEY'VE NARROWED IT DOWN TO FOUR PLACES...
WHY IS NEAR LOOKING AT THESE IMAGES? IT'S HARD TO BELIEVE THAT MELLO IS HIDING OUT IN A PLACE THE FBI ALREADY KNOWS ABOUT. IF SOMEONE CON-NECTED TO MELLO VISITS ONE OF THESE PLACES, THEN THAT MAY LEAD TO MELLO, BUT... SO THIS IS THE BEST THE SPK CAN DO SO FAR...

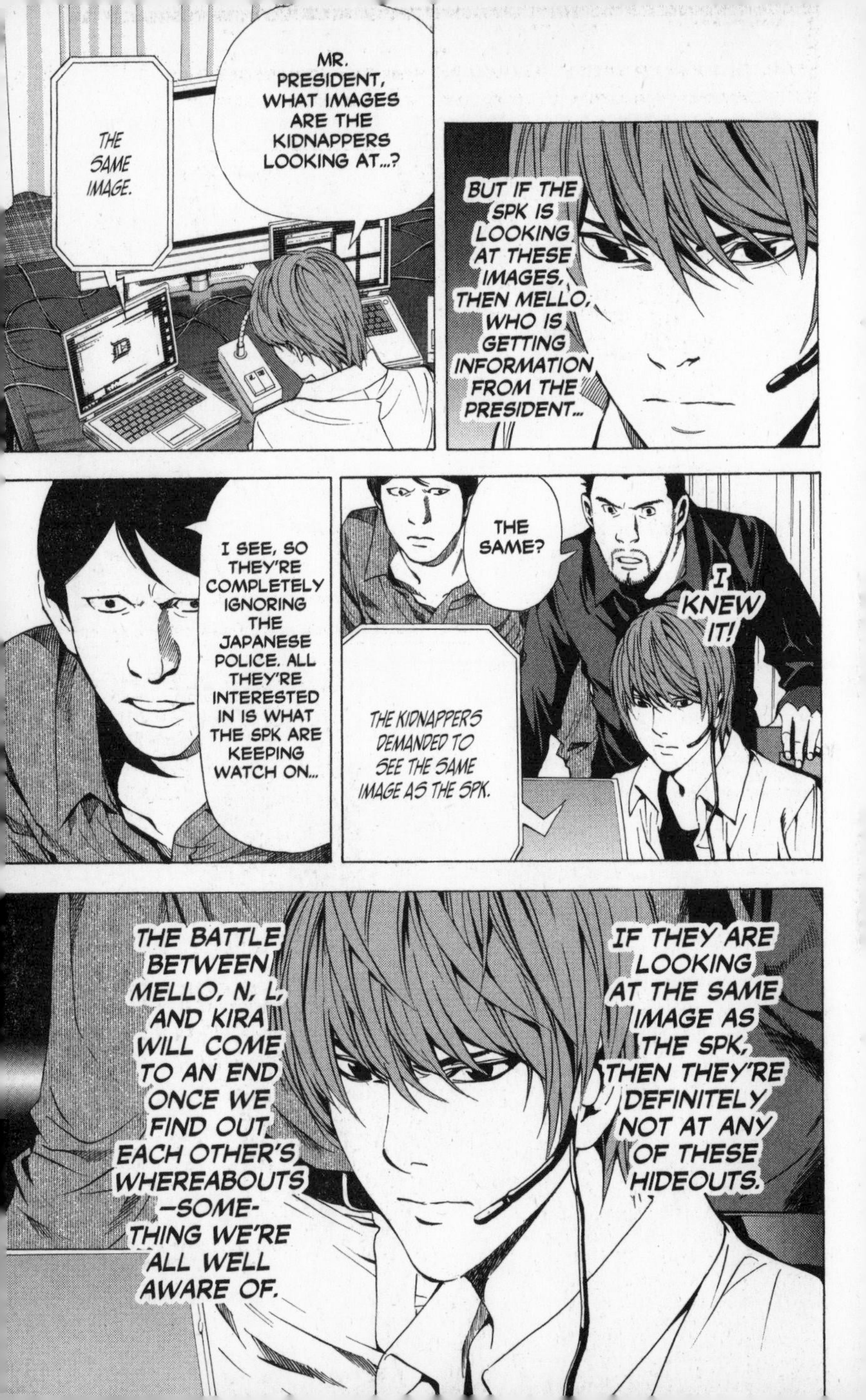
BUT IF THE SPK IS LOOKING AT THESE IMAGES, THEN MELLO, WHO IS GETTING INFORMATION FROM THE PRESIDENT...
MR. PRESIDENT, WHAT IMAGES ARE THE KIDNAPPERS LOOKING AT...?
THE SAME IMAGE.
THE SAME?
I KNEW IT!
THE KIDNAPPERS DEMANDED TO SEE THE SAME IMAGE AS THE SPK.
I SEE, SO THEY'RE COMPLETELY IGNORING THE JAPANESE POLICE. ALL THEY'RE INTERESTED IN IS WHAT THE SPK ARE KEEPING WATCH ON...
IF THEY ARE LOOKING AT THE SAME IMAGE AS THE SPK, THEN THEY'RE DEFINITELY NOT AT ANY OF THESE HIDEOUTS.
THE BATTLE BETWEEN MELLO, N, L, AND KIRA WILL COME TO AN END ONCE WE FIND OUT EACH OTHER'S WHEREABOUTS —SOMETHING WE'RE ALL WELL AWARE OF.

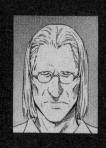

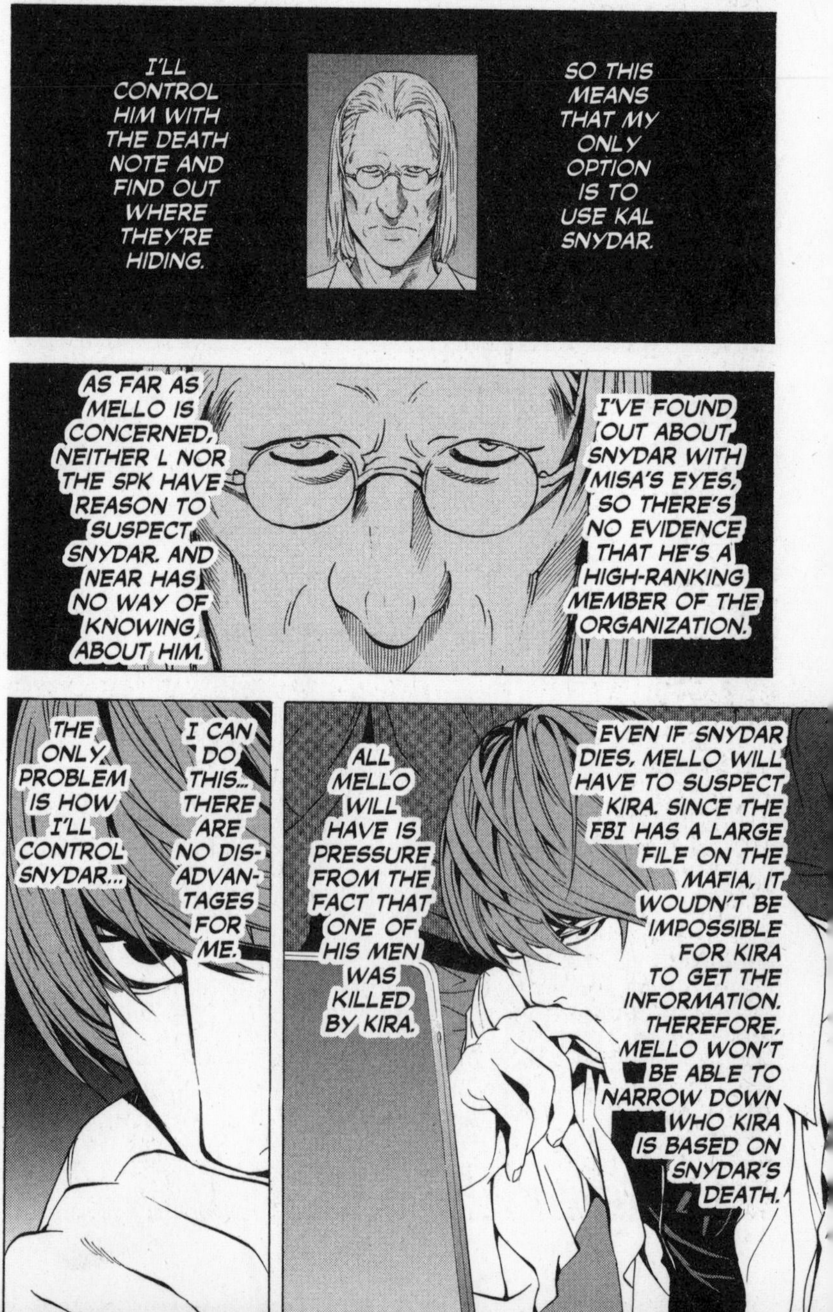
SO THIS MEANS THAT MY ONLY OPTION IS TO USE KAL SNYDAR.
I'LL CONTROL HIM WITH THE DEATH NOTE AND FIND OUT WHERE THEY'RE HIDING.
I'VE FOUND OUT ABOUT SNYDAR WITH MISA'S EYES, SO THERE'S NO EVIDENCE THAT HE'S A HIGH-RANKING MEMBER OF THE ORGANIZATION.
AS FAR AS MELLO IS CONCERNED, NEITHER L NOR THE SPK HAVE REASON TO SUSPECT SNYDAR. AND NEAR HAS NO WAY OF KNOWING ABOUT HIM.
EVEN IF SNYDAR DIES, MELLO WILL HAVE TO SUSPECT KIRA. SINCE THE FBI HAS A LARGE FILE ON THE MAFIA, IT WOUDN'T BE IMPOSSIBLE FOR KIRA TO GET THE INFORMATION. THEREFORE, MELLO WON'T BE ABLE TO NARROW DOWN WHO KIRA IS BASED ON SNYDAR'S DEATH.
ALL MELLO WILL HAVE IS PRESSURE FROM THE FACT THAT ONE OF HIS MEN WAS KILLED BY KIRA.
I CAN DO THIS... THERE ARE NO DIS-ADVAN-TAGES FOR ME.
THE ONLY PROBLEM IS HOW I'LL CONTROL SNYDAR...

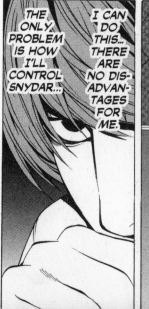

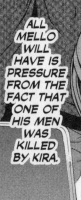

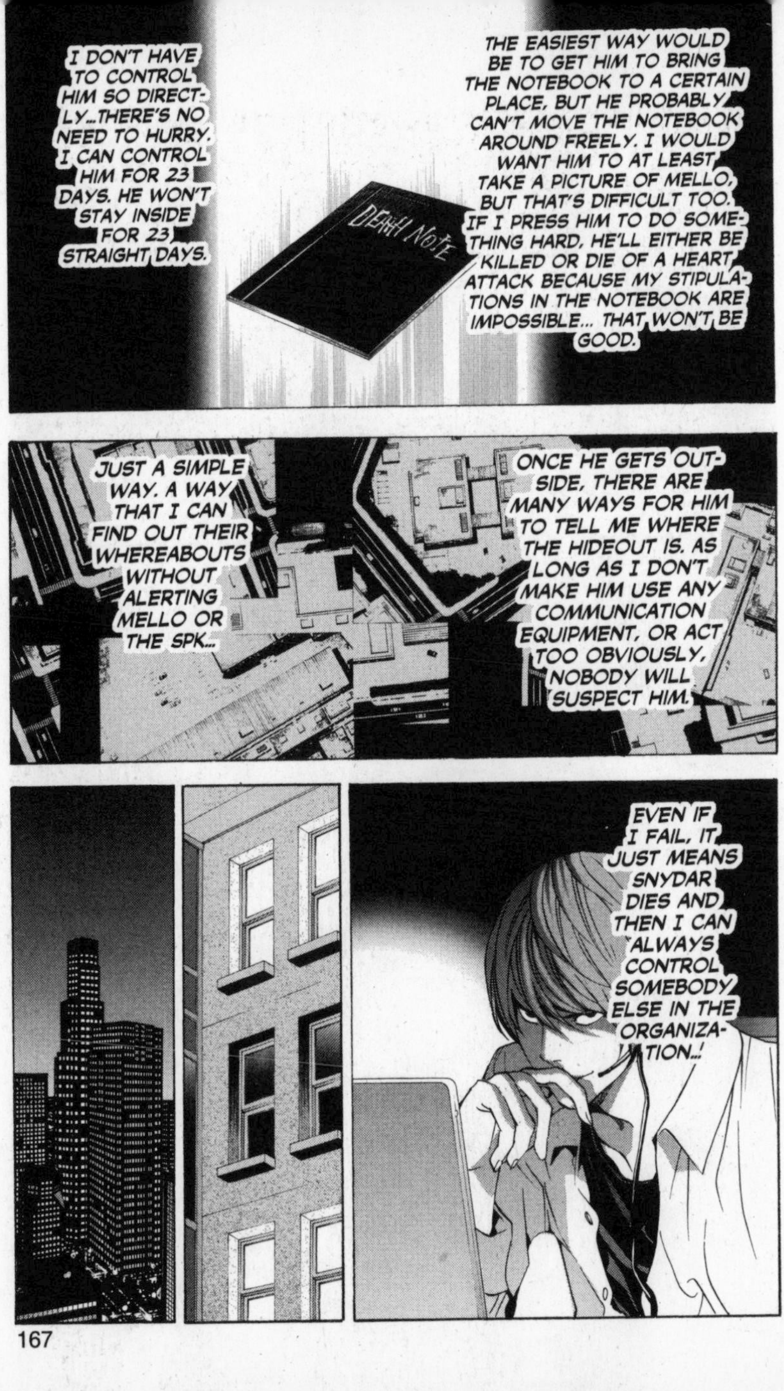
THE EASIEST WAY WOULD BE TO GET HIM TO BRING THE NOTEBOOK TO A CERTAIN PLACE, BUT HE PROBABLY CAN'T MOVE THE NOTEBOOK AROUND FREELY. I WOULD WANT HIM TO AT LEAST TAKE A PICTURE OF MELLO, BUT THAT'S DIFFICULT TOO. IF I PRESS HIM TO DO SOMETHING HARD, HE'LL EITHER BE KILLED OR DIE OF A HEART ATTACK BECAUSE MY STIPULATIONS IN THE NOTEBOOK ARE IMPOSSIBLE... THAT WON'T BE GOOD.
DEATH NOTE
I DON'T HAVE TO CONTROL HIM SO DIRECTLY...THERE'S NO NEED TO HURRY. I CAN CONTROL HIM FOR 23 DAYS. HE WON'T STAY INSIDE FOR 23 STRAIGHT DAYS.
ONCE HE GETS OUTSIDE, THERE ARE MANY WAYS FOR HIM TO TELL ME WHERE THE HIDEOUT IS. AS LONG AS I DON'T MAKE HIM USE ANY COMMUNICATION EQUIPMENT, OR ACT TOO OBVIOUSLY, NOBODY WILL SUSPECT HIM.
JUST A SIMPLE WAY. A WAY THAT I CAN FIND OUT THEIR WHEREABOUTS WITHOUT ALERTING MELLO OR THE SPK...
EVEN IF I FAIL, IT JUST MEANS SNYDAR DIES AND THEN I CAN ALWAYS CONTROL SOMEBODY ELSE IN THE ORGANIZATION...!

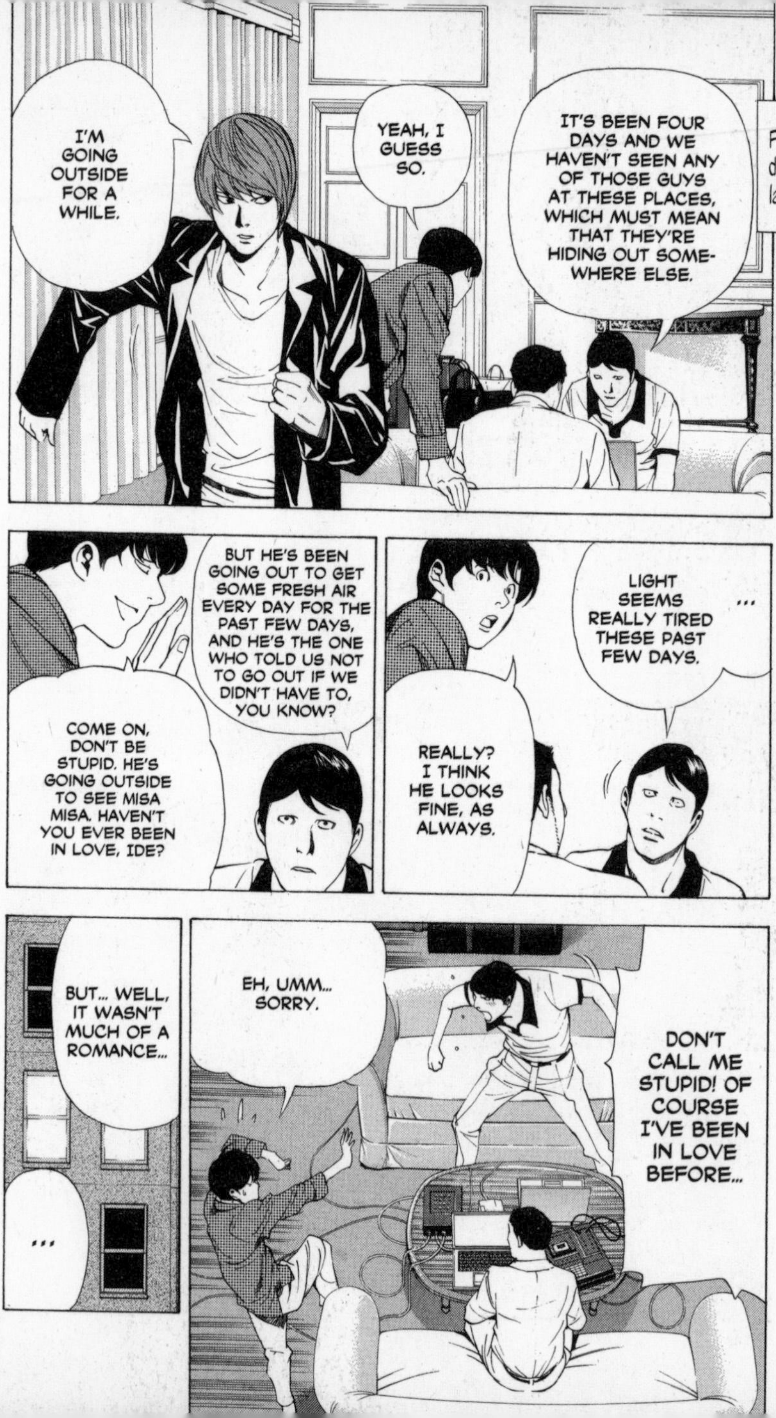
Four days later
IT'S BEEN FOUR DAYS AND WE HAVEN'T SEEN ANY OF THOSE GUYS AT THESE PLACES, WHICH MUST MEAN THAT THEY'RE HIDING OUT SOMEWHERE ELSE.
YEAH, I GUESS SO.
I'M GOING OUTSIDE FOR A WHILE.
...
LIGHT SEEMS REALLY TIRED THESE PAST FEW DAYS.
REALLY? I THINK HE LOOKS FINE, AS ALWAYS.
BUT HE'S BEEN GOING OUT TO GET SOME FRESH AIR EVERY DAY FOR THE PAST FEW DAYS, AND HE'S THE ONE WHO TOLD US NOT TO GO OUT IF WE DIDN'T HAVE TO, YOU KNOW?
COME ON, DON'T BE STUPID. HE'S GOING OUTSIDE TO SEE MISA MISA. HAVEN'T YOU EVER BEEN IN LOVE, IDE?
DON'T CALL ME STUPID! OF COURSE I'VE BEEN IN LOVE BEFORE...
EH, UMM... SORRY.
BUT... WELL, IT WASN'T MUCH OF A ROMANCE...
...

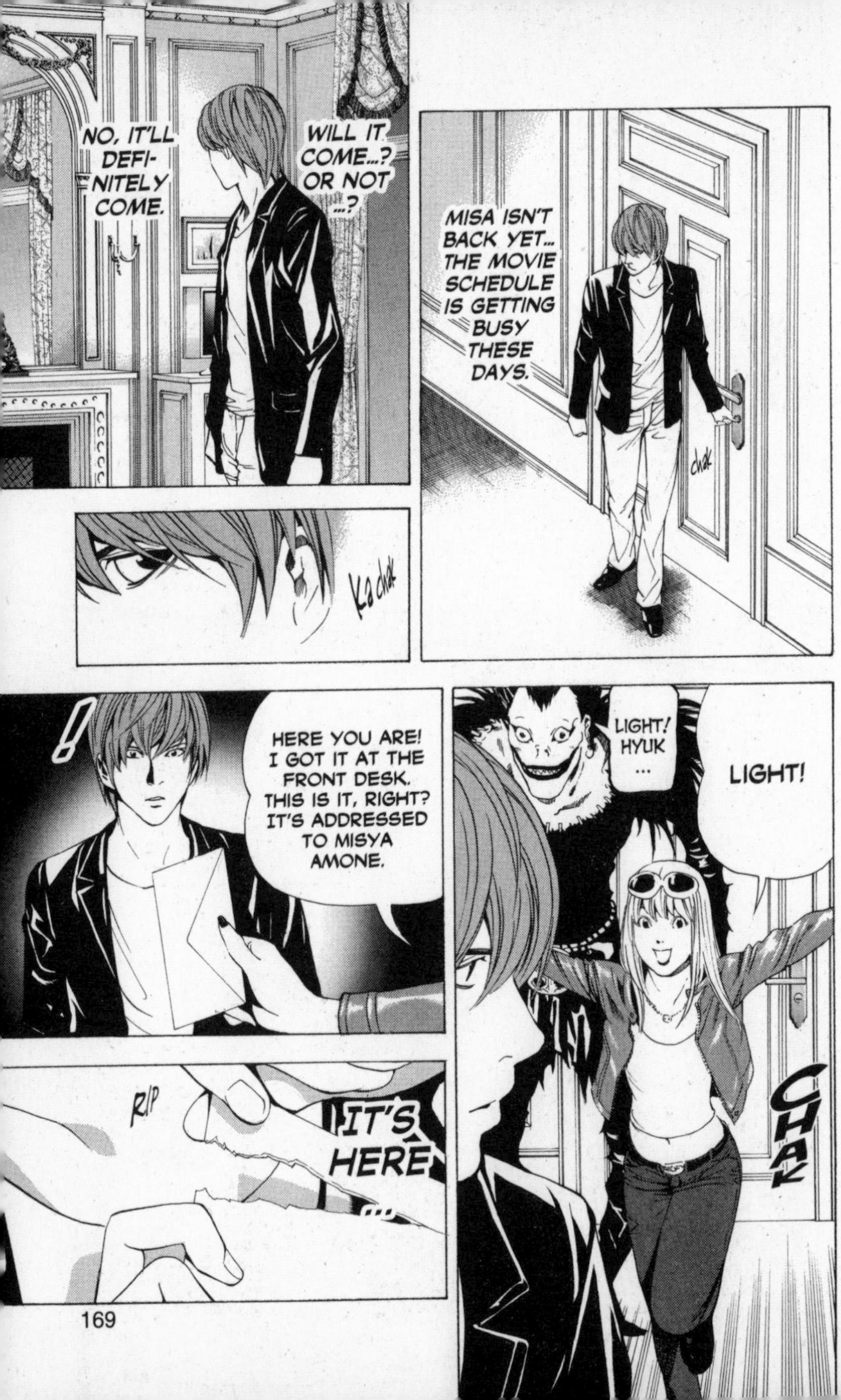
MISA ISN'T BACK YET... THE MOVIE SCHEDULE IS GETTING BUSY THESE DAYS.
chak
WILL IT COME...? OR NOT ...?
NO, IT'LL DEFINITELY COME.
Ka chak
LIGHT!
LIGHT! HYUK ...
CHAK
!
HERE YOU ARE! I GOT IT AT THE FRONT DESK. THIS IS IT, RIGHT? IT'S ADDRESSED TO MISYA AMONE.
RIP
IT'S HERE ...

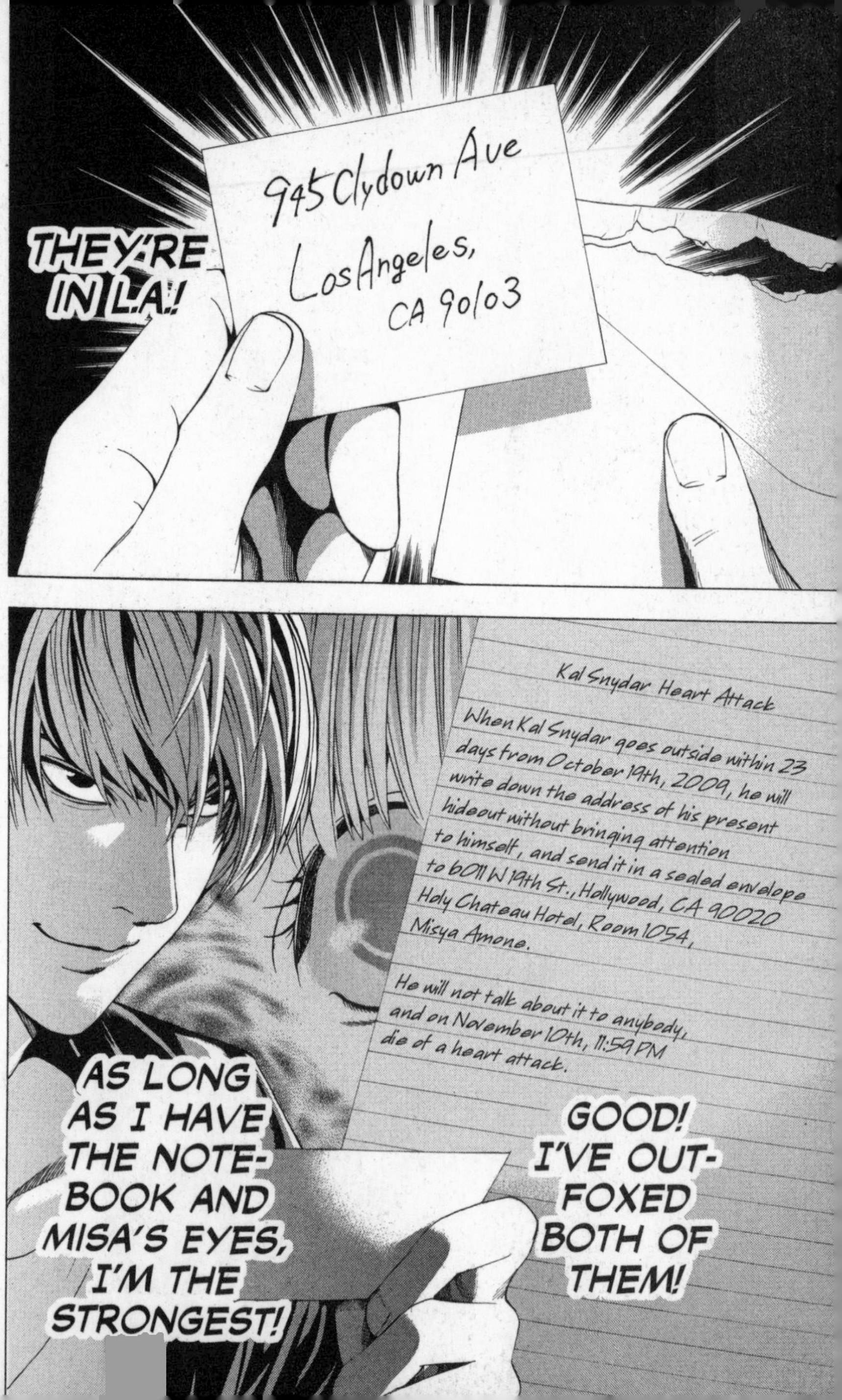
945 Clydown Ave
Los Angeles,
CA 90103
THEY'RE IN L.A.!
Kal Snydar Heart Attack
When Kal Snydar goes outside within 23 days from October 19th, 2009, he will write down the address of his present hideout without bringing attention to himself, and send it in a sealed envelope to 6011 W 19th St., Hollywood, CA 90020 Holy Chateau Hotel, Room 1054, Misya Amone.
He will not talk about it to anybody, and on November 10th, 11:59 PM die of a heart attack.
GOOD! I'VE OUT-FOXED BOTH OF THEM!
AS LONG AS I HAVE THE NOTE-BOOK AND MISA'S EYES, I'M THE STRONGEST!

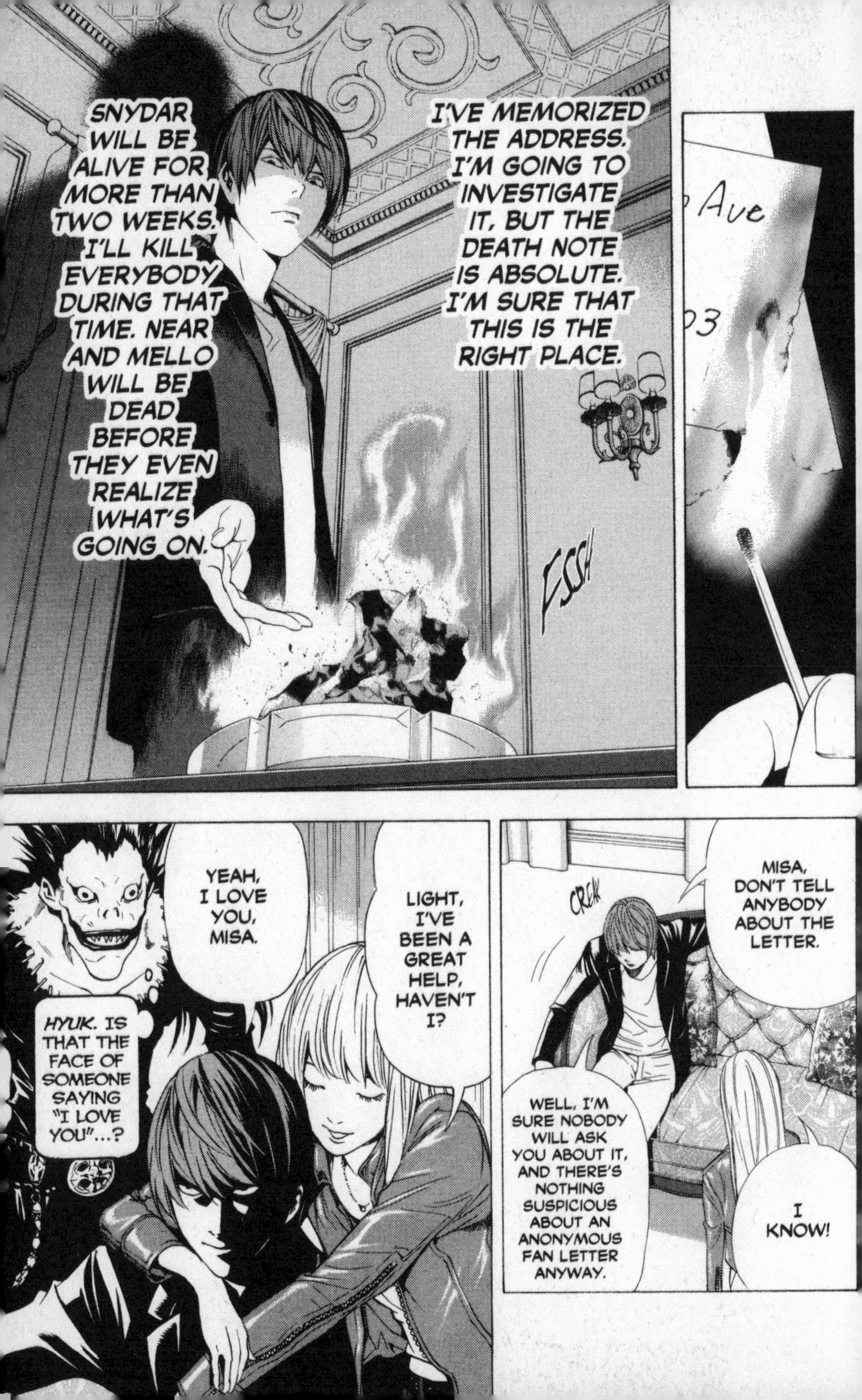
Ave
03
FSSH
I'VE MEMORIZED THE ADDRESS. I'M GOING TO INVESTIGATE IT, BUT THE DEATH NOTE IS ABSOLUTE. I'M SURE THAT THIS IS THE RIGHT PLACE.
SNYDAR WILL BE ALIVE FOR MORE THAN TWO WEEKS. I'LL KILL EVERYBODY DURING THAT TIME. NEAR AND MELLO WILL BE DEAD BEFORE THEY EVEN REALIZE WHAT'S GOING ON.
MISA, DON'T TELL ANYBODY ABOUT THE LETTER.
CREAK
WELL, I'M SURE NOBODY WILL ASK YOU ABOUT IT, AND THERE'S NOTHING SUSPICIOUS ABOUT AN ANONYMOUS FAN LETTER ANYWAY.
I KNOW!
LIGHT, I'VE BEEN A GREAT HELP, HAVEN'T I?
YEAH, I LOVE YOU, MISA.
HYUK. IS THAT THE FACE OF SOMEONE SAYING "I LOVE YOU"...?

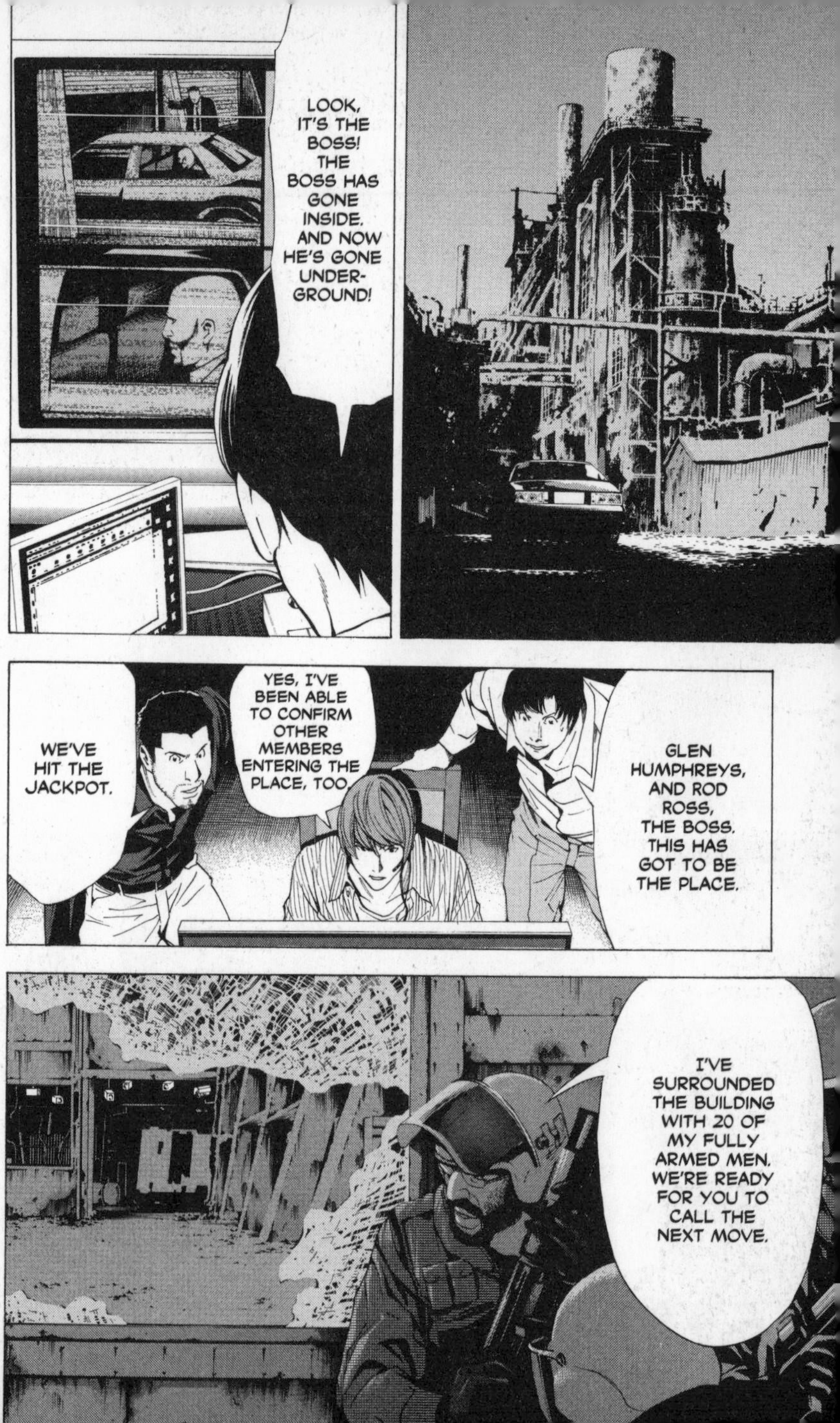
LOOK, IT'S THE BOSS! THE BOSS HAS GONE INSIDE. AND NOW HE'S GONE UNDER-GROUND!
GLEN HUMPHREYS, AND ROD ROSS, THE BOSS. THIS HAS GOT TO BE THE PLACE.
YES, I'VE BEEN ABLE TO CONFIRM OTHER MEMBERS ENTERING THE PLACE, TOO.
WE'VE HIT THE JACKPOT.
I'VE SURROUNDED THE BUILDING WITH 20 OF MY FULLY ARMED MEN. WE'RE READY FOR YOU TO CALL THE NEXT MOVE.

READ THIS WAY

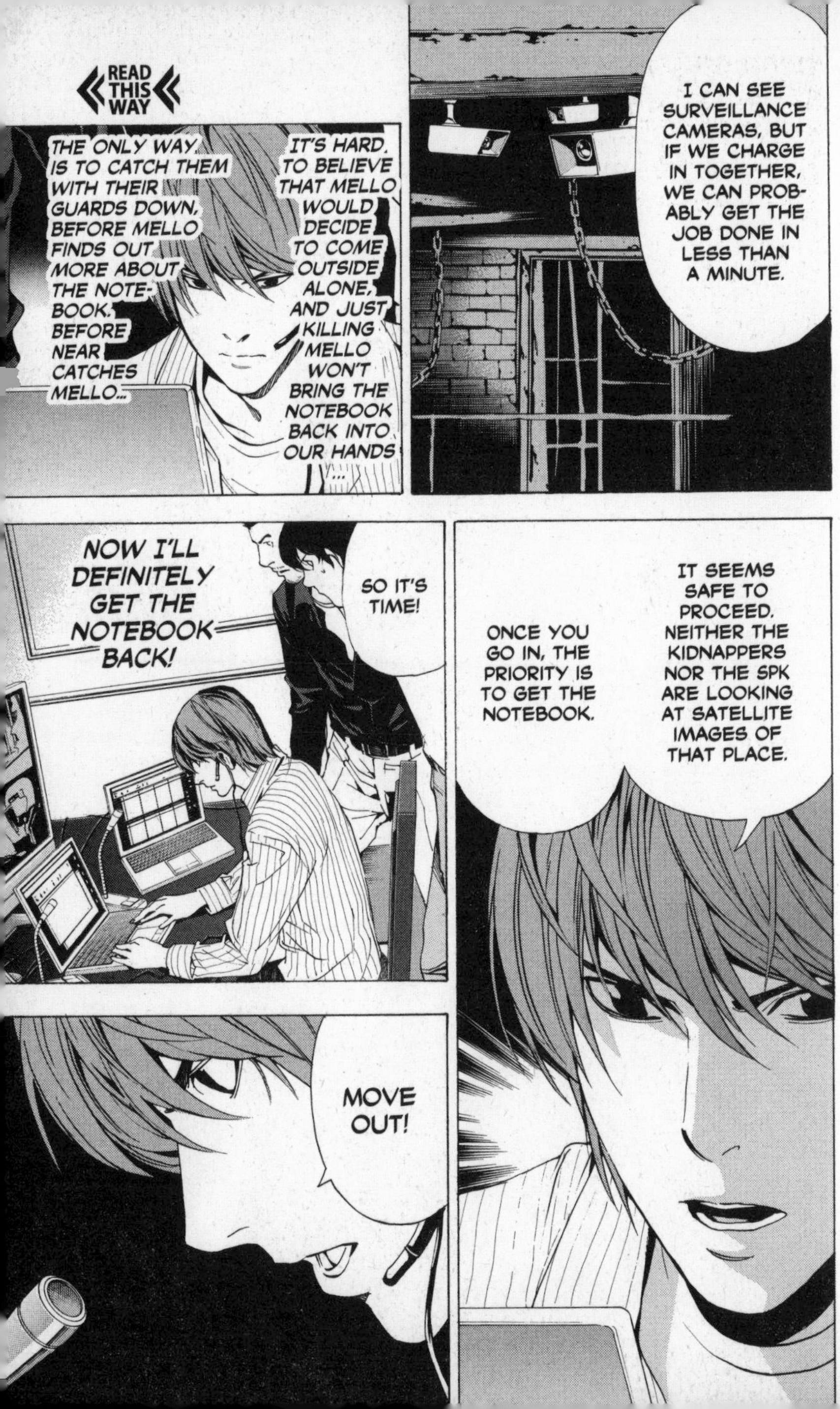
I CAN SEE SURVEILLANCE CAMERAS, BUT IF WE CHARGE IN TOGETHER, WE CAN PROBABLY GET THE JOB DONE IN LESS THAN A MINUTE.
IT'S HARD TO BELIEVE THAT MELLO WOULD DECIDE TO COME OUTSIDE ALONE, AND JUST KILLING MELLO WON'T BRING THE NOTEBOOK BACK INTO OUR HANDS...
THE ONLY WAY IS TO CATCH THEM WITH THEIR GUARDS DOWN, BEFORE MELLO FINDS OUT MORE ABOUT THE NOTEBOOK. BEFORE NEAR CATCHES MELLO...
IT SEEMS SAFE TO PROCEED. NEITHER THE KIDNAPPERS NOR THE SPK ARE LOOKING AT SATELLITE IMAGES OF THAT PLACE.
ONCE YOU GO IN, THE PRIORITY IS TO GET THE NOTEBOOK.
SO IT'S TIME!
NOW I'LL DEFINITELY GET THE NOTEBOOK BACK!
MOVE OUT!

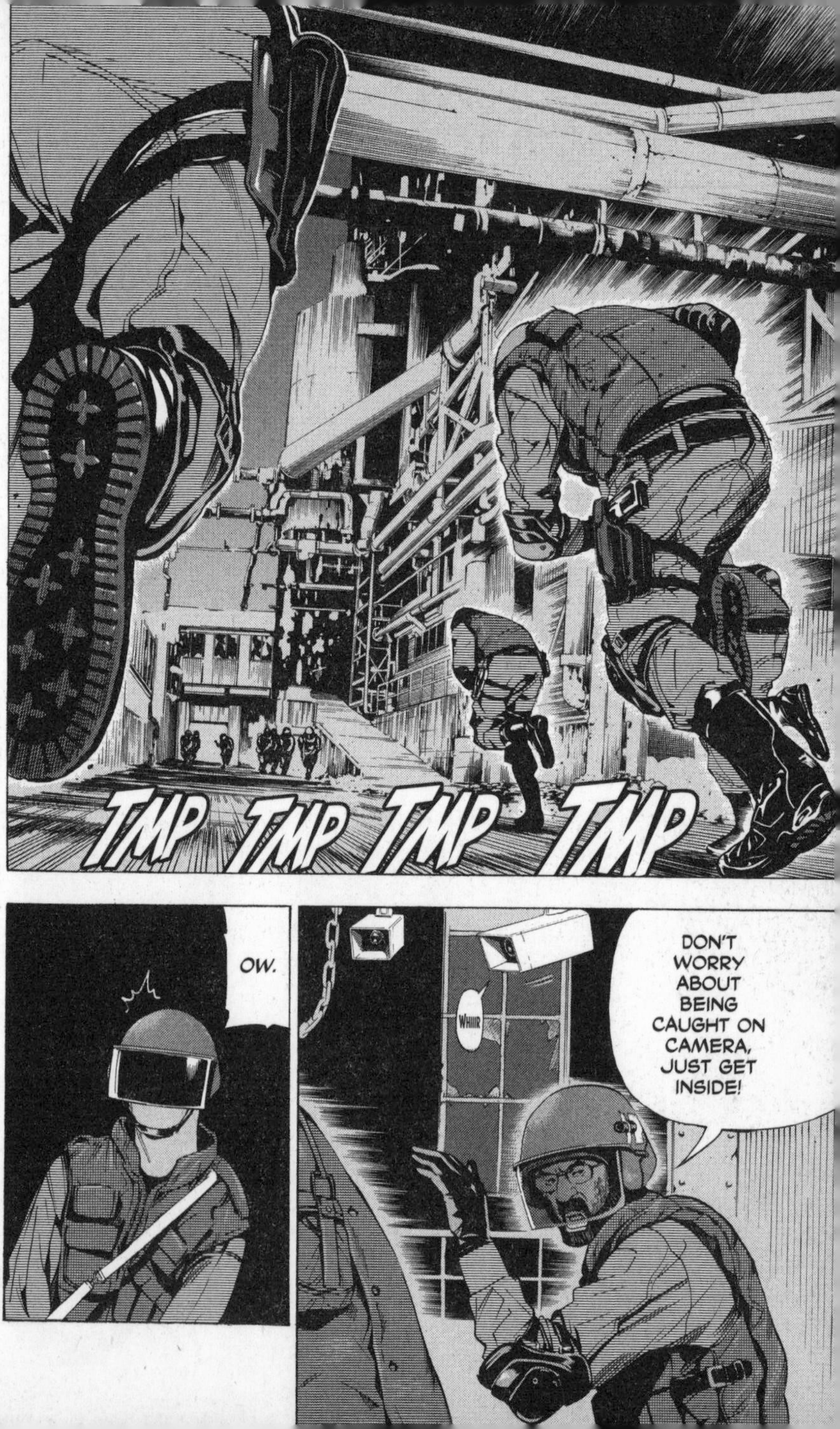
TMP TMP TMP TMP
DON'T WORRY ABOUT BEING CAUGHT ON CAMERA, JUST GET INSIDE!
WHIIIR
OW.

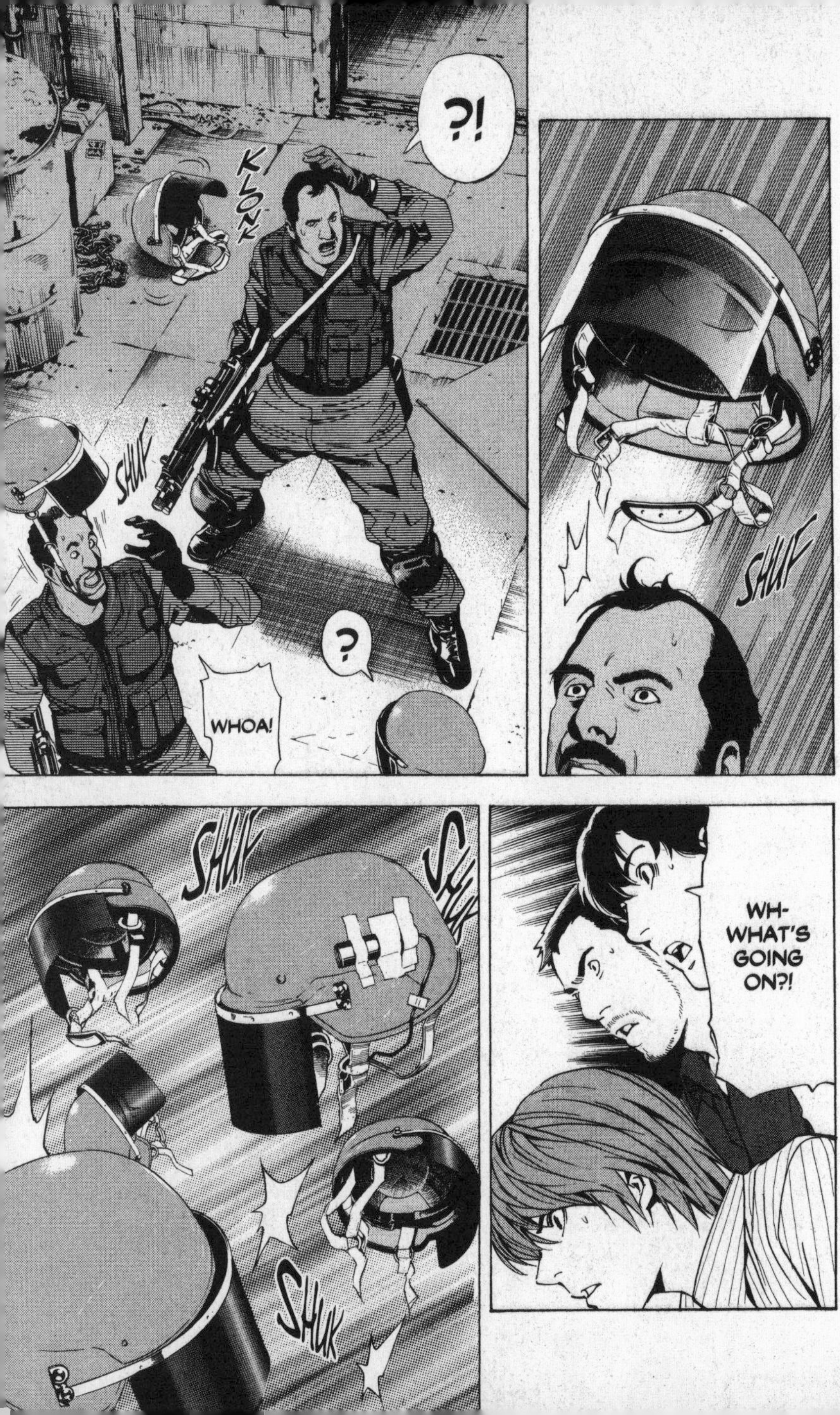
SHUF
?!
KLONK
SHUF
?
WHOA!
WH-WHAT'S GOING ON?!
SHUF
SHUK
SHUK

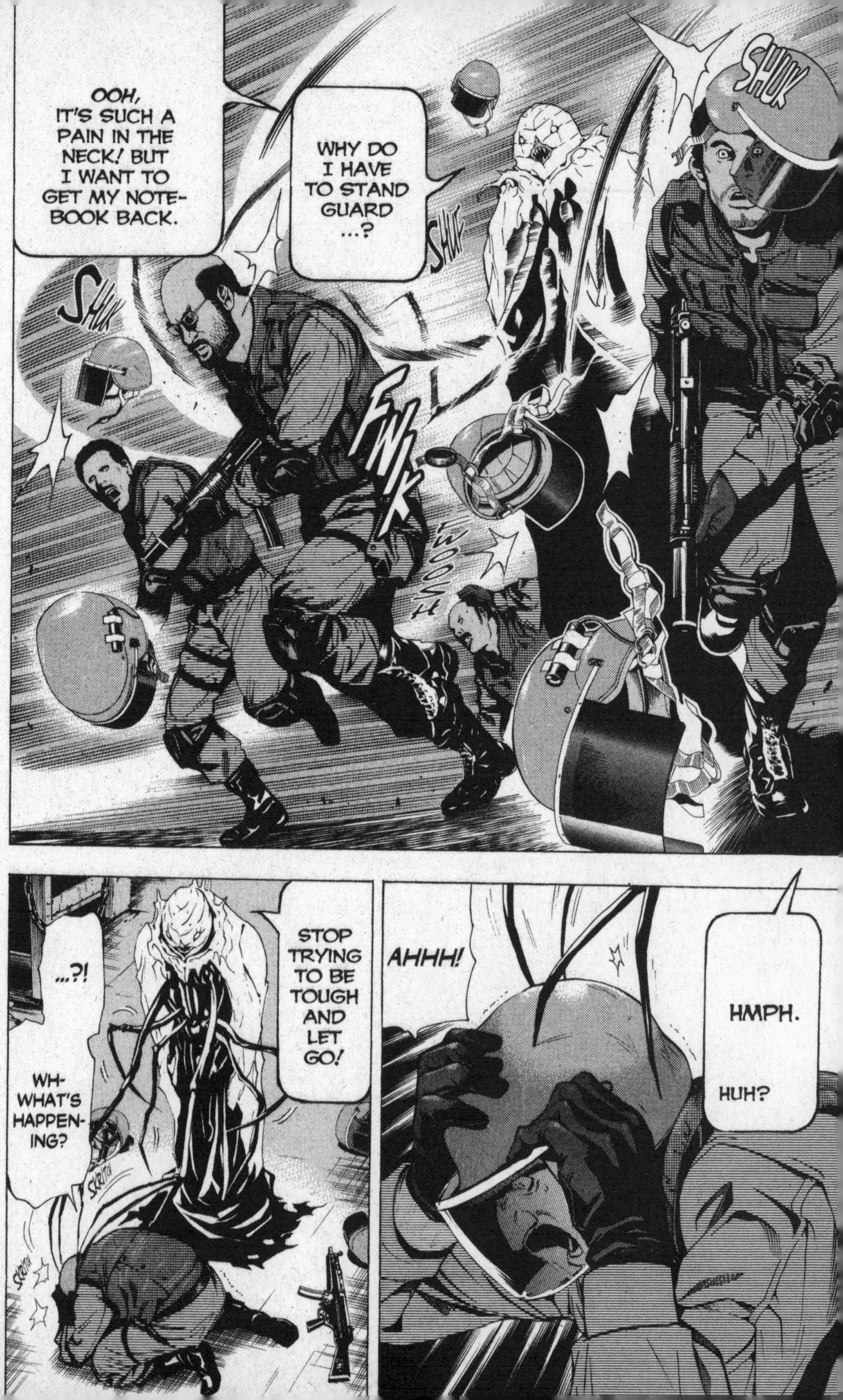
SHUK
WHY DO I HAVE TO STAND GUARD ...?
OOH, IT'S SUCH A PAIN IN THE NECK! BUT I WANT TO GET MY NOTE-BOOK BACK.
SHUK
SHUK
FWIK
HMPH.
HUH?
AHHH!
STOP TRYING TO BE TOUGH AND LET GO!
...?!
WH- WHAT'S HAPPEN-ING?

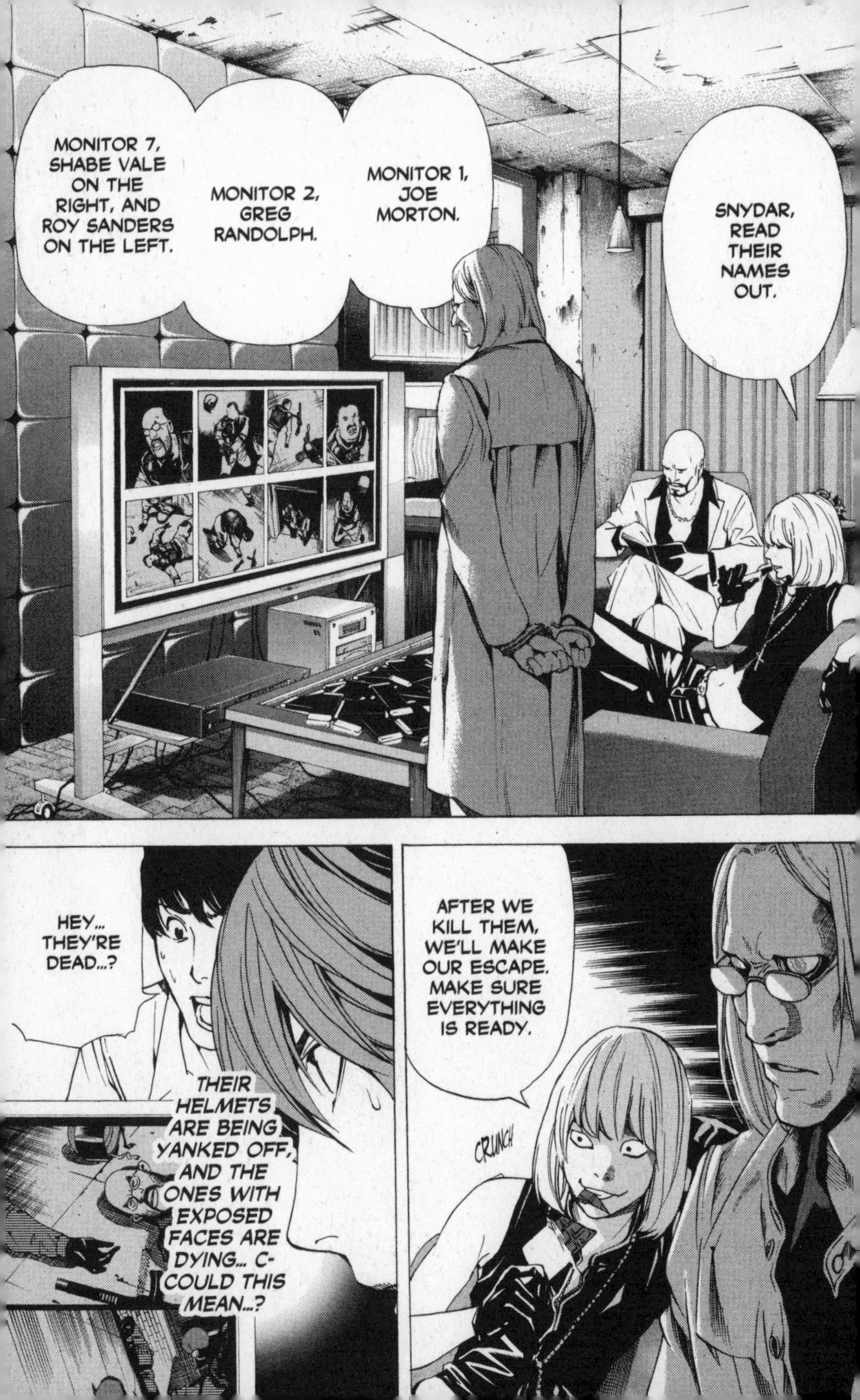

SNYDAR, READ THEIR NAMES OUT.
MONITOR 1, JOE MORTON.
MONITOR 2, GREG RANDOLPH.
MONITOR 7, SHABE VALE ON THE RIGHT, AND ROY SANDERS ON THE LEFT.
AFTER WE KILL THEM, WE'LL MAKE OUR ESCAPE. MAKE SURE EVERYTHING IS READY.
CRUNCH
HEY... THEY'RE DEAD...?
THEIR HELMETS ARE BEING YANKED OFF, AND THE ONES WITH EXPOSED FACES ARE DYING... C-COULD THIS MEAN...?

chapter 70 Tremble

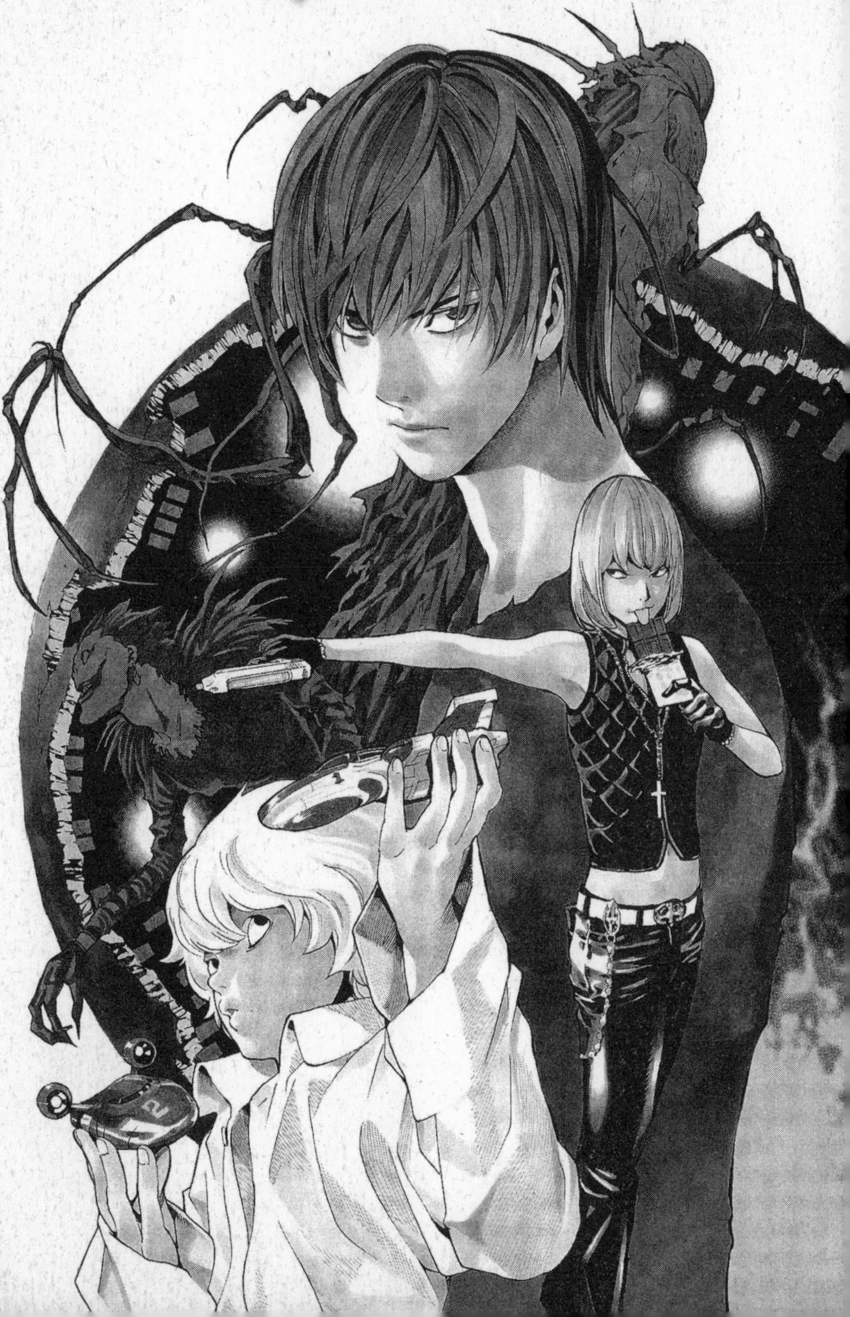

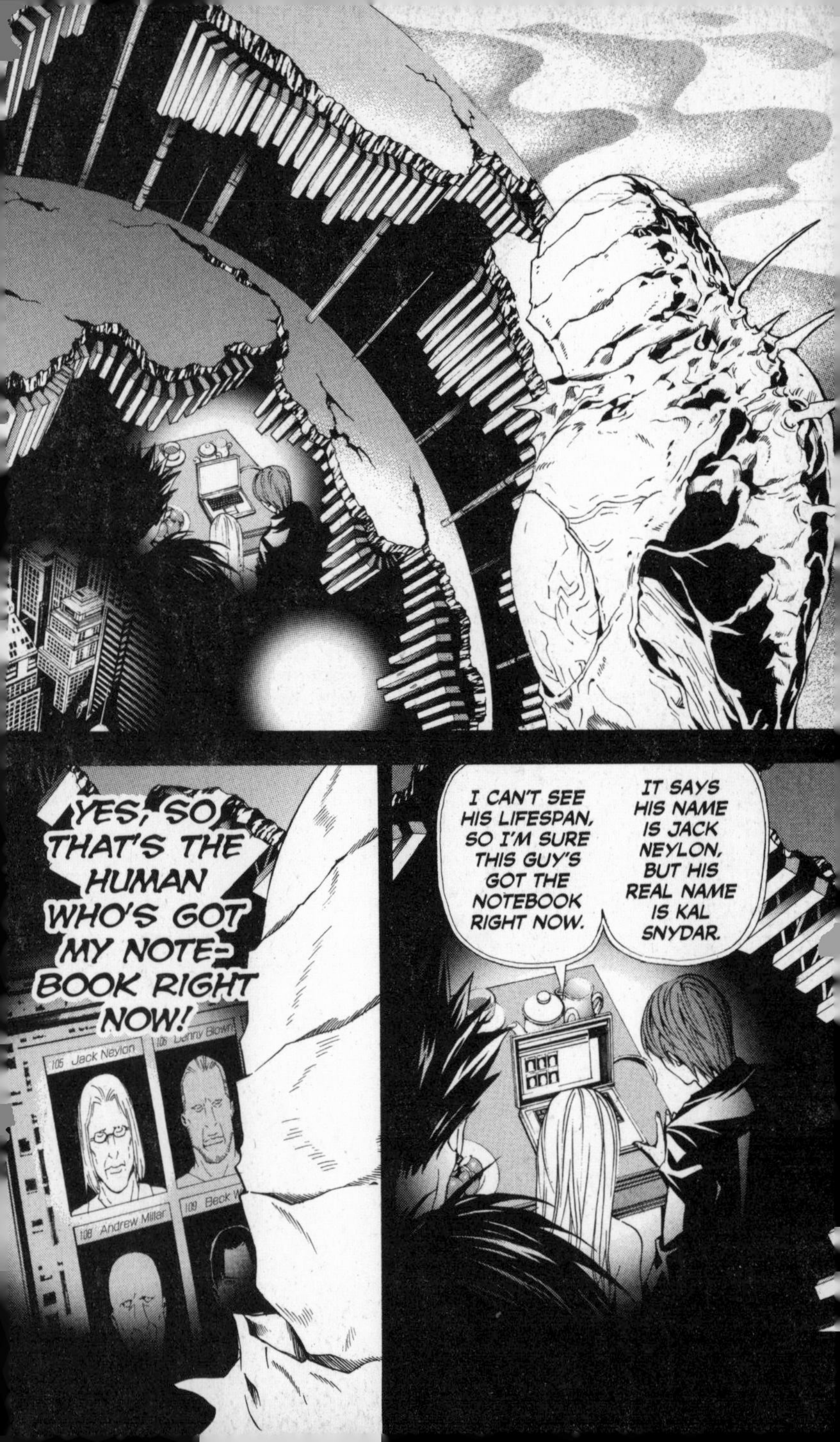
IT SAYS HIS NAME IS JACK NEYLON, BUT HIS REAL NAME IS KAL SNYDAR.
I CAN'T SEE HIS LIFESPAN, SO I'M SURE THIS GUY'S GOT THE NOTEBOOK RIGHT NOW.
YES, SO THAT'S THE HUMAN WHO'S GOT MY NOTE-BOOK RIGHT NOW!
105 Jack Neylon
106 Danny Blown
108 Andrew Miller

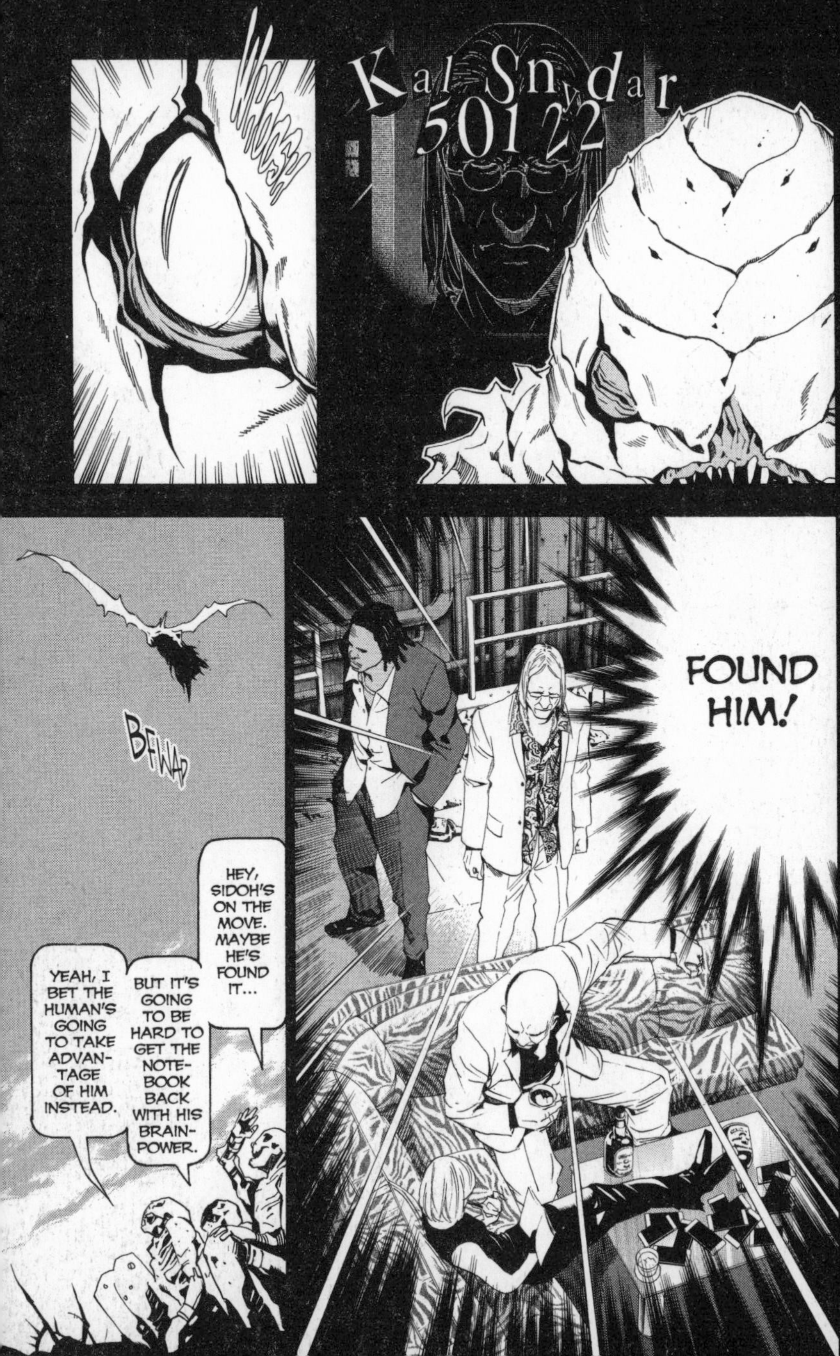
Kal Snydar
50122
WHOOSH!
FOUND HIM!
BFWAP
HEY, SIDOH'S ON THE MOVE. MAYBE HE'S FOUND IT...
BUT IT'S GOING TO BE HARD TO GET THE NOTEBOOK BACK WITH HIS BRAINPOWER.
YEAH, I BET THE HUMAN'S GOING TO TAKE ADVANTAGE OF HIM INSTEAD.

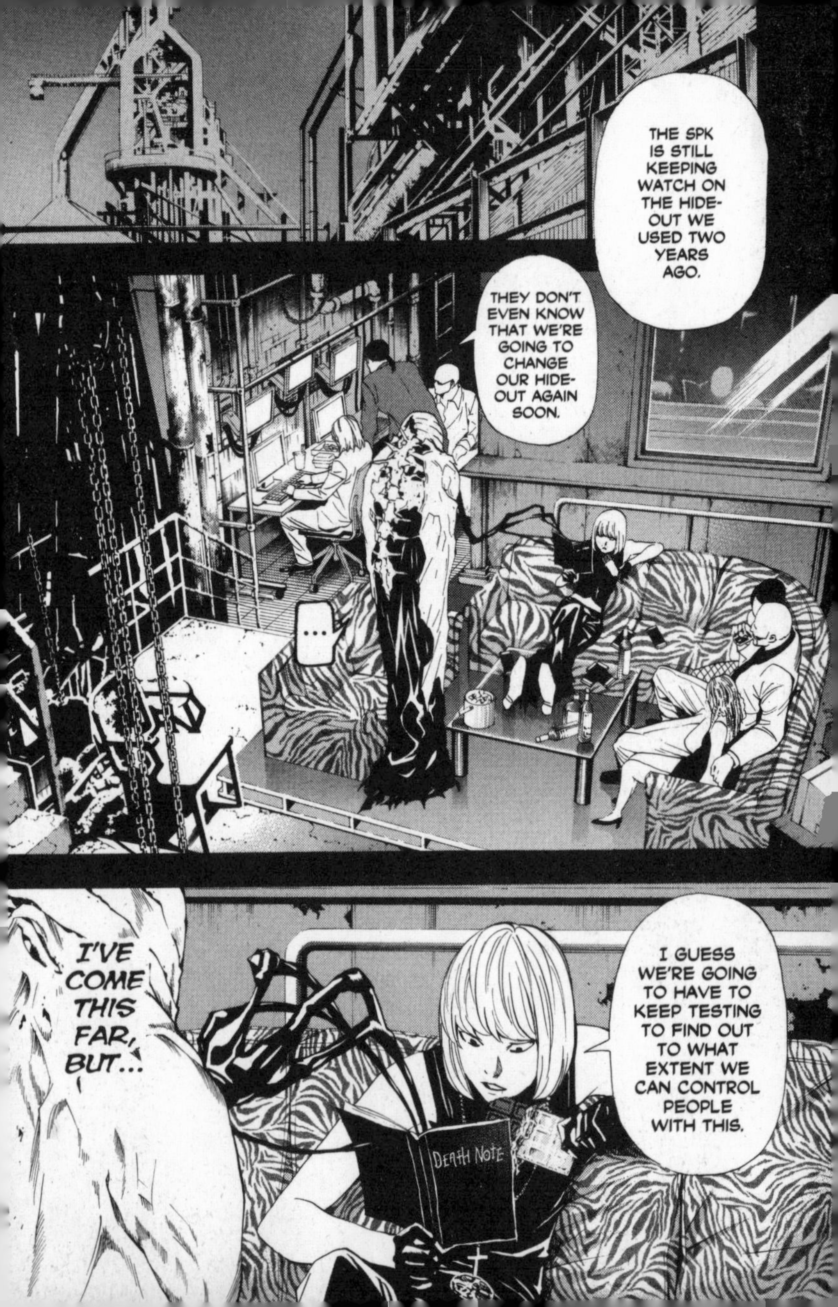
THE SPK IS STILL KEEPING WATCH ON THE HIDE-OUT WE USED TWO YEARS AGO.
THEY DON'T EVEN KNOW THAT WE'RE GOING TO CHANGE OUR HIDE-OUT AGAIN SOON.
...
I GUESS WE'RE GOING TO HAVE TO KEEP TESTING TO FIND OUT TO WHAT EXTENT WE CAN CONTROL PEOPLE WITH THIS.
DEATH NOTE
I'VE COME THIS FAR, BUT...

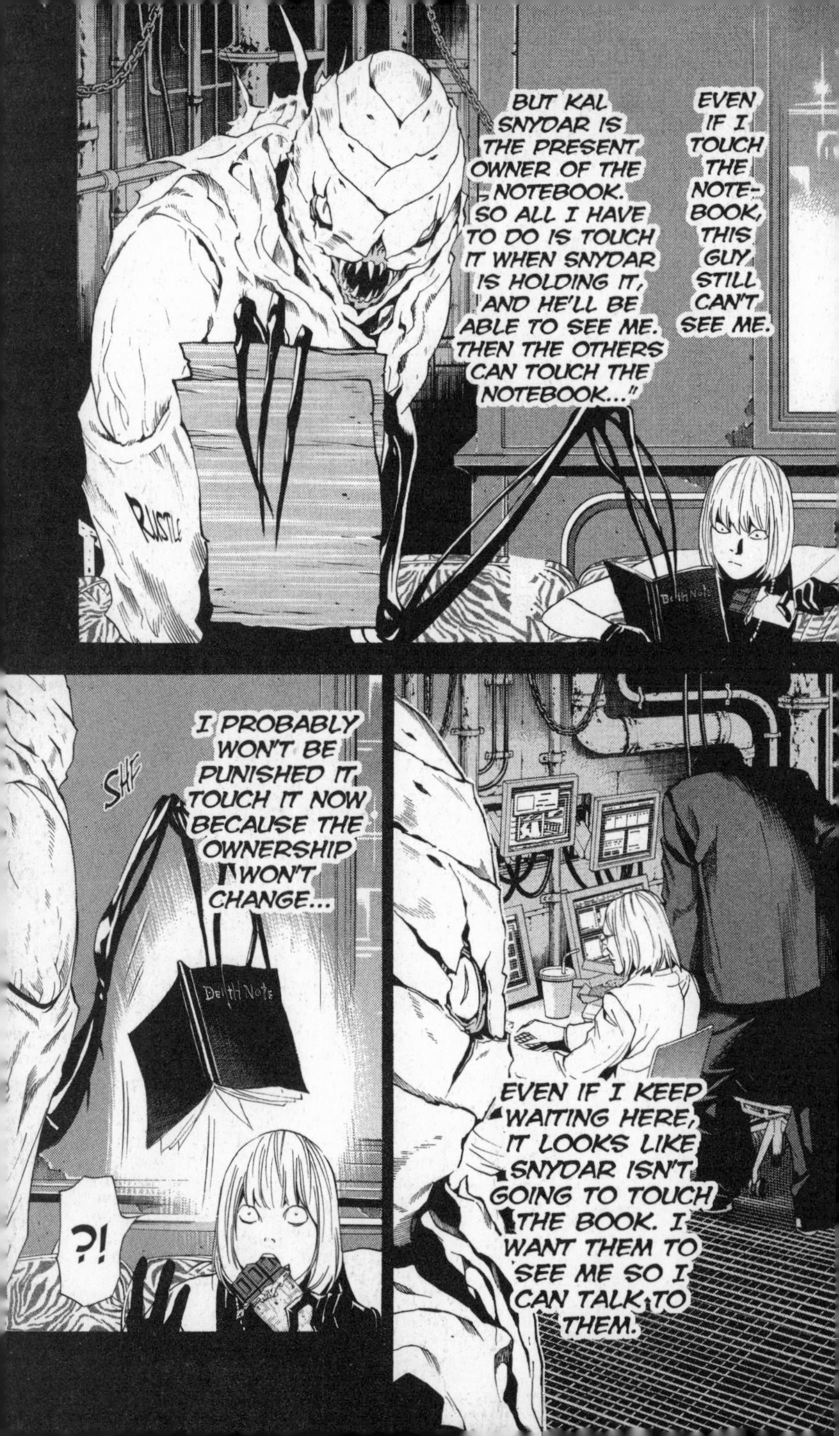
EVEN IF I TOUCH THE NOTE-BOOK, THIS GUY STILL CAN'T SEE ME.
BUT KAL SNYDAR IS THE PRESENT OWNER OF THE NOTEBOOK. SO ALL I HAVE TO DO IS TOUCH IT WHEN SNYDAR IS HOLDING IT, AND HE'LL BE ABLE TO SEE ME. THEN THE OTHERS CAN TOUCH THE NOTEBOOK..."
RUSTLE
EVEN IF I KEEP WAITING HERE, IT LOOKS LIKE SNYDAR ISN'T GOING TO TOUCH THE BOOK. I WANT THEM TO SEE ME SO I CAN TALK TO THEM.
I PROBABLY WON'T BE PUNISHED IT TOUCH IT NOW BECAUSE THE OWNERSHIP WON'T CHANGE...
SHF
?!

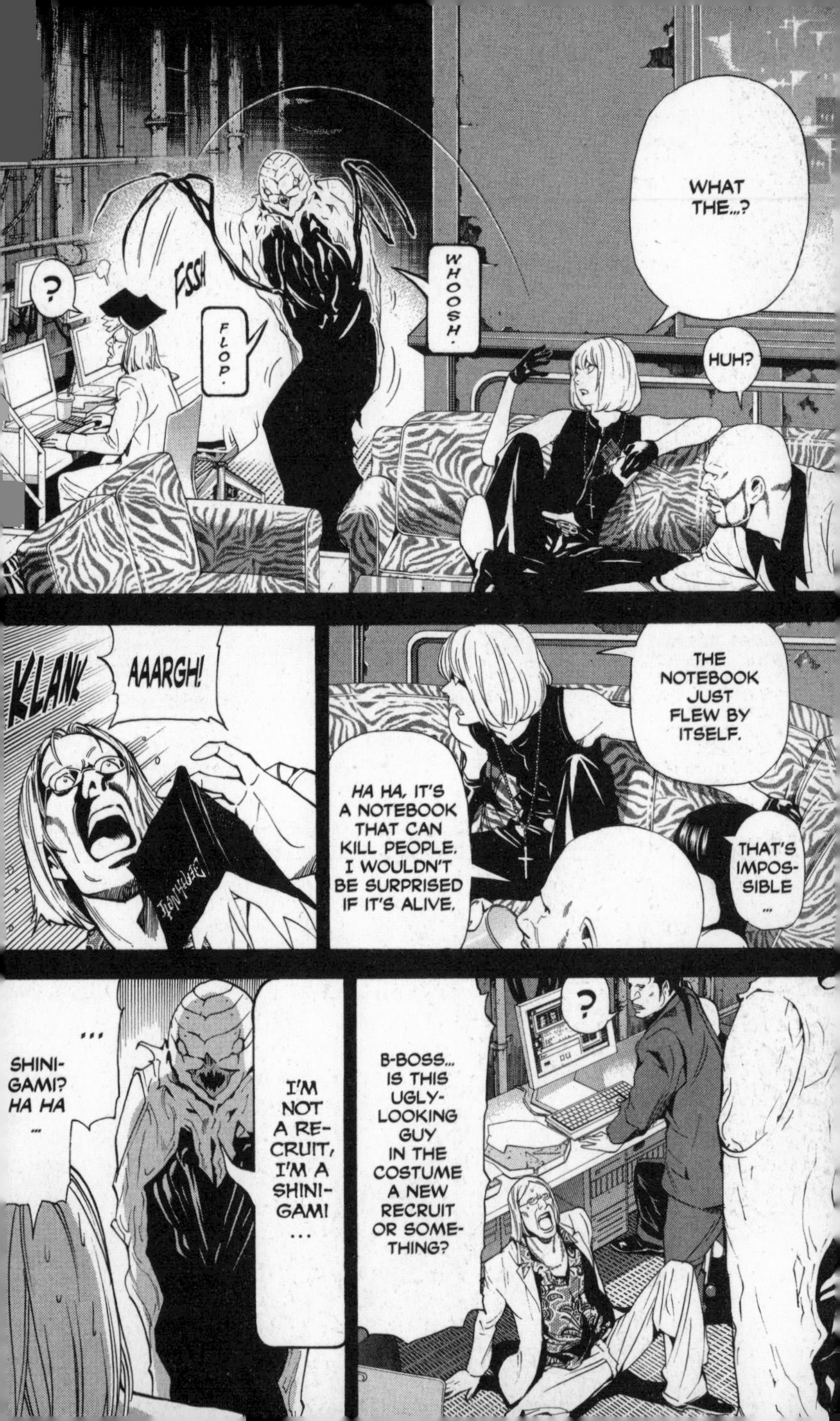
WHAT THE...?
HUH?
WHOOSH.
FLOP.
FSSH
?
THE NOTEBOOK JUST FLEW BY ITSELF.
THAT'S IMPOSSIBLE...
HA HA, IT'S A NOTEBOOK THAT CAN KILL PEOPLE. I WOULDN'T BE SURPRISED IF IT'S ALIVE.
AAARGH!
KLANK
?
B-BOSS... IS THIS UGLY-LOOKING GUY IN THE COSTUME A NEW RECRUIT OR SOMETHING?
I'M NOT A RECRUIT, I'M A SHINIGAMI...
SHINIGAMI? HA HA...
...

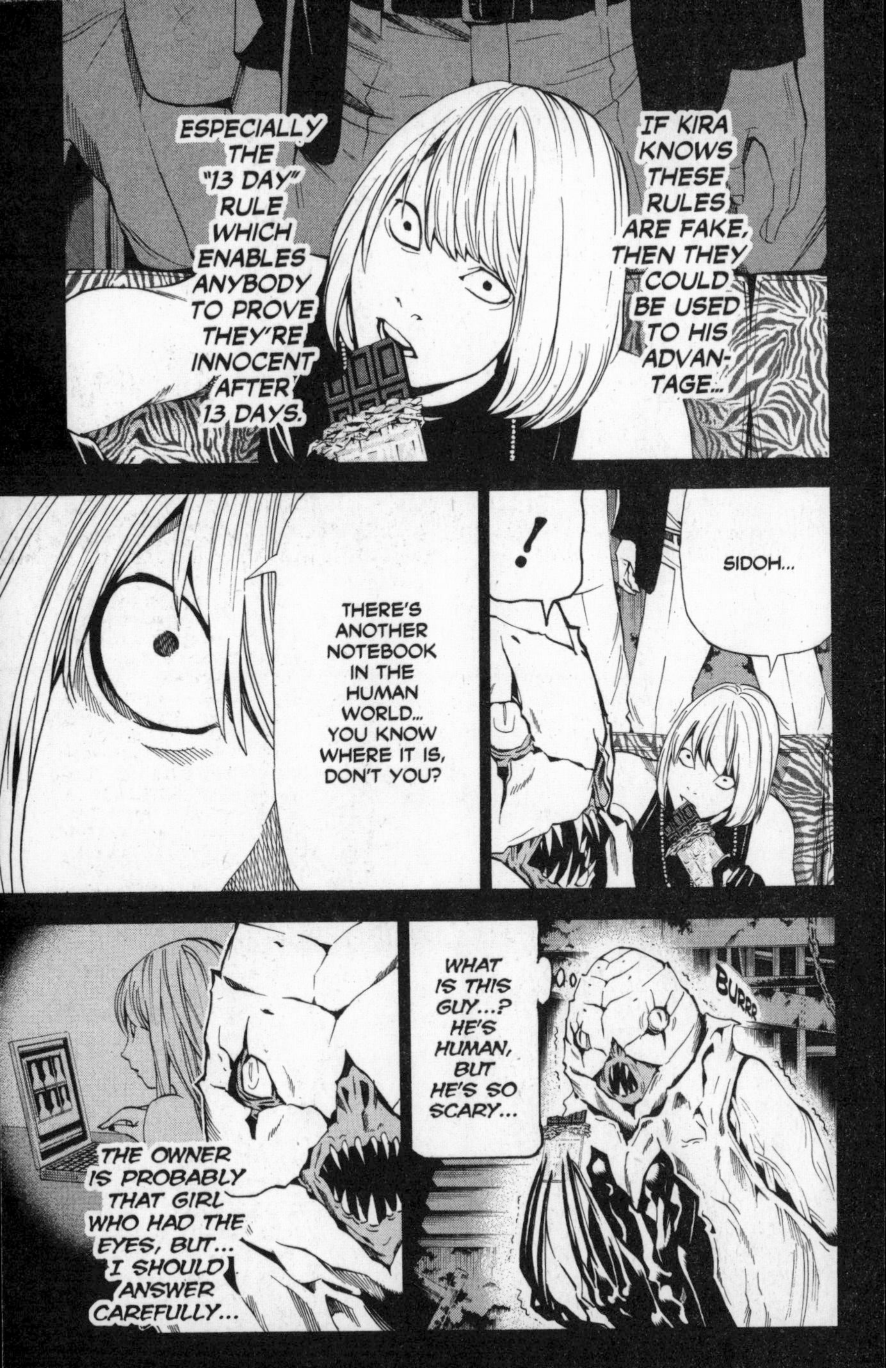
IF KIRA KNOWS THESE RULES ARE FAKE, THEN THEY COULD BE USED TO HIS ADVANTAGE...
ESPECIALLY THE "13 DAY" RULE WHICH ENABLES ANYBODY TO PROVE THEY'RE INNOCENT AFTER 13 DAYS.
!
SIDOH...
THERE'S ANOTHER NOTEBOOK IN THE HUMAN WORLD... YOU KNOW WHERE IT IS, DON'T YOU?
BURRR
WHAT IS THIS GUY...? HE'S HUMAN, BUT HE'S SO SCARY...
THE OWNER IS PROBABLY THAT GIRL WHO HAD THE EYES, BUT... I SHOULD ANSWER CAREFULLY...

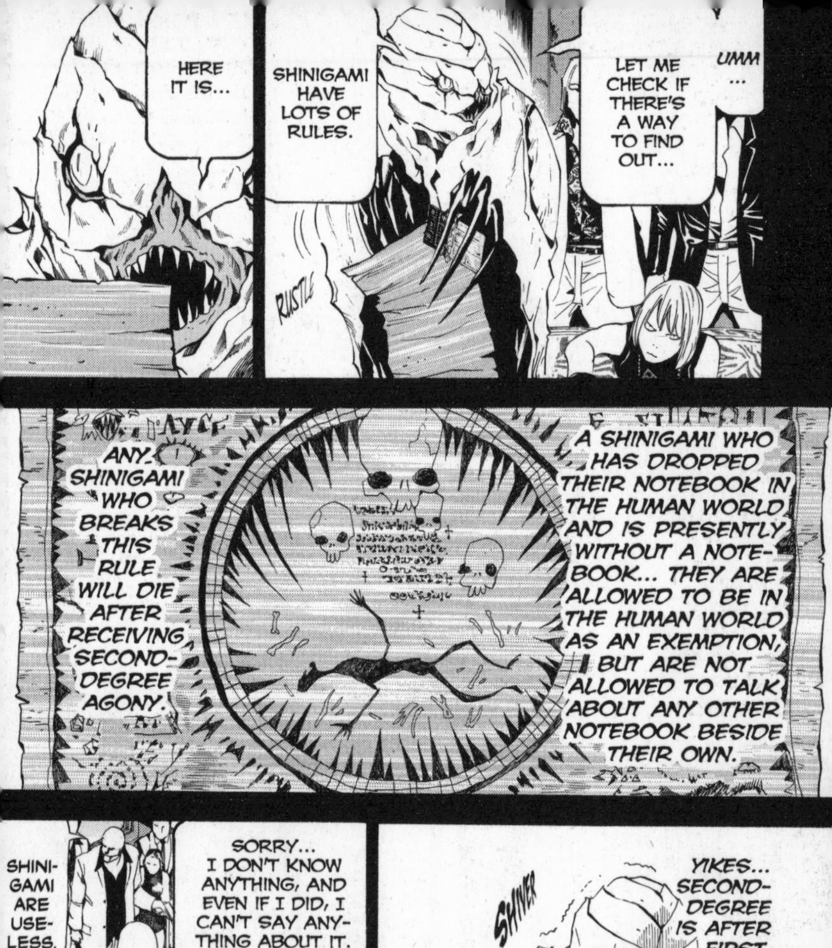
UMM ...
LET ME CHECK IF THERE'S A WAY TO FIND OUT...
SHINIGAMI HAVE LOTS OF RULES.
RUSTLE
HERE IT IS...
A SHINIGAMI WHO HAS DROPPED THEIR NOTEBOOK IN THE HUMAN WORLD AND IS PRESENTLY WITHOUT A NOTE-BOOK... THEY ARE ALLOWED TO BE IN THE HUMAN WORLD AS AN EXEMPTION, BUT ARE NOT ALLOWED TO TALK ABOUT ANY OTHER NOTEBOOK BESIDE THEIR OWN.
ANY SHINIGAMI WHO BREAKS THIS RULE WILL DIE AFTER RECEIVING SECOND-DEGREE AGONY.
YIKES... SECOND-DEGREE IS AFTER FIRST, ISN'T IT...?
SHIVER
SORRY... I DON'T KNOW ANYTHING, AND EVEN IF I DID, I CAN'T SAY ANY-THING ABOUT IT. ALL I CAN TALK TO YOU ABOUT IS THE NOTEBOOK THAT I DROPPED.
SHINI-GAMI ARE USE-LESS.
...

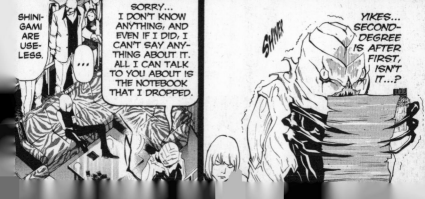

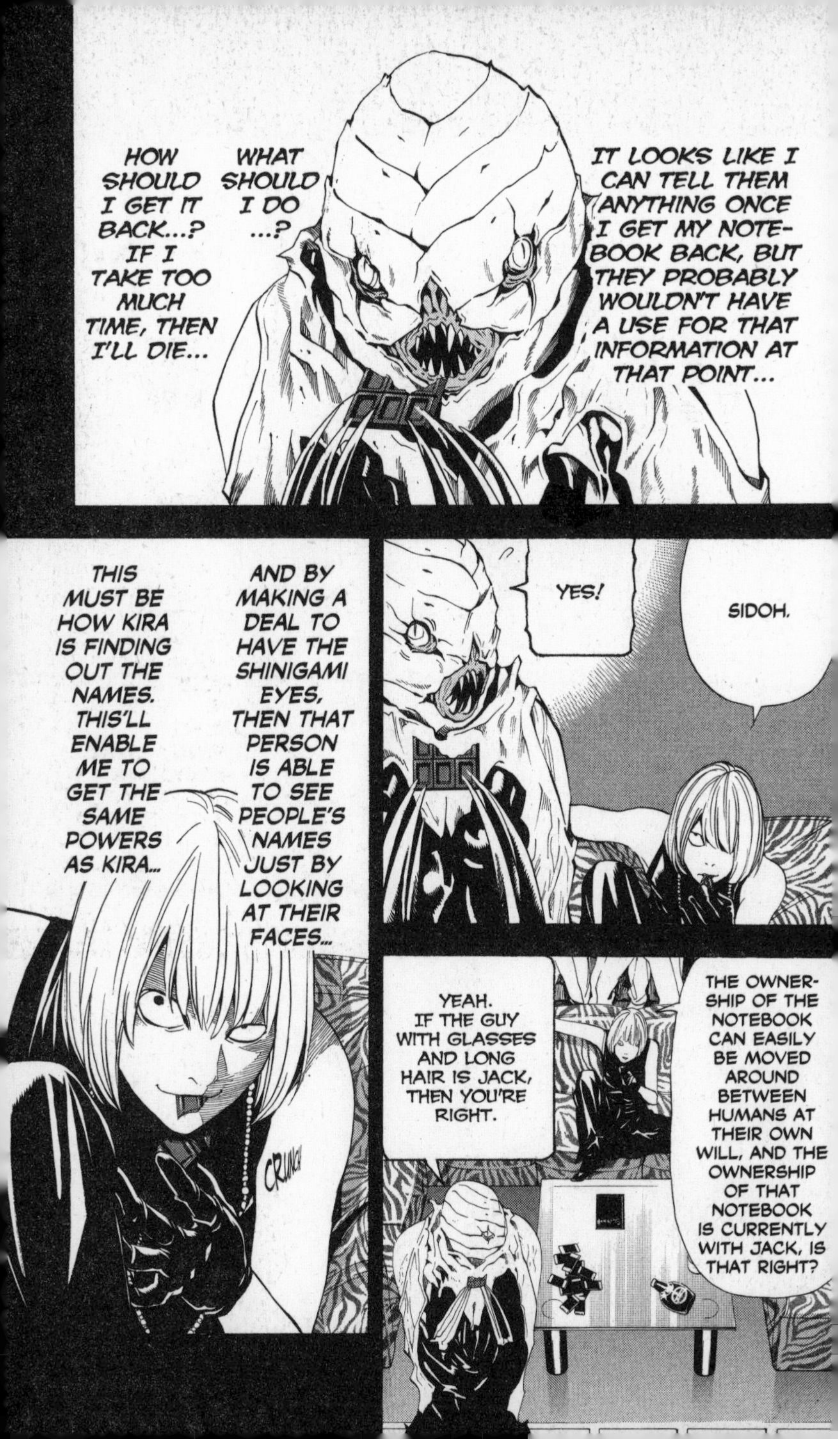
IT LOOKS LIKE I CAN TELL THEM ANYTHING ONCE I GET MY NOTE-BOOK BACK, BUT THEY PROBABLY WOULDN'T HAVE A USE FOR THAT INFORMATION AT THAT POINT...
WHAT SHOULD I DO ...?
HOW SHOULD I GET IT BACK...? IF I TAKE TOO MUCH TIME, THEN I'LL DIE...
SIDOH.
YES!
THE OWNER-SHIP OF THE NOTEBOOK CAN EASILY BE MOVED AROUND BETWEEN HUMANS AT THEIR OWN WILL, AND THE OWNERSHIP OF THAT NOTEBOOK IS CURRENTLY WITH JACK, IS THAT RIGHT?
YEAH. IF THE GUY WITH GLASSES AND LONG HAIR IS JACK, THEN YOU'RE RIGHT.
AND BY MAKING A DEAL TO HAVE THE SHINIGAMI EYES, THEN THAT PERSON IS ABLE TO SEE PEOPLE'S NAMES JUST BY LOOKING AT THEIR FACES...
THIS MUST BE HOW KIRA IS FINDING OUT THE NAMES. THIS'LL ENABLE ME TO GET THE SAME POWERS AS KIRA...
CRUNCH

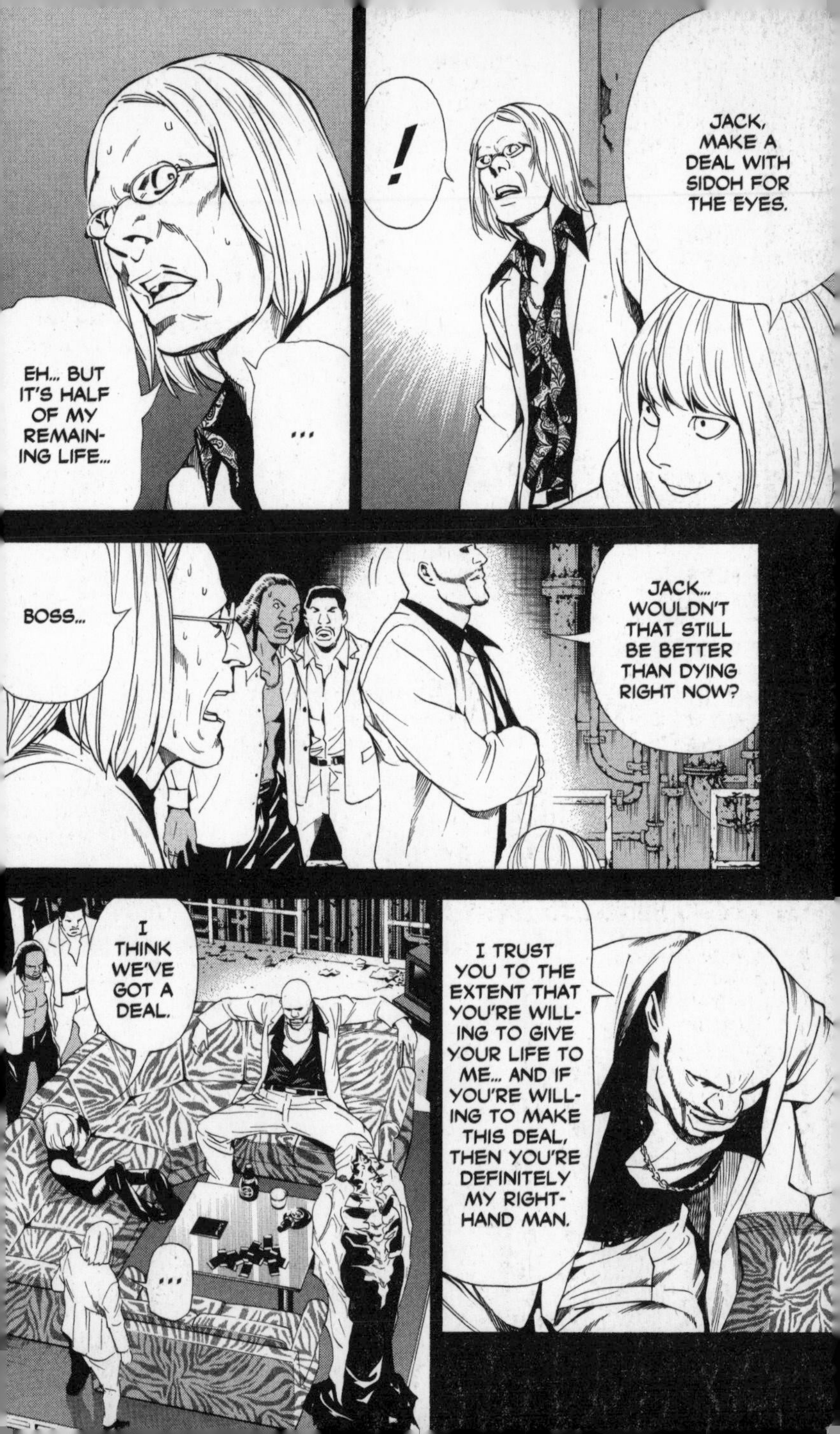
JACK, MAKE A DEAL WITH SIDOH FOR THE EYES.
!
EH... BUT IT'S HALF OF MY REMAINING LIFE...
...
JACK... WOULDN'T THAT STILL BE BETTER THAN DYING RIGHT NOW?
BOSS...
I TRUST YOU TO THE EXTENT THAT YOU'RE WILLING TO GIVE YOUR LIFE TO ME... AND IF YOU'RE WILLING TO MAKE THIS DEAL, THEN YOU'RE DEFINITELY MY RIGHT-HAND MAN.
I THINK WE'VE GOT A DEAL.
...

AWESOME. JACK, I WANT YOU TO TELL ME THE LIFESPAN OF EVERYONE, EXCEPT ME AND MELLO, LATER.

...

AND TELL ME THE REAL NAMES OF THOSE PEOPLE WITH ALIASES.

I CAN SEE IT. EVERY-BODY'S NAME AND LIFE-SPAN!

ALL HE HAS TO DO TO GET THE NOTE-BOOK BACK IS TO KILL US, BUT THERE SEEMS TO BE A RULE OR SOME KIND OF REASON FOR NOT DOING IT, SO...

THIS SHINIGAMI... EARLIER HE SAID "THAT NOTEBOOK THAT I DROPPED," SO IT'S PRETTY OBVIOUS THAT HE CAME TO GET THE NOTEBOOK BACK.

GET THE GUY OUTSIDE STAND-ING WATCH TO COME BACK IN. WE'LL ONLY NEED THE SURVEIL-LANCE CAMERAS AND SIDOH NOW.

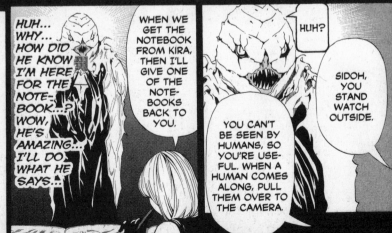

HUH... WHY... HOW DID HE KNOW I'M HERE FOR THE NOTE-BOOK...? WOW, HE'S AMAZING... I'LL DO WHAT HE SAYS...

WHEN WE GET THE NOTEBOOK FROM KIRA, THEN I'LL GIVE ONE OF THE NOTE-BOOKS BACK TO YOU.

HUH?

SIDOH, YOU STAND WATCH OUTSIDE.

YOU CAN'T BE SEEN BY HUMANS, SO YOU'RE USE-FUL. WHEN A HUMAN COMES ALONG, PULL THEM OVER TO THE CAMERA.

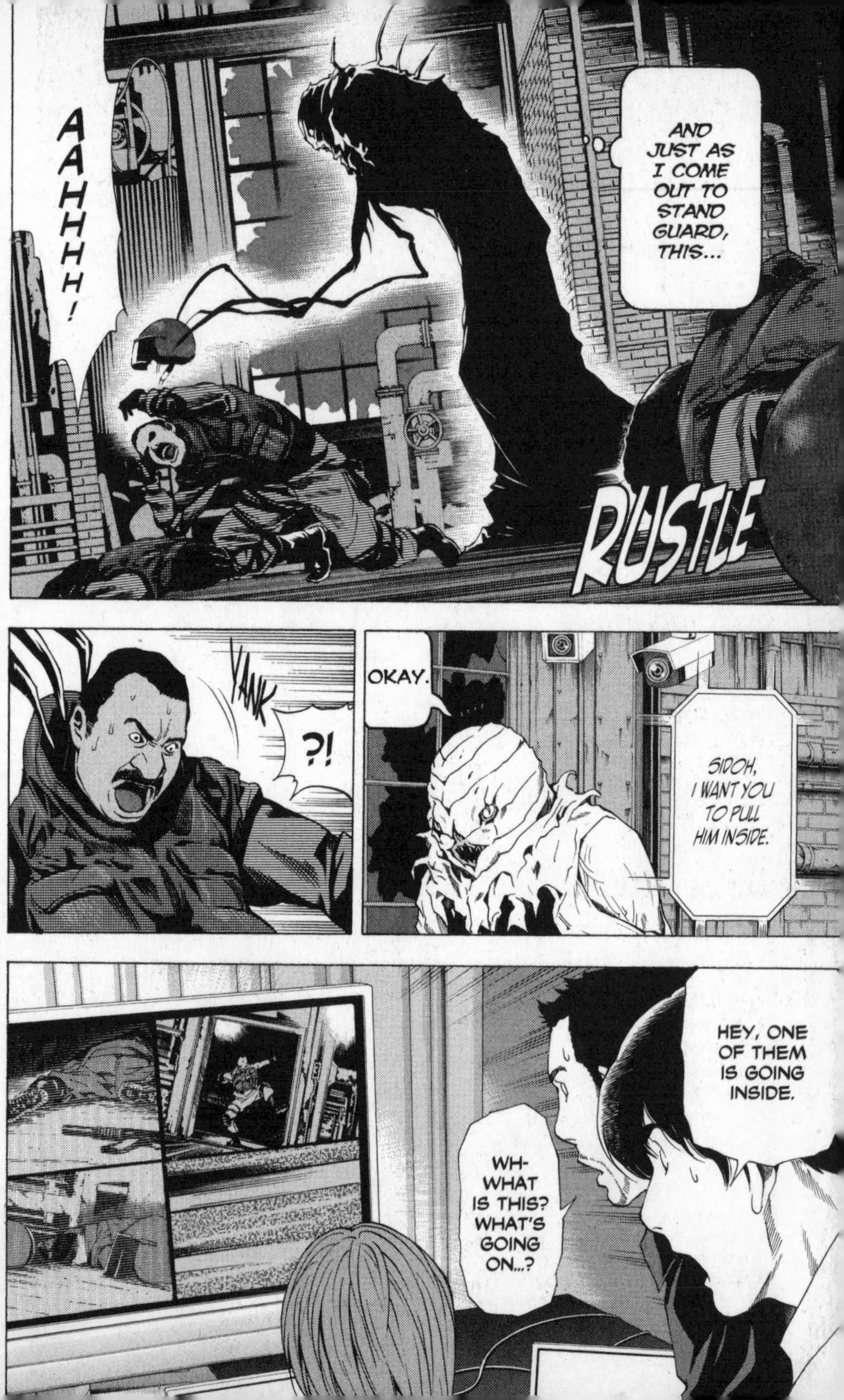
AND JUST AS I COME OUT TO STAND GUARD, THIS...
AAHHHHH!
RUSTLE
OKAY.
SIDOH, I WANT YOU TO PULL HIM INSIDE.
YANK
?!
HEY, ONE OF THEM IS GOING INSIDE.
WH- WHAT IS THIS? WHAT'S GOING ON...?

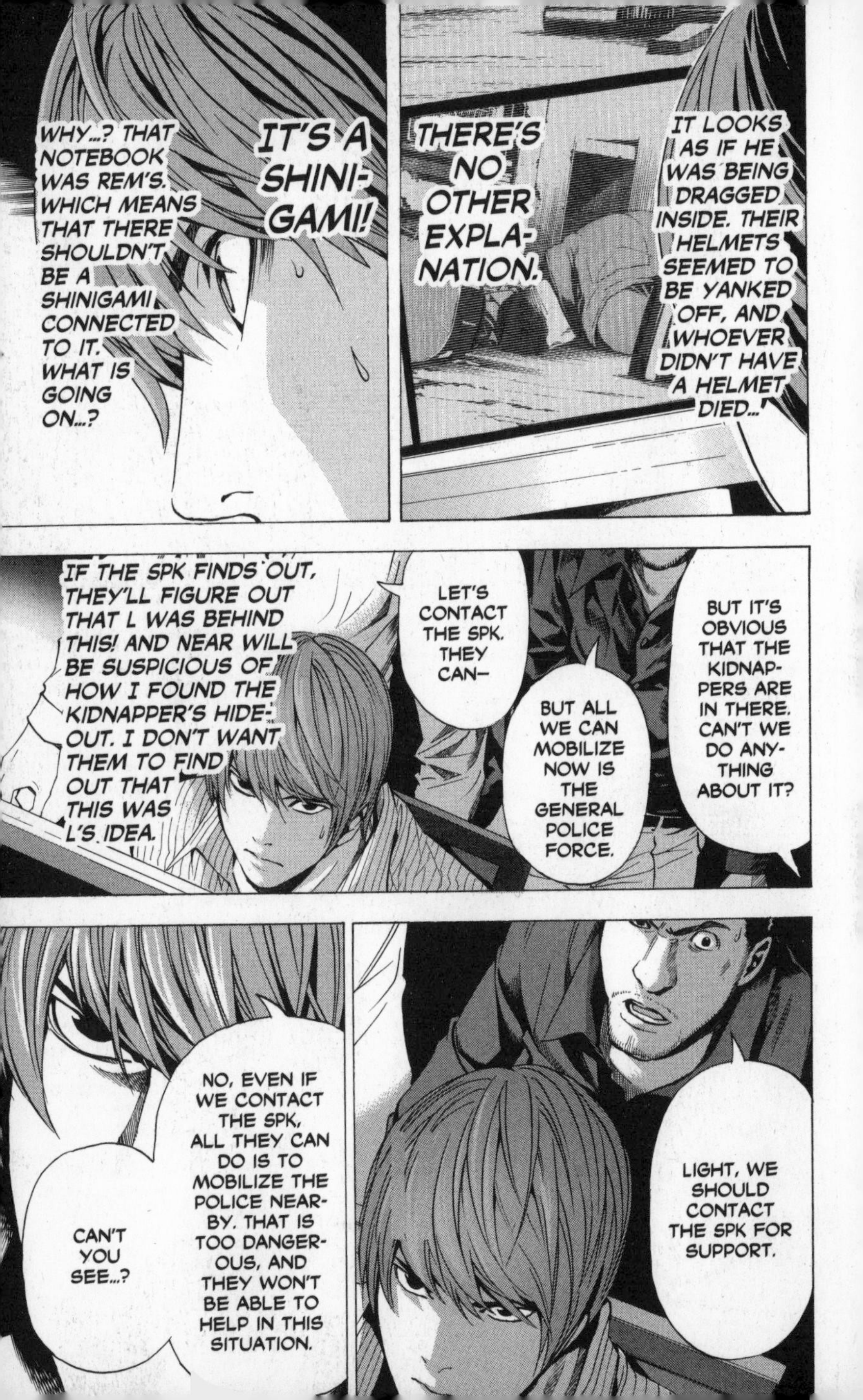
IT LOOKS AS IF HE WAS BEING DRAGGED INSIDE. THEIR HELMETS SEEMED TO BE YANKED OFF, AND WHOEVER DIDN'T HAVE A HELMET DIED...
THERE'S NO OTHER EXPLANATION.
IT'S A SHINIGAMI!
WHY...? THAT NOTEBOOK WAS REM'S. WHICH MEANS THAT THERE SHOULDN'T BE A SHINIGAMI CONNECTED TO IT. WHAT IS GOING ON...?
BUT IT'S OBVIOUS THAT THE KIDNAPPERS ARE IN THERE. CAN'T WE DO ANYTHING ABOUT IT?
BUT ALL WE CAN MOBILIZE NOW IS THE GENERAL POLICE FORCE.
LET'S CONTACT THE SPK. THEY CAN–
IF THE SPK FINDS OUT, THEY'LL FIGURE OUT THAT L WAS BEHIND THIS! AND NEAR WILL BE SUSPICIOUS OF HOW I FOUND THE KIDNAPPER'S HIDEOUT. I DON'T WANT THEM TO FIND OUT THAT THIS WAS L'S IDEA.
LIGHT, WE SHOULD CONTACT THE SPK FOR SUPPORT.
NO, EVEN IF WE CONTACT THE SPK, ALL THEY CAN DO IS TO MOBILIZE THE POLICE NEARBY. THAT IS TOO DANGEROUS, AND THEY WON'T BE ABLE TO HELP IN THIS SITUATION.
CAN'T YOU SEE...?

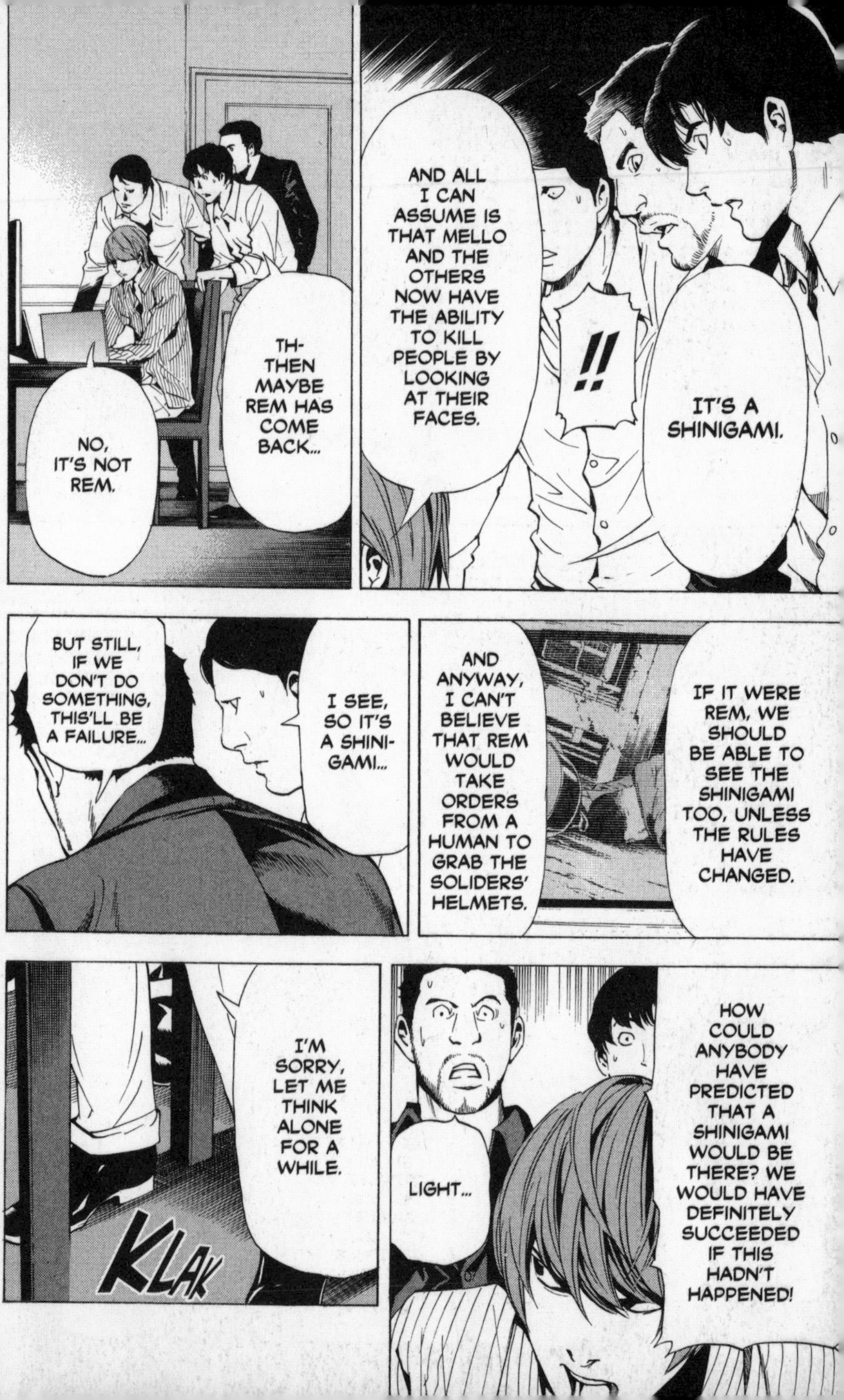
IT'S A SHINIGAMI.
!!
AND ALL I CAN ASSUME IS THAT MELLO AND THE OTHERS NOW HAVE THE ABILITY TO KILL PEOPLE BY LOOKING AT THEIR FACES.
TH-THEN MAYBE REM HAS COME BACK...
NO, IT'S NOT REM.
IF IT WERE REM, WE SHOULD BE ABLE TO SEE THE SHINIGAMI TOO, UNLESS THE RULES HAVE CHANGED.
AND ANYWAY, I CAN'T BELIEVE THAT REM WOULD TAKE ORDERS FROM A HUMAN TO GRAB THE SOLIDERS' HELMETS.
I SEE, SO IT'S A SHINIGAMI...
BUT STILL, IF WE DON'T DO SOMETHING, THIS'LL BE A FAILURE...
HOW COULD ANYBODY HAVE PREDICTED THAT A SHINIGAMI WOULD BE THERE? WE WOULD HAVE DEFINITELY SUCCEEDED IF THIS HADN'T HAPPENED!
LIGHT...
I'M SORRY, LET ME THINK ALONE FOR A WHILE.
KLAK

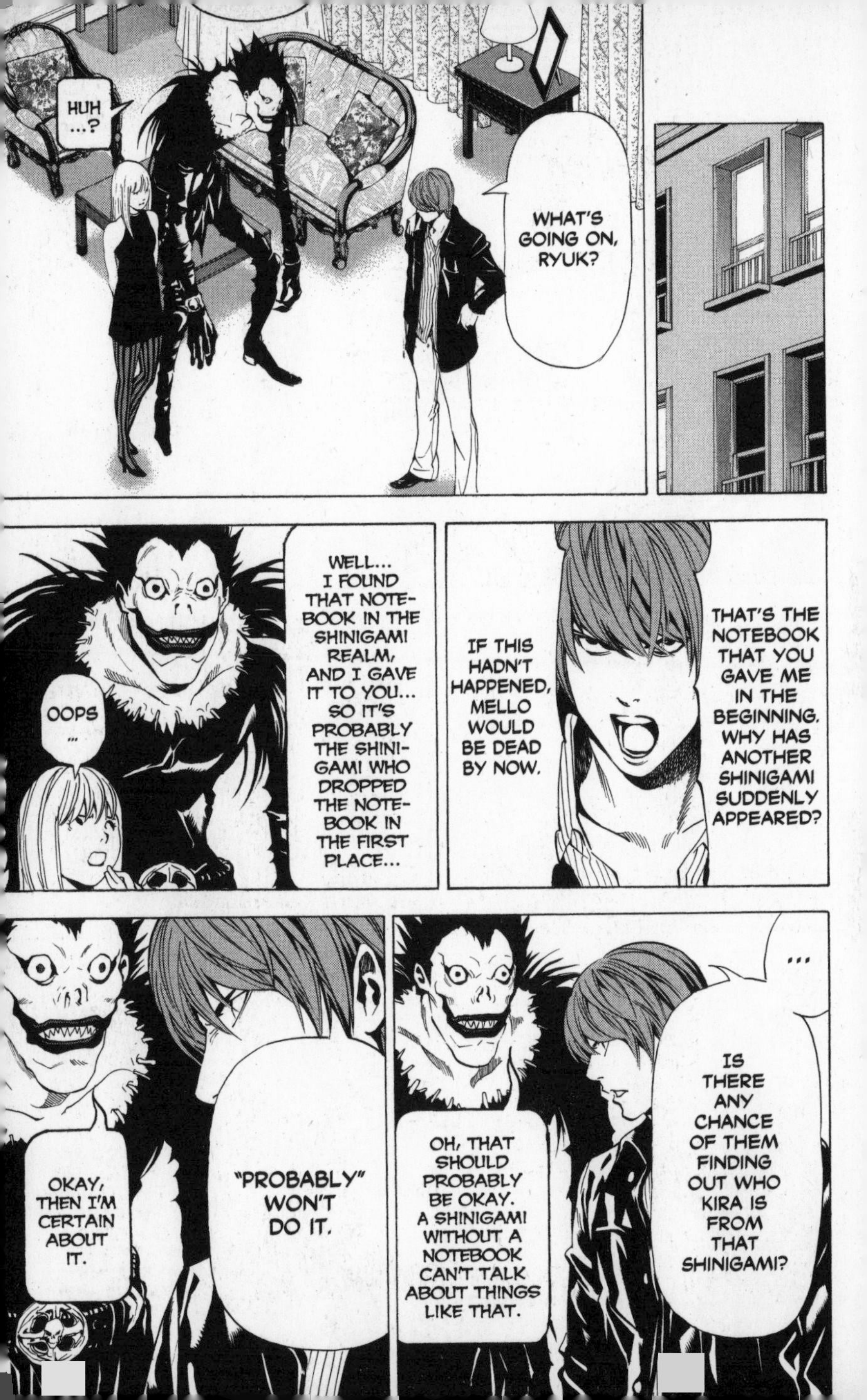
WHAT'S GOING ON, RYUK?
HUH ...?
THAT'S THE NOTEBOOK THAT YOU GAVE ME IN THE BEGINNING. WHY HAS ANOTHER SHINIGAMI SUDDENLY APPEARED?
IF THIS HADN'T HAPPENED, MELLO WOULD BE DEAD BY NOW.
WELL... I FOUND THAT NOTE-BOOK IN THE SHINIGAMI REALM, AND I GAVE IT TO YOU... SO IT'S PROBABLY THE SHINI-GAMI WHO DROPPED THE NOTE-BOOK IN THE FIRST PLACE...
OOPS ...
...
IS THERE ANY CHANCE OF THEM FINDING OUT WHO KIRA IS FROM THAT SHINIGAMI?
OH, THAT SHOULD PROBABLY BE OKAY. A SHINIGAMI WITHOUT A NOTEBOOK CAN'T TALK ABOUT THINGS LIKE THAT.
"PROBABLY" WON'T DO IT.
OKAY, THEN I'M CERTAIN ABOUT IT.

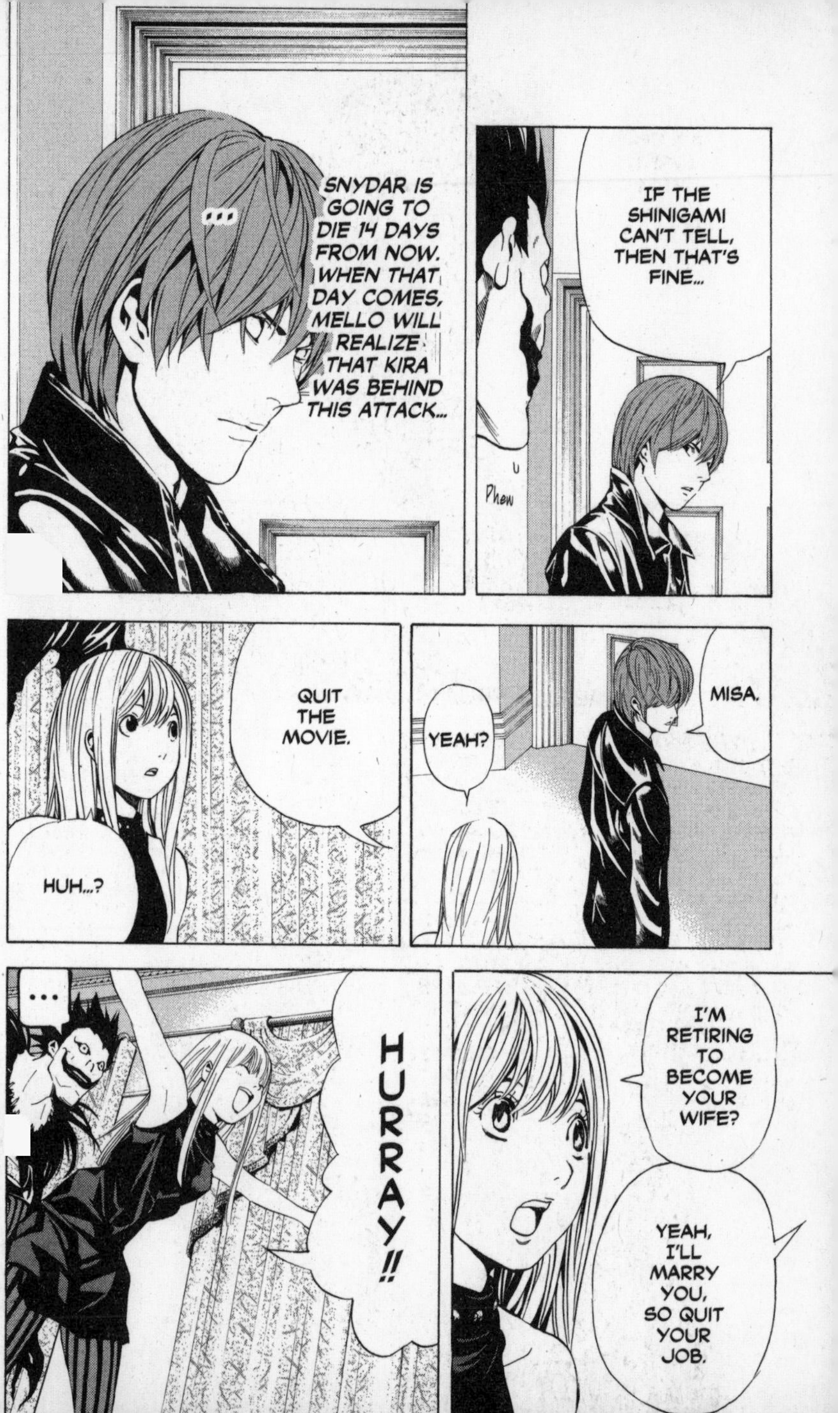
IF THE SHINIGAMI CAN'T TELL, THEN THAT'S FINE...
Phew
SNYDAR IS GOING TO DIE 14 DAYS FROM NOW. WHEN THAT DAY COMES, MELLO WILL REALIZE THAT KIRA WAS BEHIND THIS ATTACK...
...
MISA.
YEAH?
QUIT THE MOVIE.
HUH...?
I'M RETIRING TO BECOME YOUR WIFE?
YEAH, I'LL MARRY YOU, SO QUIT YOUR JOB.
HURRAY!!
...

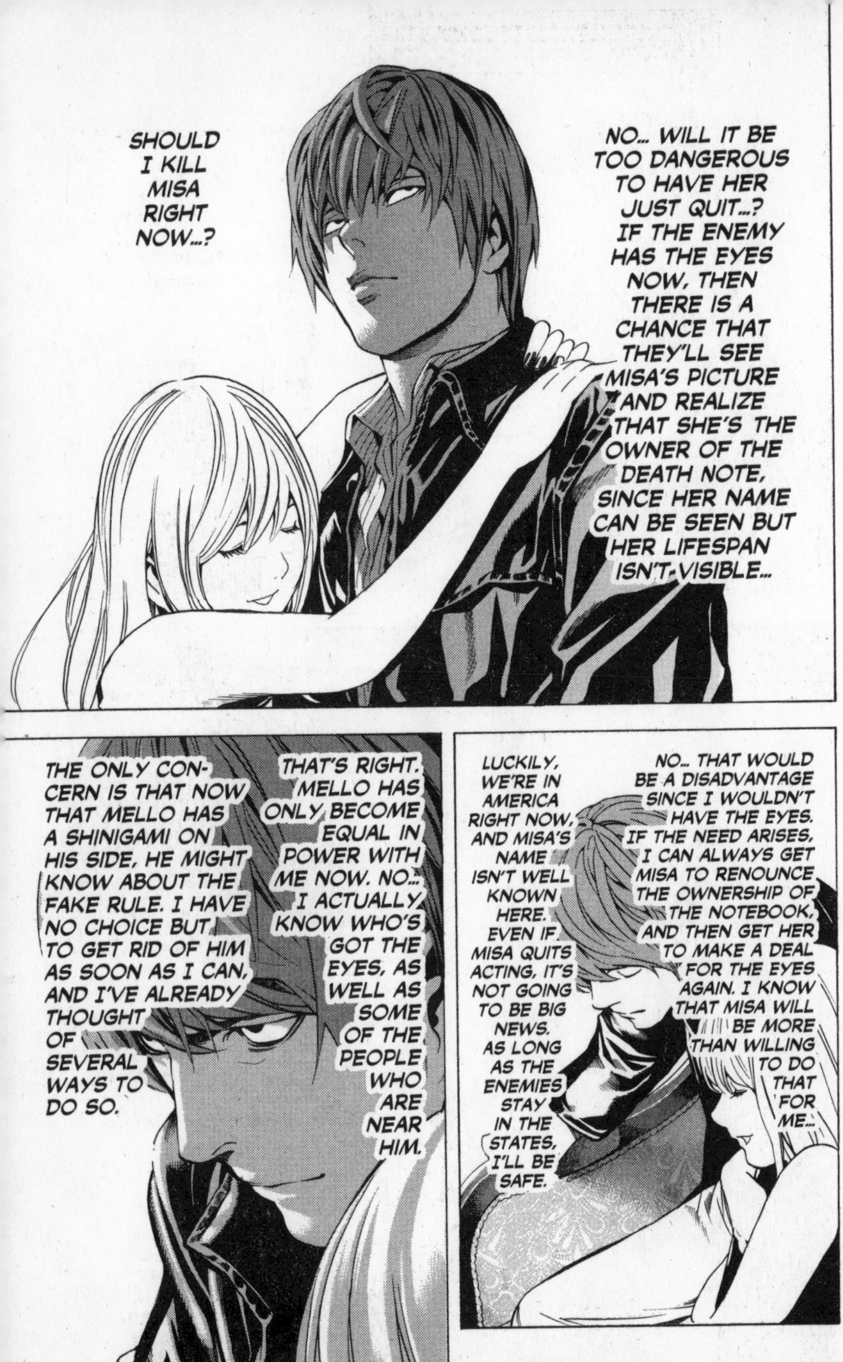
SHOULD I KILL MISA RIGHT NOW...?
NO... WILL IT BE TOO DANGEROUS TO HAVE HER JUST QUIT...? IF THE ENEMY HAS THE EYES NOW, THEN THERE IS A CHANCE THAT THEY'LL SEE MISA'S PICTURE AND REALIZE THAT SHE'S THE OWNER OF THE DEATH NOTE, SINCE HER NAME CAN BE SEEN BUT HER LIFESPAN ISN'T VISIBLE...
NO... THAT WOULD BE A DISADVANTAGE SINCE I WOULDN'T HAVE THE EYES. IF THE NEED ARISES, I CAN ALWAYS GET MISA TO RENOUNCE THE OWNERSHIP OF THE NOTEBOOK, AND THEN GET HER TO MAKE A DEAL FOR THE EYES AGAIN. I KNOW THAT MISA WILL BE MORE THAN WILLING TO DO THAT FOR ME...
LUCKILY, WE'RE IN AMERICA RIGHT NOW, AND MISA'S NAME ISN'T WELL KNOWN HERE. EVEN IF MISA QUITS ACTING, IT'S NOT GOING TO BE BIG NEWS. AS LONG AS THE ENEMIES STAY IN THE STATES, I'LL BE SAFE.
THAT'S RIGHT. MELLO HAS ONLY BECOME EQUAL IN POWER WITH ME NOW. NO... I ACTUALLY KNOW WHO'S GOT THE EYES, AS WELL AS SOME OF THE PEOPLE WHO ARE NEAR HIM.
THE ONLY CONCERN IS THAT NOW THAT MELLO HAS A SHINIGAMI ON HIS SIDE, HE MIGHT KNOW ABOUT THE FAKE RULE. I HAVE NO CHOICE BUT TO GET RID OF HIM AS SOON AS I CAN, AND I'VE ALREADY THOUGHT OF SEVERAL WAYS TO DO SO.

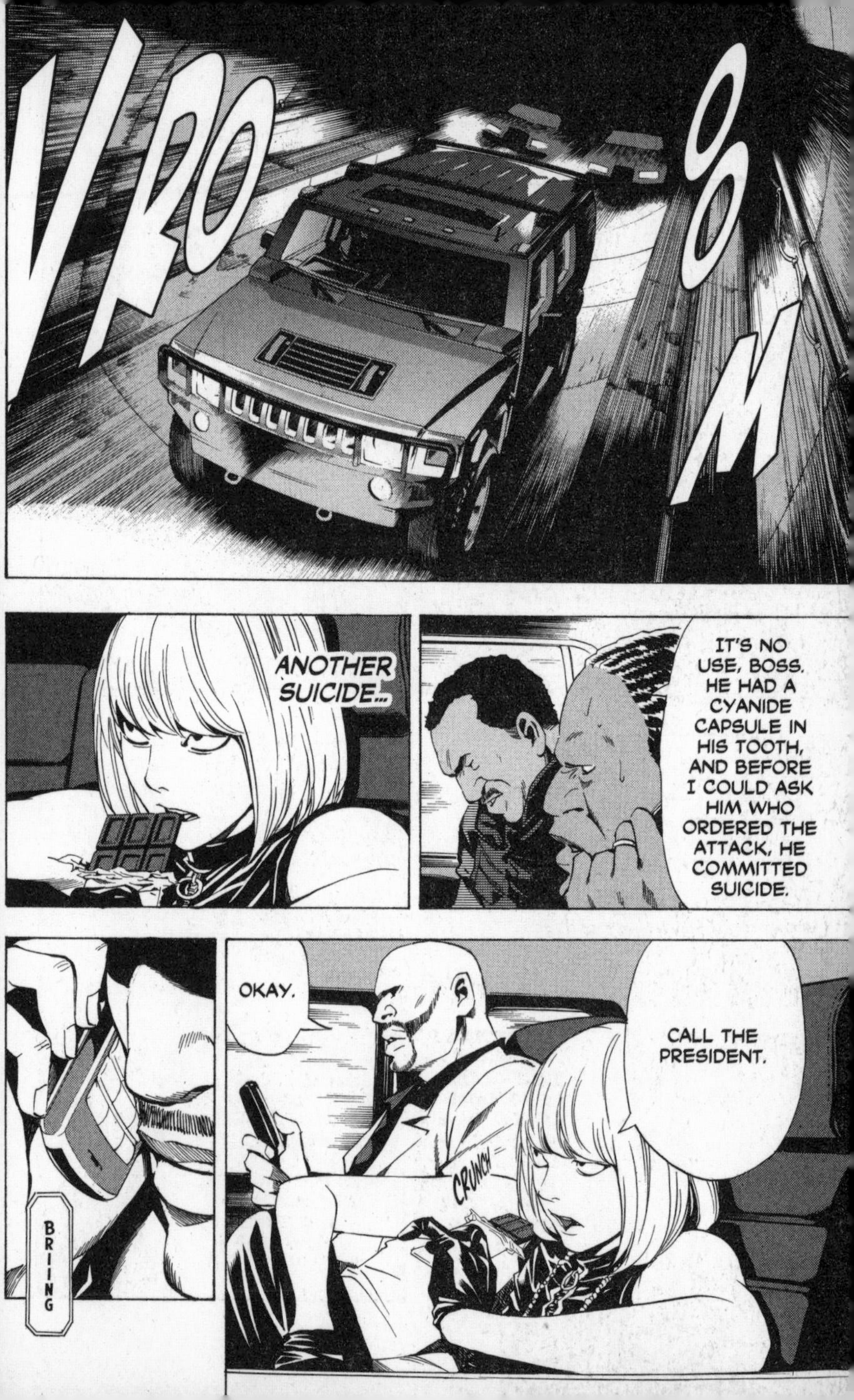
VROOOM
IT'S NO USE, BOSS. HE HAD A CYANIDE CAPSULE IN HIS TOOTH, AND BEFORE I COULD ASK HIM WHO ORDERED THE ATTACK, HE COMMITTED SUICIDE.
ANOTHER SUICIDE...
CALL THE PRESIDENT.
OKAY.
CRUNCH
BRIING

DEATH NOTE
How to use it
XLVI

- There are laws in the world of gods of death. If a god of death should break the law, there are 9 levels of severity starting at Level 8 and going up to Level 1 plus the Extreme Level. For severity levels above 8 the god of death will be killed after being punished.

死神には死神界で定められた掟があり、それを破ると、
特級・一級から八級まで九段階の罪があり、
三級以上はその罪を課せられた後、死ぬ。

- For example, killing a human without using the DEATH NOTE is considered as the Extreme Level.

たとえば、死神がデスノート以外で人間を殺す事は特級である。

In the Next Volume

L's protégés are proving more of a challenge than Light expected.
The more he tries to outmaneuver his enemies, the closer they get
to uncovering him! Will Light's quick wits be his downfall?

Available Now

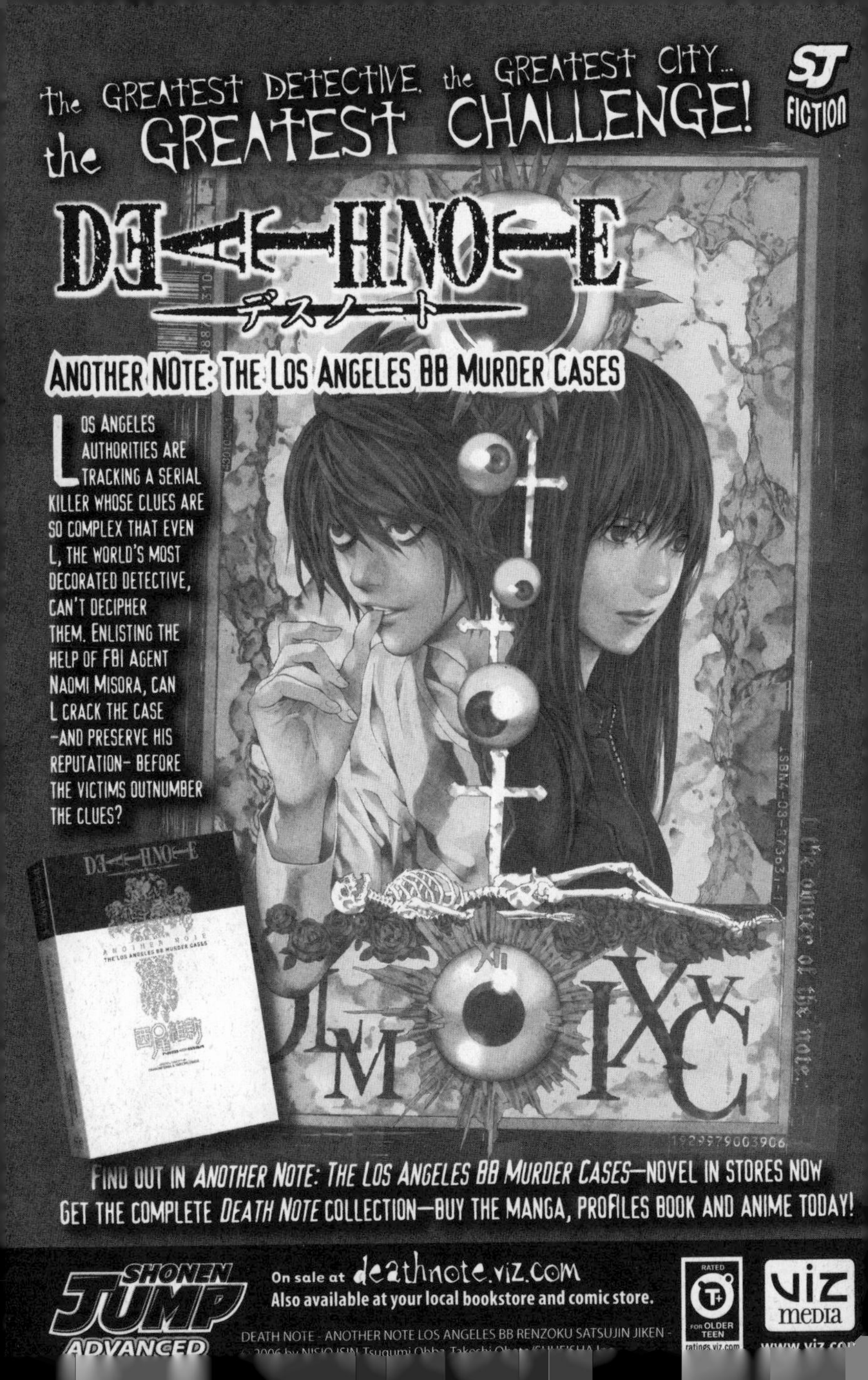
The GREATEST DETECTIVE, the GREATEST CITY...
the GREATEST CHALLENGE!
SJ FICTION
DEATH NOTE
デスノート
ANOTHER NOTE: THE LOS ANGELES BB MURDER CASES
LOS ANGELES AUTHORITIES ARE TRACKING A SERIAL KILLER WHOSE CLUES ARE SO COMPLEX THAT EVEN L, THE WORLD'S MOST DECORATED DETECTIVE, CAN'T DECIPHER THEM. ENLISTING THE HELP OF FBI AGENT NAOMI MISORA, CAN L CRACK THE CASE —AND PRESERVE HIS REPUTATION— BEFORE THE VICTIMS OUTNUMBER THE CLUES?
FIND OUT IN ANOTHER NOTE: THE LOS ANGELES BB MURDER CASES—NOVEL IN STORES NOW
GET THE COMPLETE DEATH NOTE COLLECTION—BUY THE MANGA, PROFILES BOOK AND ANIME TODAY!
SHONEN JUMP ADVANCED
On sale at deathnote.viz.com
Also available at your local bookstore and comic store.
RATED T+ FOR OLDER TEEN ratings.viz.com
VIZ media
www.viz.com
DEATH NOTE - ANOTHER NOTE LOS ANGELES BB RENZOKU SATSUJIN JIKEN -
© 2006 by NISIO ISIN, Tsugumi Ohba, Takeshi Obata/SHUEISHA Inc.

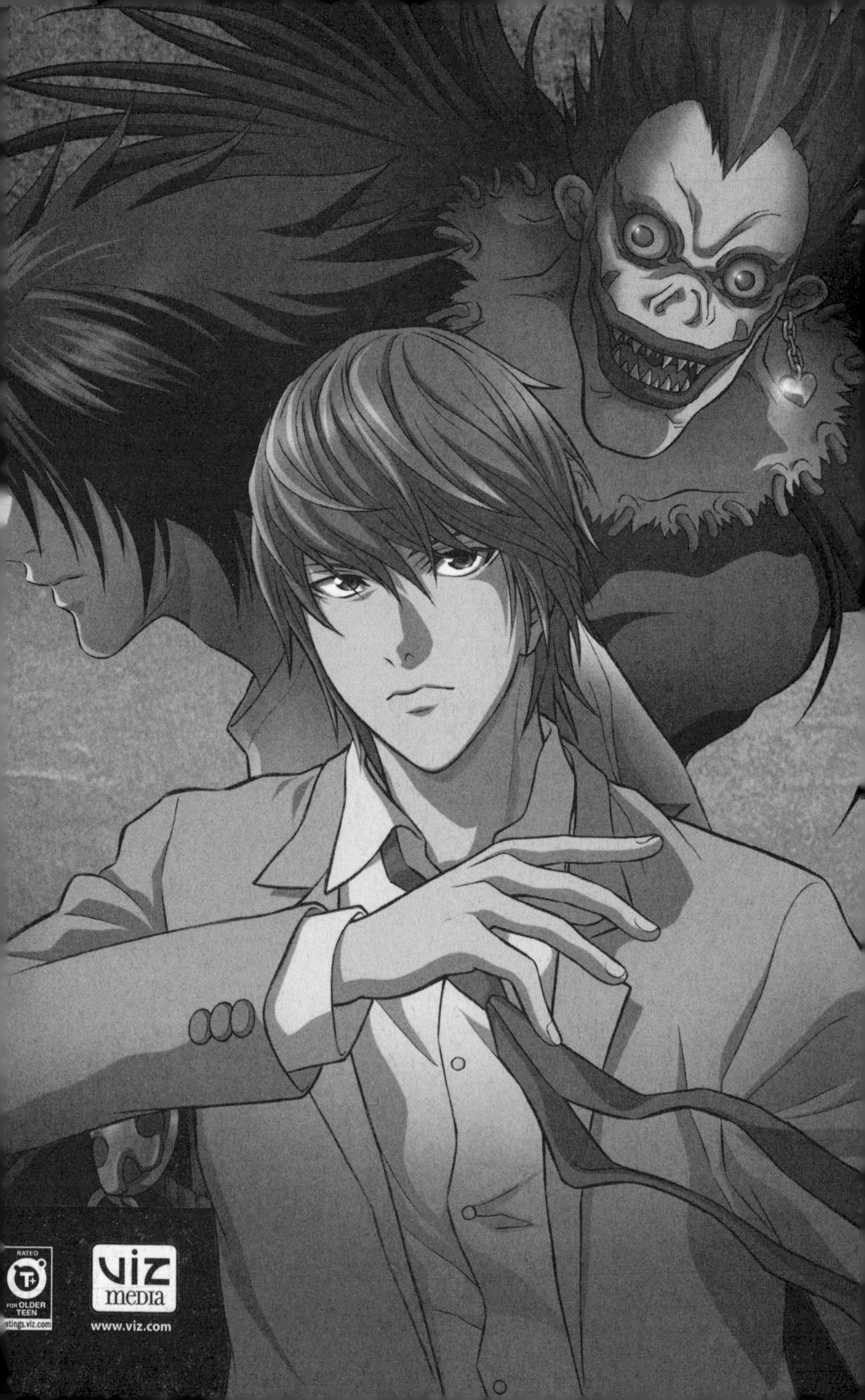
RATED
T+
FOR OLDER TEEN
VIZ media
www.viz.com

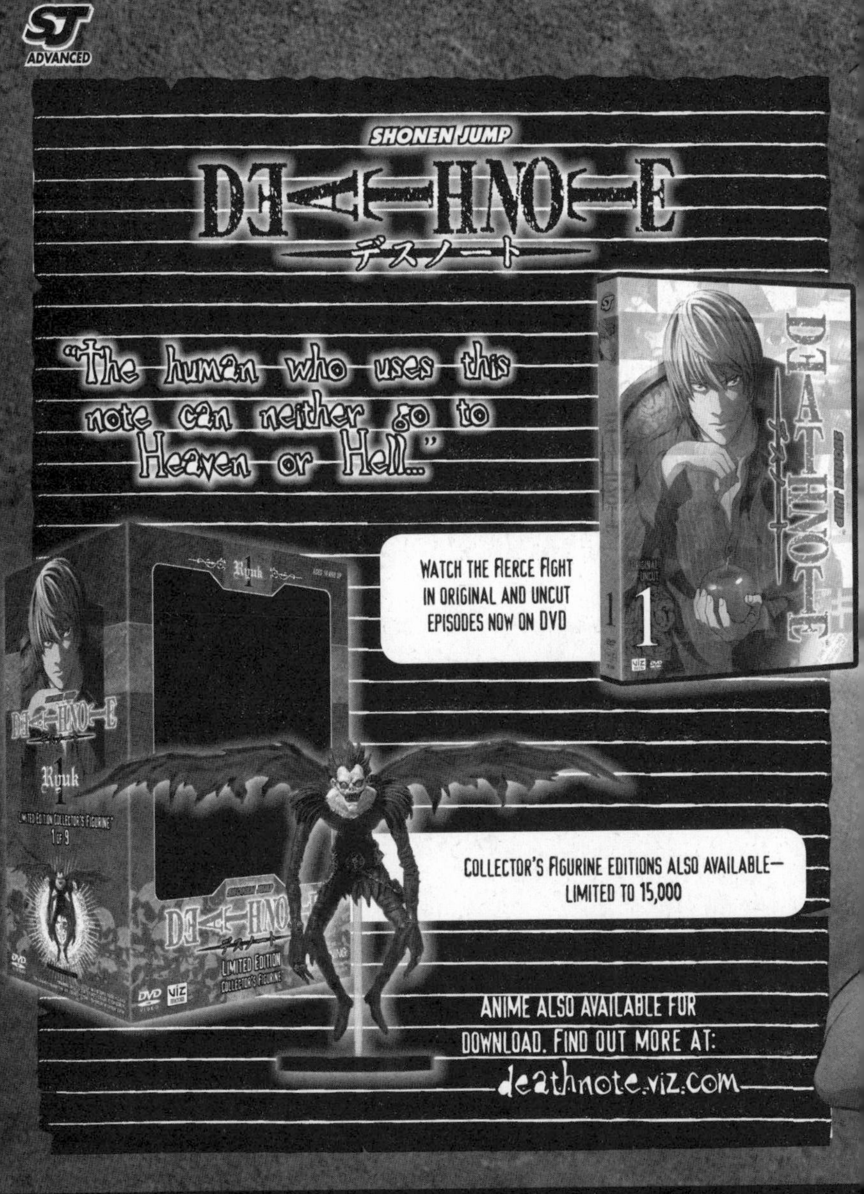

SJ ADVANCED
SHONEN JUMP
DEATH NOTE
デスノート
"The human who uses this note can neither go to Heaven or Hell..."
WATCH THE FIERCE FIGHT IN ORIGINAL AND UNCUT EPISODES NOW ON DVD
COLLECTOR'S FIGURINE EDITIONS ALSO AVAILABLE—LIMITED TO 15,000
ANIME ALSO AVAILABLE FOR DOWNLOAD. FIND OUT MORE AT:
deathnote.viz.com

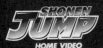

Tell us what you think about SHONEN JUMP manga!

Our survey is now available online.
Go to: www.SHONENJUMP.com/mangasurvey

Help us make our product offering better!

A WHILE AGO, WE COULD OFTEN
FIND THIS TYPE OF KEY CHAIN IN
SOUVENIR STORES AT A TOURIST
SPOT. BUT WHY IS IT THAT THEY
ALWAYS HAVE JEWELED EYES...?
- TAKESHI OBATA

Tsugumi Ohba
Born in Tokyo.
Hobby: Collecting teacups.
Day and night, develops manga plots
while holding knees on a chair.

Takeshi Obata was born in 1969 in Niigata, Japan, and
is the artist of the wildly popular SHONEN JUMP title
Hikaru no Go, which won the 2003 Tezuka Shinsei
"New Hope" award and the Shogakukan Manga award.
Obata is also the artist of **Arabian Majin Bokentan
Lamp Lamp, Ayatsuri Sakon**, and **Cyborg Jichan G.**

DEATH NOTE VOL 8
The SHONEN JUMP ADVANCED Manga Edition

STORY BY TSUGUMI OHBA
ART BY TAKESHI OBATA

Translation & Adaptation/Tetsuichiro Miyaki
Touch-up Art & Lettering/Gia Cam Luc
Design/Sean Lee
Editor/Pancha Diaz

Editor in Chief, Books/Alvin Lu
Editor in Chief, Magazines/Marc Weidenbaum
VP, Publishing Licensing/Rika Inouye
VP, Sales & Product Marketing/Gonzalo Ferreyra
VP, Creative/Linda Espinosa
Publisher/Hyoe Narita

Printed in the U.S.A.

Published by VIZ Media, LLC
P.O. Box 77010
San Francisco, CA 94107

SHONEN JUMP ADVANCED Manga Edition
10 9 8 7 6
First printing, November 2006
Sixth printing, September 2008

THE WORLD'S MOST
CUTTING-EDGE MANGA

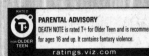

www.viz.com

www.shonenjump.com